SCIENCE AND THE PRE-ADAMIC WORLD

Science and the Pre-Adamic World

SCIENCE AND THE PRE-ADAMIC WORLD

A SCIENTIFIC PROOF OF THE EXISTENCE OF GOD AND THE MULTIVERSE.

ALFRED ADJARHO

Science and the Pre-Adamic World by Alfred Adjarho
Copyright © 2023 by Alfred Adjarho
All Rights Reserved.
ISBN: 978-1-59755-696-5

Published by: ADVANTAGE BOOKS™
  Longwood, Florida, USA
  www.advbookstore.com

This book and parts thereof may not be reproduced in any form, stored in a retrieval system or transmitted in any form by any means (electronic, mechanical, photocopy, recording or otherwise) without prior written permission of the author, except as provided by United States of America copyright law.

Unless otherwise indicated, Scriptures quotations taken from The Holy Bible KING JAMES VERSION (KJV), public domain.

Library of Congress Catalog Number: 2023931217

Name: Adjarho, Alfred, Author
Title: *Science and the Pre-Adamic World*
  Alfred Adjarho
  Advantage Books, 2023
Identifiers: ISBN Paperback: 978159756965, ebook: 9781597557030
Subjects:

First Printing: March 2023
23 24 25 26 27 28   10 9 8 7 6 5 4 3 2 1

Introduction

It has been observed that whenever humans set aside some dogmatic belief systems, much of their time and energy are channeled towards exploring their immediate environment, ultimately leading to scientific, socio-economic, and political developments. When you consider individual contributions to these developments, one would expect that they should have transformed the earth into a better place of existence for humanity. However, factors such as aging, violence, accidents, wars, natural disasters, diseases, sicknesses, etc., limit one's period of existence despite scientific discoveries and tentacles being extended to all of the cosmos. It is then obvious that death is a factor that short-circuits the human race. A simple puzzle for a philosopher could be; why then would humans, plants, animals, and even stars die, or why is violence erupting among humans and animals from one generation to another, despite global socialization and scientific and technological advancements?

Having been taught that the universe evolved from a tiny particle of matter ballooning faster than the speed of light, it seems pretty difficult to relate such a theory with reality. And, I've been puzzling if that tiny particle could have been responsible for the cosmos. And at what stage did the sun, moon, stars, fire, water, earth, plants, clouds, trees, cold, snow, and man evolve from the said hypothetical particle? Why is outer space so dark, and what could be responsible for the earth's gravitational pull? Why are the galaxies unreachable in space, but we can view them? The fastest space shuttle at this time of writing could jet off at 10,400km/h. However, it is speculated that a chemical-propelled space shuttle traveling at 58,000km/h would arrive at the nearest star in 82,000 years.

These unending puzzles got me curious, driving me into almost three decades of research that eventually produced the book in your hands. Much of the information contained in the book might sound weird, perhaps, as opposed to conventional schools of thought. Thinking, they say, is the hardest job to do because not many critically think outside the box. It's one thing to be taught and another to critically examine the knowledge impacted to find facts beyond the classroom. Some basic knowledge communicated to us in formal or informal settings has remained unchallenged, leading to perpetual errors for gullible minds.

The reality of the earth's rotation and fossil remains, which contrast views held by the theological communities, spurred my curiosity about scriptural writings relative to scientific findings. In the course of unraveling the quandary, it was observed that a huge polarity has lingered between the theological and scientific communities. This schism attributes to the lack of understanding of critical scriptural texts by some theologians. They, in turn, might have superficially concluded those texts are in error, thereby skipping applicable facts relevant to scientific discoveries.

Archeological evidence of fossil remains over the years impresses human minds with some skepticism on the stance of our theological communities. But given my understanding of scriptural mystical expressions, it's evident that scientific discoveries and the pre-Adamic world are interconnected and untapped. You'll be exposed to the basic facts of the pre-Adamic world...

Table of Contents

INTRODUCTION 5

CHAPTER 1: SCIENCE AND THEOLOGY 13
    STARS OF HEAVEN 20

CHAPTER 2: STARS ARE KNOWN 27
    SPIRIT CREATED NATURE 31

CHAPTER 3: SCIENCE AND THE GOD FACTOR 35
    ORIGIN OF THE SCIENCE WORLD 36
    CRUSADE OF CRITICISMS 39
    NIGHT NOT DARKNESS 42
    SUNLIGHT DOES AFFECT 43

CHAPTER 4: ARCTIC AND ANTARCTIC REGIONS 45
    LINES OF EQUATOR 46
    THE DARKNESS ACROSS SPACE 47

CHAPTER 5: THE UNIVERSE IN THE DEEP 54
    ATMOSPHERE FOR EXISTENCE 59
    FORMED IN THE MIDDLE 61

CHAPTER 6: FOSSILS BY ARCHAEOLOGISTS 67
    FLESH OF DIFFERENT KINDS 70
    REBELLIOUS DWELL 73
    SPIRITS FEED 74
    ANCIENT PEOPLE 77
    HIJACKED THE EARTH 83

CHAPTER 7: THE PERVERSION IN LIFE 89
    HISTORICAL MISCONCEPTION 92
    ADDING TO CREATION 96
    EXHIBIT THEIR OWN WAYS 100
    HE KNOWS EVERY SPIRIT 103

CHAPTER 8: THE EARTH UNDER DEATH 107
- River Euphrates 113
- Field of play 114
- Stop the blind arguments 115

CHAPTER 9: THE SEA OF GLASS 117
- Angels know all things 119
- The everlasting realms 121
- Son from His bosom 123
- God's direct ministers 124
- God made angels 126
- Satan was acknowledged 128
- Naturally destined 129
- Held in high esteem 131

CHAPTER 10: SONS OF GOD ON EARTHLY MISSIONS 133
- Shallow minds 136
- Hierarchy pursuits 137
- At will 141
- My servant Moses 141
- Unusual on the earth 143
- Interplay of powers 144
- Satanic onslaught 147
- Disputed with Satan 148
- Levitical priesthood 150
- Established under imperfection 152
- Visualized the agony 153

CHAPTER 11: CLOTHED IN FLESH 155
- Body of Christ 156
- Aware of His sonship 159
- Fear of death 160
- Filthy dreamers 162
- The skin of a leopard 164
- Out of the way of truth 166

CHAPTER 12: THE THEORY OF EVOLUTION 168
- REPLICATED ABSTRACT 172
- EMPOWERED TO REPLENISH 175
- POTENTIALS IN MEN 176
- CREATION OF GOD 177
- THE SAME GOD 179
- THE PERSON OF JESUS 181
- SHEW US THE FATHER 183

CHAPTER 13: ADAM WAS MADE TO RULE 185
- AIDE THE CAMP 186
- WEAK SUBSTANCES 188
- WIRED TO EXPLORE NATURE 190
- WITH STUDYING NATURE/PURSUIT OF VANITY OR SEEK GOD - NO MIDDLE GROUND. 191
- PEACE OF MIND 191
- THE FATHER'S EXPLANATION 194
- UNWITTINGLY SUBMIT 196

CHAPTER 14: AT THE GARDEN OF EDEN 198
- FASCINATED AND ENTICED 199
- MISREPRESENTATION OF THE SERPENT 203
- PROUD AND OBJECTIONAL 205
- TAKE NOTE! 207
- JUDGMENT TIME 207
- PURPOSE OF ANALYSIS 209
- REASON FOR COUNTERING 212

CHAPTER 15: CONSCIOUSNESS THAT KILLS 214
- THE BOTTOM LINE 215
- APPROVED AND DISAPPROVED 217
- PURSUIT OF KNOWLEDGE 219
- FLAMING SWORD 220
- SHUT OUT 221
- CONTROLLED BY SPIRITS TALK 222

CHAPTER 16: LUCIFER'S DEPOSITION ... 225
- Nails of brass ... 226
- Perpetual enmity ... 228
- Thoughts of overthrowing God ... 230
- Orchestrated rebellion ... 233
- Become weak ... 235

CHAPTER 17: BESSOM OF DESTRUCTION ... 238
- Multitude of iniquities ... 240
- Became a terrorist ... 243
- Sin also means violence ... 245
- But too late ... 247

CHAPTER 18: THE VIOLENCE ON EARTH ... 249
- End to violence ... 250
- Effect of righteousness ... 253
- Appropriate time ... 257
- The second heaven ... 259
- War in heaven ... 262
- Powers of heavens ... 264

CHAPTER 19: THE CONCEPT OF GOOD AND EVIL ... 268
- Appropriate or inappropriate ... 270
- No vacuum in life ... 273
- Endure hardness ... 274
- The hidden mystery ... 276
- Combat ready ... 277
- If God is all-knowing ... 280
- Why didn't God destroy Satan? ... 282

CHAPTER 20: THE SIN OF ADAM ... 284
- How about Cain? ... 285
- The knowledge of sin ... 286
- Gradual aging ... 288
- Exchanged in split seconds ... 290
- Purchased possession ... 292
- Sin and wickedness ... 294

CHAPTER 21: RELATIONSHIP WITH GOD ... 297
- Abusing God ... 298
- Make caricature ... 300
- Loving relationship ... 301
- Sins are covered ... 303
- Scarlet in color ... 305
- Efficacy of the blood ... 306
- Blood for souls ... 308

CHAPTER 22: THE ABSTRACT MAN OF DUST ... 310
- Soul is weak ... 311
- Continuous re-alignment ... 312
- Spirit of man ... 314
- Constant opposition ... 316
- The mind of the spirit ... 317

CHAPTER 23: FAMILIAR SPIRITS ... 319
- The meaning of life ... 321
- Weak through flesh ... 324
- Born again spirit ... 325
- Incorruptible seed ... 326
- Flesh to contend with ... 327
- Perfection with God ... 329
- Perfected forever ... 330

CHAPTER 24: THE GOD EXPERIENCE ... 333
- Ministry of the prophets ... 335
- Spirits listen to you ... 339
- No sinful flesh can ... 341
- Face for identification ... 342

CHAPTER 25: THE GLORY OF GOD ... 344
- Graced to relate ... 346
- Everlasting burnings ... 347
- Light generates current ... 350
- Massive in size ... 352
- Tall into the clouds ... 353
- Offspring of the giants ... 355
- Predetermining individual ... 357

Science and the Pre-Adamic World

Chapter 1

Science and Theology

Early men were somewhat ignorant about the concept of the earth's rotation theory. In our dispensation, it is scientifically proven that the earth does rotate about its axis, facing the sun and the darkness from space. This rotation is responsible for the day and night occurrences. Astronomical evidence shows that while the earth rotates on its axis, it also revolves around the sun annually. Scientific evidence concerning the earth's rotation and evolution theory has generated some controversies amidst theologians who have erroneously refuted the theory, including the archeological evidence of fossil remains which suggests the earth has been over 13.8 billion years.

Amongst theologians, it is believed that scientific theories are scripturally unfounded. Therefore, I've been searching for historical answers to these complexities so that I might find evidence connecting the pre-Adamic world to our current understanding. During this search, I stumbled upon a profound book coded with the mysteries of the 'multiverse' (not the universe as claimed in the sciences). This book details the pre-Adamic world regarding scientific discoveries in our dispensation. I spent several years studying this book and realized that scientific theories have been scripturally supported, yet these have gone unexplored.

More importantly, the evolution theory, which suggests that man was previously coined from fossil remains, categorized as beasts. As we progress through this book, you'll appreciate that science is part of God's original plan for humanity. On the flip side, it was observed that apostle Paul had refuted scientific theories in his era, warning Timothy, his son in the Lord, 'to beware of science falsely so called (1st Timothy 6:20). His assertion of science falsely in the scriptures is presumed to have had a negative impact on most of his followers dissuading many who perhaps were scared and indoctrinated to challenge his notions. Over the years, such a remark might have polarized the scientific and theological communities. And, of course, it was assumed Paul was uninterested in cosmological studies due to his perceived conflict of interest between scientific theories and his faith.

I believed such a remark might have also formed some parochial concepts about the study of science among theologians, resulting in individual retardation and disaffection for critical research about scriptural write-ups with regard to scientific discoveries. The gap is further widened and exasperated by either community out rightly rejecting ideas that could have benefited each other. And, of course, both have always been at parallel ends for tens of decades. Having studied the scriptures for almost three decades and been open to scientific views, I could understand the polarities at both ends. Science is facts finding using its processes, while theology is hinged on faith evidence. What do I mean by evidence? Theologians believed God created all things for which things of nature spoken by God are seen with the eyes. On the other hand, science assumed the universe was spontaneous without God as the Creator.

In the sciences, the slogan has been, "assume no God exists, ask questions, make a background check, construct a hypothesis and proceed with testing based on experimentations carried out, take a careful analysis of the data, draw a conclusion of the results and provide a recommendation for further testing before postulating a theory. And when these processes or methods are not adhered to, the scientific communities often disregard any thought derived from them.

Consequently, the scientific communities have unconsciously set in notions a contradiction within the theological, whose belief systems contrast with scientific discoveries. We know science is simply the study and discovery of nature to improve mankind and its environment. It is characterized by opposition to a dogmatic approach in its processes. However, some scientific theories are limited due to some 'uncertainties of assumptions.' For example, scientific theories regarding the actual causes of planet drift, earth rotation, the origin of plants and animals, gravitational pull, and the size of the rainbow are based on uncertainties of assumptions.

Whenever I drink a glass of water, I get a little bit fascinated about its origin, such a colorless substance, so nourishing and necessary for human existence. Water is the most abundant substance in nature. Similarly, I'd imagine how many grains of sand are in a city, uncountable! Look at fire, plants, birds, clouds, rocks, animals, creeping things, etc., made of various colors and textures, which are fascinating in their varieties. Having fallen over heels with nature and its source, I can vehemently say that it is evident that every substance in nature is unique, which is the God factor.

Many, if not all, inwardly attribute the earth's rotation to the Infinite One God. Generations of theologians refuted the earth's rotation theory which scientists observed, and there are still pockets of ignorant people who think otherwise about the reality of the earth's rotation. But, of course, it is 100% true the earth is rotating unstoppably - beyond scientific control. The actual cause of the rotation of the earth remains the God factor. Here, we can see scientific discoveries versus God's acts, even if some folks refuted them.

I've been privileged to experience the earth's rotation twice while standing on the earth's surface. I wouldn't know how my eyes were opened to this experience, but I saw it and knew I was moving at such a dramatic speed. This experience revolutionized my understanding of the God we are dealing with. He sets the earth and the universe in such momentum from the beginning of creation, shutting the human eyes from such visual field consciousness while on the earth. Believe me, so many are unconscious of this daily experience, with the ignorant still in doubt.

And, I'd like to applaud the scientific communities who doggedly refused to die in ignorance because ignorance has been the bane of men. Of course, it was written in the scriptures that God concealed things so men would search them out. "It is the glory of God to conceal a thing: but the honor of kings is to search out a matter" (Proverbs 25:2). Science has searched out things hidden from men in fulfillment of the scriptures. And based on scientific theory as regards the earth's rotation, I can vehemently say that scientific theories are the background checks of scriptural write-ups. Are you wondering what I mean? You will have a better understanding after reading this book.

I vividly remember gazing into the sky one morning and focusing on the top of a high-rise building relative to the sky. Suddenly, my eyes were opened, and I noticed that I was traveling on the earth at the speed of an airplane along with the buildings. This was no vision or dream. I repeated my focus and noticed the same view, but it was a frightening experience to behold. I then said to myself, "I've been on this earth for some years, and it didn't occur to me that such a thing had been in existence?" For me, it was profound. For the next two weeks, I was immersed in the understanding that on earth, I was unaware that I was in constant motion (rotation). As a result, I found it difficult to sleep.

I began studying the scriptures to search out why these things weren't written in the book of Genesis. In the course of my deep meditations, the scriptures were unveiled to my understanding by the Spirit of God. It became obvious that the earth's rotation causes day and night, and it has existed for several billion years, even far more than the 13.8 billion years that scientists proclaim. The problem is that most theologians aren't studying the scriptures thoroughly despite scriptural writes-up being latently coded. They rely on what higher authorities have told them in theological schools. Perhaps, many are scared of criticizing scriptural writings where necessary. I believe in science, but more importantly, I had to ensure a critical analysis of the background knowledge of scriptural writings relative to scientific discoveries. And this has opened me up to many wonders of this universe we live in, which comprises innumerable shaped planets.

I have found that the book of Genesis is concise regarding man, planets, galaxies, sun, moon, and fossils currently being unraveled by our scientific communities. The planets and galaxies were all captured in the book of Genesis, and further scriptural references point to these galaxies and planets, which pre-existed the Genesis of recreation. However, planets and galaxies were expanded into infinite positions during the recreation. For example, Isaiah 40:22 says that God stretched out the heavens (clouds or planets) as a curtain and spread them as a tent to dwell. In other words, our universe is made of the endless expanse of innumerable planets in space. Hence the scripture says, "Who can number the clouds (planets) in wisdom?" (Job 38:37).

In context, who can give an accurate number of planets that exist? The heavens (planets) were shaped to be habitable. The scripture was specific. These planets were spread like a tent to dwell in. It shows planets are like the earth in shape with various sizes. So it is no big deal if men discover these planets configured like the earth to dwell on. The challenge is that some of these planets lack oxygen or rainfall, unlike earth. "In the beginning, God created the heaven and the earth. And the earth was without form, and void; and darkness was upon the face of the deep. And the Spirit of God moved upon the face of the waters" (Genesis 1:1-2).

Many are unaware that God carried out a recreation of things in the book of Genesis. Things formed or "created and made" according to Genesis 2:3 had existed before the recommencement of time being submerged. It means time had begun several billion years before Genesis. New species of animals, fishes, birds, creeping things, man, etc., were formed from the previous breeds, indicating that things were refurbished and rebranded.

Recreation in the book of Genesis talked about the re-illumination of the stars or galaxies, sun, and moons that formed the universe once under the darkness. It involves the recreation of the current firmament over the earth's sphere (but exclusive of several planets in space identified in the form of dry lands, oceans, rocks, and fire) and calling forth of the earth out of the great deep waters wherein the earth was submerged with the intent to replenish or repopulate the earth planet once again with a 'new set of people called the Adamic race.

The emphasis on recreation was the reclamation and refurbishment of the earth and the spreading of the galaxies and planets outside space under the darkness. "And the earth was without form and void, and darkness was upon the face of the deep." The word void implies devoid of animals, humans, sun, moon, plants, fishes, creeping things, etc., just the chaos seen.

The universe then was comparatively narrow before the chaos. When God began the refurbishment of the planets, galaxies, and earth in Genesis, it was understood the darkness in space reflected over the waters in which the earth was submerged to a given height. The darkness in space stretched across all of the cosmos. Although, I had been reticent on the term 'universe or cosmos' to have implied all created things in existence. I believe the word 'universe' is restricted to all galaxies, planets, animals, birds, sun, moon, and earth found under the darkness of space and time.

Since the light zone universe above the darkness in space wasn't taken into cognizance, nor has it ever been a subject of discourse in the sciences, not even in the theological communities. I'm aware that the majority are unaware of 'the light zone universe,' which is bigger than our universe established under the darkness. It means we're limited to the concepts of the term 'cosmos' to have included all created things because 'the light zone universe above' also consists of galaxies, planets, spirit beings, plants, animals, birds, etc., which formed parts of things that exist.

Of course, one might unhesitatingly contend that spirit beings or aliens are unscientific in the sciences, but they've unwittingly become some puzzles currently being explored in our universe, which our scientific communities are fascinated about. Wondering what I mean by "puzzles currently being explored?" You'll find out soon! The Book of Genesis tells us that darkness covered the earth, and several other planets that hosted fallen spirit beings were shut down and placed under darkness. And the scriptures confirmed these planets; galaxies, including the earth, were then enlarged or expanded in size. This shows the sun and moon were also stretched to their current size, having pre-existed the chaos.

The distance between the darkness in space and the earth's surface is yet unknown. However, scientists have estimated various distances from the earth to some galaxies as several million or billion light-years. A Light-year is approximately 9.5 trillion-kilometer distance, and if we have to factor in the black darkness covering space above the stars, then we might as well have several million light years from the positions of the stars. Since I studied mathematics, I'd like to break it down mathematically for those who may not understand these parameters.

The farthest point of our firmament called forth in Genesis over the earth's sphere (exosphere) is about 100 kilometers above sea level. Usually, a passenger airplane cruises at an altitude of 36,000 to 40,000 feet above sea level. Now, 1km is approximately 3,281ft, or 1km is 0.62137 miles. It means 1-foot equals 0.00030405km. But let's make use of the kilometer distance. It means the passenger airplane would cruise at an altitude of 10.946km (36,000ft) above sea level, and the speed is usually around 900km/hr. Supposedly, a passenger airplane can travel the earth's diameter (12,756km) at 900km/hr in just over 14 days.

The fastest jet at this time of writing could travel at 7,200km/hr. It would take approximately 42 hours to cover the earth's diameter. And the fastest space shuttle travels at 10,400km/hr, and we hope to have a 58,000 km/hr space shuttle in the near future. If science succeeds in producing a space shuttle that can travel to the nearest star, it will take 81,500 years. From the time Adam was created until now is about 6,346 years as of this time of writing. So, when science uses the term light year, it means the distance light travels in 356 days at the speed of 300,000,000 m/s, or 300,000 km/s which is a 1.95 trillion-kilometer distance. The reason for this little math exercise is that many don't seem to appreciate the vast universe we live in outside space under the darkness. This math might help comprehend the various distances of the stars from the earth.

The earth's firmament was re-shaped over a void of existing dry land, forming a planet that God called earth. It was initially earth several billion years before the refurbishment in the book of Genesis. God called forth an existing firmament (sunk) inside the deep waters in which the void land, earth, was submerged to form a given-shaped atmosphere. At the same time, the rotation continued, and He later called forth the dry land from the same deep waters. But the earth was found to have been narrowed in its landmass when it was called forth out of the deep. The scripture says God had to enlarge the earth by stretching its landmass to its current size, as recorded in the scriptures.

Isaiah 44:24 says, "I am the LORD that maketh all things; that stretcheth forth the heavens alone; that spreadeth abroad the earth by myself." God made all things from the beginning several billion years ago, which is not the very beginning captured in the book of Genesis. Once smaller in size, the earth was further expanded by God's hand. So also, the heavens or universe were enlarged infinitely. This is precisely what the scripture meant by 'spreadeth abroad' or 'stretcheth forth.' According to the scriptures, there are uncountable numbers of planets in the universe, and no man can number the planets because our universe is infinite in space under the darkness.

Remember, we are considering this universe under space darkness and not the 'light zone universe' above the darkness, which is several trillion light-years away. Are you wondering how I know this? The scriptures described our universe as being under the space darkness and also talked about the light zone universe, which has never been a subject of discourse by our scientific communities. The book of Genesis identified the space-darkness spread as our universe. The book of Genesis 1:1 says, "In the beginning,

God created the heaven and the earth." The 'heaven' here should read 'heavens,' which implies the planets. So we can say, "In the beginning, God created the heavens and the earth. It then went further to say, "And the earth was without form, and void, and darkness was upon the face of the deep" (Genesis 1:2). The deep is the distance between the space darkness comprising several trillions of planets. The emphasis was then switched to the planet earth and how it was in a chaotic state with darkness covering the face of the deep, for which the earth was one of the planets of the deep. Consider Genesis 1:17, which says, "And God set them in the firmament of the heaven to give light upon the earth." It denotes the 'heaven' in which the lights were set remains the same heavens used in Genesis 1:1. Because the firmament over the earth was also called heaven, which is not the same as the heavens used in Genesis 1:1. The planets have been in existence in space for billion years, so also are the galaxies but the galaxies were not positioned to such degree of infinite space as it were today.

Innumerable planets and galaxies (stars) were captured succinctly during the recreation in Genesis. They were distinguished from the submerged earth being refurbished or recreated. The scriptures conclusively referenced these planets and galaxies in Genesis 2:1, saying, "Thus the heavens (planets) and the earth were finished, and all the hosts (galaxies or stars) of them" (Emphasis mine). The hosts of them are referred to as the galaxies. In contrast, the heavens refer to the planets. This corroborates my earlier point in Genesis 1:1 that the heaven used in Genesis 1:1 implied heavens, as emphasized in Genesis 2:1.

One of the proofs from the scriptures that these planets pre-existed recreation in Genesis was found in the book of 2nd Peter 3:5, which says, "…The heavens were of old (ancient), and the earth standing of the water and in the water." This tells us the planets pre-existed the chaos but were expanded in what the scriptures inferred by the phrase 'were finished. All planets under the darkness, including the earth, had existed for several billion years before Genesis. However, the earth was the focal point for man's existence and survival. God simply repopulated the dry land (earth) with plants, animals, fish, birds, and creeping things for man's consumption since a set of people had once lived on this earth for several billion years before Genesis. I will show you shortly from the scriptures these people and their behaviors, which led to God destroying them.

Thus, planets and galaxies were revisited once again during the recreation which took place in Genesis. There are several planets as lands in the heavens. Isaiah 33:17 talks about the land that is far off – signifying a planet. "…They shall behold the land that is very far off." Although the scripture here talks about heaven being the angels' abode, it is evident that the scripture gave us clues into the existence of land in the heavens other than the earth. So, you cannot ignore scriptural writings because you lack a proper understanding of the scriptures, and neither can you disregard the sciences because you cannot relate scientific findings to scriptural writings.

Science evolves daily, and I am open to new discoveries. Still, more importantly, I connected current findings to scriptural writings. God opened my understanding to know that the earth we live in also breathes, having cardiac rhythms. Hence the vegetation grows just like the stars or galaxies are giant spiritual beings, with some larger than our sun or moon in space. You may question this, but you will find these truths in the scriptures as I did as we progress through this book. As mentioned earlier, these things are coded in the scriptures. Until I expound on them, you may not be able to comprehend their context even if you read the scriptures repeatedly. I know someone thinks these are heresies, but they are not. I had my understanding enlightened to these scriptural mysteries, which I never thought I'd come to know in my lifetime. Please read on to learn these truths.

Stars of Heaven

God used the black darkness seen in space to shut down the activities of previous people who once lived several billion years back on this earth. They were shut down under darkness for thousands or even millions of years. Let's distinguish these three sets of people created by God several billion years back, comprising of cherubim, angels, and ancient giant men and women - who once procreated this earth. Of course, they were not all created at the same time. In general, they were sets of people made of precious stones, such as gold, jasper, brass, diamonds, brass, onyx stones, bdellium, beryls, etc., as their skeletal structures. However, they weren't made of the same substance in their skeletal structures or outward flesh (I'll expound on this as we progress). The Adamic human race, mandated by God to run the activities of this earth, was made of skeletal bones and covered with sinews and clay flesh.

These ancient people, who are still alive spiritually, and sometimes incarnate physically, differ in hierarchies, as we shall discuss in much detail. Angels were made with substances of light of fire, in addition to substances of beryl, brass, diamonds, etc., several billion years back, with some angels bigger than our sun or earth planet. These once lived in the "light zone universe," much bigger than our universe. They were messengers of God visiting the previous giant people (men and women) on this earth before Adam was brought into human consciousness. Some angelic beings created with the substances of light and precious stones were shut down under our universe in darkness covering space which formed part of the reason for the chaos in the book of Genesis.

They were innumerable giant spirit beings who once lived in heaven - the light zone universe but were cast down, while the spirit men and women who lived on this earth for several billion years were submerged in great waters recorded in Genesis 1:1-2. Both exhibited behaviors hostile to God's nature, which I'll also touch on. And so, God withdrew light from these spirit men and women by darkening the sun and moon over this earth and withdrew light from fallen angels. The earth then was flooded in deep waters before covering the entire universe with a thick darkness, which we can see covering space.

However, after a long while of lockdowns under the darkness, perhaps, millions of years, God decided to modify and upgrade fossils of previous beasts to become a new set of people adopted - the current human race that God called Adam. I will come to several proofs from the scriptures that man was coined or recreated from previous animals as we progress. God simply began a process of reclamation and refurbishment in the book of Genesis. Still, these people, including angels, giant men, and women who once lived on this earth, now spirit beings, were confined and dispersed under the darkness universe as they have been forever banished from accessing the light zone universe above.

Genesis 2:1 says, "Thus the heavens and the earth were finished and all the host of them." In context, the constellations of the heavens, which talked about the galaxies and the planets, were reactivated once again, having undergone closure under darkness for a period of time, perhaps millions of years, but still under the darkness to date. The earth, which had existed for several billion years, was made to resurface from the great deep waters. By implication, the sun, including galaxies in space, were re-illuminated or reignited with light, having pre-existed the recreation in Genesis.

So when God said, "Let there be light" in Genesis 1:3, it lit up innumerable spirit (light) beings once formed with the substance of 'lights of fire' and precious stones, gold, brass, beryl, clouds, pearls, diamond, etc. God re-illuminated the universe with light once again because he had dreamt of modifying and adopting a new set of people whose fossil remains were from the previous earth sunk in the deep waters under darkness, recorded in Genesis 1:2. God remembered this universe under darkness and decided to revive fallen stars that were shut down (as black holes) once again hence the scripture wrote: he made the stars also (Genesis 1:16).

A new species from the previous breed of irrational animals were recreated, not evolved in the process – the current human race on the earth. I'm aware some religious folks might be infuriated and agitated over this statement as heresy, but please be patient until I prove these claims from the same scriptures, not necessarily the book of Genesis alone. And so, God expanded the universe under darkness and dispersed these reignited spirits (light) beings (stars) far apart several million light years from this refurbished earth because God had revisited the darkness zone - our universe in the deep.

The intent was to replenish the earth with the Adamic human race instead. God revived the stars in Genesis once shut under the darkness. These two sets of beings put together are in multitudes, as some spirit men and women, great or small, were dispersed to the unseen world of waters, which is under the earth, and others to various planets in space, while the majority as stars of heaven formed our current galaxies or stars. I know this might sound weird to us, but I'll show you proof from the scriptures. The stars that form our galaxies are celestial beings unknown to Adam and his descendants (our scientific and theological communities).

The scripture in the book of Job 38:31 says, "Canst thou bind the sweet influences of Pleiades, or loose the band of Orion? Canst thou bring forth Mazzaroth in his season? Or Canst thou guide Arcturus with his sons?" Stars (light beings made of precious stones burning like the sun) were spread abroad to various positions and were made incommunicable to humans currently occupying this earth. I wouldn't know if they would communicate or respond to us from space in the nearest future.

Several galaxies comprising trillions of stars and dust matters weren't the focal point in the book of Genesis. Still, according to the scriptures, they were reignited in the recreation in Genesis. The dust matter seen alongside these stars indicates certain mysteries, which I'll touch on shortly. The reason is that the scripture was given to us humans to know what concerns the earth alone, as angels also have scriptures that detailed their time of existence several billion years back. At least I've been privileged by God once to read a verse of their scriptures in my vision, written exactly like the King James Version. Having regained consciousness, I searched my earthly scriptures. Still, I found the references were completely different in content. Individual destinies were written inside angel scriptures. And, of course, I'm talking about angels above the darkness in space.

Mighty spirit beings made with substances of light that once lived in the light zone universe were made to reflect light as stars under the darkness in our dispensations far apart. Each star is known by name because God does call the stars by their names irrespective of their numbers. Psalms 147:4 says, "He (God) telleth the number of the stars, he calleth them by their names." God alone knows the number of stars that are innumerable to humans. Some of these stars have sons, like humans procreating children. They exist as children to parent stars under the darkness in space. Just like several galaxies have spiral structure arms containing younger stars spiraling out from older stars. We saw Arcturus with his sons mentioned in the scriptures.

These are mighty stars in space that scientists are still puzzling about to date. Stars below the darkness in space are made according to their previous relevance several billion years back, which is why we see them in various sizes. They were revived in the book of Genesis as light was once withdrawn from them for a period of time. Job 38:15 says, "And from the wicked, their light is withholden, and the high arm shall be broken." This dictates God had once withdrawn light from fallen stars and has revisited these stars after several thousand or million years of lockdowns.

These innumerable light beings formed with substances of lamps of fire in space do communicate with God directly, which you and I cannot detect their modes of communication. We can only view them from afar. In the language of the spirit world, they exist as beings and can also die like humans since they were revived under the darkness in space, having been previously shut off under darkness. As we progress, I will discuss what the darkness in space signifies in the scriptures. Let me quickly take you through scripture substantiating that God communicates with stars like humans since he formed them as beings with light. Job 38:35 says, "Canst thou send lightnings that they may go, and say unto thee, here we are?" This shows God communicates with lightning or stars who give feedback to God about their locations in space.

God is the Father of lights (James 1:17). God is light. Light begat lights, and their languages are unknown to humans. For instance, the scripture talks about stars praising God in Psalms 148:3 which says, "Praise you him, sun and moon: praise him, all you stars of light." In other words, the galaxies are light beings that praise God in their own style and language. Stars in their courses above means they exist, carrying out various activities as humans do on earth. They were revisited during the recreation in Genesis; hence the scripture clandestinely wrote, "He made the stars also" (Genesis 1:16).

I'll show you scriptural proof that God often conveys meetings with fallen angels made of light substances and precious stones cast down from the universe above to this universe under darkness as we progress. The communication link was once re-established from the recreation in Genesis, but that doesn't mean they have been discharged and acquitted. They are simply awaiting the judgment of the great day, in which even humans adopted as new sons of God will also be made to judge fallen stars. Hence, the scripture wrote, "Know you not that we shall judge angels? how much more things that pertain to this life?" (1st Corinthians 6:3). And of course, believers in Christ will judge fallen angels under the space darkness. Angels are innumerable stars seen at night or daytime in the sky from the earth's surface. Revelation 1:20 says, "...The seven stars are the angels of the churches...."

But these stars often turn humans to infiltrate this earth. Let's look at some scriptural proofs. Judges 5:20 talks about "stars in their courses fought against Sisera." This scripture may not make sense to many people who may have studied it for decades because some scriptural writings were coded so that an amateur may not comprehend its context. The above scripture denotes stars beings infiltrated the earth. Their courses imply they are in their world, busy like us humans but far apart. Galaxies or stars exist in their world and perform certain activities, such as driving ships, playing, replicating, walking, eating, fighting, praising God, or listening to God's command as we humans do. Psalms 103:20 says, "Bless the LORD, ye his angels that excel in strength, that do his commandments, hearkening unto the voice of his word." This talked about God's angels in heaven listening to God's command, but we also saw fallen angels fighting against Sisera in the scriptures performing God's command. Someone might say, "How can you say stars fought against Sisera? These are just scriptural allegories" No. These are no scriptural allegories.

Let me show you scriptures that prove these stars turned humans and physically fought against the company of Sisera on earth in the days of Deborah. Judges 5:18- 20 says, "Zebulun and Napthali were a people that jeopardized their lives unto death in the high places of the field. The kings came and fought, then fought the kings of Canaan in Taanach by the water of Megiddo; they took no gain of money. They fought from heaven; the stars in their courses fought against Sisera." It is crystal clear that amongst the people who came out from the tribes of Zebulun and Naphtali, the stars of heaven turned into humans and joined the Israelites in this war unknown to them. The reason is that the opposite camp, the children of Israelites, were fighting also were angelic beings (in human forms) referred to as the mighty dressed in chariots of iron drawn from river Kishon. The river Kishon, an ancient river, predated the chaos in Genesis, like the river Hiddekel. The LORD ordered some stars to fight against these chariots of iron (stars); hence, the angel of the LORD cursed Meroz, a set of people, who did not take part in the battle which the LORD muttered (Judges 5:23). Of course, the Israelites then had no clue about stars turning into humans on earth. Stars often infiltrate this earth to date as humans unknown to us. Stars that fought for the Israelites returned to space after the war; hence the scriptures talked about stars in their courses fought from heaven. The scriptures say that they took no gain of money after the war. They fought freely and went back to space, just as Lucifer often returns to space after entering earth at will. You may be wondering how. Later in this book, I will show you scriptures corroborating Lucifer's ability to infiltrate the earth.

Of course, there are also female stars, as you will soon find out. The sons of Arcturus referenced in scripture implies that the parent star split apart to yield smaller stars because God formed subordinate stars. Although this suggests copulation amongst stars to engender new stars (sons), I wouldn't know if stars are still capable of reproducing in space. However, as you will soon find out that these stars were found to have defiled pre-Adamic people who once lived on this earth; I believe they can copulate and reproduce. Some of the stars re-illuminated are much bigger than our sun. The book of Second Peter 2:11 says, "Whereas angels which are greater in power and might...." This implies that light or celestial beings are much mightier than the sun or earth in space. However, whenever they appear on earth or in dreams and visions, they seem condensed into human shapes convenient for us to relate to.

The book of Revelations 10:1-2 says, "And I saw another mighty angel come down from heaven, clothed with a cloud: and a rainbow was upon his head, and his face was as it were the sun, and his feet as pillars of fire...he set his right foot upon the sea and his left foot on the earth." This angel of God's presence, who in a real sense is far bigger and mightier than the sun in size, would descend to earth during the tribulation. Outside the earth's spheres, these mighty star beings shine in space and seem like the sun. Many are unaware that we have stars in capacities much bigger than our sun planet.

Let me quickly substantiate this from Genesis 2:1, cited above, which talked about planets, earth, and all the host of them being completed. Daniel 8:10 says, "...And it cast down some of the hosts of heaven; and of the stars to the ground, and stamped upon them." It's crystal clear the 'host of them' spoken about in Genesis 2:1 implies the galaxies of stars that were reignited and re-illuminated once more, having undergone lockdowns in darkness for several million years. Stars in space have rulers over them in what the scriptures denote by a host of them. The host of them implies a band over the stars in space. We refer to them as galaxies (of stars), but in reality, they are mighty princes over smaller stars. We can also refer to these princes as archangels. In generic terms, the 'host of heaven' implies 'stars of heaven' under the darkness zone universe.

Just like hell planet has a prince over it. So also, stars have a prince. "Yea, he magnified himself to the prince of the host...." Daniel 8:11. Archangels in charge of fallen stars in space are usually hotter than the rest of the stars. In other words, they are bigger, like the prince of Persia, which I'll expound on much later, who is also a mighty archangel over other stars in space. So, we read from the scriptures that an opposing personality (Antichrist) was seen to have magnified himself against the prince of the host (archangel over stars) in space. It is observed in the proceeding verse that this opposing personality was given a host (band of stars) to accompany him. They will infiltrate this earth in human flesh, having subdued the archangel in charge of the stars in space before infiltrating the earth to rule some regions of the earth (all of Asia, the Middle East, Europe, Africa) by flatteries, and he will disregard religious gatherings.

His will exercise his powers over the archangel in charge of stars to forestall a breakdown or repeated similar occurrence in which stars of heaven turned men and fought against stars (men) drawn from river Kishon. So this personality anointed by Lucifer will, first of all, ascend to space, subdue the archangel overall stars suspicious of opposing his mission on earth, and then take one-third of the stars in space. After that, they will descend to earth in human flesh. This is what the scriptures meant by Lucifer's tail drew the third part of heaven's stars, and cast them to the earth...." (Revelation 12:4). And because stars are much mightier and stronger than humans, they will subdue the earth, ruling amongst men. That does not suggest that they can't be killed physically.

Chapter 2

Stars are Known

All stars existing under the darkness in space are subject to die like humans giving off the breath of life, as in stars losing their illumination. That is why they usually fall from space, giving off their life span. Of course, Astronauts sometimes view stars exploding in space. When the scripture says, "The stars are not pure enough in God's sight it implies stars seen under the darkness in space are classified unclean before God because they were once shut under the darkness of the deep, having sinned in the pre-Adamic world (Job 25:5). Their impure or colored nature explains why they currently radiate color light, such as green, red, brown, black, yellow, purple, blue, etc.

All stars of heaven under the darkness in space will eventually die off. Jesus said, "And the stars of heaven shall fall" (Mark 13:25). Implying all stars will die since they were re-illuminated in Genesis with light from God, who gave them the opportunity under darkness to relate with God once again until the number of human race expected is accomplished, and the curtain is drawn. Whenever these stars sinned, they die like humans, and light is withdrawn from them. They form what science calls 'the black holes in space, which implied the law of sin and death (light withdrawn) descending into earth, or some planets in space since stars don't die eternally as spirit beings. Some give off light to form black holes as thick black darkness and descend beneath to planets, while others incarnate or infiltrate the earth turning into humans. Of course, some return to positions in space as we have seen stars that came to planet earth, fought for the Israelites and returned to space. When they return to space, they form a new star or appear somewhere else in space as they were.

They simply shed off their illuminated bodies and fall into innumerable planets in space, turning into diamonds, gases, and precious stones. This has resulted in debris - floating particles, gases, asteroids, or metals as waves in space. These stars maintain strong magnetic flux despite giving off illumination in space. Their forces of attraction can pull any substance that comes in contact with a dead star (black hole) in space, acting as waves or gravitational pull after falling, yet alive in darkness as spirit beings acting as demons or simply turning into humans on earth dwelling amongst us. Let's look at the scriptures to buttress these points.

The book of Jude 1:12-13 says, "These are spots in your feasts of charity, when they feast with you, feeding themselves without fear: clouds they are without water, carried about of winds; trees whose fruit withereth, without fruit, twice dead, plucked up by the roots; raging waves of the sea, foaming out their own shame; wandering stars, to whom is reserved the blackness of darkness forever." So these stars are 'twice dead' in that they were once shut down under the black darkness before the Genesis of recreation, and that in the course of their exploding, they cannot give off water, what the scriptures meant by clouds without water or planets without water.

Stars in space are in the form of clouds but without water. Similarly, most planets are brazen clouds, having no dew or rainfall, but precious stones or several elements will be found there. Most planets are the dwelling places for alien beings or stars, which often infiltrate our planet in human form.

We saw this played out in the book of Revelations 9:1, which says, "And the fifth angel sounded, and I saw a star fall from heaven (space) unto the earth, and to him was given the key of the bottomless pit. And he opened the bottomless pit, and there arose a smoke out of the pit, and the sun and the air were darkened because of the smoke of the pit". The bottomless pit means endless depths into which some fallen stars from space that formed black holes also descend, and in the near future, the sun will be affected by the smoke emanating from the bottomless pit.

The star we just read about was addressed as a person using the personal pronoun in the objective case 'him' since stars (light beings) exist before God as mighty beings for which God calls them by their names. This star had the power to open the bottomless pit, indicating that they don't eternally die after exploding in space. Still, their lifespan has expired in space like humans also die on earth decaying into sand, with the soul and spirit in oneness alive in the abstract realms to paradise or hell or reserved under the cloud on earth. On falling from space, this star must have turned into a black hole immediately after being assigned to planet earth.

Jesus, while on this earth, once sighted Satan as lightning that fell into the earth. Luke 10:18 says, "...I beheld Satan as lightning fall from heaven." This was a clear case of Lucifer descending into the earth and maintaining his position in space. Satan was seen in the Old Testament walking to and fro, up and down earth (Job 2:2). The up and down movements indicate trafficking back to space and returning to earth at will. Hence, he was seen descending into the earth as lightning. So Jesus saw him when he entered planet earth as a light substance (lightning). It means that when appropriately viewed, black holes will have light substances descending into the earth. That doesn't mean he won't return to his abode in space as the biggest star in the universe's darkness. His routines have been ups and downs, to and fro on the earth.

In Revelations 8:10, it says, "And the third angel sounded, and there fell a great star from heaven, burning as it were a lamp, and it fell upon the third part of the rivers, and upon the fountains of waters, and the name of the star is called Wormwood: and the third part of the waters became wormwood, and many men died of the waters because they were made bitter." Stars are suns burning with the light of fire. The above scripture emphasized this star was burning as a lamp (light substance) descended upon rivers and streams, polluting the waters, which resulted in difficulty in drinking fresh water. Such pollution may probably cause massive death like the covid 19, killing millions to date.

There are innumerable planets and galaxies in space since most planets are reserved for fallen stars and ancient people. You can see that the above star was identified by named wormwood. Stars are known by names because God calls them by name, and whenever a star explodes or falls, it turns into a spirit being back to hell or falls into one of those planets in space awaiting judgment day, a hidden mystery from sons of men over thousands of years.

Let me show you a typical example of a star in the darkness of space capable of illuminating all of the earth. Revelations 18:1 says, "And after these things I saw another angel come down from heaven, having great power; and the earth was lightened with his glory." This tells you that there are mighty angels whose light can illuminate the entire earth. This angel would be more powerful than the sun and could walk into the sun. We saw this from the scriptures. Revelations 19:17 talks about an angel standing in the sun unhurt. Our sun is just one of the stars in space.

When people worship stars, they are indirectly worshipping light spirit beings, of which many are aware that these spirits (gods) communicate to them in their spirit. We saw this in the books of Amos and Acts, in which the Israelites once worshipped Moloch and Chuin as their God using images in the form of stars. "But you have borne the tabernacle of your Moloch and Chuin your images, the star of your god, which you made for yourselves" (Amos 5:26). We saw from the scriptures that these stars have the names Moloch and Chuin. And that is why you see many religions unwittingly use stars and moon in their flags, signifying the spirits they worship as a nation. Many people are unaware that worshipping stars or moon suggests their choice of whom they have chosen to worship, for which they will be cast into hell at last. They ignorantly claim to worship the same God who made the stars or gods they worship. No. They are worshipping the host of heaven.

Apart from the New Testament, the scriptures recorded that all re-illuminated stars in space from the recreation of Genesis will fall. Isaiah 13:10 says, "For the stars of heaven and the constellations (galaxies) shall not give their light...." You can see that the scriptures actually talked about galaxies already and that a time will come when all galaxies shall fall from space only when the sun will be finally darkened. The moon will cease to reflect light from the sun during the great tribulations.

One of the common features of stars under the darkness in space are incapable of is the capacity to give off water on explosion, even if they are like planets in the form of clouds in wavelike motions. The dust or cloud formed around these stars is what scientists see as dark matter. No star can give off water on explosion. Galaxies above the darkness in space are bigger than some galaxies found in our universe under the darkness.

Fortunately, in the universe above the darkness in space, Jesus is the bright and morning star, not Lucifer, wrongly translated in some books or Bibles. Jesus is the biggest Star-light who became flesh and blood for the sake of relating with humanity, just like fallen stars infiltrate this earth dwelling amongst us as humans, which we just saw in the scriptures that they feast amongst us in our earthly parties. And Jesus confirmed this in the book of Revelation 22:16, which says, "I Jesus...I am the root of David and the bright and morning star." He is the Chief Morning star, and he also imparts the 'morning star' status to his chosen ones as well.

The prophecy about Jesus' emergence as a Star from Israel could be dated 3,890 years ago when a prophet from the east named Balaam predicted a Star that would arise from Israel. Numbers 24;17 says, "I shall see him, but not now: I behold him, but not nigh: there shall come a Star out of Jacob, and a Sceptre shall rise out of Israel..." The same Jesus Christ you must have read about was also a Star in the universe above from the pre-Adamic world. For these reasons, the wise men (astronomers) from the east traced the star they sighted to Bethlehem of Judah until the star stopped.

Matthew 2:1-2, 9 says, "Now when Jesus was born in Bethlehem of Judaea in the days of Herod, the king, behold, there came wise men from the east to Jerusalem, Saying, Where is he that is born King of the Jews? For we have seen his star in the east, and are come to worship him...and lo, the star, which they saw in the east, went before them, till it came and stood over where the young child was...When they saw the star, they rejoiced with exceeding great joy." Just like the fallen stars we read about in the book of Revelations turned into human flesh, so also Jesus, who is the Light (Star) incarnated as a human clothed with flesh and blood by birth. As you'll soon find out, Jesus created all stars above and beneath, but he also became a star to relate with. So also, he became flesh and blood to relate with us humans.

Theologians have told us that Lucifer was a light bearer. They taught that theory in assumption. Lucifer wasn't a light bearer but a superior star; hence he was called the son of the morning in Isaiah 14:12. "O Lucifer, son of the morning! The phrase' son of the morning' denotes "son of the Morning Star." Lucifer was called the son of the morning because he was created by the bright and morning star. Just like Arcturus, a fallen star has sons, so Lucifer was once the son of the morning star (Jesus Christ), but Lucifer rebelled. So when theologians say Lucifer was a light bearer, very beautiful, they do not understand that Lucifer was Giant Star, not a light bearer. A light bearer means someone who goes before God, which is incorrect. His name as one of the stars was Lucifer, just like other stars have names. We saw Orion, Arcturus, Wormwood, Moloch, Gabriel, etc. An anticipated question might be, "Are you saying God created darkness?" I'll come to how the darkness existed later in this book.

As an interlude, let me use this opportunity to salute the scientific communities who explore these planets, galaxies, and the earth and have educated us in detail about their characteristics. Without scientific discoveries, I couldn't have been able to research in much detail what the scriptures meant as it relates to the darkness covering space, stars, man, and other planets. Thanks to the founding fathers of science, Aristotle, Plato, Isaac Newton, and our current scientific communities. I'm not suggesting that science should discard these fascinating discoveries, but studying and analyzing them helps us appreciate God's wonders. The universe is filled with the wonders of God, who formed all things from the beginning.

Spirit created nature

"...And the Spirit of God moved upon the face of the waters" (Genesis1:2). A detailed study of the book of Genesis revealed all created things in the universe under darkness were set in motion, drifting with respect to the recommencement of time immediately, when the Spirit of God moved upon the chaos. The move of the Spirit was upon the face of the waters wherein the earth was submerged, and this move also included the galaxies and planets. It kick-started the motions of every substance and beings shut under the darkness, indicating the reviving of life under the darkness once again, resulting in planet drifting associated with rotation, revolution, orbiting, and gravitational pull.

This means the earth, sun, moon, stars, and planets would experience constant drifting associated with rotation, revolution, and orbit—a continuous motion of things touched by the spirit of life once again. Once darkened, the sun would rotate on its axis and, at the same time, drift, so the earth, stars, moons, and other planets in their respective positions would also experience drifting.

God decided to revisit this universe for the purpose of expansion and resumption of activities. He needed to reactivate the moribund universe shut under darkness, but with a careful planning process adopting Adamic race humans as his sons and daughters.

Immediately, he began this refurbishment process. The scriptures recorded that the morning stars and all the sons of God shouted for joy together" (Job 38:7). This means angels in heaven and spirit men and women who were adopted into heaven before the chaos rejoiced together shouted for joy. They knew God was about to enlarge heaven's population by adopting humans as a new set of the sons of God and angels.

This does not suggest that the sons of God under the great darkness ceased to exist spiritually during those periods (millions or thousands of years) of lockdowns since they were already spirit beings that live forever. Still, they had no light, nor did they reflect light throughout this period. They were locked down under darkness without food for thousands of years. In other words, they had their bodies removed under death, like humans dropping the physical body by death, but spiritually alive. When these sons of God saw the move of the spirit upon the darkness, they sang together, rejoicing that God had revisited them under the darkness once again because the scripture was emphatic that all the sons of God shouted for joy together. Unfortunately, sons of God under the darkness were only given a little time spanning from the time of Adam till the end of this age, in what the scriptures meant by this life.

The move of the Spirit of God is like a force that I'd like to designate as 'the force of consistency of life' associated with the constant drifting of all planets and galaxies into endlessness. There is no end to the universe under the darkness after the recreation in Genesis. It became infinite in space. The move of the Spirit of God sets the chaos in motion before the spoken Word of God, 'Let there be light,' was introduced upon the chaos. The Spirit of God is still moving hence the drifting of the earth, sun, moon, and galaxies which are in constant motion even when we can't perceive it. The move of the Spirit is responsible for the earth's rotation and the motions of all galaxies and planets under the darkness. The declarative Word of God, "Let there be," actually upheld all things by the force of the Spirit because by Him (the WORD) all things consist" (Colossians 1:17, Hebrews 1:3).

The Word introduced into the chaos carried out manual recreation of things that were preconceived or invented by the Spirit of God; so that "the things which are seen, were not made of the things which do appear" (Hebrews 11:3). In other words, the Word formed 'things' which were preconceived (created or invented) and manifested as substances. Things here imply nature and man. Most of the things formed were taken from the previous earth sunk to form new species. The previous earth had things formed that differed from the things seen after recreation, but not all things, as some are reshaped and repeated. It means a new species of animals, not the dinosaurs anymore. New species from previous breeds' fossil remains in the old earth were used to form new species. Hence the scriptures recorded that things formed were from the dust of the ground. This implied the remains of fossils that pre-existed recreation in Genesis.

This shows that the move of the Spirit created nature, such as trees, birds, animals, flowers, man, fish, creeping things, firmaments, galaxies, sun, moon, earth, planets, etc. The spoken Word proceeded the move of the Spirit under darkness because the Spirit knows the mind of God (1st Corinthians 2:10). The heavens and the earth, and all therein are outcomes of the preconceived spoken Word. However, the Word performed the activities of recreation. Things formed were created and made. In other words, mental and physical works were carried out by a personality. "And God blessed the seventh day and sanctified it: because that in it he had rested from all his work (activity) which God created and made" (Genesis 2:3; Emphasis mine). The sun was re-arranged and reignited/re-illuminated, having undergone darkness before Genesis, and the earth, once sunk, was manually bolted to stones of the great deep waters during the universe's expansion in Genesis (Genesis 1:17, Job 38: 4-6).

Manual works were carried out in the process after spirit inventions. Hence, the universe was created and made (Genesis 2:3). "Where wast thou when I laid the foundations of the earth? Declare it if thou hast understanding. Who hath laid the measures (measurements) thereof, if thou knowest? Or who hath stretched the line upon it? Whereupon are the foundations thereof fastened? Who laid the cornerstone thereof?" (Job 38:4-6, emphasis mine). The earth was laid with lines of measurements as in precision of actual diameters and fastened to stones of the great deep before the recreation in Genesis. Are you wondering what I mean by recreation? Let me quickly show you from the scriptures that this present earth once existed and was sunk before Genesis.

Isaiah 41:22-23 says, "Let them bring them forth, and shew us what shall happen: let them shew the former things, what they are, that we may consider them, and know the latter end of them, or declare us things for to come. Shew the things to come hereafter, so that we may know that you are gods...." The scripture was crystal clear here about the previous earth signified by the former things and their latter end. This implies that the previous earth had dinosaurs and different creatures whose fossils are currently being discovered by our scientific communities. That pre-Adamic earth ended and time suspended.

Then the scripture talked about things to come, which means this present earth from Genesis of recreation to date. Then it spoke of things to come after that, which implies after shutting down activities of this present earth, there will be recommencement of another earth's activities. This indicates that the book of Genesis 1:1 was a synopsis of the previous earth sunk by God in the great deep waters. It was not sunk by demons as popularly taught in some quarters. As we progress, I will show you further scriptural proofs that denote people who once existed on the earth before the recreation in Genesis. Each stage of the new earth formed would have different species of organisms; created from previous fossils. I will come back to the origin of the concepts of good and evil as well.

Chapter 3

Science and the God Factor

The fossil remains of the new man Adam were retrieved from the old earth and recreated with new flesh. Of course, I'll take you through scriptural proofs as we progress. Adam was part of God's plans, hence the visitation of this universe under the darkness. The fossil remains of previous earthly beasts were upgraded to the image of God to dominate and give names to things formed. The actual reasons for modifying an earthly beast into a rational being will be discussed in due course. The upgraded irrational beast, now named Adam, was endowed with consciousness, capable of communicating directly with his Creator.

Of course, all living and non-living things communicate with God, just that not all can reason, unlike previous men and women in the pre-adamic world who possessed a higher faculty of reasoning. Ancient people (referred to as sons of God in the book of Genesis and Job) who once occupied this earth, knew that the fossil remains of irrational male and female beasts they coexisted with during the preadamic era, were converted and modified by God (after the lockdowns) to form the Adamic human race. With evolving developments, the Adam's descendants had intended to form a code name (scientists) for themselves but were once restrained by God in Genesis from accessing space for some reasons unknown to them at that time, for which they were scattered abroad to all the face of the earth.

In our dispensation, the same Adamic descendants have finally emerged with the code name 'scientists' and have named the force (move) of the Spirit in the recreation in Genesis as gravity, and that was the name thereof in the world of men because whatsoever Adam's descendants called every living creature, that was the name thereof since things formed were made for the natural man Adam to take pleasure in God's handiwork (Genesis 2:19). This force of gravity which attracts all things into its center on the earth planet is spiritual a force hence, it is impalpable lines of force in the sciences. The descendants of Adam and Eve were once restrained from accessing space, which I think it's a natural curiosity in humans, and all created things on the earth to often aspire to move upward or downward in search of the unknown.

Scientific discovery of the earth's rotation became a plus to the world of men, searching out hidden mysteries of the Creator. Although the word 'rotation' wasn't used in the book of Genesis, there are scriptural references in the book of Jeremiah that denotes the earth's rotation. Jeremiah 4:24 says, "I beheld the mountains, and lo, they tremble, and the hills moved lightly." Take note of the phrase "moved lightly" This implies the earth is rotating slowly with the hills. Mountains and hills are currently spread over the earth. The mountains and the hills rotate with the earth in their large masses; Adam's descendants have simply discovered the earth's rotation. The rotation of hills and mountains on the earth began when the Spirit moved upon the chaos in Genesis already explained.

Further scriptural references regarding the earth's rotation can be found in Isaiah 24:20, which says, "The earth shall reel to and fro like a drunkard, and shall be removed like a cottage, and the transgression thereof shall be heavy upon it; shall fall, and not rise again." To reel means to roll or rotate about a fixed point. It means there is a fixed north and south pole upon which the earth is hinged. The earth shall spin, and the transgression, which is heavy upon the earth, shall drop off, never to rise again. Both scriptures talked about the earth's rotation like a globe in the office hinged on the north and south poles. As I said, critics who lack an understanding of scriptural writings do that in ignorance.

God arranged the hills and mountains. God girded the mountains when he prepared them in different parts of the earth and on several planets in space. Psalms 65:6 says, "Which by his strength setteth fast the mountains; being girded with power." In other words, the mountains were piled upwards high by force. It is like humans trying to construct a high-rise building and would need compact pillars to make the building withstand winds. Similarly, God girded the high hills and mountains by his strength (force).

Origin of the science world

Advancement in science and technology had been predicted in accordance with scripture that Adamic descendants would increase in knowledge rapidly. "But thou, O Daniel shut up the words and seal the book, even to the time of the end: many shall run to and fro, and knowledge shall be increased." (Daniel 12:4). God needed to prove to the fallen stars and sons of God that he can bring something out of nothing. God then decided to use the animals they knew in their era to confound these fallen stars and sons of God. The scripture implied this when it wrote, "But God hath chosen the foolish things of the world to confound the wise, and God hath chosen the weak things of the world to confound the things which are mighty" (1st Corinthians 1:27). God told Daniel that science (knowledge) will increase and that because there will be an increase in knowledge, many shall be confused. The newly recreated Adamic race will invent artificial intelligence in which robots will obtain consciousness to deal ruthlessly with humans as well, through the instrumentality of a fallen spirit being in human flesh, as I will expound on shortly.

Over 2370 years ago, the scriptures foretold this increase in science-based knowledge amongst men. This shows it is part of God's plan to have men explore nature through science. Hence he taught Adam how to form things from the ground and give names to things. Scientific discoveries do not threaten God because he enjoys our discoveries even if they miss God. Daniel was a science student, and he understood science 2370 years ago. However, as men began to explore their world, they felt comfortable setting aside the God factor in their research and began to focus on experimental analysis. The concept of discarding the abstract world has revolutionized the human race in terms of physical developments, but it hasn't stamped out the reality of life - violence, conflict of wars, aging, natural disasters, accidents, death, poverty, pains, sorrows, sickness, diseases, etc.

There is a trend of societal disregard and criticism of the scriptures because men have formed a philosophy that without God, man can explore its world. The same man coined from beast once endowed with consciousness is now civilized to ignore God. Of course, the scriptures typified Cain, who left the presence of God, yet he built a city. In other words, man, setting aside the God factor, doesn't exclude him from reasoning or being creative, having been upgraded to the image of God – reasons like God, or having been endowed with consciousness. Man as an entity was recreated from irrational beasts (fossil remains) to join rational stars and sons of God in reasoning capacities.

The book of Genesis 2:19 says, "And out of the ground the LORD God formed every beast of the field and every fowl of the air, and brought them unto Adam to see what he would call them: and whatsoever Adam called every living creature, that was the name thereof." This was the origin of the science world. God knew that the new upgraded beast Man would have to be a tutor about things just like man is teaching animals or robot consciousness abilities nowadays. This was the order of things until man was fully adapted to reasoning and acquainted with his Maker. Of course, it was at this early stage of cognitive learning that Lucifer took advantage of man, swindling Eve. As I said, I will come to these details in the scriptures as we progress.

God formed things from the ground and brought them to Adam to name them according to the scriptures. And whatsoever Adam called things formed, that was their name, incontestable and approved based on the mandate given to them over all the earth. It implies Adam was introduced to study nature, create things and give names to things formed. I see no reason for the polarity between science and the scriptures over the years. God knew science would emerge according to the scriptures because he knows the end from the beginning.

Man's adventures into planets began in the book of Genesis when early men attempted building a tower (of Babel) into the clouds, which I believe was the great pyramid of Egypt built in conjunction with giant beings who once re-populated this earth through the copulation of Ham and his wife. God had to interrupt primitive men's plans because he needed them to be spread to all parts of the earth first. "And the whole earth is one language and one speech. And as they journeyed from the east, it came to pass that they found a plain in the land of Shinar; and they dwelt there. And they said one to another, Go to, let us make bricks and burn them thoroughly. And they had brick for stone, and slime had they for mortar. And they said, Go to, let us build us a city and a tower, whose height may reach unto heaven; and let us make us a name, lest we be scattered abroad upon the face of the whole earth" (Genesis 11:1-4).

These were early men (approximately 5,000 years ago) attempting to build a tower into the heavens. Studying and exploring nature is part of man's assignment. When early men lost contact with God, they resorted to exploring nature through God's divine abilities in them. We can see here that whenever God is not in view, man would always be preoccupied with thoughts of exploring the earth and the universe. God never said man could not function in the capacity to think anymore because they didn't believe in Him. Don't blame man, as we cannot sit idle doing nothing. Early men were interested in exploring the heights of the heavens, which we call planets or space.

Curiosity in man is natural, not sinful. Man was given consciousness and grew into the capacity to think, and so the only reason God had to distort early men was because he told Adam and Eve to replenish the earth. To replenish means to fill up or refill the earth once submerged in deep waters. "…Be fruitful, and multiply, and replenish the earth, and subdue it…" (Genesis 1:28). God wants the earth populated. God needed humans to fill the earth's land mass, which he stretched like the stars upon covering all space. This is exactly what the scripture meant when it says: "…The whole earth is full of his glory" because "man is the image and glory of God" (Isaiah 6:3, 1st Corinthians 11:7).

But men began to feel pride because of their achievements. Like the early men, they intended to make themselves a name (science) when they embarked on planetary exploration by constructing a tower that would reach the heavens. The name they intended to make in the early age has been achieved in our time. Some say, "Where is the light God spoke about in Genesis since it had been discovered that the sun regulates the day and night experience?" By so doing, they spurn scriptural writings ignorantly without taking time to search the scriptures. They erred in not knowing the scriptures.

Crusade of criticisms

I believe such ignorant remarks were made to smear God in their hearts. And guess what? There's a bandwagon effect of such criticisms. I think it is appropriate to consider these areas of criticism as we go through this book. For example, the eclipse of the sun was referenced in Amos 8:9, which says, "I will cause the sun to go down at noon, and I will darken the earth in the clear day." In context, a solar eclipse will take place on the earth. Early men also gave names to natural disasters, which the book of Acts 27:14 described as Hurricane Euroclydon. Nowadays, scientists also call some natural disasters (tornados and hurricanes) by names; hurricane Florida, hurricane Mary, etc. As you can see, the eclipse of the sun had been written in the scriptures, but many critics, who lack understanding of the scriptures, hurriedly jump to conclusions criticizing scriptural writings.

Although I will discuss the emergence of the darkness cited in Genesis as we progress, here I will talk about the light on the first day of creation, which has been the subject of criticism amongst many. Though scriptural writings are close-lipped, which forms the reasons for the polarity between science and scriptures over the years, many people do not take time to study the scriptures to match scientific discoveries to scriptural writings; they criticize from afar in ignorance.

Let's look at creation from the first day in Genesis 1:3-5 says, "And God said, "Let there be light, and there was light. And God saw the light that it was good: and God divided the light from the darkness. And God called the light day, and the darkness he called night: and the evening and the morning were the first day." Having studied the scriptures in depth, I knew apostle Paul was wrong when he wrote that God called light out of the darkness (2nd Corinthians 4:6). But as earlier explained, the light declared on the first day lit up fallen stars in space, including the sun, moon, and waters of the deep in which the earth was submerged under darkness. God re-introduced light on the first day of recreation, which revived all galaxies in the cosmos.

However, the light spoken under the darkness as it concerns the earth's sphere needs to be clarified here because the sun as a star was once darkened for many years during the lockdowns (being unperfect) before Genesis and was once again reignited and repositioned on the fourth day of recreation. So I will discuss the light on the first day of recreation apart from innumerable 'light beings' or "stars" that were re-illuminated in space as galaxies.

Let's go through the scriptures again in Genesis 1:2, which says, "And the earth was without form, and void, and darkness was upon the face of the deep. And the Spirit of God moved upon the face of the waters." This tells you that the darkness was upon the face of the deep waters. It means there was a mist of darkness upon the face of the waters. The waters were below while the darkness covering space beamed over the waters in the deep. Then God said, Let there be light", and there was light. Now, the light spoken on the first day of creation refers to the morning, which is often experienced in the early hours characterized by the morning dew. The morning dew phases out at sunrise since the heat content of the sun would melt out the morning dew. Scripture talks about the morning dews in Hosea 13:3. It says, "Therefore they shall be like the morning cloud, and as the early dew that passeth away..." The morning clouds come with dew which phases out as soon as the earth begins to face the sun. Proverbs 3:20 says, "...the clouds drop down the dew," indicating dews dropping from the clouds of waters above the earth.

The book of Job referred to it as the "day spring." "Hast thou commanded the morning since thy days, and caused the dayspring to know his place?" (Job 38:12). So, we can say the light spoken into existence from the first day of creation dispelled the mist darkness upon the face of the waters of the great deep before the sun was declared to rule over the daylight on the fourth day of creation. The light declared on the first day to rule over the earth wasn't the sunlight. The Spirit of God had already moved, causing the chaos to rotate and drift. And that means the light on the first day of creation introduced into the already rotating waters shone on the surface of the waters. "And God divided the light from the darkness." (Genesis 1:4). This shows the earth's rotation had commenced before the light spoken on the first day since a segment of evening and morning rotation of the earth forms a complete circle of a day.

The light shone and dispelled the darkness upon the deep waters where the earth was submerged. The brightness of the first daylight upon the deep waters was separated and was called day, while its reflection over the darkness was called night. But given that the rotation had commenced via the move of the Spirit before the light was introduced, God called the rotation of the light upon the waters day. Then the rotation of the reflected light in the darkness was called night. The light introduced on the first day of creation continued until the fourth day, and this light was very cool and did not radiate heat. It is associated with dew and was very refreshing. It was upon the face of the waters. And when God called for a firmament from the midst of the waters, the light was absorbed with the firmament alongside the waters above that moved upwards and continued to shine inside the clouds or firmaments.

This light absorbed into the clouds is characterized by coolness often noticed in the early hours of the morning or evening when the earth rotates away from the sun's heat; hence, it is recorded evening and morning. And that is why you and I experience coolness in the morning or evening. This light runs through the day and the night inside the firmament above the earth. That means whenever the earth is not facing the sun, the clouds will still be brighter than space's darkness. It is a half-truth that the sun only reflects over the earth when the earth faces the darkness covering all of space.

And so, we can see that this first daylight continued until the fourth day before God decided to utilize sunlight over the daylight absorbed in the firmaments. In other words, we can say the first daylight introduced the dayspring before the sunlight overshadowed the daylight since God made the sun to rule over the daylight. "And God set them in the firmament of the heaven to give light upon the earth, and to rule over the daylight and the night, and to divide the daylight from the darkness: and God saw it that it was good" (Genesis 1:17-18, Emphasis mine). The sun was set or arranged in the firmament of the heavens to outshine the existing daylight over the earth's spheres.

This means the sun must have been an existing planet several billion years ago among other planets but was reignited once again. Of course, we have proved that already. But to explain this further, let's take a clue from Ecclesiastes 12:2, which says, "While the sun, or the light, or the moon, or the stars, be not darkened...." If this verse of scripture is juxtaposed with Matthew 24:29, which says, "Immediately after the tribulation of those days shall the sun be darkened, and the moon shall not give her light (reflect), and the stars shall fall from heaven..." it is evident the sun and moon were darkened before the recreation in Genesis and will be darkened once more.

Night not darkness

The earth's rotation causes the day spring with morning dew to phase out before sunrise, or we can say before the earth gets the sunlight. We can all attest that 4:30 am through 6:45 am isn't always sunrise. It is called the 'morning.' The morning dew or dayspring often turns into fog, or what the scriptures call 'clay.' Job 38:14 says, "It is turned into clay to the seal, and they stand as a garment." And in the same book of Job 38:38 says, "When dust growth into hardness and the clods cleave fast together." In other words, the dayspring or dews, on being heated by the sunlight, turns into fog or clay, which evaporates back to the clouds standing as a garment. This is why grey or ash color forms in the clouds on a sunny day. Of course, it also depends upon the amount of air pollution in that given environment.

The sun was re-arranged to overshadow the morning clouds or dayspring to give brighter light upon the earth. Did you get that? The Scriptures revealed that the sun, moon, and stars were formed and set in their positions to give light to the earth and regulate the day and night seasons. "And God said, Let there be lights in the firmament of the heaven to divide the day from the night and let them be for signs, and seasons, and days, and for years. And God made two great lights; the greater light to rule the day, and the lesser light to rule the night: he made the stars also" (Genesis 1:15-16). Please note the phrase, 'to divide the day from the night. In context, the day already had the first daylight spoken; hence it is called day, and the night already had the same first daylight coined from the darkness, but the sun and moon were made to add illumination to the existing 'day and night time.

This means the interest is to have the sunlight and the dayspring during the day and part of the sunlight to illuminate the night. In other words, illuminated darkness equals night. Psalms 104:20 says, "Thou makest darkness, and it is night…." In other words, darkness was turned into night by the introduction of light spoken on the first day. The word night came into existence by adding light to darkness equals night. Contextually, night isn't the same as darkness. The sunlight contributes to a brightening of the clouds at night in addition to the light spoken on the first day absorbed in the clouds. This was captured in the scriptures already. Genesis 1:18 says, "And to rule over the day and the night, and to divide the light from the darkness…."

To divide the light from the darkness implies distinguishing between the darkness and the earlier introduced light of the first day. If you'd recollect, the first daylight had already divided the darkness producing two equations: day and night, respectively

(Genesis 1:4). In either case, the light spoken had been operational as day and night. It's crystal clear the sun and moon were positioned to ensure more illumination on the earth in addition to light spoken on the first day, which produced the night. Therefore, it's untrue that the sun's reflection is fully responsible for the bright clouds at night when the earth faces the darkness because the sun radiates heat all the time, but with the cool light spoken on the first day rotating in the clouds provides coolness that refreshed the earth during the night into the morning. It is crystal clear the day spring existed before the sunlight.

Sunlight does affect

God set them, implying he did some work, not just speaking. God positioned the sun, moon, and stars in their various axes, having expanded the universe under the darkness. The scriptures talked about the gigantic size of the sun, which forms our solar system. Psalms 19:6 says, "His going forth is from one end of the heaven, and his circuit unto the ends of it: and there is nothing hid from it." The sun's circumference is enormously large, radiating heat to planets orbiting around its circumference. The sun was made to regulate the daylight period of planets within its circumference; these include Mercury, Venus, Jupiter, Earth, etc.

It is scientifically proven that the moon has no light but reflects light from the sun. This puts things in proper perspective from a scriptural point of view as well when it refers to the sun being darkened and its effect on the moon. Joel 2:15 says, "The sun and the moon will be darkened...." The first event in which the sun and moon were shut down under darkness took place on the previous earth; God revisited the universe once shut under darkness. And Job 25:5 says, "Behold even to the moon and it shineth not...." In context, the moon has a limited reflection of light from the sun.

Jesus also foretold the end of this world when he said, "...The sun will be darkened, and the moon shall not give her light..." (Matthew 24:29). In context, sunlight does affect the moonlight, an indication that science and scriptures are in tandem as regards the reflection of the sun by the moon. In Revelation 8:12, it says, "And the fourth angel sounded, and the third part of the sun was smitten, and the third part of the moon, and the third part of the stars; so as the third part of them was darkened, and the day shone not for a third part of it, and the night likewise." From this scripture, it is evident that the sunlight does affect moonlight.

But it has been a sort of argument and criticism by some schools of thought that the scriptures recorded the sun stood still without going down for a full day which is the reason for 366 days leap year calendar. And this has generated some criticisms as well, citing the book of Joshua 8:29, which says, "...The sun stood still, and the moon stayed...so the sun stood still in the midst of heaven, and hasted not to go down about a whole day" (Joshua 10:13).

Given the narratives, it is understood that these were archaic languages, as contemporary English is concerned. However, technically speaking, it is scientifically proven that the sun does rotate about its axis once in 25 days; an indication that the sun standing still in scriptures is applicable here. Since the sun does rotate about its axis (once a month) with the gravitational pull of attraction on the earth planet in orbit because the earth's gravitational field around the sun is generated, it implies the sun's rotation within its axis was stopped (or stood still). It shows the field effect was also restrained for 24 hours by God. Don't forget the sun was made to regulate the earth's daylight.

Now, let's consider a typical example of the event which took place in the land of Egypt 3,890 years ago, in which the land of Egypt, in isolation, experienced total darkness, which in modern-day is an eclipse of the sun. But I wouldn't call it a solar eclipse because the Egyptians did not experience night. Instead, they experienced black darkness for three days, while other parts of the earth experienced a typical day and night period. Exodus 10:21-23 says, "And the LORD said unto Moses, stretch out thine hand toward heaven, that there may be darkness over the land of Egypt, even darkness which may be felt. And Moses stretched out his hands towards heaven, and there was a thick darkness in the land of Egypt three days: And saw not one another, neither rose any from his place for three days: and all the children of Israel had light in their dwellings."

This was no solar eclipse in the land of Egypt, but what the scripture described as 'thick darkness. People can move from one point to another when they experience a solar eclipse of the sun. However, in Egypt, God brought a thick cloud of black darkness over Egypt for three days, and they were immobilized in one spot while the earth still rotated, producing daylight and night to other parts of the earth. God made nature, so he can interrupt nature anytime because the world and everything in it belongs to him. "The earth is the LORD's, and the fullness thereof; the world, and they that dwell therein" (Psalms 24:1). Men can only analyze nature but cannot control nature. Meteorologists often forecast winds, storms, and tornados ready to strike a given geographical location, but they cannot control nature.

Chapter 4

Arctic and Antarctic Regions

What I've found in my further studies is that the earth has foundational pillars laid by God not captured in the book of Genesis. "Where wast thou when I laid the foundations of the earth...whereupon was the foundation fastened? or who laid the cornerstone thereof "(Job 38:4). These pillars were referenced in the scriptures as North, East, South, and West poles. The north and south hemispheres were captured in the scriptures. God confirmed the pillars which sustained the earth were bored up by Him. "I bear up the pillars of it" (Psalms 75:3).

These pillars rotate alongside the earth's sphere. Some pillars were kept in the Arctic and Antarctic regions of the earth. Job 37:9 says, "Out of the south cometh whirlwind: and cold out of the north" This implies the north and south poles would be drifting. The north and south poles would constantly change positions, with both poles producing extreme cold because the Spirit is still moving. Jesus specifically told us that lightning comes from the east to the west (See Matthew 24:27. An indication that he knows how the earth was configured since he was the actual personality on the ground as a spirit being by whom God created the earth and universe including the universe above the darkness.

You may be confused, saying, "What do you mean by personality on the ground?" John 1:10 says, "He was in the world, and the world was made by him, and the world knew him not." I'll expound on this scripture aside from the book of John to show you that Jesus Christ had been in existence before water, sand, planets, stars, rocks, animals, plants, mountains, hills, thunders, storms, clouds, etc., were formed several billion years back. So, when Jesus talked about the movement of lightning from the west to the east, He knew how the earth was configured because He created it.

Frost and snow came from God at the beginning of creation. The scripture captured this in Job 38:29-30, which says,' Out of whose womb came the ice? And the hoary frost of heaven, who hath gendered it? The waters are hidden as with a stone, and the face of the deep is frozen." This showed the arctic and Antarctic regions were all captured in the scriptures. God issued out frozen temperatures from his womb as snows. The scripture says that the waters are hidden or turned into stone ice under the oceans. As a matter of fact, the scripture says that God casteth forth his ice like morsels: who can stand before his cool?" (Psalms 147:17). In context, God issues out extremely frozen waters from his womb, and there are various levels of cold in the universe above the darkness that cannot be withstood by any man. The extreme cold was found to preserve certain creatures without food for thousands of years in our universe before Adam was formed.

According to the scriptures, we have tidal waves on earth caused by interactions of lights. For example, Job 38:24 says, "By what way is the light parted, which scattereth the east wind upon the earth? In other words, the interaction of the sun and moonlight causes tidal waves. In science, it is called the moon's and sun's gravitational force. The word parted means divided, which implies the sun and moon interactions or moonlight interactions.

The south wind also blows upon the earth (Exodus 10:13). The most fascinating aspect of the scriptures is that the imaginary lines (axis) were all captured. Job 38:5 says, "Who hath laid the measures thereof… who hath stretched the line upon it?" Isn't this amazing? The latitude and longitude lines were captured and stretched on the earth during the recreation.

Lines of equator

God stretched out the lines upon the earth from the beginning, which have magnetic flux. Science discovered these things in our times. "Have you not known? Have you not heard? Had it not been told to you from the beginning? Have you not understood from the foundations of the earth? It is he that sitteth upon the circle of the earth, and the inhabitants thereof are as grasshoppers…" (Isaiah 40:21-22). "Hast thou perceived the breadth of the earth?" (Job 39:18). The breadth of the earth refers to the lines of the equator, and the circle of the earth refers to the axis upon which the earth rotates. God, by his Spirit, ensured the rotation of the earth on its axis constantly while the earth drifts at the same time slowly. How did he ensure such an accurate measurement of the size of the earth?

Scriptures revealed God had a compass by which he did some measurements during the creation of the earth. Proverbs 8:24-29 says, "…When he set a compass upon the face of the depth. When he established the clouds above: when he strengthened the fountains of the deep: When he gave the sea his decree, that the waters should not pass his commandment: when he appointed the foundations of the earth." This means God knows the exact measurement of the depths of the heavens from below the bottomless pit. He fixed the earth's foundation upon four rotating pillars in the floods of waters. The above Scriptures refer to creation before time began. That is the formation of all things - the universe above and beneath. Science is yet to breakthrough on the age of fire, water, clouds, etc. The 13.8 billion year estimate of the age of the earth is based on certain assumptions, and it tends to limit further research on fossils above 20 billion years.

How about the rainbow, which is undoubtedly seen during a rainfall in the sky? God set his bow upon the cloud after the floods of Noah, according to the scriptures. And we're all witnesses of the rainbow appearing in the sky to date. However, science is yet to determine the actual size of the rainbow. "And God said this is the token of the covenant which I make between me and you and every living creature that is with you, for a perpetual generation: I do set my bow in the cloud, and it shall be for a token of a covenant me and the earth. And it shall come to pass that when I bring a cloud over the earth, that the bow shall be seen in the cloud" (Genesis 9:13-14). The rainbow cannot be found in space or on any other planet in the universe because it was established in the clouds for humans living on earth. Man can analyze nature but can't create it.

The darkness across space

Many schools of thought believe that the darkness in space was a huge challenge to God. We've got a lot of junk sermons over the years, with some people alleging that God was equally faced with challenges because there was darkness seen in Genesis before creation. Some preach these misconceived sermons as preachers of the gospel. Some say, "God did not create darkness and that God is chasing the darkness away." I do not mean to talk down on any, but we must thoroughly search the scriptures before making certain utterances. I'm not criticizing the apostle Paul, who erroneously wrote in the scriptures that "God commanded light to shine out of darkness." He implied darkness existed before light or God met darkness during recreation in Genesis – wrong!

Some religious folks might say, "But the scripture says all scripture is given by the inspiration of God." Yes, but there are certain scriptures in which the author wrote based on his depth of knowledge extracted from the Old Testament, and if not careful, he may erroneously summarize the scriptures in ignorance, which I believe we should correct. Similarly, many songs that were ignorantly produced from this scripture must also be corrected. God never called forth light out of darkness as erroneously written by the apostle Paul. Many are bewildered, wondering, "How come there was darkness at the beginning of creation?"

Others alleged the darkness was due to the activities of demons or fallen spirits who fought and destroyed the earth resulting in chaos. Such notions weren't the actual events that resulted in the darkness. If fallen spirits fought and destroyed the earth, which led to chaos, what stops them from destroying this present earth immediately after Adam fell to Satan's deception? Why can't demons stop the day and night occurrence?

According to the scripture, God created darkness himself. God said, "I form light and create darkness" (Isaiah 45:7). God formed the darkness we read about in Genesis across space (our universe) which we have discussed already. The darkness was formed several billion years back as one of his arsenals. Job 38:9 says, "When I made the cloud the garment thereof, and thick darkness a swaddling band for it...Where is the way light dwelleth? As for darkness, where is the place thereof, that thou shouldst take it to thy bound thereof, and that thou shouldest know the paths to the house thereof...Hast thou seen the treasure of snow? Or hast thou seen the treasure of the hail which I have reserved against the time of trouble, against the day of battle and war?" (Job 38:9, 19-23) These verses of scriptures dictate that God formed darkness and light several billion years back and kept darkness as his weapon for the imprisonment of deviant spirits.

We saw from the scriptures that snow, hail, and darkness were God's arsenals for war or in times of trouble. God foreknew spirit beings would fail or rebel, and he had to prepare darkness in store against the time of trouble which he used in flooding the universe before the recreation in Genesis. Isaiah 50:3 says, "I clothe the heavens (all of this universe) with blackness, and I make sackcloth their covering." And the book of Nahum 1:8 says that darkness shall pursue God's enemies, indicating that God used darkness as one of his arsenals in times of trouble. A typical example was seen in the land of Egypt, in which hail and darkness were used in the days of Pharoah. God still has so many reservoirs of asteroids in space ready to launch during the great tribulation that will come upon this earth for those who refused the gospel of Jesus Christ. Asteroids are floating pieces of rocks split by electromagnetic wind (storms) on various planets in space. There are stormy winds of greater magnitude than what we experience on earth. As a matter of fact, the velocity of the space shuttle does increase due to these stormy winds in space.

Spirit beings have a strong force of currents which they often generate as storms over cities, causing disasters that we sometimes attribute to God in our ignorance. I've had several experiences in which storms arose over my roof, and when I perceived that such storms came from the devil, I would take authority in the name of Jesus Christ over the storm, which immediately ceased. Unfortunately, science has no clue about demonic storms, and many have suffered catastrophically untold hardship due to stormy winds or tornados. The scriptures acknowledged four principal powers over the heavens (universe under darkness) responsible for strong winds. However, God's wind current is the strongest of all.

A typical manifest presence of God resulting in the formation of asteroids was seen in the scriptures. 1st Kings 19:11 says, "...And behold, the LORD passed by, and a great and strong wind rent the mountains, and broke in pieces the rocks before the LORD...." We can see that the presence of God generates winds so strong that rocks are shattered into asteroids. The strongest of all winds is from the LORD. Nahum 1:6 says, "...His fury is poured out like fire, and the rocks are thrown down by him." God's arsenal in space was once utilized on the earth to destroy His enemy nations. God had used hailstones for trouble times as his arsenal on earth. "And it came to pass, as they fled from before Israel, and were going down to Beth-horon, that the LORD cast down stones from heaven upon them unto Azekah, and they died: they were more which died with hailstone than they whom the children of Israel slew with the sword" (Joshua 10:11).

The above scripture talked about Adoni-zedek, a one-time king of Jerusalem discomfited in battle by the Israelites. In the ensuing battle, God had to cast hailstones from heaven upon Adoni-zedek's people. It is obvious God reserved hail for a time of war, according to the scriptures. In the near future, God will launch his reserved hailstones weighing as much as 100 pounds on this earth again to strike humans who have spoken against him or rejected the gospel. We had previously talked about the thick darkness over the land of Egypt, which lasted for three days. God foreknew the event in the land of Egypt. God sees the end from the beginning. He has the foreknowledge of several billion years to come as the author of life. He has the foreknowledge of his angels and ancient men and women going astray. So he prepared the darkness to shut down the activities of fallen stars and ancient people before Genesis.

As earlier mentioned, recreation in Genesis was for the recommencement of time in our world aimed at adopting a new set of sons of God from among irrational beasts modified from ancient people. Ephesians 1:5 talks about "the adoption of children by Jesus Christ unto himself according to the good pleasure of his will." This means God is pleased by adopting children from the earth to join his kingdom as a set of people. This he purposed in himself before the recreation in Genesis. He had purposed to adopt a new set of beings into his kingdom before the foundation of the world (universe under darkness). There were once people who lived on this earth several million back during the pre-Adamic world, who were adopted as current spirit men into the light zone universe above before Genesis. In contrast, others were shut under the darkness. I'll prove these from the scriptures as well.

Fallen stars in various hierarchies as galaxies of stars, including ancient men and women who sinned in the pre-Adamic world, were arrested and banished under chains of darkness. "And the angels which kept not their first estate, but left their own habitation, he hath reserved in everlasting chains under darkness (in space) unto the judgment of the great day" (Jude1:6). As we progress, I will touch on the men who were also ordained to condemnation with these angels. So God had to roll out darkness from its reserved place across all of space. God withdrew light covering all of the universe from these rebellious stars thrown out of the light universe into this universe before recreation in Genesis. This was earlier captured in the book of Job that God withdrew light from the wicked.

We all live in a universe under darkness, and many are ignorant that our universe under darkness in space is like a prison zone. It was once a place where deviant spirits were locked up, even on the earth. John 1:5 says, "And the light shineth in the darkness (zone); and the darkness (universe) comprehended it not" (Emphasis mine). In other words, Jesus came into this realm of our dark universe (once a prison zone), and the people under the dark universe don't seem to understand him. They were already conformed to the behaviors and ways of fallen ancient men and women banished under darkness where evil thinking exists. The Adamic human races to date are simply used to the darkness and evil, being ignorant of the light zone universe above where darkness or evil thought does not exist. For these reasons, John 3:19 says, "And this is the condemnation, that light came into this world (the dark universe), and men loved darkness rather than light because their deeds were evil." It is obvious the scriptures interchanged 'the darkness' with 'the world' in the same book of John. The world speaks of the universe. The world is a mixture of previously fallen spirit men and stars capable of turning into human flesh dwelling amongst us, teaching us wrong ways.

Our universe is not all there is. The earth was founded under the dark zone universe with fallen angels and spirit beings still under the same universe with us. You've got to understand that there exists a much bigger universe where saints in light dwell. Colossians 1:12 says, "Giving thanks unto the Father, which hath made us meet (fit) to be partakers of the inheritance of the saints in light" (Emphasis mine). So, when the scripture says, "If we walk in the light as he is in the light…" (1st John 1:7). The saints in the light speak of the universe in the light zone in which Abraham, Enoch, Adam, Samuel, Paul, and saints are currently in existence like you and I, are alive here on earth, but these possess celestial bodies.

It means the sun, moon, planets, galaxies, earth, etc., which make up the cosmos are under the darkness. God also confirmed that he made outer space with thick darkness. When the LORD rebuked Job, he said, "When I made the cloud as garment thereof, and thick darkness as a swaddling band for it"

(Job 38:9). It's evident that the outer space sky was once full of light like our current cloud in the day, the difference being God rolled out thick darkness over space. This explains why space is very black to date. The question is, "Why would God establish man under darkness if he loves man?" A good response to that question is given as we progress. But let's consider some of the merits and demerits of the darkness.

The scriptures say that 'God made darkness His secret place, and his pavilion round about him were dark waters and a thick cloud of the skies' (Psalm 18:11). God hid in darkness. Psalm 97:2 says, "Clouds and darkness are round about him" God kept a spiritual vial between himself and man, making God inaccessible. The darkness round about God implies the darkness in space was meant to obstruct man or fallen spirit beings from accessing God, who is in the light zone universe. The thick darkness in space could be far more than 90km in thickness by which the earth's spheres compass the surface of the earth. In addition, the darkness is fortified with thick chains and black sack clothes, which barricaded the darkness zone universe. The darkness also functioned as a covering for God. That is why the scriptures say dark waters and thick clouds of the skies surrounded God. God is above the thick darkness covering space several trillion miles of light years away. Outside the darkness universe, God is seen upon the throne in the light zone universe with innumerable mighty stars. It's a zone of sparkling, beautiful lights. There's no nighttime in the light zone universe above.

However, whenever God descends into this dark universe, he is covered with darkness or thick clouds. In Genesis 15:12, the scripture records,"...An horror of great darkness fell upon him", and God spoke in the darkness by assuring Abram that all the land of Ham, which includes the Amorites, Jebusites, Girgashites, Canaanites, Hittites, Kenites, recorded in Genesis 10:6-18, were Abram's and his descendants for possession. So, God changed his name from Abram and named him after the land of Ham by changing his name to Abram-Ham, in one word, Abraham. The father of many nations - Amorites, Jebusites, Girgashites, Canaanites, Hittites, Kenites, etc. (See Genesis 17:4). God also changed Sarai to Sara-Ham, pronounced Sarah. God Almighty gave them these lands for an everlasting possession.

Another reason for the darkness in the context of our existence was to account for days and years while the earth remains. Scripture says, "And God said, Let there be lights in the firmament of the heaven to divide the day from the night, and let them be for signs, and for seasons, and for days, and for years." (Genesis 1:14) And Psalms 104:20 says, "Thou makest darkness, and it is night." Without night, we cannot sleep properly in this earthly realm. At night, the moon reflects the sunlight, which causes vegetation to grow before daybreak. The night also functioned in the growth of a child. When a child is born, it would be observed that over time, as the day breaks and the night falls, the child is growing due to sleep at night. Some animals, birds, fishes, and creeping things feed at night. So, we can see some usefulness of darkness in our natural world. As humans, we also convert waste into useful materials. After several million years, God's aim of forming darkness was later converted to serve a useful purpose.

God made the darkness and called it night in order to have humans rest. "The night cometh when no man works" (John 9:4). "Man goeth forth unto his work, and to his labor until evening. (Psalm 104:23). However, God sees through the darkness as daylight. "Yea, the darkness hideth not from thee; but the night shineth as the day: the darkness and the light are both alike to thee" (Psalms 139:12). Some animals see clearly at night. Humans and fallen spirit beings have their eyes behold darkness. But, of course, fallen spirit beings are used to the darkness, already carrying out mischievous acts of violence in the dark.

Chapter 5

The Universe in the Deep

Before picking up my pen to write these mysteries, I was inspired by the Spirit of God, who gave me insights into the scriptures of truth. Of course, I spent a lot of sleepless nights reasoning and analyzing scriptures bit by bit, comparing scriptures with scriptures, and I then realized that creation began at a point. And so, basically, I'll be delving deeper into the creation of all things. That is prior to the emergence of the multiverse. Since it's understood that there was a timeless beginning' or what I'd refer to as the none-existences of life-or-death concept, as in no water, heavens, deep, earth, mountains, galaxies, light beings, animals, plants, etc., just a state of nothingness except for God. I'll be considering an approach to the non-existence of space and time.

As with the sciences, one might presume 'life or light' was the commencement of time, but that is untrue! However, let's zoom in on the concept of 'life or existence. The first sign of life was 'light' according to the scriptures, which talked about 'the light of life, an indication that light emerged from life (John 8:12). The big bang theory was premised upon an explosion of a mass of matter under high density and temperature ballooning a tiny particle of matter (as the origin of the cosmos) outwardly faster than the speed of light around 13.8billion years ago. Although this postulation is basically an imaginary conjecture, nevertheless, on scrutiny, it fundamentally contains some elements of ambiguity. I believe this postulation was deposited in cognizance of the galaxies in space. Of course, the galaxies in space have been demystified in this book; however, prior to the emergence of the book, those of us in the sciences have classified these galaxies as inanimate substances; hence they were referred to as matters from which the big bang theory was postulated. However, suppose we assumed this 'mass of matter' under high density and temperature to have been a non-living thing. In that case, its internal energy must have been greater than its region of explosion - the Arctic or Antarctic not negligible here since it was presumably the origin of the cosmos, which evolved into space, time, galaxies, sun, moon, beasts, etc.

Given that the mass of matter possesses a high density and temperature, it's anticipated that an opposite mass of matter should be responsible for the arctic and antarctic regions since you can't give what you don't have. One might contend that the exploded particle of matter became cool over time. If it became cool, what made it cool? Who created that cool environment? Could the same particle of matter become cool and at the same time get hotter than the sun over time to form the galaxies since it was ballooning faster with such a high density and temperature? We all know that natural radioactive disintegration is made possible because a given atmospheric temperature and pressure exist in a region in which the atomic nucleus radiation was factored. If the atomic nucleus was stored in an arctic region, then radiation couldn't have been possible, and disintegration not in view.

On the other hand, the assumed 'mass of matter' in consideration is a 'non-living particle' because if it's 'living,' it automatically implies a being. But let's assume a non-living matter producing living organisms sounds ridiculous - whoosh! Suppose a force greater than the speed of light was imputed to have been responsible for the ballooning particle within the mass of matter (in an uncharted region). It unalterably implies light was created from a source greater than it. And from the scriptures, light was created, since God said he formed light (Isaiah 45:7). It means light as a sign of life was created from a given source. Which shows life was created as a concept. Hence Jesus said, "...I am the life" (John 11:25). In addition, John 1:4 says, "In him was life," which shows life which is manifest in the form of light came from an immeasurable being. Of course, when I mean light, it contextually includes 'light of fire,' which depicts the characteristics of the galaxies.

God lives outside time and space but created time and space as a concept from which all things (life or death) consist. We read earlier in Colossians 1:17 that He is before all things, and by Him, all things consist. It means the concept of death and life (as things) was formed in the mind of God. It shows life was a concept created by the spirit of life. The spirit of life means the force that engendered the concepts of life and death. If life was a concept, it means the force that produced the light of life is greater than the speed of light. Hence it is the spirit of life or light capable of moving faster than light and capable of giving life to dead things because dead things can only be injected with the spirit of life. Romans 8:2 talks about 'the law of the spirit of life in Christ Jesus....' Which shows life as a concept came from a Spirit. The spirit does infuse life into lifeless materials, causing it to acquire a living status.

A typical example is found in Revelation 11:11, which says, "And after three and a half days, the Spirit of life from God entered into them, and they stood upon their feet...." The law of the spirit of life activates non-living things to life, and this spirit of life came from God, who is a Spirit. Science posited the universe's expansion (under darkness) to have been greater than the speed of light. Contextually, a force that created light, matter, space, and time must have been responsible - the Infinite One, who upholds all things in their respective order from colliding with one another.

God came from the everlasting realms but began his' kingdom of life in the spiritual realms several billion years back in the light zone wherein 'time' began. Scripture says, "God is light" (1st John 1:5). God is light, capable of replicating himself. You cannot give what you don't have (Nemo dat quod non habet). God formed light himself, and his kingdom is made of sparkling lights with his angels and cherubs radiating lights of fire far brighter than the sun. The core personality of God isn't light, but being a Spirit, he radiates light. So, when Scripture says, 'God is light, it unreservedly dictates he radiates light like the sun.

The truth is God wrapped himself with light as a garment. "Who covereth thyself with light as with a garment..." (Psalms 104:2).

In other words, God is clothed with light, but he isn't light in his core personality since he created light. God literally radiates light far more than all galaxies in space; hence the Scripture says, "Who only hath immortality, dwelling in light, which no man can approach..." (1st Timothy 6:16). God had immortality (everlasting life) dwelling in light. In context, he originated the concept of life. He formed light dwelling in the light of fire which no human can approach, and he literally shines brighter than all galaxies in space. When we describe a person, we say, "He or she is fair or dark in complexion." God shines like the sun, as a purer white (snow) light, not scorching as the solar sun. "For the LORD God is a Sun and a shield" (Psalms 84:11). God radiates light that shields. In other words, very cool light and, at the same time, a consuming fire.

The light zone universe above consists of galaxies and planets. Jesus is the biggest star in that zone and the sun of righteousness. However, his angels also radiate sun light as well. Malachi 4:2 described Jesus as the sun of righteousness, an indication that our solar sun is unrighteousness dwelling under the death zone universe; hence it is impure and subject to be darkened in the near future. The book of Job 31:26-28 corroborates God as a person is a Sun in the light zone universe. It says, "If I beheld the sun when it shined, or the moon walking in brightness; my heart hath been secretly enticed. This is also iniquity to be punished by the judge: for I should have denied the God that is above (higher in space than our solar sun, including all stars under the darkness)." (Emphasis mine).

As you can see from the scriptures, God dwells several trillion light years above our solar sun. God is to be worshipped, not the sun, moon, or other galaxies under darkness.

"He walketh in the circuit of heaven" in the light zone universe as the sun (Job 22:14). In other words, God as a person radiates light as the sun, and walks in the circuit of the heaven in the light zone universe above, brighter, cooler, and whiter than snow, indicating holiness environment. We read previously that Jesus is the bright and morning star. This denotes he isn't scorching to the saints and angels above.

Let's consider the Scripture, which says, God formed light and created darkness" (Isaiah 45:7). If we expound on the darkness, it becomes immeasurable, but light under the darkness is measurable. Now, supposed God existed infinitely before forming the light, given His principle of dual formation of things, for example, heat and cool, what would you deduce from this axiom? I'd leave that to your sense of judgment. Someone might hastily quote, 'God is light, in him is no darkness at all,' citing 1st John 1:5. Of course, that emphasizes love substituting light. The context of that Scripture is God is 'love' being interchanged with 'light.' What would you make of the scriptures which depict God making darkness his secret place? (Psalm 18:11). We saw thick darkness preceded God's visitation to Abraham in a vision because God sometimes wrapped himself with darkness as well. Psalms 97:2 says, "Clouds and darkness are round about him...."

Let's get back on track about the universe at creation from the beginning of time, not the Genesis of recreation. To be a king, you'd have to establish a domain. Malachi 1:14 says, "God is a great King." So, God, being a great King, set out the creation of his kingdom of life upon the floods of waters, having formed the measurable light, considering the above axiom. The number of years he pre-existed before forming light remains unsearchable. Water and light were formed in sequence by God as a sign of life for created things to breathe in, having predated life, dwelling inside fire, the everlasting realms from which he created the spiritual and the natural world. Men and women who once dwelled on this earth, designated as aliens, were natural but were moved into the abstract world for the sake of the Adamic human race.

Fallen spirits as ancient people who may have disdained the current Adamic human races adopted to run the activities of this present earth are dazed by the inventions of humans at measuring the universe (even if not accurate) because God wants to prove a point; hence he endowed us with so much potential. God loves the human race He formed on this earth, even under the darkness. He is pleasured by our inventions, as stated in the scriptures, that all things are and were created for his pleasure. Revelations 4:11 says, "Thou art worthy, O Lord, to receive glory and honor and power: for thou hast created all things, and for thy pleasure, they are and were created." In other words, ancient people were created while the current Adamic race, including the future people, are created for his pleasure. Hence, they were (past) and are (present) created.

Created things were formed in light, which is life. Scriptures talked about the light of life. But things created in light weren't made from the things that appear in the light. Hebrews 11:3 says, "...things which are seen were not made of the things which do appear." Technically, this implied a source greater than light is absolutely responsible since the concept of life came from an immeasurable source. Was there ever a state of nothingness? The scriptures stated a lifeless and timeless period when the cosmos did not exist, perhaps, similar to the big bang theory. That doesn't mean God is likened to a particle here. He emerged massive, and his creatures – the gigantic galaxies much larger than the sun planet- are also massive.

Delving into creation at the 'very beginning' (not the recreation in Genesis), as referenced in the scriptures, put things into perspective. Proverbs 8:24-28 says, "When there were no depths, I was brought forth; when there were no fountains abounding with waters...while he had not made the earth, nor the fields, nor the highest part of the dust of the world (both worlds). When he prepared the heavens, I was there: when he set a compass upon the face of the depth. When he established the clouds above: when he strengthened the fountains of the deep." And if you connect Psalms 104:3-4, which says, "Who layeth the beams of his chambers in the waters; who maketh the clouds his chariots: who walketh upon the wings of the wind: who maketh his angels spirits; his ministers a flaming fire." It's obvious the components of the universe stand out from these scriptures.

Although the scriptures never indicated when fire was formed, we saw a timeless period when there was no existence of fountains of waters, clouds, galaxies, stars, sun, sand, angels, man, rocks, trees, birds, animals, etc. God began his kingdom of life concept with light which proceeded from Him – the immeasurable source. Scriptures earlier read showed God used a set of compasses while establishing the measurement of the deep, which is all of space and time, in both the light and darkness zone. This means the universe wasn't initially vast but was blown into endless depth, height, and width, similar to the big bang theory. Nature was formed several billion years back.

Regarding our universe, the number of years varies due to multiple discoveries and figures posited by various archeologists. In reality, things formed were made to experience death or life. Some of the things formed were made to join the forever living stream of life or death concept.

However, in an attempt to unify the varieties of things formed under the darkness, science unanimously named things seen under darkness as the universe or cosmos.

However, I'd prefer the terminology of the scriptures "the worlds," which implies the universe under the darkness and the universe above the darkness of space and time, as captioned in Hebrews 11:3, which says, "...The 'worlds' were framed by the word of God." The 'worlds' here encapsulated the everlasting realms, which is a separate universe that differs from the light and darkness zones, hence the term multiverse. God envisioned the conceptualization of life. So basically, I'll be expounding on the systems upon which God formed 'the worlds.' And this has to do with the 'light of fire and waters' encompassing a wide range of things, such as clouds, deep or space, earth, darkness, planets, angels, cherubs, man, plants, animals, fishes, birds, galaxies, etc. into an ensemble.

Atmosphere for existence

Psalms 29:10 says, "The LORD sitteth upon the flood; yea, the LORD sitteth King forever." God rules over all creation from the heights of the floods. The flood here denotes the waters in which the clouds were formed. Clouds are frozen waters mixed with fog, air, and other trace elements. God is seated at the peak of the great floods of waters, implying the peak of the clouds in the light zone universe above the space darkness. So when the Scripture says the LORD seated upon the floods or established his chambers upon the waters, it substantially denotes various planets such as fire planets, ocean planets, snows, rocks, arctic, Antarctic regions, etc., found in both worlds. According to the scriptures, both worlds can be referred to as the deep.

Space and time represent the deep, which I'd designate as part of the great floods upon which the LORD is seated. The dark universe was made dry and referred to as 'mist darkness. That is, without air, in space darkness'. 2nd Peter 2:17 says, "These are wells without water, clouds that are carried with a tempest; to whom the mist of darkness is reserved forever." This means all of space and time was suspended and flooded with a mist of darkness, indicating a mid-point in the great floods. Several millions of planets in our universe were also suspended from water, except God opened the windows in them. That doesn't suggest that there are no planets in our universe without water or life apart from the earth. There are planets full of water in our universe. The light zone universe has clouds that are full of water-like frost. So also, the cloud over our earth's sphere is full of waters as in frost and natural waters being the land of the living, hence the rainfall and dews for sustenance.

God dwells in and above the light zone universe, interacting with his creatures - angels and sons of God who live in the light zone universe. Inferentially, just as our dark zone universe is wrapped with blackness, so also the light zone universe is wrapped with light, with God as the sun. That doesn't suggest God's core personality can't be seen in the light zone (the angels' abode) upon which he established his throne in the kingdom of heaven. His disposition suggests his angels in heaven can look up to him. Jesus said, "...Angels do behold the face of God in heaven" (Matthew 18:10, paraphrase). Heaven here presupposes a planet coined with clouds of frozen waters. God's hands formed the waters. "The sea is His, and he made it..." (Psalms 95:5). Humans breathe under the firmament, which is over the earth's sphere, so spirit beings live in waters as their natural habitat and in planets without water for those under the darkness in space.

Natural seawater may not be the habitat for humans, just that ancient people, now spirit beings, inhabit the oceans and seas. They don't get suffocated living in the oceans, rivers, and sea waters since the atmosphere in the waters looks similar to earth's atmosphere. In the land of the living, life cannot be sustained without water of life. Water, as a sign of life, proceeded from God. "And he shew me a pure river of the water of life, clear as crystal, proceeding out of the throne of God." (Revelation 22:1). In Psalms 65:9, it says, "...the river of God, which is full of water..." Water came forth from the throne of God at the beginning of His works, and he made all things inside the flood of waters. All of life is situated in the flood upon which God is seated on his fiery throne. What do I mean? All created beings - spirit beings, human souls, and their hosts were formed in the floods of waters, for which humans also breathe in air, which contains water molecules for survival. Angels in the universe above also breathe in fire as well as water molecules.

We currently live in the midst of waters and clouds, with some waters suspended in volumes such as ice, snow, water, and mists. Clouds were created to form a garment over the earth, as with other planets, so also, there are clouds in heaven above where angels dwell. Clouds are angels' habitats, and they also walk on lands similar to the earth in heaven. The scriptures corroborated this when it says, "...They shall behold the land that is very far off." (Isaiah 33:17). The land in heaven, the light zone universe, is wrapped with gold. The substances in the light zone universe are similar to those found in our universe, indicating elements of nature.

Of course, nature was created before the angels, cherubs, and ancient people were formed. God utilized light and elements of nature in the formation of spirit beings. We saw certain substances of nature used in the formation of Lucifer as described in Ezekiel 28:13, which says, "...Every precious stone was thy covering, the sardius, topaz, and the diamond, the beryl, the onyx, and the jasper, the sapphire, the emerald, and the carbuncle, and gold...." As you would soon discover, angels are made with elements of nature, like the clouds. The Scripture says, "Who maketh the clouds his chariots." (Psalms 104:3). In other words, angels are God's chariots, made with substances of clouds, in addition to other element of nature, such as beryl, sapphires, gold, diamond, and other precious stones. In Revelation 1:7, it says, "Behold, he cometh with clouds..." (Revelation 1:7). And as a matter of fact, the Scripture says, "God's strength is in the clouds" (Psalms 68:34). God dwells in fire and clouds. So also, spirit beings dwell in clouds and fire. The book of Exodus 13:21 talks about the LORD through his angel appearing in a pillar of cloud and fire, giving light to the children of Israel by day and night.

God exercises his strength in the clouds (angels). The book of Psalms 103:20 says, "Bless the LORD, you His angels that excel in strength, hearkening unto the voice of his word." So, when the Scripture says God's strength is in the clouds, it implies that God formed angels with light and clouds and made the angels his chariots. This was also revealed in the book of Daniel 7: 13, which says, "I saw in the night visions, and behold, one like the Son of man came with clouds of heaven and came to the Ancient of days, and they brought near before him." The kingdom of heaven is made of clouds, gold, trees, rocks, animals, birds, mountains, hills, flowers, precious stones, etc.

Formed in the middle

If you recall the recreation in Genesis, God had to split the waters in which the earth was submerged into parts: some waters suspended above as ice, others beneath. "And God said, Let there be a firmament in the midst of the waters, and let it divide the waters from the waters. And God made the firmament and divided the waters under the firmament from those above the firmament: and it was so." (Genesis 1:6-7). The firmament above the earth has volumes of water suspended by gravity.

Similarly, uncountable planets in space are made of water, fog, and some trace elements, while others are dry as mists of darkness covering all of space suspended from rainfall or dews, depicting a brazen firmament. Deuteronomy 28:23 says, "The heavens over you are brass." This denotes that some clouds in space have cloud waters suspended and are very cool, while others are without just brazen brass form of clouds.

The waters above the earth precipitate seasonally, and there're waters in the cloud over the earth known as 'windows of heaven,' so much in store than the oceans and the seas (Genesis 7:11). I'd like you to recollect the thickness of the spheres of clouds above the earth's surface. The opening of the 'windows of heaven over the earth denotes similar apertures exist over some other planets to downpour if God so desires. We also have waters upon which the earth was founded, referred to as waters of the great deep (Genesis 7:11). The earth was founded and established upon the deep waters. "...For he hath founded it upon the seas, and established it upon the floods" (Psalm 24:2). The pillars of the earth were established in the deep floods. The book of 2nd Peter 3:5 says, "...The earth standing out of the water, and in the water." The earth in the middle of waters implies the great sea referenced in the scriptures.

As earlier said, some planets are very cool due to suspended waters over them, but the ground remains dry. The earth once had clouds full of water suspended in Genesis. The Scripture says, "...For the Lord God had not caused it to rain upon the earth, and there was not a man to till the ground" (Genesis 2:5). It means the brazen clouds over several planets had suspended volumes of ice as waters. Job 38:37 says, "...Who can stay the bottles of heaven? This means only God suspended the waters or air over all of space.

God laid the earth's foundations upon the floods of waters, which sustained the pillars or poles of the earth, and then suspended the earth in space to drift relative to our sun planet. Psalms 18:15 talks about "The channels of waters seen with the foundations of the world" The channels of water seen dictate that the earth and the universe was established upon the floods of waters but suspended. We're in the midst of deep waters with the sun, earth, moon, clouds, planets, and galaxies hanging in space. Job 26:7 says that God hanged the earth upon nothing. This earth is floating in the middle of space and time, including several planets sustained by His word. It means the solar system was formed in the midst of deep clouds, as already explained. We're in the midst of the deep waters when viewed from the third heaven above the darkness, which the scriptures referred to as seas. Hence the Scripture referred to this realm as a 'sea of glass,' which I'd expound on much later.

The space created by the suspension of the firmaments above the earth is called the "atmosphere." Psalms 104:6 says, "...The waters stood above the mountains." Waters stood above the mountain, indicating that clouds made of water in the form of ice mixed with fog and other elements were suspended by the force of gravity over the earth, including several planets. The earth's atmosphere is saturated with oxygen and other gases, which are comfortable for human existence; water and sunlight also sustain plants and animals. God is the fountain of life in all of existence. "For with thee is the fountain of life..." (Psalms 36:9). Interchangeably, one can say, for with God is the water of life. God becomes the breath you take in since he's the fountain of life, and that is why you can't stop thinking about Him over and over.

Life was premised upon the floods of water, but then, we've stars breathing in fire though still under the mist of darkness in space, which we have discussed before. It means life is composed of water and fire atmosphere of existence. If you'd recollect, the light of fire and water were the fundamental substances upon which life was formed. Those in the land of the living breathe under clouds containing water molecules, while the stars as lamps of fire under darkness without water molecules, yet sustained in mist darkness, which came from the same immeasurable source of life. By implication, life is sustained by clouds of water or the light of fire, but the lights of fire interconnect both life and death. If you'd recall, we talked about water proceeding out from the throne of God, which is the source of light of fire. The galaxies (stars) in our universe have obtained the forever-living nature of God - the light of fire.

Psalms 33:6 says, "By the word of the LORD were the heavens made and all the host of them by the breath of his mouth." If you recall a similar scripture in Genesis 2:1, which we've expounded on earlier, referencing the heavens and their host. Psalms 33:6 corroborates the heavens – as planets and the host of them – as galaxies, The Milky Way, etc. These were initially created at the 'very beginning' and breathed out from God's mouth.

Now, from the waters of the great deep, God formed several planets and designated a planet formed for human existence - earth. Inside the great deep floods, the gates of death and the shadow of death, which are mighty principalities, were kept under darkness (prison) before recreation in Genesis. Job 36: 16-18 says, "Hast thou entered into the springs of the sea? Or hast thou walked in search of the depth? Have the gates of death been opened unto you? Or hast thou seen the doors of the shadow of death? Hast thou perceived the breadth of the earth? Declare it if thou knowest it at all."

The deep has a pit, several dry lands (planets) with a brazen cloud of darkness in which fallen, rebellious spirits were shut down. Psalms 69:15 substantiates this when it says, "Let not the water flood overflow me; neither let the deep swallow me up, and let not the pit shut her mouth upon me." This means spiritually, down the depth of the seas, there is a hollow spot called a 'pit' where no water is. Under the seas lies a deep pit leading to a reservoir storing souls who have passed out of planet earth. For this reason, the sea will give up the dead in it on the Day of Judgment (Revelation 20:13).

Also, there is spiritually a pathway from under the earth to some planets in space which expand daily, perhaps, corroborating scientific claims that our universe is expanding. The Scripture was very clear that the hell planet is a reservoir pit for departed souls awaiting judgment. From what I saw in my vision, hell has no literal fire burning, just heat waves as in 'flame' radiating from an unseen inferno. Although I didn't access all of hell in my vision, the LORD showed me. But, of course, we are aware that under the earth, there is a massive, impenetrable fire that pops up as molten lava and gases erupting as volcanoes. "As for the earth...under it is turned up as it were fire" (Job 28:5).

I would not know if the flame from the fire under the earth radiates to hell planet, the abode of unrepentant souls, which might be why hell is very hot and unconducive. It's a reserved place of darkness for the unrepented and wicked souls. Job 21:30 says that the wicked are reserved for the day of destruction and that they shall be brought forth in the day of wrath." Hell is a planet as a pit, beneath the earth as a reservoir, and its occupants will be sentenced to the lake of fire planet(s). In hell, the stars of heaven cannot be seen in space. How did I know all this? I had been caught up there, which spurred my further research into the universe we live in. Black clouds of darkness without stars or moon hover over the planet hell. The planet enlarges itself as people descend into it after death every minute.

The Scripture says, "Hell hath enlarged herself, and opened her mouth without measure: and their glory, and their multitude, and their pomp, and he that rejoiceth shall descend into it" (Isaiah 5:14). Hell planet does enlarge unstoppably every day. Aside from the pit known as hell, there's what the Scripture describes as the bottomless pit. This is a different pit that is endless; even if all spirits beings were thrown in it, they'd keep descending through a billion years, incapable of landing. The scriptures talk about a bottomless pit into which Satan will be cast, and he would fall for a thousand years without landing at the base of this pit. The book of Revelation 20:3 says, "And cast him into the bottomless pit, and shut him up, and set a seal upon him, that he should deceive the nations no more, till the thousand years should be fulfilled: after that he must be loosed a little season." It denotes that the universe under darkness seems endless in depth.

There is an endless depth beneath the earth planet and an endless height above the heavens: the multiverse is infinite in space. Proverbs 25:3 says, "The heaven for height, and the earth for depth, and the heart of kings is unsearchable." I believe the adjective 'unsearchable' implies infinity in space, and it is obvious that we live in a world without end outside space. If you would take a space shuttle and embark on traveling outside the earth sphere, northwards, southwards, eastwards, and westwards to any direction of choice, you cannot arrive at the end of the universe in a billion years; it does expand daily.

Similarly, there is no end to existence once a being is formed. It moves from one phase of existence into another, spiraling into everlasting or the forever stream of life or death concept. As it is written: "...World without end" (Ephesians 3:21, Isaiah 45:17). Infinity outside time does not impair the Spirit's capacity to keep moving even when the activities of the universe under the darkness were shut down for a period. Time was still counting in general because the Spirit can't stop moving in the universe above. However, the reintroduction of the Spirit move was manifest once again in the dark zone universe, resulting in the drifting, rotation, and orbiting. Many are unaware that the earth, the moon, and the sun are drifting while the rotation and revolution subsist.

Many, if not most people, ignorantly think God formed the earth in the book of Genesis, but that isn't what the Scripture says. The scriptures didn't say God formed the dry land earth in the book of Genesis. The Scripture says that God made the waters to pave the way for the existing dry land earth to appear. "And God said, Let the waters under the heaven be gathered together into one place, and let the dry land appear: and it was so" (Genesis 1:9). God parted the waters of the great deep, separating the waters with a firmament, and then gathered the waters into one place, this he called seas, oceans, rivers, etc. to make surface the old earth in the deep waters. An indication of an existing dry land in the great deep is evident when we consider the definite article 'the' used here. Therefore, we can say that the dry land earth existed in the midst of the great deep waters. It was called dry land in Genesis because there were no trees, animals, birds, creeping things, humans, etc. I think some creatures in the great deep waters might survive in the waters from the old sunk earth.

The earth became a prison yard for fallen spirit men and women. Some of which came forth dwarf spirit beings as aliens, which I've literally seen walking on the river. At another time, I saw a spirit dwarf run through a wall. So I knew these aliens came from some planets under the space darkness. Sometimes you may not see these spirits if your eyes are not opened, but at other times they're found around oceans or forests. Normally, spirits operate in sea waters and oceans of the world. They walk on waters like Jesus did. Water and land became their habitation as soon as God recreated the earth in Genesis. They were shut down in deep water for several millions of years when the earth was submerged before Genesis. And because they were made spirits having put off flesh which is not the type of human flesh, the water became solid ground.

Jesus Christ demonstrated walking upon waters before his disciples. He demonstrated his nature as a spirit being in human flesh. He didn't perform a miracle walking on sea waters unaided. "And the disciples saw him, walking on the sea, they were troubled, saying, it is a spirit; and they cried out for fear" (Matthew 14:26). His disciples were astonished and yelled out that Jesus was a spirit. Peter stepping upon the water is a miracle, but to Jesus, it is natural.

Similarly, it's natural for spirits to walk on water easily because water seems firm before them. One time, an angel stood upon water while talking to Daniel. "And one said to the man clothed in linen, which was upon the waters of the river..." (Daniel 12: 6).

So, Jesus walking upon water wasn't a miracle, but the reality of his personality as a Spirit being in human flesh dwelling among men. For this reason, Jesus literally ascended up the clouds when he left planet earth in the presence of people. We saw from the scriptures that angels do fly and, at the same time, stand between the earth and the heavens at will. 1st Chronicles 21:16 says, "And David lifted up his eyes, and saw the angel of the LORD stand between the earth and the heaven, having a drawn sword in his hand..." This angel was seen standing in the air, unaffected by gravitational pull because angels are spirit beings.

Unlike spirit beings, Natural Adam's descendants are incapable of walking in sea waters. Natural man was made from the dry land called out of the deep waters and would depend on water for survival. The clouds, earth, water, fire, etc., are spirit substances formed by God. It means the supernatural sustains both the natural and supernatural man since water sustains man on earth. Scriptures also talked about fallen spirits that often proceed from the seas. The book of Daniel and Revelation both talk about beasts in the shapes of rams, goats, and frogs as fallen spirits proceeding out of the seas.

Chapter 6

Fossils by Archaeologists

When the waters of the great deep were gathered into one place, forming seas or oceans, footprints of dead species, including skeletons of pre-Adamic creatures, were found in rocks. This underscores the presence of fossil remains by various archaeologists of our times. The fossil remains of pre-Adamic creatures serve as food for people of old times. Fossil remains were predicted to be found in rocks in line with scriptural provisions. A typical scriptural example of fossil remains predicted to be found in rocks was captured in Ezekiel 26:4-5, which says, "...I will also scrape her dust from her, and make her like the top of a rock. It shall be a place of spreading the nets in the midst of the sea: for I have spoken it saith the Lord God...." This explains why fossil remains were found in most rocks, sea beds, and earth crusts. If you'd take the time to go through the entire chapter, it significantly denotes a typical desolation event of the pre-Adamic earth.

In context, God submerged this earth in pre-Adamic time, perhaps, for several million years with people of old times, including creatures of dinosaurs, birds, frogs, dogs, creeping things, etc. Living creatures in the pre-Adamic time perished, being congealed in rocks or sea beds, which are currently being excavated for analysis by our scientific communities. The race of people (men/women/children) who once lived on this earth formed with skeletons of precious stones and covered with the flesh of brass were giant beings with long fingers and toes based on the visions seen. They had snow-white colored skins speckled with black (large round spots), similar to jaguars, all over their bodies, and they were very beautiful.

Searching through the scriptures to substantiate the vision God showed me, I was amazed at my findings, having read the scriptures repeatedly for decades. I discovered that the vision aligned with the pre-Adamic people's scriptural accounts. 2 Peter 2:13 is direct to the point when it says, "...Spots they are, and blemishes, sporting themselves with their own deceivings while they feast with you." Pre-Adamic men and women were people of whitish snow skins speckled (large black or grayish) patches all over their bodies. It is like manufacturing 60 by 60 tiles with a pure white base and embellishing it with black circles in the middle, just like a typical football played on the pitch. Jude 1:12

is also a pointer to the fact that pre-Adamic people, known as 'ancient people' in the scriptures, were reckoned to have spotted bodies: "These are spots in your feasts of charity, when they feast with you, feeding themselves without fear...."

So, the scripture gave us clues as to what these ancient people seemed like who usually infiltrate this earth, dining with us as humans to date. Of course, they usually don't surface on earth with their spotted bodies, but they're spiritually known to the angels. I can't say if the large black round spots (speckled) seen in their snow-whitish bodies might have been due to their indulgence in sin. Perhaps, they were originally formed with snow-white skins, not blonde color. I doubt if the round large speckled (black) depicts sins committed since the Adamic human race doesn't have the effect of sins committed sticking to their flesh.

A typical clue from the scriptures about ancient men/women in human forms is that they often associate among themselves. Probably, they form clubs and secret societies in an attempt to associate closely with Adam's descendants, and of course, they possess inherent abilities to speak different languages. In other words, whenever they associate among themselves (say four or five of them) mingling with Adam's natural descendants (humans), their objective is to deceive and corrupt them, especially in the area of sexual immorality, and castigate God or Jesus without fear. They are known for maligning God at will.

Let's consider another scriptural account depicting pre-Adamic men and women who were speckled in their skins. Zachariah 1:9-10 says, "I saw by night, and behold a man riding upon a red horse, and he stood among the myrtle trees that were in the bottom; and behind him were three red horses, speckled, and white. Then said I, O my Lord, what are these? And the angel that talked with me said unto me, I will shew thee what these be. And the man who stood among the myrtle tree answered and said, these are whom the LORD sent to walk to and fro through the earth." Three men were found riding upon red horses, white and speckled. Speckled implies spotted or blemished, which aligns with what the LORD showed me about ancient people. And I cannot formulate what God didn't show me. I saw pre-Adamic men and women in a clear vision.

When the scripture says, 'these are they,' it implies the men (not the red horses) sent forth to walk to and fro the earth spiritually. Chariots or horses in the scriptures often dictate someone riding upon the horses. And of a truth, I least expect the vision the LORD showed me. I was amazed by God's love in revealing such mysteries to mortals. I guess it was for a purpose. Having seen a glimpse of pre-Adamic men and women, my perspective on life changed. I was inquisitive and got more engrossed about these ancient people who lived on this earth for several billion years, procreating the earth before the Genesis of recreation (Genesis 1:1-2).

In my curiosity, I discovered that the principality named 'Death' placed in charge of planets under darkness also rode upon a grizzled horse in the spiritual realms. That is, Death rode on a speckled horse in the spiritual realms. Zachariah 6:1- 7 talked about this ancient principality called 'Death' as a mighty prince roaming the earth in the spiritual realms. "And I turned, and lifted up my eyes, and looked, and behold, there came four chariots out from between two mountains, and the mountains were mountains of brass...the third chariots white horses, and the fourth chariots grisled and bay horses. Then I answered and said unto the angel that talked with me, What are these, my Lord? And the angel answered and said unto me: "These are the four spirits of the heavens, which go forth from standing before the Lord of all the earth. Get you thence, walk fro and to the earth, So they walked to and fro through the earth."

Death in association with three mighty spirit beings (personalities) were found to have been responsible for famine, violent tendencies in humans, conflicts of wars, sickness, disease, and hunger. The scriptures just read said, 'these proceedeth forth from mountains of brass.' Please note the 'element of brass' used in this context in relation to these ancient people. Creatures of birds, dinosaurs, dogs, man/woman beasts, crocodiles, etc., in the pre-Adamic times, were made of bones and flesh, which served as food to ancient people. The demised skeletons of the pre-Adamic animals were congealed in rocks over thousand/million years of lockdowns in deep waters under the darkness. God utilized these creatures' fossil remains to form new species during the Genesis of recreation.

We saw from the scriptures: Genesis 1:24 says, "Let the earth bring forth living creature after his kind, cattle, and creeping thing, and beast of the earth after his kind: and it was so." The old earth sunk brought forth cattle, beasts, and creeping things that differed or looked similar to pre-Adamic world creatures, of which God utilized the same skeletons or fossil remains. It's like calling forth the seabed to the surface, having dead bones of animals, birds, and creeping things that were parts of current fossil remains found in rocks or sea beds. "And out of the ground, the Lord God formed every beast of the field, and every fowl of the air..." (Genesis 2:19). It means God recreated cattle, beasts, birds, man, reptiles, etc. from the old earth once submerged in deep waters. However, creatures like behemoth and leviathan recreated during the Genesis were made of elements of brass and iron in addition to flesh of clay, indicating a pre-Adamic beast world emergence since brass is superior to clay - flesh and bones.

Flesh of different kinds

It was observed that pre-Adamic men and women were made of flesh of brass and precious stones or iron, forming their skeletal structures. These men and women who once lived on this earth perished with their flesh of brass, alongside their skeletons made of precious stones, not bones, according to the scriptures. Unlike the current human race, Adam adopted to run the activities of this earth, which were made from fossil remains of pre-Adamic animals having flesh and bones, categorized as 'weak' substances. I saw from the scriptures a spirit being who once lived in the pre-Adamic times testified to this in the book of Job 4:17-19, which says, "Shall mortal man be more just than God? Shall a man be purer than his maker? Behold, he put no trust in his servants, and his angels he charged with folly: How much in them that dwell in houses of clay, whose foundation is in the dust, which are crushed before the moth?" Whose foundation is in the dust implies the human races were taken from the earth's crust coined from previous animals, which served as food to ancient people. This particular spirit (ancient man) said that the current human race from Adam dwells in houses of clay, which are inferior to the types of houses ancient people of old dwelled in.

A detailed study of the scriptures dictates two sets of people pre-existed the Genesis. They were men and angels, which we have noted. If you've highlighted what this spirit being (sons of God) whispered to Eliphaz the Temanite, one could identify two sets of people - servants and angels. The word servant here implies men as 'sons of God who once occupied this earth several million years back. While the angels who were charged with folly are current stars of heaven - once stars of God. That is why you've Job 38:7 distinguishing the stars of God from the sons of God. Take note of the word 'stars of God', stars of heaven. You must understand that 'stars of heaven' implies stars forming our galaxies under the darkness zone universe, while 'stars of God' implies stars in the light zone universe.

If you attempt to produce a telescope to view the light zone universe, capturing images would make no sense because the light zone is extremely bright, such that light generated by a scientific telescope would be insignificant. In addition, you would find a gigantic Sun (not scorching) in the light zone 100 times larger than the largest star in our universe under darkness. The scripture explicitly describes God in the light zone universe as the sun there and as a person, which has been extensively discussed. God walking in the circuit of the heaven as the sun in our earlier scripture implies our solar sun is a man angel walking. Hence the scripture, when emphasizing the sun in Psalms 19:6, described the sun as a man using the possessive pronouns 'His going forth....'

Now, when you compare Psalms 19:6, which says, "His going forth is from the end of the heaven, and its circuit unto the ends of it...." It typically describes our solar sun radiating across some planets. Similarly, the scriptures described God as the sun in the universe above the darkness. The scripture in the book of Job 22:14 says, "...thick clouds are a covering to him, that he seeth not?" In other words, God is far above the thick darkness covering all of space, but he sees through the darkness in space from the height of his throne down to all planets in space, including the planet called hell. We saw earlier that night and darkness are alike unto God.

So, when the scriptures say, "thick clouds are a covering to him that he seeth not," it means darkness is not obstructive to God's eyes. He sees through darkness just like a lion sees through darkness at night. But given the distances of several trillion light years, he had to manufacture a device by which he monitors the universe even if he is omnipresent. God has his own device used in covering distance, which the scripture described as a 'sea of glass like unto a crystal, and I'll expound a little more as we progress. With this device, God sees all activities going on in the darkness zone universe, including the thoughts of our hearts. He sees all of hell, planets, galaxies, earth, and space. Job 26:6 says that "hell is naked before him." All activities in our universe are naked to him, and he can issue orders through his device (sea of crystal glass), which is audibly transmissible to any spirit or human.

Let's get back on track regarding the sons of God and stars of heaven. The stars of God, as well as pre-Adamic people, were once under God's rule of righteousness and peace. As time passed, some stars from the universe above began to pervert righteousness on earth, mingling with the men and women on earth in sexual perversions. So God cast them down by engaging other stars of God in a fierce battle that drew swords against rebellious stars. We saw the scriptures captured a similar scenario when it talked about Lucifer's deposition in Isaiah 14:19, which says, "But thou art cast out of thy grave like an abominable branch, and as the raiment of those that are thrust through with a sword, that go down to the stones of the pit...." This was a perfect pictorial event of what transpired when angels who sinned were cast out of the light zone universe.

They were chased out with swords by armies of God during the pre-Adamic times. Lucifer wasn't part of this whole drama, even if we just borrowed a clue from a similar event of what took place as the angels who sinned were once thrust through with a sword down to the stones of pit hell. Lucifer was still with God as a cherub during the chase. Several billions of stars cast down to this dark zone universe were found guilty of having cross-breaded sexually with ancient men and women. That is why the scriptures talked about angels who sinned, having left their habitation, he hath reserved under chains of darkness unto judgment day (See 1st Peter 2:4, Jude 1:6). The question is, "Who taught them?" You'll find a good answer to that question as we progress.

They were locked under chains of darkness in space despite God's visitation in Genesis, pending the judgment of the great day. You should understand that stars cast down to this darkness zone universe conspicuously seen above in space are referred to as 'stars of heaven. However, the scriptures categorized them as sons of God in generic terms in some parts of the scriptures. For example, the book of Job 38:7 puts a distinct difference between the actual 'stars of God' from the 'sons of God. So we can say the sons and stars of God in the light zone universe were referenced in Job 38:7. These were all formed with precious stones and covered with flesh of different kinds. The scriptures distinguish different kinds of flesh when it states: "All flesh is not the same flesh: but there is one kind of flesh of men, another flesh of beasts, another of fishes, and another of birds. There are celestial bodies and terrestrial bodies: but the glory of the celestial is one, and the glory of the terrestrial is another. There is one glory of the sun, another glory of the moon, and another glory of the stars: for one star differs from another in glory" (1st Corinthians 15:39-41).

As you can see, there are celestial and terrestrial bodies, and the glory or features of the terrestrials differ from the celestials. Sons of God as pre-Adamic men and women are distinct from stars of heaven despite the fact they were fallen spirits under the darkness. These two sets of people weren't made of the same material components in their formation stages, hence the perversions by crossbreeding hyper sexually. It is like a man or woman sleeping with cows or dogs, even if both are made of flesh and bones but with different skin textures. The difference in the skin textures was the reason the book of Genesis kept emphasizing that every living thing created was made after his kind (Genesis 1:17-25). Angels and ancient men/women of pre-Adamic ages were made of different precious stones in their skeletal structures and flesh of different textures, even if the angels might appear like them.

The concept of precious stones in the skeletal structure of pre-Adamic men was coined from the various scriptural accounts of angels, men/women, Lucifer, etc., formed with gold, pearls, precious stones, brass, iron, diamond, etc. The scriptures expressly told us that pre-Adamic men and women weren't made of flesh and bones, but were also flesh, just not the Adamic human type flesh. The scriptures already distinguished different types of flesh made by God, hence things creatures formed were made after their kind. And, I can categorically say that if there're archeological records of fossil remains in resemblance to current human skeletons found in rocks or sea beds/earth crust exceeding 7,500 years (as of this time of writing), such fossils remains were primitive beasts - man (as irrational beasts in the pre-Adamic age) redesigned by God in the Genesis into his own image and likeness. As earlier said, I will expound on the accounts of the current human ancestry, once regarded as irrational beasts recreated and endowed with consciousness into God's image in Genesis.

While the actual pre-Adamic people (men, women, or children - now spirit beings) were dispersed to various planets, oceans, seas, and rivers as spirits, some planets were named after these fallen ancient men. We saw this in the book of Acts, in which the Lycaonians captured Mercury and Jupiter: "And when the people saw what Paul had done, they lifted up their voices, saying in the speech of Lycaonia, The gods are come down to us in the likeness of men. And they called Barnabas: Jupiter; and Paul: Mercurius because he was the chief speaker. Then the priest of Jupiter was before their city...." (Acts 14:11-13). Mercurius was the chief speaker, implying Mercury planet would be the first planet near the sun. And these ancient people have human priests who worship them since humans are fond of worshipping the hosts of heaven. Unfortunately, some have infiltrated the earth by incarnation or sudden appearance from the seas since the days of Adam/Eve. You already saw how these ancient people were equally drawn from the river Kishon, mingling with humans to fight physical battles on earth. They often access our planet earth as they love to return to their previous earth of old, leaving the dry places (planets in space) – their habitation designated by God during recreation.

Rebellious dwell

God formed the dry land himself at the beginning of his works several billion years back. Psalms 95:5 says, "...His hands formed the dry lands" Several planets in space were designated heavens in the scripture. Apart from the earth, innumerable planets under the darkness are currently dried as they became a place for rebellious spirits to dwell. Psalms 68:6 says, "...The rebellious dwell in a dry land or dry places." The concepts of dryness (i.e., suspension of rainfall or plants) in several space planets undoubtedly served as punishments for fallen ancient people, now spirits. God had a clairvoyance of spirit beings rebelling; hence he prepared dry lands under darkness at the beginning of time before ever forming any star or ancient people. I'll shortly show you from the scriptures that God foreknew some pre-Adamic people, now fallen stars, and ancient people, including our current human races, would sin against him.

The scripture was emphatic about rebellious spirits dwelling in dry lands (Psalms

68:6). Some rebellious stars, including men and women in the pre-Adamic times, would have their portion in dry lands. I guess you're familiar with the term 'dry land' depicting the dry planets. There are no rainfalls, trees, plants, water, animals, fish, or creeping things in the dry land. I already told you that stars that fell from space often shed off their bodies, losing their precious stones or elements – metals or non-metals in these planets. Hence you may find these different elements in those planets. Rocks in the form of asteroids might be seen floating or found on some planets as they are shed off bodies of stars, while others fell from other planets in space.

The dry land or dry places was referent by Jesus in the scriptures when he said, "When an unclean spirit is cast out of man, he walketh through dry places (planets), seeking rest, and findeth none." (Matthew 12:43, emphasis mine). This means when demons (ancient people who once lived on earth) are cast out of a man (Adam's descendants), their first port of call is the dry places, the dry land in the deep as in various planets formed within/outside our solar system. It takes less than 2 minutes for a demon to move from planet earth to Mars, Saturn, or any other dry planet in space. Usually, they travel much faster than the speed of light. Therefore, they don't need a space shuttle. Jesus was specific when he said the unclean spirit we read about on discovering that the person from whom he was cast out had become docile to his antics. The same spirit will then beckon on seven other spirit beings more wicked than they are. They will possess the person's heart with inordinate ungodly behaviors that would aggravate the situation.

For example, someone prone to depression might have one demon (spirit being) in control. But whenever Satan wants that individual destroyed, he sends more spirits to occupy that individual to the extent that a great state of depression is built up until that individual decides to commit suicide. Others might be anger, sex, alcohol, lesbians, homosexuals, addictions, greed, etc. These spirits often continuously interpolate ungodly voices/suggestions in the human mind, regardless of your personality, which we attribute to thoughts we unwittingly yield. Most evil thoughts originate from them as a way of suggestion in humans and are built up with pressure on that individual. Deviant spirits shut in the dry places under darkness were once people of old, which we saw earlier in the scriptures.

Spirits feed

Let's consider the later part of the scriptures typifying the historical desolation of the pre-Adamic earth. "For thus saith the Lord GOD; When I shall make thee a desolate city, like the cities that are not inhabited; when I shall bring up the deep upon thee, and great waters shall cover thee; When I shall bring thee down with them that descend into the pit with the people of old time, and shall set thee in the low parts of the earth, in 'places of old, with them that go down to the pit,' that thou be not inhabited; and I shall set glory in the land of the living" (Ezekiel 26:19-20).

Those scriptures say, "I shall bring up the deep upon thee." In context, in pre-Adamic times, God sunk the previous earth, flooding it with deep waters, and then cast previous people who sinned to hell. Of course, not all men and women in the pre-Adamic earth were submerged. Some saved people (now spirits) went to heaven as sons of God, and I'll shortly expatiate about their incarnations to earth for special assignments. Notwithstanding, we saw some pre-Adamic men in the scriptures riding upon red horses in the spiritual realm on this current earth. They were saved pre-Adamic men who went to heaven – the light zone universe. They are sometimes assigned to perform certain functions (as watchers), coming to earth as servants or sons of God. In contrast, the unsaved or rebellious men and women or children act as demons on earth which Jesus referenced as unclean spirits.

God speaking in Job 40:12, said, "Look on every one that is proud and bring him low, and tread down the wicked in their place (earth). Hide them in the dust together; bind their faces in secret." God trod them down under the earth by flooding it with water under darkness. They were proud and wicked as sinners before God. As you can see from the scriptures, demons weren't responsible for the darkness in space, but God sunk the earth, which led to the chaos. We can draw a simple analogy to the time of Noah, in which floods of water covered the earth, and all living substances died.

Creatures that served as food also died due to the darkness, though some that lived in water might survive. While these people were shut down in the darkness, their spirits were sustained by the power of life in death (darkness). And after several million years of lockdowns, God revisited the universe under darkness, intending to form a new man for himself whom he would adopt as sons of God and stars of God. During the recreation, he revisited the stars, which we discussed earlier. However, their food chain was changed because stars cast down to the universe under darkness (death) would have to feed on the blood of animals or dust matters. When Lucifer sinned in the Garden of Eden, his food was also changed. God changed the food chain of Lucifer, who was once a cherub beast (a higher type of star). "...And dust shall thou eat all the days of thy life" (Genesis 3:14).

Lucifer, the largest star, I suppose, in all of space, would have dust matter around it in space as its current food chain. So also, several stars would have dust matters around them. Some ignorant people are alleging that spirits don't eat. They assumed that a spirit could live on and on without food. That is ignorance! Psalms 78:25 says, "Man did eat angels' food..." So, we can see that spirits do feed. Spirits also rest when fatigued. God rested on the seventh day after all his work (Genesis 2:2). God neither faint nor weary, scripture says God rested after the recreation of this earth (See Genesis 2:2). He didn't create the earth alone in Genesis. He did some serious work expanding planets under the dark zone universe into innumerable planets and spreading the stars into their positions, which are infinite in number. He could have been tired of working, hence he rested.

Spirits are invisible beings to the human eye that require food, water, dust, manna, etc. In the Wicca world, witches and wizards depend on blood for survival. Jesus said, "I will not eat of this fruit of this vine until I eat it again in my father's kingdom." (Luke 22:18). And then he expounded further by saying, "That you may eat and drink at my table in my kingdom, and sit on thrones to judge the twelve tribes of Israel." (Luke 22:30). If Jesus talked about his kingdom, of which he told Pilate his kingdom is not of this world, it explicitly means he was referring to eating and drinking in the kingdom of heaven from where he came.

God categorized spirit beings under the darkness as sinners/wicked in the past, so God had them shut down in this realm of darkness - prison. These fallen spirit men are in our societies, churches, government, industries, schools, families, etc. They often crave for positions in every gathering to influence or rule over Adamic descendants. And if you'd recollect the event which took place between Moses versus Koran, Dathan, and Abiram, instigated by 250 fallen spirit men amongst the Israelites then, when they led a rebellion against Moses in the wilderness, scriptures recorded, "the ground clave asunder that was under them, and the earth opened her mouth, and swallow them up, and their houses, and all the men that pertained unto Koran, and all their goods. So all that pertained unto them, went down alive into the pit, and the earth closed upon them, and they perished from the congregation" (Numbers 16:32-33).

The identities of 250 princes of the assembly then were captured in the scriptures as 'men of renown, which implies offspring or fallen spirit men of old who once occupied the earth dwelling among the Israelites. God sank the company of Koran into the pit beneath, shutting them into "the lowest pit, in darkness, in the deeps" (Psalms 88:6). God, the most Mighty, often throws out rebellious humans or spirits into a reservoir – hell planet; like government, authorities apprehending deviant social behaviors on earth.

If we consider the case of the mad man in the country of the Gadarenes, the fallen spirits in the mad man pleaded with Jesus not to send them back to the deep. "And they besought him that he would not command them to go out into the deep" (Luke 8:31).

Demons don't like occupying the deep, but the earth. They pleaded with Jesus not to send them to the deep, which implies the dry places or planets. The deep here implies the dry land or planets in space. Demons on departing to these planets, if cast out of a man or woman in the name of Jesus Christ, often tend to return to the body on earth from which they were driven out. They hardly give up, always checking on their victims, feeding them with inordinate immoral thoughts, and they have repulsive odors at a close range. An anticipated question might be: "Why would the dry land be a place to cast demons?" It's simply because it remains their habitation prepared by God for the rebellious spirits.

Ancient people

The scriptures referenced God as the 'Ancient of days, which implies God is the oldest of all spirits, being the Creator and the Father of light and spirits (James 1:17; Hebrews 12:9). God is the Father of stars and spirit beings implied. Daniel 7:9 says, "I beheld till the thrones were cast down, and the Ancient of days did sit...." So often you see the scriptures capturing 'ancient men,' it implies people of old times who preexisted the Genesis of recreation. There's a complete difference between when the scriptures used elders from ancient men.

The word ancient used in describing God as ancient of days was used for ancient people, which generally comprises cherubs, angels, and spirit men formed with different materials composition skeletally and outwardly covered with flesh. The composition of an angel (as stars or light beings) capable of radiating such a high level degree of heat like the sun is much higher in comparison to ancient people made of lower material components. For instance, the cherub Lucifer as a mighty star has higher material configurations than nominal angels. The material components used in the formation of Lucifer (a cherub) differ from that used in forming angels. Ezekiel 28:13 says, "Thou hast been in Eden the garden of God; every precious stone was thy covering (makeup), the sardius, topaz, and the diamond, the beryl, the onyx, and the jasper, the sapphire, the emerald, and the carbuncle, and gold: the workmanship of thy tabrets and thy pipes was prepared in thee in the day that thou wast created."

Lucifer being a created high-ranking cherub (star), would reflect flashes of lightning made of fire since cherubs reflect lights of fire like the angels. "As for the living creatures, their appearance was like the burning coal of fire, and like the appearance of lamps...out of the fire went forth lightning" (Ezekiel 1:13). This lamp of fire characterizes our solar sun, which we have already acknowledged that the sun is classified star positioned to give light to planet earth. The scriptures told us that God made two great lights, and if stars are light of fire, it means the sun is a star, as earlier mentioned. However, our objective here is to distinguish the material components differentiating Lucifer from angels and that of angels from spirit men and women of the pre-Adamic times. These three sets of ancient people weren't made of the same material components.

Let's carefully analyze the material component of a given cherub. Ezekiel 1:5 describes the four living cherubs in God's kingdom as men. "...And this was their appearance; they had the likeness of a man." Zooming in on the texture of skin compositions, Lucifer can be looked into. Ezekiel 1:7 described these cherubs as having burnished brass feet which aligns with Lucifer's foot as seen in Daniel 7:19, which says, "...whose teeth were of iron and his nails of brass...."

Lucifer has iron teeth, a foot of brass, and possibly a head of gold in one body, which reflects light. Though Lucifer's hands were cut off in Eden, we saw from the scriptures that cherubs have hands that might look like man's hands, probably made of different materials. Ezekiel 10:21 says, "...The likeness of hands of a man was under their wings." Meaning hands similar to man. Psalms 68:13 describes the wings of a dove covered with silver and her feathers with yellow gold. A cherub has wings and eyes all over his body. They were made of iron teeth, brass feet, elements of gold, etc.

We can then connect the image King Nebuchadnezzar of Babylon saw in his dream and was interpreted by Daniel: "Thou O king sawest, and behold a great image. This great image, whose brightness was excellent, stood before; and the form thereof was terrible. This image head was of fine gold, his breast and his arms of silver, his belly and his thigh of brass, his legs of iron, his feet part of iron and clay" (Daniel 2:31-33). Of course, these scriptures depict an overall pictorial view of God's program for the earth from the days of Nebuchadnezzar of Babylon. Suppose I'd borrow a clue from this image. In that case, it constructively denotes various stages in God's handiwork in forming cherubs, angels, ancient men, and humans, using different precious stones, onyx, brass, beryl, and finally applying clay for humans before rounding off his mystery of the universe, and then making all things new once again.

Angels were made of different substances of light, clouds, beryl, brass, gold, and precious stones. Daniel 10:5-6 described a little fraction of the composition of angels. "Then I lifted up my eyes, and looked, and behold a certain man clothed in linen, whose loins were girded with fine gold of Uphaz: His body also was like the beryl, and his face as the appearance of lightning, and his eyes as lamps of fire, and his arms and his feet in color to polished brass, and the voice of his words like the voice of a multitude." It means angels have some body parts of beryl, brass, and gold in addition to various precious stones which form their skeletal structures. For stars to shine in that capacity, they might have been made of higher precious stones.

Job 6:12 talks about flesh of brass and the strength of stones, which typifies skeletal strength made from precious stones. The body of this angel was like beryl stones, but the arm and foot were of brass. We read that angel's feet are made of brass, and we also know that they have faces shining with lamps of fire. However, their body might be made of different material components. The element brass is a common denominator, even when Jesus was seen in the spirit realm. Revelation 1:15 says, "And his feet like unto a fine brass as if they burned in a furnace." What furnace? Furnace - lamps of fire.

These are stars in their various capacities, with Jesus being the biggest star who became prince over all archangel status to relate with the angels like he became human to relate with us. Hebrews 2:16 says, "For verily he took not on him the nature of angels, but he took on him the seed of Abraham. In context, he didn't incarnate with his angelic body but became flesh as a human. We already talked about Jesus as the bright and morning star. But we also saw how Jesus held seven stars in his right hand. Revelation 1:16 says, "And in his right hand seven stars; and out of his mouth went a sharp two-edged sword: and his countenance was the sun shining in his strength."

John the Revelator had no idea about stars which are bigger than our sun planet in space in his days, so he identified the sun's maximum strength, which Jesus shone in that revelation. It means Jesus was transformed back to his initial bright and morning star body after departing planet earth and went straight to the throne, where he proceeded before creating all things. I will show scriptural proof of Jesus's return to his glory shortly. However, Jesus often utilizes his earthly body he exchanged in the cloud to access this planet earth in the spirit realm every morning, pending the day he will resurface again with human flesh. The truth is Jesus comes to planet earth every morning in the spiritual realm, which I've seen in my vision because he promised in his word, 'I will not leave you comfortless, I will come to you (John 14:18).

Ancient men and women were clothed with 'flesh of brass' differing from angel's skins. We read that angel's feet are made of brass, and we also know that they have faces shining with lamps of fire. However, their body might be made of different material components. The book of Ezekiel 40:3 referenced a pre-Adamic man – a spirit man whose appearance was like that of brass. The scripture only gave us a clue that fallen men (now spirits) were also flesh, not the same as ours, even if they could transform into human flesh as spirits. Genesis 6:3 says, "And the LORD said, My spirit shall not always strive with man, for he also is flesh....." This scripture verse refers to the sons of God who infiltrated the earth to

Science and the Pre-Adamic World

teach humans violence and immorality. God had to cut shut the human race during Noah's time to minimize such pervasive aberrancy in the earth. God submerged the earth in deep waters before Genesis, indicating that pre-Adamic men and women's flesh was subject to destruction. Their skeletons were made of iron or precious stones, minerals or non-metals, brass, and iron deposits under the earth.

For this reason, the book of Genesis clandestinely highlighted the fall out of the pre-Adamic world, of which precious stones like onyx, bdellium, and gold were recorded in Genesis 2:10-14, which says, "And a river went of Eden to water the garden, and from thence it was parted, and it became into four heads. The name of the first was Pison, which compasseth the whole land of Havilah, where there's gold: there is bdellium and the onyx stone. And the name of the second is Gihon: the same is that compasseth the whole land of Ethiopia. And the name of the third is Hiddekel: that is it which goeth east of Assyria. And the fourth is the river Euphrates" In other words, ancient people once lived in these geographical regions in the pre-Adamic age; hence the reformed beast-man was made to begin his journey within the east.

We saw gold and onyx were some of the material compositions of Lucifer's formation stage, even if Lucifer was not part of those locked down. It is obvious that ancient men and women had bdellium and onyx stone in their structure but were clothed with flesh of brass (copper and zinc). The precious stones captured in the scriptures in Genesis indicate the skeletal structures of these ancient men and women submerged in the flood for several million years, and that means there will be many deposits of brass (copper and zinc) in the east, denoting the decomposed flesh of ancient people captured in the scriptures. Just like the scripture has also pre-informed us about certain inhabitants of this earth whose bodies (human flesh) will be consumed with fire, turning them into heaps of brimstones (thick sulfur) after this earth has been reeled of this current Adamic age, perhaps for millions of years again. This is already written in the scriptures of truth.

I believe the elements of gold found in Genesis might represent ancient men's buildings or streets since we already read the admission of an ancient man (spirit) who testified that the Adamic races were inferior, dwelling in clay houses. As an interlude, a usual anticipated question might be: "If they perished, how come they are active again on earth?" Simple, I will respond to that question when I talk about the soul and spirit of man. But it proves true that archeological records of ancient beasts and solid minerals will be found in these regions specified in Genesis before the earth was stretched to its current size.

Jesus, one time playing with the little minds of men, said to the Jews, "Think not that to say within yourselves, we have Abraham to our father: for I say unto you, that God is able of these stones to raise up children unto Abraham." He was indirectly playing with the little minds of men indicating God's ability to make precious stones as lively stones once again which had been the past about ancient men, and will yet do it again. 1st Peter 2:4-5 says, "To whom coming as unto a living stone, disallowed indeed of men, but chosen of God and precious. You also as lively stones are built up a spiritual house...." An indication that the current human race made of flesh and bones will be made into spirit beings (lively stones) to conform to spirit beings standard bodies. That is why the scripture says, "And many of them that sleep in the dust of the earth shall awake, some to everlasting life, and some to shame and everlasting contempt. And they that be wise shall shine as the brightness of the firmament; and they that turn many to righteousness as the stars forever" (Daniel 12:2-3).

The saved souls made from flesh and bones will be transformed into precious stones skeletons and clothed with the flesh of brass and beryls (glorious body) in the resurrection to come (after the great judgment), while the unsaved souls from this earth since the time of Adam will remain flesh and bones in an everlasting burning furnace because they will be charged with 'everlasting contempt charges' hence they will suffer everlasting contempt or shame as well. In the courts of law, whenever one is charged with 'contempt of courts,' a warrant of arrest can be placed by the jury on the accused. This is because he's liable for contempt of courts as charged. Those who refused the free gift offer of Jesus Christ as Lord and Savior will be charged with everlasting contempt.

On the flip side, everlasting contempt also means everlasting shame, which is a complete regret in the lake of fire, saying, 'had I known, I'd have listened to people who told me about Jesus Christ, my only hope, but it's too late. 2 Thessalonians 1:8 says that God, in flaming fire, will take vengeance on them that know not God, and that obey not the gospel of our Lord Jesus Christ. When you missed Jesus Christ before you take your last breath on planet earth, it's over. No more hope for your soul. Ancient people amongst us often instigate men against Jesus Christ, as you will find out shortly. They're not afraid to speak against God on the earth because of their temporal advantage. They will face everlasting shame because they also rejected God's salvation in their days on earth.

Ancient people once dwelled under God's rule when the universe was not expanded compared to its current infinite structure. God refers to these ancient people while dealing with the Israelites, saying, "And who, as I, shall call, and declare it, and set it in order for me since I appointed the ancient people? And the things that are coming, and shall come, let them shew unto them" (Isaiah 44:7). God is throwing a challenge here, asking questions. He said who can be compared unto God who once created ancient people who lived upon this earth several million years back. And that he is going to form a new set of people, in what the scriptures meant by 'things that are coming, and shall come.' God notified ancient people about creating a new set of people - the current human race from Adam to date.

And presently, God is saying that he will surely redesign a new set of men after this world is over by transforming existing bones buried in the graves. Jesus said the current human bones buried on this earth would resurface from the earth's crust for judgment. John 5:28 says, "Marvel not at this: for the hour is coming, in which all that are in the graves shall hear his voice, and they shall come forth; they have done good, unto the resurrection of life; and they that have done evil unto the resurrection of damnation." This tallies with what we read earlier in the book of Daniel. Innumerable human skeletons will be clothed with flesh and brought forth from the days of Adam to the judgment, and after that, the good ones will be transformed into lively stones and stars forever.

In another scripture, God called them 'people of old times.' "When I shall bring thee down with them that descend into the pit with the people of old time..." (Ezekiel 26:20). Both scriptures contextually refer to current spirit beings, which were men of old – men and women who once lived under God's rule but began to manifest unwanted behaviors, such as violence, clamoring, anger, bitterness, fighting, cursing, wrath, immorality, gossiping, murmuring, complaining, malice, wars, evil speaking, pride, hatred, etc. A typical example of one of the women who preexisted Adam could be found in Isaiah 47:1-15, which described this hierarchical lady over the kingdom of Babylon.

She was reputed in the spirit realms to have been very attractive and exquisitely fine, subtle, and acceptable to all. But she rules over the kingdom of Babylon through her manipulative power of sorceries. She is known to have enticed people into her kingdom on earth by practicing stargazing and monthly prognostication. I saw another spirit woman in the scripture whose name was wickedness with smaller spirit women in subjection to her (See Zachariah 5:1-11). Spirit women operate like spirit men, having existed on this earth for several billion/million years. At least, I had seen a spirit lady whom I knew on earth, she died early at 25 years of age, and after 17 years of her demise, she was seen in the spirit as a principality over a city. They often access the earth in human flesh, of which Cain married one of these spirit women in the land of Nod. And that is the reason why the scriptures ended the genealogy of Cain and began with Seth from Adam. This was explicitly written in the scriptures.

Hijacked the earth

Now, one of the puzzling circumstances on which much time was expended thinking through, was that ancient people were found to have also hijacked this present Adamic earth from God. Of course, one would say Lucifer did, but they were also happy to have joined Lucifer in the coup d'état since they had previously rejected God's righteous style of living over the earth several million years back, which resulted in their destruction being submerged. I was struck with bewilderment when the scriptures wrote, "...The kingdom of this world have become the kingdoms of our Lord, and of his Christ, and he shall reign for ever" (Revelation 11:15). Not taking anything for granted, I began another scriptural research to know why and how? Because I was wondering, "How could that be possible?"

The scriptures in Job 22:15 says, "Hast thou marked the old way which wicked men have trodden? Which were cut of time, whose foundation was overflown with a flood? Which said unto God, Depart from us: and what can the Almighty do for them? Please note the phrase, 'cut out of time,' which implies time was ticking from the pre-Adamic times and was suspended for thousands or millions of years before the Genesis of recreation. At first, I had thought this scripture was referencing Noah's flood, but that wasn't the case. There was no place in the scriptures where the men of Noah's time rejected God outrightly, uttering such comments. I then traced back to pre-Adamic times. And I ask myself this question: "Why didn't God save them like he did in our times? I then realized that men of old rejected God's righteous living, having hijacked the pre-Adamic earth for their pleasure due to what the scriptures referred to as 'because of advantage.' What advantage?

They felt they were already created with similar material components as God, so they rejected God's righteousness rule in their days, giving themselves over to sexual immorality with several million stars of God which led to the flooding of the earth for several million or thousands of years. The overthrow of the universe then with darkness signifies death to innumerable stars who colluded in sexual immorality with these ancient men and women, submerged in floods of water under the darkness. Such mingling of different kinds of flesh in acts of sexual perversions was despicable to God.

Of course, the darkness used in flooding this universe was regarded as the first death since the second death in the scriptures means the destruction of the principality called death and hell. As earlier noted, two prominent personalities in the pre-Adamic world were the principalities named Death and Hell, amongst three other high-ranked principalities who ruled over several billions of smaller spirits. Death, an archangel status, was in charge of all planets under the darkness zone universe (including the earth), just like we have archangels over fire, water, and a bottomless pit. I already told you that the flooding of this universe with black darkness signified death.

It means the archangel named 'Death' was superior to fallen angels cast down under his command, including fallen ancient men and women. But scripture confirmed that Death came under Lucifer at last when Lucifer sinned. We saw this from the scriptures, which confirmed that death, alongside other mighty spirits, stopped walking with God, of which I'd tell you the reasons for their decision in due course. Of course, the angel Death, including other mighty spirits, didn't discontinue with God because of immorality but because of certain decisions God took, which led to Lucifer's rebellion. The scripture was explicit that death, as one of the four spirits of the heavens, rebelled at last. Zachariah 6:5 was directly on point: "These are the four spirits of the heavens, which go forth from standing before the Lord of the earth."

Take note of the phrase 'from standing before the Lord of the earth.' In other words, they stopped walking with God; hence death and hell will be cast into the lake of fire at last (Revelation 20:14). This means death as a spirit will be thrown under another death called the second death. But the angels called Death and Hell, having discontinued with God and joining Lucifer, were occupied with the assignment of devouring human lives, just like Lucifer is currently obsessed with walking up and down, seeking whom he may devour. Lucifer was a higher hierarchy star whom all stars of heaven and stars of God, including the principality death, usually submit to. I'll soon expound on how Death submitted to Lucifer from the scripture for which the scripture wrote that Satan had the power of death.

Now, given the fact that ancient men and women were extremely immoral, having encountered stars in cross-breeding sexual relation, for which they derived pleasures therein. The scriptures described these ancient men as "certain men who crept in unawares, who were before of old ordained to this condemnation, ungodly men, turning the grace of our God into lasciviousness" (Jude 1:4). The pleasures they derived in immorality and violence led to their proud speeches rebelling against God saying, "What can the Almighty do for them?" (Job 22:15).

Of course, perpetuating such a level of insurrection in the pre-Adamic world would automatically resort to violence amongst angels and ancient people who were for and against God's rule. One should expect a scenario of the antagonists versus protagonists of God's rule of righteousness and peace. Although they were submerged and flooded under darkness for several million years, it is obvious from the scriptures that final judgment and sentencing were not passed on them because God intended to unfold his next agenda of creating a new set of humans and then deliver one judgment day for all for those who will live after that after their conducts. Only Lucifer was judged during Genesis; hence Jesus said that the prince of this world is (or had been) judged (John 16:11, emphasis mine).

Jude 1:14-16 captured Enoch, the seventh from Adam, prophesied of these, saying, "Behold, the Lord cometh with ten thousands of his saints, to execute judgment upon all, and to convince all that are ungodly among them of all their ungodly deeds, which they have ungodly committed, and of all their hard speeches which the ungodly sinners have spoken against him. These are murmurers, complainers, walking after their lusts; and their mouth speaking great swelling words, having men's persons in admiration because of advantage." What advantage? They were all spirit beings as well who could change forms. Like many ignorant people talk carelessly about Jesus to date because he came in the flesh, they also took advantage of speaking against God since they were created with precious stones in the form of God. They are murmurers and complainers against righteousness living because they want to continue in their invented carnal ways.

Enoch, who existed before Noah's flood, had prophesied about these ancient men's judgment day, which tallies with Job's account of these wicked ancient men and women reserved to the day of destruction (Job 21:30). They were ordained or appointed to condemnation. I believe God gave dominion of that earth to them like he gave to Adam. They were hard in speech against God, saying, "What can the Almighty do for them?" What an insult! Just because of the temporal pleasures of sex. Men began to speak against God. And the scripture confirmed that yet God filled their houses with good things (Job 22:18). The same men of old, upon gaining access to the earth through Lucifer, also mingled with Adam's descendants (women) in the time of Noah, for which God swept this earth with floods again. I'll expound on how these men of old resurfaced again after the floods of Noah.

1 Peter 2:4 says, "To whom coming as unto a living stone, disallowed indeed of men, but chosen of God, and precious." It is evident that fallen ancient men disallowed God's righteous and peaceful rule in their days. They invented their selfish ways by rejecting God's rule of righteousness and peace in their era. So God shut them down for several million years in darkness and began recreation with a new set of people (humans) for himself with the intent to have humans replenish the earth instead, just that these gained access again through Lucifer's subversion of God's trust in the Garden of Eden which will be expounded shortly.

However, the scripture says God went ahead with his plans since his righteous rule was rejected. During the pre-Adamic times, God sent his Son, who also appeared in the type of flesh they were, but they rejected God outrightly, saying, "Depart from us" They rejected their savior. As a result, few men who worshipped God in the pre-Adamic time were redeemed, while others were submerged in floods of waters. God then purposed to go through the human flesh to establish his reign on the earth.

The book of Psalms 2:2-6 was a clear narrative of what transpired in the spiritual realms that the kings of the earth set themselves, and the rulers take counsel together, against the LORD, and against his anointed, saying, Let us break their bands asunder, and cast away their cords from us. He that sitteth in the heaven shall laugh, and the LORD shall have them in derision...yet have I set my king upon the holy hill of Zion." What bands and cords? The rulership is represented by bands and cords of righteousness, love, and peaceful living, which is the scepter of righteousness.

These stars of heaven infiltrated the earth during Jesus's days on earth in the land of Israel, and they actually opposed him and eventually had him killed, even if Jesus came to die. I'll show you from the scriptures that they were amongst the soldiers and Pharisees who had Jesus killed as humans in the flesh. A common characteristic of ancient people is the propensity at which they often clinch power on earth, meting out wickedness to humanity in their leadership style. It's not unusual that ancient people often occupy positions in synagogues, churches, and government, being rulers of mortal men in human flesh. They are obsessed with domineering attitudes on earth wherever they're found, always craving positions to lead unsuspecting mortals with cruelty; the same becomes the behavior of their offspring everywhere.

Remember, as we have seen, the same ancient people surfaced during the days of Moses and Ezekiel. In Ezekiel 9:1-11, scripture talks about six watchers (spirit men who once lived on earth, now sons of God) who God instructed to sweep through the land of Israel, killing both small and great, but that they should begin with these 'ancient men.' Scripture says, "Slay utterly old and young, both maid, and little children, and women: but come not near any man upon who is the mark; and begin at my sanctuary, Then they began at the 'ancient men which were before the house" (Ezekiel 9:6).

As rulers in Israel, these ancient men were spiritually appointed to destruction already as infiltrators on earth amongst the Israelites; hence, the book of Peter emphasized that ancient men disallowed God's righteousness over them. "Unto you therefore which believed he is precious: but unto them which be disobedient, the stone which the builder disallowed, the same is the head of the corner. And a stone of stumbling, a rock of offense, even to them which stumble at the word, being disobedient: whereunto also they were appointed" (1st Peter 2:7-8). Did the scriptures use the word 'disallowed'? Yes. They had disallowed God's rule of righteousness and peace when the earth was handed over to them like Adam.

They were the builders (spirit beings made of stones) who rejected God's principles of righteousness on the earth because they had converted the earth to immoral grounds and violence living in the pre-Adamic times. Note the last phrase, 'whereunto they were appointed to destruction already (paraphrase). They refused God's salvation in person during the pre-Adamic times, continuing in their ways of ungodliness until they were locked in darkness and submerged in floods. So even though the scripture says all Israel shall be saved, these ancient people who infiltrated the Israelites alongside their offspring on earth are predestined to destruction. And I told you spirit men were fashioned with precious stones, so also Jesus is a living stone – Rock, whom they rejected in their days, and after the recreation of the earth will rule over them in the long run. Jesus, whose name was Melchizedek, left them during their days and had to come through Adamic human flesh - 'the weak and foolish things which they least expected.

For this reason, 1st Peter 1:18-20 says, "Forasmuch as you know that you were not redeemed with corruptible things, as silver and gold, from your vain conversation received by traditions from your fathers; but with the precious blood of Christ, as of a lamb without blemish and without spot: Who verily was ordained before the foundation of the world, but was manifest in these last times for you." The scripture here isn't talking about money typified by silver and gold. No. Because money couldn't have been vain conduct or nature impacted or received by traditions from our fathers. The scripture used the term 'as silver, and gold connotes spirit beings formed with precious stones bodies who corrupted the human race. The word 'corruptible things' implies spirit beings capable of corrupting. As you'd discover, the word 'things' implies 'created spirit beings,' which you'll find in Colossians, Corinthians, etc.

In context, the scripture is saying that you weren't redeemed through the type of bodies fallen spirit beings had – precious stones type of bodies, having infiltrated the earth through Adam down to your fathers with their conducts or nature of rebellion, but by the precious blood of Jesus who came 'without spot and blemish type of body, a lamb - with flesh and bones body, weak and despised. And that Jesus had already been programmed to die before the foundation/recreation of the world in Genesis – the universe under darkness zone, and that his death was only fulfilled in the last days.

"Who verily was foreordained before the foundation of the world" implies Jesus was programmed to die through human flesh to obtain the keys of death and hell as part of God's mystery plan for the Adamic human races. Hence, the stone which the builder (ancient men made of precious stone skeletons and flesh of brass) rejected or disallowed, the same (stone in ancient times) has become the head corner - reclaiming the hijacked earth back from them to establish his rule/kingdom they once rejected. For this reason, God admonished them in advance to "kiss the Son, lest he is angry, and you perished from the way..." (Psalms 2:12). The same chief cornerstone (Rock) was seen by Daniel, who became mighty upon the earth taking possession of the earth. Some people think these ancient men will resurface with the same giant type of bodies as in the days of Noah. Unfortunately, that won't happen forever. As you'll soon discover, these ancient, incarnated beings were amongst the Israelites when Jesus walked upon the earth, so don't expect giants in these last days.

Chapter 7

The Perversion in Life

Some time ago, I had someone visit my office who presented a fantastic business proposal, to which I consented. But until the LORD whispered to my hearings that this guy had an ulterior motive, he'd have succeeded in his antics, and I couldn't have been able to figure out his underlying motives. Amazingly, I said, "How could this guy attempt swindling me?" And I heard the LORD say, "They don't change." Similarly, hordes of darkness can never change their ways. There's virtually nothing God can do to have them change their ways. And neither your sympathy nor mine can effectively bring about any desired change. They were created spirits possessing free will capabilities, so whatever forms of perverted concepts they may have invented could be likened to permanent dipole-dipole attractions of molecules.

Hordes of darkness were initially made upright but, over time, perverted knowledge and wisdom of uprightness, inventing their own ways, which impacted existence in the dark universe. Their inventions were contrary to God's righteous ways. These inventions impacted the Adamic human race. Consequently, the Adamic human race is found to have exhibited ancient characteristics such as violence, immorality, wickedness, abusive language, envy, anger, wrath, lesbianism, cursing, etc., having partaken of the forbidden fruit of ancient civilization, classified as death. This doesn't suggest that the Adamic race is devoid of their inventions. Adamic offspring were found to have invented smoking, drunkenness, guns, engines, chemical weapons, electricity, nuclear weapons, cars, computers, phones, warships, jets, etc., unlike ancient civilizations that stopped at the swords.

In general, created things invented certain concepts permeating existence on earth. An anticipated question might be: "If these hordes of darkness had the capacity to originate certain concepts which perpetuated existence, it substantially makes them gods in status." Yes. Does this mean that created spirit beings are gods, like God, who invented the concept of life? Yes! Being gods implies they were smaller spirits capable of permeating human consciousness and also girding mortals, just like God spiritually has control over humans. One of the functions of God is to gird. To gird means to encompass or enclose or surround. Isaiah 45:5 says, "I am the LORD, and there is none else, there is no God beside me: I girded thee, though thou hast not known me." God does gird or surround. God also influences your actions, so also these spirits influence the Adamic race.

Adamic men often depend on spirits to defend and assist them on the battlefields. Up to date, certain countries celebrate their gods as their girds. If we expound on the term 'LORD,' it also depicts someone in charge or control or an instructor. Spirit beings gird those who depend on them for guardians. Lucifer became a god of this world when Adam submitted to him. Meaning Lucifer began to gird the affairs of humanity for those who willy-nilly followed his guardians. Lucifer was also a higher hierarchy spirit in God before he fell, having attained a higher realm of spiritual manipulations of the weak Adamic human races. He was once God's minister in a flaming fire as a cherub higher than angelic beings except for the Prince over all archangel stars.

As you will come to understand that the presence of Cherubs indicates the presence of God. Cherubs are God's direct ministers who sometimes inform angels what God would have them do. The scripture described "the noise of the wings of cherubs as the voice of the Almighty, the voice of speech, as the noise of a host...." (Ezekiel 1:24). This shows cherubs were respected in ranks as God possessing higher authority than angels or spirit men/women and can speak as God. A personal assistant would usually get acquainted with the director's modus operandi and, perhaps, speak on his behalf. Lucifer was rated very high as a cherub in spite of the fact that he was created. Lucifer's hierarchy in God would necessitate the LORD to address him as thus: The LORD rebuke you.' This was written in the book of Zachariah 3:2, which says, "The LORD said unto Satan, The LORD rebuke thee, O Satan...." Implying nominal angels or archangels don't dare talk to Lucifer rudely. Lucifer remains a personality respected in the rank despite his demise in God's kingdom.

Lucifer invented the concept of perverted truth, known as 'deception' or 'lie,' into this dark universe, which has permeated all fallen spirits, including the humans in this universe. His antecedents were imbibed by fallen spirits who fell before him and used his invention to manipulate humans on earth to date. The manipulations of humanity by hordes of darkness were made possible because humans were regarded as 'the weak and foolish things of this world, just as humans manipulate artificial intelligence robots to perform certain functions. Fallen spirits influence the natural tendency for humans to premeditate evil thoughts constantly. The book of Peter calls it vain conversation or vain conduct received from forefathers through corruptible things (fallen spirits).

When Lucifer engaged Eve in the Garden of Eden, the narrative was that she would be like the gods (spirit beings) who already possessed the knowledge of good and evil. God confirmed Lucifer's words, saying, 'Man has become one of us.' Man has acquired the nature of spirit beings that pre-existed Adam. Take note of the phrase 'one of us, not 'everything about us. Of course, there are still unattained natures of 'gods' man is yet to acquire. Don't forget the actual meaning of the word 'God' implies a 'Spirit.' Jesus told us that God is a Spirit (John 4:24). So God created spirit beings (gods) like himself who also originated certain concepts within his world even if they all belong to him. In other words, they have the same forms of God since they were created with precious stones or lamps of fire, like God who is a Rock (like unto jasper and sardine stone), and at the same time, everlasting burnings.

God replicated himself in nature by forming creatures that evidenced his personality. God declared in the scriptures saying, "The world is mine and the fullness thereof" (Psalms 50:12). And Colossians 1:16 says, "For by him were all things created, that are in heaven, and that are in earth, visible and invisible, whether they be thrones, or dominions, or principalities, or powers: all things were created by him and for him. God alone initiated and originated 'the concept of life and death, for which he also participated in his concept of life together with his creatures to pleasure himself. God the Father (inventor) of glory (light) brought forth a Light being from himself as the morning star. This star has the exact composition of the Father. The difference in features being the Father remains a Rock, while the star is made of light and rocky substances. We saw Jesus, the bright and morning star (substances made with a lamp of fire) associated with the cherubs, galaxies, and stars dwelling amongst them as a star.

Jesus (not his name then, as it were) once obtained an angelic body for several billion years as the Son of God, who incarnated eventually to become Jesus Christ in human flesh. It shows God participated in his own concept of life with his creatures. Jesus was made so much better than all angels. I'll expound on the concept of Jesus as Son from God the Father and at the same time, God the Father as we progress. Hebrews 2:4 says, "Being made so much better than the angels, as he hath by inheritance obtained a more excellent name than they." He obtained a more excellent name than all stars put together. In other words, he was a star but a special and superior type. He shined so much brighter than all stars of God. Although I had earlier touched on this, I think the onus lies on me to prove beyond a reasonable doubt from the scriptures that Jesus was once a star and a spirit man who incarnated flesh and blood.

Historical misconception

Now, let me expound a little bit on this: The book of Hebrews just read says that Jesus obtained a more excellent name than they (angels); hence the scripture says, "For unto which angels said he at any time, Thou art my Son, this day have I begotten thee...?" (Hebrews 1:5). Now, what the scripture is saying here is, amongst the angels of God, to which angel did God the Father at any time said, 'Thou art my Son? In other words, Jesus was an angel among the hosts of angels. And so God said to Jesus (then), thou art my Son, implies 'You came from me,' while other angels were created by you. We already saw that all things were created by him (Jesus). While addressing the Son from his own body, God the Father said, "But unto the Son, he saith, thy throne, O God, is forever and forever..." (Hebrews 1:8).

The scriptures continued, "...Therefore God, even thy God, hath anointed thee with oil of gladness above thy fellows." Fellows denote associates or companions - a group of syndicates performing similar/related activities. This shows God brought forth himself, a star, who participated amongst the stars. This is what the scripture meant by only begotten of the Father. Of course, he was the first star amongst all cherubs and angels of God, a Giant star splitting apart to produce another star. God, even thy God, implies God the Father replicated himself with an angelic body who's also God in status as a creator. Hence God also addressed the Son as 'O God' amongst the angels of God. Meaning Jesus, as God, created the cherubs and angels.

We already saw in the scriptures that Lucifer was called son of the morning. When the cherubs, archangels, and angels were created, they saw God the Son, and God the Father, whom they worshipped, but the Son amongst them was a fellow star made so much brighter than they all. Jesus made the world but came and dwelt amongst us (humans) so that all glory might go to God the Father - the object of worship even if he was the Father.

When the scriptures wrote: "This day have I begotten you," it means God, in every phase of his creatures, declared the birth of the Son in the spiritual realms, having earmarked a day to have him birthed amongst humanity by incarnation. God dwelled and mingled with his creatures just to taste what they felt. Jesus confirmed he was the bright and morning star, as we've seen earlier. Psalms 68:17 further substantiates Jesus was a Star. It says, "The chariots of God are twenty thousand, even thousands of angels: the Lord is among them as in Sinai, in the holy place." The scripture says that when the LORD visited the Israelites at Mount Sinai in the days of Moses, thousands of angels accompanied God from heaven to Sinai. I studied the scriptures thoroughly and discovered that the trumpet's sound came from the thousands of angels who were his entourage.

Angels were responsible for sounding those trumpets at Mount Sinai, not the Israelites since the Israelites had just come out of Egypt on the third month, and there were no trumpets amongst them. Little wonder the book of Hebrews says, 'Moses exceedingly fear and quake' (Hebrews 12:21). The scripture says, "And it came to pass on the third day in the morning, that there were thunders and lightnings, and a thick cloud upon the mount, and the voice of the trumpet exceedingly loud; so that all the people that were in the camp trembled." (Exodus 19:16). The children of Israel were amazed and trembled on hearing the sounds of trumpets upon the mountain, the trumpeters being invisible.

The sounds of trumpets were in their thousands, getting louder and louder, but they could see no one, just a thick cloud of darkness with smoke and fire. Of course, it calls for alarm. If you heard the sound of trumpets in an isolated compound when no one is there, you might dash out of that building to safety, knowing fully well that no one in the neighborhood possessed such volumes of trumpets. The Israelites heard trumpets which made them tremble. The book of Joshua identified the first set of trumpets (ram's horns) the Israelites made. So this was a clear-cut case of angels in their thousands surrounding Mount Sinai.

The LORD instructed Moses to allow the people to come up only when they heard the sound of the trumpets at the highest pitch. Moses spoke at the highest pitch, and God responded with a voice. The scripture declared the Lord was among the twenty thousand angels who came down on Mount Sinai as the commander-in-chief. It is obvious that Jesus's name amongst the angels then was 'Lord.' That was the name more excellent than they all. Isaiah 13:4 says, "…The LORD of hosts mustereth the host of the battle. Jesus was Lord by name, who mustered battle among the angels. To muster a battle is congregating or putting together, as in marshal plans of tactical commands.

As you'll come to understand, this same Jesus, whose name was Lord amongst the stars several billion years back, visited Abraham one-on-one, having transformed himself into a man, which I'd expound much later. The book of Hebrews 1:10 further confirmed his name was Lord when God the Father said unto him, "And, Thou, Lord, in the beginning, hast laid the foundation of the earth; and the heavens are the works of thine hands." He created the heavens and the earth. The book of Malachi 3:1 says, "…The Lord whom you seek shall suddenly come to his temple." Psalms 110:5-6 says, "The Lord at thy right hand shall strike through kings in the day of his wrath. He shall judge among the heathen and fill the places with dead bodies...." You can see that he was known as Lord amongst the angels.

Jesus knew so many doctors of the law in Israel were ignorant that he was also the Lord, so he tested their knowledge of God, quoting what they seemed to have misconstrued in the scriptures. He asked thus: "Saying, What think of Christ? Whose son is he? They say unto him, the son of David. He saith unto them, How then doth David in spirit call him Lord, saying, The LORD said unto my Lord, Sit down on my right hand, till I make thine enemies thy footstool? If David then calls him Lord, how is he his son?" (Matthew 22:42-45). Jesus indirectly corrected a historical misconception of the scriptures, which many are still confused about to date. He was dispelling an age-long religious notion enlightening little minds that he was the LORD himself, operational as the Father in the Old Testament. The Father is LORD by name, so the Son as a star also bears the name LORD amongst the stars of heaven as the commander of the armies of heaven.

Malachi 4:5-6 expressly told us, "Behold, I will send you Elijah the prophet before the coming of the great and dreadful day of the LORD: And he shall turn the heart of the fathers to the children...lest I come and smite the earth with a curse." Did you notice the phrase, 'the coming and dreadful day of the LORD'? If the scripture used the word LORD here, it is crystal clear Jesus, who will return to planet earth, was the LORD himself from the Old Testament. Then verse 6 says, lest I come and smite the earth with a curse. Please take note of the pronoun I will send you, Elijah the prophet. And then lest I come. He proceeded from the Father, as LORD dwelling amongst the hosts of angels, being called LORD by the angels. Zachariah 1:12 typified his actual name amongst the angel: "Then the angel of the LORD answered and said, O LORD of hosts...." The question is, "Where is the Father? He's the same Father upon the throne. The scriptures gave us clues about this one God in three forms.

For example, the scriptures would sometimes say: The word of the LORD came again unto me, saying, Son of man, prophesy and say, Thus saith the Lord God...." (Ezekiel 30:1-2). He was the Lord, who's also God, as LORD. He can speak as the Father and sometimes speak as an angel by the name Lord or LORD. For instance, the scripture says, "And the LORD said unto Satan, The LORD rebuke thee, O Satan, even the LORD rebuke thee...(Zachariah 3:2). This means the bright and morning star LORD said unto Satan that the LORD (Father) rebuked thee, Satan. Trust all clear.

Many ignorantly think and teach their congregation that God is completely different from Jesus, even when Jesus told his disciples that he was also the Father. Many ignorant teachers assumed Jesus only heralded from the New Testament times, just as some alleged the Holy Ghost came only after Jesus had gone to heaven. They erred by not knowing the scriptures.

I've heard many preachers floundering over the mystery that Jesus was God the Father. I knew he was the Lord all through the Old Testament until he incarnated as Jesus in the flesh. It wasn't a coincidence that mortals intuitively recognized his angelic name 'Lord' in the New Testament and began to address him by the name Lord, even at age 30. He was a star amongst the angels and cherubs, being the Morning Star, which is also the glory of God in the Old Testament. He is known as the LORD of hosts. For this reason, the scriptures described the Son as The mighty God, The everlasting Father, the Prince of peace, etc. (Isaiah 9:6).

As earlier noted, the Father replicated himself as the WORD. He also became a spirit man who once mingled amongst men in the pre-Adamic world. And his name then was Melchizedek which I'll prove in the scripture. Though, he was rejected by pre-Adamic men. He was reputed to have been the Prince of princes (principalities) amongst hosts of angels. Jesus was referred to as the 'Prince of princes' described in Daniel 8:25, corroborating Isaiah 9:6. If you'd recollect, the galaxies of stars signified several princes or principalities over innumerable stars across both light and darkness universe. Archangel Michael was a great prince as one of the princes (See Daniel 12:1), while Jesus was referred to as the 'Prince' (Daniel 9:25).

The proper noun 'Prince' denotes a Prince who loves peace; hence he was known as the Prince of peace. Because on a given playing field, this Prince over princes was observed to have been an icon of righteousness, which connotes 'peace' as you will soon understand. He was the most peaceful among all angels, despite wielding enormous powers as the commander-in-chief amongst the hosts of angels since he participated amongst his own creatures to understand what they loved most and what they felt. Their true nature and desires were revealed when tested with the waves of good and evil concepts. He is the same God upon the throne as the Father and Lord of hosts. And this makes it clear that the Father sent the Star, Lord (now Jesus), amongst the angels to planet earth to be born of a virgin girl named Mary while the Father was still on the throne as God. This is where many get confused, asking if Jesus could be God himself. This is the puzzle the world is trying to unravel.

In every phase of existence, he partook in the people he formed to have a feel of what his creatures love most between the current of good and evil. Hebrews 2:14 says, "Forasmuch as the children are partakers of flesh and blood, he also himself took part of the same...." And from my in-depth studies, I realized that God is the same 'Everlasting burnings or devouring fire,' who chose to undertake a form of God as a Rock, and at the same time, the Morning Star, named Lord over galaxies of stars, being the Son of God (ancient) and the Son of Man (in human flesh) because created things couldn't have been able to relate with everlasting burnings form of Giant devouring fire. God became a star, ancient man, and son of man to feel his creature's experiences.

Adding to creation

God provided a level playing field for his creatures to manifest their underlying preferences, which birthed perversion over time. God said, "...I make peace and create evil: I the LORD do these things." (Isaiah 45:7). In other words, He initiated the concepts of evil and peace, but individuals formed within time and space were at liberty to choose between what is good and evil. The scriptures undoubtedly confirmed God initiated the concepts of good and evil. The book of Isaiah 41:23 further corroborates this when it says, "Shew the things that are to come hereafter, that we may know that you are gods: yea, do good or do evil, that we may be dismayed, and behold it all together." In context, spirit beings cannot create the future since they never had what it takes to create time and space. Nevertheless, this is exactly what the scripture implies.

It is worthy of note that fallen spirits, over time, do not possess the quality of manifesting righteousness anymore, having adapted to their wicked ways. The ways of fallen spirits became permanently evil, incapable of reverting to any form of righteousness they once possessed. They were inclined to evil ways. Similarly, spirits in the light zone retained righteousness, peace, and love only. Fallen spirits are incapable of changing their evil ways once deviated, just like God cannot change from righteousness to evil, which is exactly what the scripture meant when it says, "For I am the LORD, I change not..." (Malachi 3:6).

Although, God said he is capable of doing good and evil without permanently being evil (his disapproval). His actual preferences remain righteousness, justice, peace, love, and equity. And his 'evil dispositions' denote his retribution of evil to those who deserve it. So God knew fallen spirits are incapable of ever manifesting righteousness attributes once perverted hence he threw a challenge to them, saying,"...Yea, do good or do evil, that we may be dismayed, and behold it all together." And, of course, God originated the concepts of good and evil but has his preference for righteousness.

In the pre-Adamic times, ancient people exhibited preferences for curses, violence, hybridized forms of sex, pride, and abusive language. However, God, having recreated the Adamic human race, saw that the imaginations and the thoughts of the Adamic human hearts often tend towards the evil paths continually because Adam acquired the nature of fallen spirits. The scriptures talked about some fundamental attributes of fallen spirits that impacted the Adamic race. A typical attribute that impacted the human race is the concept of lie or deception, which is perverted truth initiated from the days of Adam by Lucifer.

The scriptures also captured the inventions of a principal woman designated 'wickedness,' whose inventions from the pre-Adamic world perpetuated existence only in this dark universe. We saw in the scriptures that this woman (queen of heaven) established her base in the land of Shinar. Zachariah 5:6-11 says,"…This is their resemblance through all the earth. And, behold, there was lifted up a talent of lead: and this is a woman that sitteth in the midst of the ephah. And he said, 'This is wickedness'…to build a house in the land of Shinar. It shall be established and set there upon her own base." The land of Shinar encompasses Mount Seir, which is the border of wickedness, a people against whom the LORD hath indignation forever" (Malachi 1:4).

This ancient spirit woman designated wickedness was the mother of harlots and abominations of the earth, according to Revelation chapter 17. She has permeated the human race with her inventions, prostitution in the pre-Adamic era, with other women, as lesbians. Her inventions on earth amongst the daughters of men are currently being practiced. Nahum 3:5 says, "Because of the multitude of the whoredoms of the well-favored harlot, the mistress of witchcrafts that selleth nations through her whoredoms, and families through her witchcrafts." She was the inventor of whoredom, using sorcery in her inventions; hence she was reputed as the mother or inventor of promiscuity in the universe under darkness.

Her inventions were simply the perverted wisdom and knowledge of righteousness. For example, the wisdom of God approves male and female intercourse within the same kind of flesh, but a perverted version is female to female, male to male intercourse, including crossbreeding sexuality. That is, humans were, in the context of 'righteousness,' approved to mate between males and females of the same kind of flesh. But a perverted version is homosexuality or lesbianism, and by extension, an excessive lust in humans mating with dogs/cows or horses, or spirit beings turned human, mating with human flesh, which is perversion as in the case with Sodom and Gomorrah. These perversions infiltrated the Adamic race.

Another form of perversion might be the art of spellbinding, often practiced by those in the Wicca world, mimicking angelic beings which were initially made to fly as spirit beings. This mistress of witchcraft introduced witchcraft practices to Adam's descendants, enabling some humans to fly by transforming into a hawk, owls, rats, cows, and other creeping things aimed at haunting the unsuspecting victims. Sometimes, this art enables them to communicate with the dead in the grave. The art of spellbinding or bewitching unsuspecting victims has infiltrated many nations of the earth. Sexual perversions, sorceries, and violence are mechanisms by which wickedness is propagated in the land of Shinar and, by extension, to all nations of the earth, as written in the book of Revelation. These perversions characterize the inhabitants of Mount Seir; hence it is called the border of wickedness ruled by the queen of heaven.

Similarly, we have spirits, namely: Destruction, Death, Famine, etc., whose inventions currently perpetuate existence in our universe under darkness. We read about Mammon, a fallen spirit being in the land of Assyria that invented the concept of money, which is being used to date. Hence Jesus was quoted as saying, "...You cannot serve God and Mammon" (Matthew 6:24). In other words, you cannot secretly worship the principality called Mammon in an attempt to attain earthly wealth and at the same time seek to worship God of truth who made the heaven and earth. If your means of getting money is through occult or secret societies or performing certain diabolic means, you cannot worship the true living God at the same time except you repent. You can't serve two masters. As a fallen spirit, Mammon originated the concept of money on this earth thousands of years back. He was regarded as a principality in the heavenly realms under the dark universe; hence Jesus said you cannot serve two masters.

Mammon's invention (money ought to be amoral amongst humanity, however, when people become greedy by craving its invention, it might lead to the direct or indirect worship of its source or inventor, or what the scripture described as the root of all evil. This means an obsession with the pursuit of money - the Mammon spirit might take full control of people's minds. That is to say, people's submission to Mammon's spirit nature of obtaining money (his invention) generates greed, selfishness, envy, immorality, pride, anger, lies, murder, robbery, craftiness, bitterness, hatred, idolatry, witchcraft, etc. Jesus was quoted as saying, "...The mammon of unrighteousness..." which dictates this spirit being Mammon was a fallen spirit under the darkness universe (Luke 16:9). His invention perpetuated life on earth only, not the light zone universe. There is no money in the light zone universe above, not even a dollar.

On the flip side, there were also spirit beings who loved God's righteousness lifestyle, of which the angels of 'goodness and mercy' were found righteous. When the scripture says that goodness and mercy shall follow me all the days of my life, it means angels of goodness and mercy shall follow me all the days of my life. These angelic beings, several billion years back, manifested God's attributes of showing mercy and exhibiting goodness. So they were named according to their preferences for God's nature. You can take a clue from children in their tender ages by critical observations: one of them might love giving out things, while the other might be avaricious. Another might always love striking with the fist, while the other is peaceful and calm. It's easier for a parent to categorize such children by observations. So also God observed angels who loved certain traits which aligned with his true nature of righteousness and goodness. We have established that the bright and morning Star angel loved righteousness and peace and hated violence and wickedness.

However, spirits who perverted righteousness living seem incapable of changing their ways back to righteousness, and this tallies with what God told me:' they don't change.' Those who love good stuck to good, and those who love evil also stuck to evil forever. You're what you manifest in life. A tree is known by its fruit. What you love most is deeply rooted in your thought life, which automatically pops up as soon as an opportunity presents itself. Humans who exhibit traits of perversion to righteousness and truth under the dark universe are programmed for destruction, even if such perversions have impacted existence for hundreds of decades. The perversions they exhibited cannot be changed, and those who partook of their inventions are denied access to God forever except they repent.

Perversion portrays what the scripture meant by men having devised many inventions. The book of Ecclesiastes 7:29 says, "God made man upright from the beginning, but man had sought out many inventions." Man sought many inventions to dictate freedom granted individual beings to manifest certain traits. We are created to please God from the time of Adam by our inventions. Our inventions are valuable to God even if he knows all things; hence the scriptures acknowledge some human inventions which speak volumes as their contributions to life. For instance, Jabal was recognized as the father of tent-making "And Adah bare Jabal: he was the father of such as dwell in tents, and of such as have cattle. And his brother's name was Jabal: he was the father of all, such as handling the harp and organ. And Zillah bore Tubalcain, an instructor of every artificer in brass and iron; and the sister of Tubal was Naamah" (Genesis 4:20-22).

Abraham was credited to have been the first man who invented the well of water in all of human history. So also, Albert Einstein would be credited with his inventions in heaven as well if he made it. In the days of Uzziah, the scripture captured cunning men who invented engines that could shoot arrows and stones. (See 2nd Chronicles 26:15).

Perversion in any field of life is common amongst humanity, especially people who manipulate other persons with their God's given potential aimed at defrauding them. For example, a true man of God, who had the gift of prophecy, may mislead unsuspecting members to obtain money or property, all in the name of the LORD. Of course, such a level of perversion is a direct twist of uprightness. It seeks ways of contradicting righteousness standards. Similarly, God formed man upright, but man's inquisitiveness under darkness, has resulted in deviating from the known to the unknown.

Given a level of curiosity towards the unknown, the knowledge gained in searching for the unknown might be a complete departure from the known, leading to error, and such error could be adopted by a set of people who crave knowledge of the unknown, unwittingly clustering into an arena of death and destruction. Obviously, the perversion to righteousness and truth comes with its consequences. Adventuring the new often comes with its rigorous advantages/disadvantages. Are we saying new adventures and innovations are necessary evil? No. But changing nature against nature is a bend in itself in most cases.

For example, it is pathologically assumed that the origin of HIV disease is traceable to homosexuality on earth. However, this perversion was captured in the book of Romans 1:27, which says, "And likewise also the men, leaving the natural use of the woman, burned in their lust one toward another; men with men working that which is unseemly, and receiving in themselves that recompense of their error which was meet." The scripture was explicit regarding what homosexuals practice, but there was a just recompense for their error which they deserved. HIV diseases become the consequence earned for the perversion of the natural use of the opposite sex to the unknown.

Exhibit their own ways

Given that the free will right was granted to every spirit and human being alike, it dictates God's unreserved pleasure in watching his creatures imagine and dream things into existence. God invented the concept of freedom because he expects us to put our minds to work, thereby providing humanity the capability of reasoning and contributing their innovations to life. Isaiah 1:18 says, "Come now, and let us reason together, saith the LORD..." In other words, engage your mind to think in righteousness. It means God needed diversities of thoughts aligning with righteousness, peace, and truth. For instance, David dreamt of building God a house, and such a notion emanated from his essence. The scripture wrote that God was pleased with the thought generated and thereby reciprocated in kind, having sworn to give David a throne perpetual with his dynasty.

This capacity to dream or imagine good or evil things is exclusive to individual spirits or human beings at any point in time. Abraham had to reason within himself that if God provided Isaac at an old age and requested him to sacrifice, it meant he was equally able to raise him from the dead if he so wished. So he trusted God with Isaac and was willing to let go. God appropriated such an act of faith as righteousness which aligned with God's ways. This faith in God automatically made Abraham the 'Father of faith,' which was also an expression of God's attributes, like the angels of goodness and mercy who manifested God's attributes in their times. Abraham was oblivious if his actions would spur God to swear, but having drawn on that virtue, it compelled God to swear about the Abraham kind of faith, given the diversities of thoughts expected from his creatures.

God was pleased with Abraham since his action proceeded of his volition and not compulsion. And such expression of faith indicates pleasantness or good thoughts about God. Those who frequently think evil are categorized evil, while those who frequently think good thoughts are categorized good: 'As a man thinketh in his heart, so is he.' The products of our hearts are perceived in the spirit realms. Titus 1:15 says, "To the pure all things are pure, but to the defiled and unbelieving is nothing pure."

Your greatest asset is your ability to reason, which makes you a free moral agent differing from animals. If you recollect, Moses once produced compelling reasons why God should turn from his fierce anger. Exodus 32:12 says, "...Turn from thy fierce wrath, and repent of this evil against thy people." This was a mortal man negotiating with his Creator. It denotes God's exclusive free will authority granted to man, possessing such capability to think/reason outside the box. Moses's suggestions were classified as thoughts of righteousness, peace, and justice. And so, his concepts were deemed 'good.' He didn't hurriedly accept the offer to have God wipe off the stiff-necked Israelites, who quickly forgot what God had done. Moses did reason with God by suggestion, unlike Lucifer, who enforced his opinion about God's choice of endowing pre-Adamic man-beasts with consciousness to rule the earth.

We also read from the scriptures how God intended to destroy Sodom and Gomorrah, engaged Abraham before executing judgment. Why? God was seeking Abraham's opinion over his decision. Of course, Abraham had no idea of the gravity of the offenses committed by the men of Sodom and Gomorrah. They were indulged in homosexuality which has gone wild as far as desiring cross-breeding sexual intercourse with angels (stars) whose skins they lusted after (Genesis 19:24). You know Satan makes people slave to sex such that some humans are degraded to desire to sleep with animals or fowls. They were exhibiting the same traits of pre-Adamic men and women submerged in the flood of waters with fallen angels cast down into the darkness zone before the recreation in Genesis. Abraham was emotionally sympathizing with humanity. However, God seeking human input or opinion about his righteous judgment indicated that he needed man to see his just ways of reasoning. So, eliciting a response from mortals implies seeking human concepts to life.

As we have read above, Moses contributed to life by reasoning. The scriptures recorded that the LORD repented of the evil (unpleasant) actions he intended to execute, having listened to Moses's points of view. Of course, this is no case of God influencing man's heart, but man's capacity to love righteousness or peace, reasoning with God on earth. God has no control over your capacity to reason; hence he made you in his image (semblance) and likeness (rationale). He deals with you as a personality who takes decisions and implements them on earth, having handed over the earth to man. Similarly, ancient people, including the stars of heaven, were formed with free will capabilities.

Isaiah 1:2 says, "Hear, O heavens, and give ear O earth: for the LORD had spoken, I have nourished and brought up children, and they have rebelled against me." Does this sound strange to you? That is a typical example of what transpired between God and fallen spirit beings. God created them as free morals, but they rebelled at last. Just like we humans are currently rebelling against God. I know the scripture was talking about the Israelites, but this scripture is typical of ancient people who rebelled against God and said, "What can the Almighty do for them?" They invented perversion in life, refusing to change their ways. The perversion in life was fundamentally the 'evil' classification initiated at the beginning of creation. The ability to pervert righteousness couldn't have arisen if God hadn't dreamt or conceived beings who would fall to the evil side of his concepts; hence he created darkness as one of his arsenals reserved for troubled times.

As seen in the scriptures, God foreknew some spirits beings and human souls would fail (See Isaiah 57:16). The scriptures confirmed God invented both concepts of evil and peace. But we saw spirit beings leveraged on that and became proud speaking against God. Perhaps they felt they possessed the authority to corrupt humans, which God had made for himself. So they wholeheartedly gave in their hearts to work evil. Like Pharoah, whose heart was hardened by God, ended up leveraging that window of opportunity to resist God. Exodus 9:16-17 says, "And in very deed for this cause, have I raised thee up…as yet exaltest thou thyself…." The scriptures expressly told us that Pharoah exalted himself against God. And so we must understand that when potentials are put to work in forms of contributions to life and death concepts, it shouldn't get into our heads, but respect the fact that God assigns us for a purpose within his concept of good and evil.

For this reason, God himself treads down any spirit or human being who assumed a prideful state of the heart because of the free will authority. Unfortunately, so many spirits don't know these things that God originated the concepts of good and evil. They felt they were powerful as gods and became rebellious, and they had their cases foreclosed for judgment. We're privileged to know these things in our dispensations. People often ask, "How could created spirits rebel if God is all-knowing?" Simple! Just as God delights in love, peace, righteousness, and justice – his ways, he also created beings to choose what they love – the evil ways. Even humans are entitled to their opinions and can act similarly to spirit beings, with some alleging God doesn't exist. While others alleged the earth expanded from a small particle on its own, that animals originated from nowhere, and that man evolved from those animals, which have been proven untrue that evolution does not exist, but the man-beast had been in existence in the ancient earth and was endowed with consciousness in the recreation in Genesis.

Some say food, the substances found on earth, showed up without a thoughtful planning process. Water, mountains, sand, and flowers evolve from nowhere. That is the height of ignorance in men, trying to figure out things beyond their scope. For every effect, there is a cause – universal law. God never asked man to invent airplanes, computers, bombs, cars, etc. he simply created man to have his own inventions.

Similarly, these fallen spirits loved the opposite of what God loves. They violated God's rule against cross-breeding; they went off course, departing into wrong ways classified as evil ways. The scripture wrote: "They have no fear of God in them. Hence they have no changes – no intention to repent." (Psalms 55:19).

They knew they were created to live forever, having obtained the forever-living nature of God. They were created spirits and cannot be eternally annihilated. They can only be punished and banished from life into the death zone, where they continue existence in everlasting punishment, being shut out of light. I once heard someone quote the scriptures of context, alleging that demons can be destroyed entirely. He quoted the book of Mark 1:24, in which demons asked Jesus, "art thou come to destroy us?" And because he felt he was anointed, he was teaching gullible minds that demons can be destroyed. And you know, we've got a lot of ignorant people who call themselves "demon destroyers" in the third world.

He knows every spirit

There's a final judgment for demons which is torment in the lake of fire. It is their punishment. That is what the scriptures meant. Of course, God has the power to recreate their skeletons in life if so wished. However, the scripture tells us that all things under the darkness zone are subject to change. This includes the stars, ancient men, and humans. The book of Matthew 8:29 puts things in proper perspective that demons can only be tormented, not obliterated eternally. So, these fallen spirits are aware that they cannot be destroyed; that is why they speak against God. Daniel 11:36 says, "...and shall speak marvelous things against God...." These ancient spirits boast, saying, "...With our tongue will we prevail; our lips are our own: who is lord over us?" (Psalms 12:4)

As earlier mentioned, Lucifer wasn't part of fallen spirits chained in the darkness of the deep before the recreation in Genesis. Lucifer was still active with God as a cherub, not a nominal angel, but as a higher hierarchy angel than all archangels, angels and spirit men in the dark universe. Please follow on to know the truth as we progress. These are not religious traditions taught you over the years. These spirits knew God was by nature the most peaceful, upright, longsuffering, and just. But as time passed, they chose to exhibit their own ways. As the scripture puts it, "He went on frowardly in the way of his heart." (Isaiah 57:17).

God said, "...For the spirit should fail before me, and the souls which I have made." God foreknew some spirit beings would sin, and so also the souls of men. And one might ask, "Why would God know that they would fail and still banished them?" It is simply because the spirits themselves did not see any need to change or repent, and they have no fear of God in them (See Psalms 55:19). Someone else might ask, "How did you know what transpired?" These things were written in the scriptures already. I began this research by reading the account of Job's friends: Eliphaz the Temanite, Bildad the Shuhite, and Zophar the Naamithite. These all came to console Job over his predicaments and got me researching the scriptures about the pre-Adamic world. The scriptures recorded that Job's friends were astonished at Job's situation, sympathizing with him. Job, who once had ten children, lost all in one day, including his source of livelihood. In addition, he was afflicted with diseases all over his body, being struck by Satan.

Job's friends were speechless for 168 hours straight, and they didn't eat or drink anything during that time. It might lead to supernatural encounters when humans fast for such a time. During this empathetic consolation with Job, one of the spirit beings spoke to Eliphaz the Temanite, saying, "Shall mortal man be more just than God? Shall a man be purer than his maker? Behold he (God) put no trust in his servants (spirit men); and his angels he charged with folly, how much less is man that was made of dust...?" (Job 4:15-20; emphasis mine). You can see that this particular spirit gave us clues into how

Science and the Pre-Adamic World

God once dealt with spirit beings which were ancient people. It showed that there was orderliness in the kingdom of God. Scripture says even the angels were browbeaten, much less man, who is made of dust.

You know the scriptures talked about God's style of disciplining and scourging every son whom he received into his kingdom. (Hebrews 12:5-6). God knew that some spirits would sin and rebel. If you study the scriptures in detail, you will find other scriptures in which these fallen spirits speak blasphemous words against God. Revelation 13:6 talks about a fallen beast that opened his mouth in blasphemy against God, to blaspheme his name, his tabernacle, and them that dwell in heaven. They invented abusive language, sexual perversion, and violent living. So, God also countered them with the sword and thrust them into the darkness prison, which is our dark universe.

Similarly, some human souls in hell, a planet in our dark universe, often blaspheme God in the agony of thick darkness, heat, lack of water, and frustrations they currently go through in hell. Someone might ask, "If they were created perfect, how come they rebelled?" Simple! A child left to himself will self-destruct: "...a child left to himself bringeth his mother to shame" (See Proverbs 29:15). When a child is left to have his own way, he will destroy things while thinking it is the right thing to do. Freedom sometimes leads to pride and self-destruction. There is no way a child can equal his parents in experience. Sons of God already possess the knowledge of good and evil, having learned God's ways.

God, by nature, loves anyone who admits his folly. God dwells on high with the contrite and humble spirits. "For thus saith the high and lofty One that inhabiteth eternity whose name is Holy; I dwell in the high and holy place, with him also that is of a contrite and humble spirit, to revive the spirit of the humble, and to revive the heart of the contrite ones." (Isaiah 57:15). God weighs the actions of every creature. Those who repent and acknowledge their folly, he revived them. Those whose hearts love violence, hypocrisy, wickedness, envy, malice, oppression, fighting, and abusive words are known by him. He knows every spirit or soul. He would strengthen such a one if genuine repentance existed, but God "shall wound the head of him that goeth on still in his trespasses" (Psalms 68:21).

These ancient people formed hatred toward God because God loves a kingdom of peace and righteousness. God is the most powerful but also the most peaceful. Therefore, he is called the God of peace. He is non-violent by nature, and he loves righteousness and justice (Psalm 33:5). "For the righteous LORD loveth righteousness; his countenance doth behold the upright." (Psalms 11:3). God loves peaceful, upright, and truthful living. This is just his nature, and he does not intend to change from his nature of truth and righteousness.

That is why he keeps warning wicked humans to change, or else they will be cut off from the earth like those fallen spirits cast out in darkness. But this time, the fallen spirits and all wicked human souls will be thrown into the lake of fire. God is opposed to any who loves wickedness or perversion. "The face of the LORD is against them that do evil, to cut off the remembrance of them from the earth." (Psalms 34:16). God is still warning the sons of men from previous generations that "The wicked shall be cut off from the earth, and the transgressors shall be rooted out of it." (Proverbs 2:22, Psalms 37:38). But you know what? Many people won't take heed. They move on in their wicked ways until death comes unaware.

Chapter 8

The Earth Under Death

As you are aware, there are uncountable planets (earth inclusive) in space under the darkness, which is death. And as earlier noted, the earth is hinged on nothing in space while spinning and drifting at the same time slowly. The sighting of the earth under the darkness could be synonymous with placing the Israelites amongst enemy nations. It means the earth (the land of the living) is surrounded by fallen principalities and powers of darkness once shut out under darkness, death. As soon as Adam fell, he had, by omission, given access to these fallen spirit beings (stars and fallen sons of God under darkness) in space to encroach on planet earth. And this speaks volumes why God cautioned Adam that on the day he ate the forbidden fruit, he shall surely die; by implication, is the intrusion of these fallen spirits into the earth planet to cause destruction and death upon humanity.

As mentioned earlier, the darkness covering our dark universe came about as a kind of prison environment for deviant stars and ancient people due to their perverted ways. It's expected that certain attitudes such as fear, oppression, fighting, contention, and survival mentality coupled with greed, unruly behaviors, depression, frustration, bondage, and starvation characterize the lifestyle of spirits imprisoned under the darkness. Inmates sometimes behave unruly due to frustrations or depression, with some becoming abusive and recalcitrant. Fallen ancient men and women submerged under this dark universe began sourcing food.

You are already aware that ancient people once fed on animals made of flesh and bones, which are dinosaurs, gorillas, and man-beasts, amongst others, in the pre-Adamic earth. These ancient people, having infiltrated the earth, began to feed on the blood of animals and, over time, developed an interest in human blood. And so, in the process of time introduced idolatrous living as a means of drinking human blood because they knew God took fossil remains of the pre-Adamic 'man beast' and reformed them to God's resemblance. They knew man's origin was beasts recreated and endowed with consciousness in reasoning and responding like ancient people and stars of heaven.

Given such pre-knowledge about the origin of man, they had so much disdain towards humans - their previous food chain for which God forewarned Adam that death would feed on him once he ate of the forbidden fruit of the knowledge of good and evil. We saw how one of these spirits spoke up that humans dwell in inferior houses made of sand and also affirmed humans came from the dust (fossil remains); hence they are easily crushed to death, being destroyed from morning to evening across the globe and continue without checking out why they are being destroyed (See Job 4:19-20). Hordes of darkness as giant beings had no regard for man-beasts in the pre-Adamic times.

We have established that these spirits turn flesh and procreated giants into humans, from which Goliath, amongst several thousand giants, were descendants of these giants' procreation in human flesh. The height of Goliath, when compared to David, could result in disdain giving such a competitive advantage. They initiated idolatrous living amongst primitive men sacrificing humans, which has become the culture in many heathen nations. Humans were sacrificed to spirits (gods) by offering their blood to spirit beings in different nations, communities, languages, and tribes of the earth. Some nations incremating their dead, while others allow children to pass through fire. God distastes such practices.

The Israelites were forewarned by God, saying, "There shall not be found among you anyone that maketh his son or his daughter to pass through the fire, or that useth divination, or an observer of times, or an enchanter, or a witch, or charmer, or consulter with familiar spirits, or a wizard, or a necromancer...because of these abominations the LORD thy God doth drive them out before thee" (Deuteronomy 18:9-12). And we know one of the reasons God asked the Israelites to dispose these nations in those days was because they were practicing idolatry, wasting human lives as a sacrifice to fallen spirits that feed on human blood as food. The scriptures refer to these hordes of darkness as the 'thrones of iniquity. Psalms 53:4 says, "Have the workers of iniquity no knowledge who eat up my people (humans) as they eat bread..." You may wonder what the scriptures meant by eating up my people as they eat bread?

Hordes of darkness indulged in drinking human blood, deviating from animal blood to human, disdaining humans as once animals in the pre-Adamic times. Daniel 7:5 describes a fallen angel in the form of a beast in bear shape authorized to devour much flesh on earth, which dictates these gods still maintain the notions of seeing the Adamic human race with a mindset of once a beast, always a beast. Demons often search for food as the blood of animals or humans. I believe this account for the presence of blood particles (in spatial forms) as dust matters seen revolving around stars in space, which is their food. Blood is reserved for spirit beings under darkness. So when the scripture says, "...The devil as a roaring lion, walketh about, seeking whom he may devour" (1st Peter 5:8). It means the devil is seeking for human flesh to devour since he was cursed to eat dust (blood) all the days of his life (Genesis 3:14).

His food chain was changed to dust, which implies the blood of animals and, by extension, humans. Although I've established from the scriptures that dust also implies animals or fossil remains generically, I'd like us to look at one more scripture substantiating humans as 'dust' referenced in the scriptures. Habakkuk 1:1-17 says, "O LORD, how long shall I cry, and thou wilt not hear! Even cry out unto thee of violence, and thou wilt not save! Why dost thou shew me iniquity and cause me to behold grievance? For spoiling and violence are before me, they shall gather the captivity as sand, they shall heap dust, and take it, thou art of purer eyes than to behold evil, and canst not look on iniquity: wherefore lookest thou upon them that deal treacherously, and holdest thy tongue when the wicked devoureth a man that is more righteous than he? And make men as the fishes of the sea, they catch them in their net, and gather them in their drag...."

The dust here refers to humans who were gathered as fishes in the net being devoured by the wicked. And God kept quiet; hence the prophet cried out. Humans are wasted daily by death and destruction spirits. Hence I said in my heart concerning the estate of the sons of men that God might manifest (show) them and that they might see that they themselves are beasts. For that which befalleth the sons of men befalleth beasts, even one thing befalleth them: as the one dieth, so the other...." (Ecclesiastes 3:18-19). Satan came to kill and destroy human lives by utilizing hordes of darkness to manipulate plane crashes, accidents, communal wars, violence, etc., in order to feed on blood emanating from such disasters in the spiritual realms.

As long as humans are on this earth, there will be daily death experienced through violence, sickness, diseases, accidents, famine, wars, etc. These death events characterized media reports, of which not all death catastrophes are reported. Psalms 94:4-20 says, "...the workers of iniquity boast themselves. They break in pieces thy people, O LORD, and afflict thine heritage. They slay the widow and the stranger and murder the fatherless...shall the throne of iniquity have fellowship with thee, which frameth mischief by a law? They gather themselves together against the soul of the righteous and condemn the innocent blood."

There is a distinctive difference between 'Throne of Iniquity' and 'Workers of iniquity' described in the scriptures. The throne of iniquity remains the citadel of powers in space, while workers of iniquity are wicked people, comprising men and women currently dwelling on the earth working with these spirits. Workers of iniquity are humans consciously working for Satan in conjunction with fallen spirits in human flesh as powers of darkness. The 'throne of iniquity' often afflicts the innocent with sicknesses and diseases in a dream or hypnotic state. These afflictions are the avenues by which death eventually comes and takes such life. Death being a principality over the universe under darkness, was permitted to feed on humans as soon as Adam disobeyed.

So many people are ignorant that the same humans in the flesh represent these powers of darkness on earth. You know we've got some ignorant teachers who tell you the devil in the spiritual realms is your real enemy, not humans in flesh. They might quote the scripture saying, "For we wrestle not against flesh and blood, but against principalities and powers," ignorantly thinking that the enemies always act in the abstract realms. But the enemies are the same humans walking with powers of darkness in the abstract realm. The powers of darkness are human agents in families, neighborhoods, offices, schools, marketplaces, or worship centers, perpetuating acts of wickedness on the earth unknown to many. They live amongst us, familiarize themselves with people, and use their mystical powers to oppress and maim their unsuspecting victims; hence they are referred to as workers of iniquity.

They are the wicked ones on the earth. Wickedness, as the word implies, is a deliberate act of unkindness, oppression, or violence. The art of oppression comes in various forms, such as bewitchment or spellbinding, or suppressing, while at other times, oppression comes through governmental powers, societies, associations, and traditions of men. And if we take this into context, it shows the wicked oppress the poor or fatherless on the earth. The book of Psalms 27:2 says, "When the wicked, even mine enemies and foes, came upon me to eat up my flesh, they stumbled and fell." So we can see that the iniquity workers delight in humans' death and destruction, and they ignorantly assume God does not see their evil works under the dark universe.

The wicked said in "his heart, God hath forgotten: he hideth his face; he will never see it" (Psalms 10:11). They say among themselves: "…How does God know? Can he judge through the dark cloud?" (Job 22:13). Hordes of darkness are aware of the light zone universe exist; hence they said, "Can God judge through the darkness covering all of space?" Even the queen of the heavens also thought in her heart that her wicked deeds of sorceries, enchantments, and immoralities over nations are unknown unto God. Hence God replied to her, saying, "For thou hast trusted in thy wickedness: thou hast said, None seeth me. Thy wisdom and thy knowledge, it hath perverted thee…" (Isaiah 47:10). The incursions of these wicked hordes of darkness into the earth resulted in the suffering of humanity on the earth. And as earlier noted, these spirits dwell amongst us in the flesh, impacting their nature of wickedness to humans who join in the crusade of oppressing the poor (defenseless) or needy of the earth.

The book of Job 24:4-16 says, "They turn the needy out of the way: the poor of the earth hide themselves altogether. Behold as wild asses in the desert, they go forth to their work, rising before betimes (midnight before daybreak) for a prey; the wilderness yielded food for them and their children…they cause the naked to lodge without clothing…they pluck the fatherless from the breast, and take a pledge of the poor…they take away the sheaf from the hungry; which make oil within their walls, and tread their winepresses, and suffer thirst. Men groan from out of the city, and the soul of the wounded crieth out: yet God layeth not folly to them. They are of those that rebel against the light; they know not the ways thereof nor abideth in the paths thereof. The murderer rising with light killeth the poor and needy, and in the night as a thief...in the dark, they dig through houses, which they have marked for themselves in the daytime: they know not the light" (emphasis mine).

The hordes of darkness rebelling against light, dictates their opposition to the kingdom of God in the light zone universe above. They refused to abide by the rulership of God, perverting their ways, and now recruited humans who delighted in their wicked ways, teaching them how to oppress the poor of the earth. The fatherless are being oppressed, and the needy go naked. Workers of iniquity violently take away the fruit (inheritance) of the poor of the earth. The earth has become a place of suffering, tears, oppression, and pains. Men groan in tears being oppressed, with some government in power as representatives of these hordes of darkness taking leadership positions as kings or rulers on earth to perpetuate wickedness. Women are being raped, and some are incarcerated and tortured. No wonder the Psalmist cried out, saying, "Have respect unto the covenant: for the dark places of the earth are full of habitations of cruelty" (Psalms 74:20). To be cruel means to cause misery or pains to others or to be destitute of sympathetic kindness and pity. The wicked have no pity in their hearts telling lies in hypocrisy.

One of the signs of the wicked is that they are full of lies. Psalms 58:3 says, "The wicked are estranged from the womb: they go astray as soon as they are born, speaking lies." They blink no eyes telling lies in hypocrisies. They are swift in cooking up lies, being hardened in hearts. The wicked shed blood without feelings. They don't have sympathy. Hence the word 'wicked' also implies being unmerciful, ungrateful, proud, haters of God. They lure the innocent ones of the earth and kill them. The wicked have multiplied themselves on the earth. The mistress of witchcraft was seen to have wasted so much blood on the earth. "And I saw the woman drunken with the blood of the saints and with the blood of the martyrs of Jesus..." (Revelation 17:6). We can see from the scripture that fallen spirits feed on human blood; hence they corrupt the human race to drink blood through witchcraft, idolatry, cultism, etc.

For example, most secret societies of the world were formed solely to waste human lives. Their objectives remain the destruction of humans. So when the scriptures talked about a woman drunken with the blood of the saints, it denotes the multitude of people under her influence will be obsessed with immoral and violent living – shedding human blood, like Nineveh and Babylon. The nations under her influence will have no regard for human lives. And going by her inventions designated 'wickedness,' it goes to show that wickedness is all about perversions, oppression, and blood lettings.

River Euphrates

The incursion of fallen spirits into the earth began from the recreation in Genesis. Now, before the fall of Lucifer after recreation in Genesis, fallen spirits banished under darkness were parted into various planets, oceans, rivers, and seas which we have discussed earlier. The Scriptures talked about a river in Eden that splits into four heads, of which river Euphrates was identified as one of these. Some other rivers mentioned in Genesis are Pison, Gihon, and Hiddekel. "And a river went out of Eden to water the garden, and from thence it was parted into four heads...And the fourth is the river Euphrates (Genesis 2:10-14). In the great river Euphrates four principal angels were locked down in chains of darkness before Adam was formed. "Saying unto the sixth angel which had the trumpet, Loose the four angels which are bound in river Euphrates" (Revelation 9:14). These four principal angels had been locked down in chains of darkness since the commencement of the lockdowns several million years back, even when other stars were re-ignited or re-illuminated during the recreation in Genesis.

They will regain freedom for a while during the great tribulations which will come upon this earth. According to the scriptures, these four principal angels rule over 200 million fallen demons (Revelation 9:16). The great river Euphrates was predicted to dry up in the last days. It is pertinent to know that spirits often thrive in waters invisible to humans. It means these spirits were right inside the rivers unknown to Adam. Adam had no knowledge of these gods until Lucifer beguiled Eve, who eventually enticed Adam to acquire such knowledge of the gods by partaking of the forbidden fruit. It means these spirits had no influence over Adam despite their presence in Euphrates, in so far as Adam was unmindful. It suggests that if man had set aside the acquisition of the knowledge of good and evil, it wouldn't have diminished his potential in any way. Adam was out there exploring his world when Eve ate of the forbidden fruit - indicating that whenever man sets aside a dogmatic belief system, it does not diminish his reasoning capacity.

Adam and Eve, having acquired such knowledge, will have to live with it until the end of this age. Of course, man would be recreated again, exclusive of the knowledge of good and evil knowledge. God will start all over again with man, devoid of the knowledge of good and evil, but the selected few from this current Adamic race will then act as sons of God in that world.

To establish that spirits live in rivers before the days of Adam, let's take a typical study case from the book of Daniel. And if you would recollect, the river Hiddekel was mentioned in Genesis. Daniel was by the side of the great river Hiddekel where he saw one of the sons of God who communicated answers to his prayers. "In the four and twentieth day of the first month, I was by the side of the great river, which is Hiddekel; Then I lifted up my eyes, and looked, and behold a certain man clothed in linen, whose loins were girded with fine gold of Uphaz: His body was like beryl, and his face as the appearance of lightning, and his eyes as lamps of fire, and his arms and his feet like the color of polished brass, and the voice of his words like the voice of a multitude." (Daniel 10:4-6). Daniel was also said to have been by the river Ulai where he saw spirits as well (See Daniel 8:2). One time, in a night vision, Daniel saw the four winds of heaven strove upon the great sea with some beasts coming out of the sea, of which the scripture recorded that one of the beasts transformed into man (See Daniel 7:2-3).

The prophet Ezekiel was also by the river Chebar when he saw visions of God with four cherubs (See Ezekiel 1:1-28). We have so many people who ignorantly think that rivers or seas often indicate the marine kingdoms, and they teach against nature as in seas or oceans upon which the earth was founded. I am not saying that evil spirits don't operate in waters, but we saw from the scriptures that angels and cherubs were also seen at some rivers. The earth was founded upon waters. The stars, clouds, and rivers are the avenues by which spirit beings penetrate the earth at will. The earth was refurbished upon the floods, under darkness. Hence the scripture says in Psalms 22:15, "...Thou hast brought me into the dust of death." This scripture was a prophetic declaration of Jesus' incarnation into the dark zone universe – earth.

Field of play

The dust of death means land under the darkness in which fallen spirits once lived and were imprisoned for several million years. Mankind is currently coexisting in the same universe with fallen stars and spirits. Ecclesiastes 5:15-17 acknowledges the fact that man was born under the darkness universe; hence the scripture says, "As he came forth of his mother's womb, naked shall he return to go as he came, and shall take nothing of his labor…all his days he eateth in darkness, and he hath much sorrow and wrath with his sickness." Under the darkness are mad men and women, lame, blind, deaf, dumb, deformed, sick, weak, destitute, oppressed, poor, etc. Humanity was made to labor under hard bondage, trying to survive under darkness in sorrow, pain, stress, and sickness after the fall of Adam. And sometimes, these fallen spirits oppress and possess humanity.

They sometimes transform into smaller size imps with the intent to possess the human heart, as in the case of the madman of Gadarenes, where the demons responsible for his mental dysfunctionality were two thousand. "And the devils besought him saying, "Send us into the swine, that we may enter into them. And forthwith, Jesus gave them leave. And the unclean spirits went out, and entered into the swine: and the herd ran violently down a steep place into the sea, (they were about two thousand)

Stop the blind arguments

It's pretty difficult to determine the accurate age of the earth before Genesis. Some scientists have speculated that the earth is 13.8 billion years. But as earlier noted, we've had conflicting figures from various archeological reports about some species found to have been over 25 billion years. Conversely, many theologians got it wrong, erroneously refuting archaeological evidence of fossil remains. In my opinion, scientists should be appreciated because their contributions have overly impacted our world and indirectly shown the potential in men and women capable of exploring the universe despite being tagged as foolish things of this world by ancient people.

Many theologians think the earth's age is proportionate to the available chronological records from the Genesis of creation, so they erroneously refute scientific claims of fossil remains dictating several billion years. The arguments regarding the earth's age could be traced to Paul's era, in which the apostle Paul discarded the idea of science which delved into the chronological age of the earth. I believe some theologians borrowed similar arguments of discarding science from the writings of Paul in the scriptures, which I have expounded on earlier.

Though science began before the birth of Jesus Christ, Paul strictly warned Timothy to avoid "oppositions of science falsely so called" (1st Timothy 6:20). Paul was unaware that the earth was much older than the recreation in Genesis. Similarly, some theologians are ignorant to date. Perhaps, the apostle Paul might have skipped scriptural accounts of the book of Daniel, which foretold the emergence of science in the last days. The scriptures tell us that Daniel was a science student. The scripture said that Daniel was one of those chosen to serve King Nebuchadnezzar due to his qualifications as a science student in the land of Babylon.

In Daniel 1:4, the scripture says, "Children in whom there is no blemish...cunning in knowledge and understanding science..." And because of this scientific knowledge coupled with his curiosity, God sent a watcher to inform Daniel that "many shall run to and fro (confused), and knowledge (science) shall be increased" (Daniel 12:4, emphasis mine). In other words, science will emerge. Daniel, a science student, was still serving God as well, and his curiosity brought him into spiritual depths, for which mysteries were revealed to him. Spiritual secrets are not given to mindless persons but to hearts that are beloved of God. All of life is a script written by God. Created things are the players in this field.

Albeit, there are many religious minds indoctrinated to discard scientific views. Science is man's way of enhancing his world. It shouldn't be rejected. Scientific findings have immensely contributed to saving lives and also destroying lives. To a large extent, significant progress in research was made into scriptural accounts of science and scriptures due to some scientific findings. The earth, including the planets, stars, moon, and sun, existed for several billion years before Genesis. Theologians should accept the facts and stop the blind arguments. Unfortunately, there are still theological schools of thought who think that one day of creation in Genesis translates into one thousand years, which they erroneously assumed from scriptural references of 1000 years to a day in God's eyes (2nd Peter 3:8). Such assumptions are completely out of context. The earth was refurbished in six consecutive twenty-four-hour days as we know them.

Chapter 9

The Sea of Glass

As earlier noted, the Scripture talked about the sea of glass crystal in front of God's throne in heaven by which God monitors various activities being undertaken in our universe. God's crystal device in modern times could be likened to satellite systems by which God sees the deep. "And before the throne, there was a sea of glass like unto crystal..." (Revelation 4:6). Now, before expounding further about the sea of glass, I'd like us to have a retrospect on scientific claims concerning space travel with no God in sight, which has led to erroneous conclusions about the non-existent God being ignorantly taught in our schools, for which many gullible minds have joined the bandwagon. So far, science has not scaled past the stars and penetrated through the darkness above the stars, and I knew such claims of no God in sight were incorrect and myopic.

Therefore, I contend that if the stars (light beings) are visible to everyone on earth, it shows science is absolutely wrong in its assumptions of no-God-in-sight because the galaxies made by God are proofs of stars existing in their world just as humans exist on earth. Scientists lack understanding and are looking for someone that looks like a human in the flesh, as the God they seek in space travel. They are ignorant of light beings as spirits. When you view the stars in our dark universe, you will find them walking and interacting amongst themselves. They live in their world.

God lives in a separate realm above the light zone universe.

The scriptures talked about the heaven of heavens, which implied a planet above the planets under the darkness. "Behold the heaven and the heaven of heavens is the LORD'S thy God, the earth also and all that are therein" (Deuteronomy 10:14). In context, there's a heaven planet that rules over innumerable planets, which shows the Scripture was specific to details about these three levels of heavens indicating the domains of the stars of God, stars of heaven and the earth planet. Paul, the apostle, confirmed he was once caught up in a vision when he visited the domain of the stars of God in his vision. We know that visions, trances, and dreams are confined to the abstract world, and they are not subjects of discourse in the sciences; however, we must admit that a major breakthrough in the structure of benzene molecules was obtained in the dream state – the abstract realm.

The abstract world exists side by side with us, and we have seen individuals testify of deceased people appearing to the living in a dream state and disclosing some secrets regarding things on the earth. It shows the departed souls of men and women are actively conscious in the abstract world. You cannot deny dreams in which certain secrets were told to you, and it was discovered that such secrets were found true on earth. I knew a lady who survived an auto crash in which her close friend died on the spot in the accident. The deceased friend appeared to her in a dream and told her the whereabouts of a missing item they had been searching for at the scene of the accident for three days which they couldn't find. This lady immediately went to the exact spot-on, regaining consciousness from the dream, and found the missing item right at the specific place.

Many have been fooled into thinking that God does not exist, which has been disproved because man has all these years thought God is flesh and blood mighty being that they have been searching for. They've been ignorant, thinking that whatever seemed unscientific is not factored in the natural realm of existence, not knowing we live in a universe under darkness. The universe under darkness is the natural realm of existence which we are concerned about, but that nature was not made from nature. Nature was made from the supernatural realm; as a result, "the things which are seen were not made of the things which do appear" (Hebrews 11:3). For instance, sand was not made from any physical substance, neither was the firmament made by chemical combinations. The supernatural hands of God formed the clouds. When we name elements of water which we call hydrogen and oxygen molecules, the question is, "Where did oxygen come from?" A possible answer could be plants. But, then, "Where did plants come from?" In other words, the things which are made were not made from the substance of the things which do appear.

The evidence of God's existence is searchable since he is also in the natural realm in and above the light zone universe, being a Spirit, just like the stars of heaven are seen in our universe. However, his core personality is in the abstract world, which is the spiritual world. God is a Spirit, and they that worship him must worship him in spirit and truth" (John 4:24). God lives in the everlasting realm, which is endless - out of time and space. His ways are everlasting: two steps away from the natural realm. Habakkuk 3:6 says, "...His ways are everlasting." Scripture says, "God inhabits eternity" (Isaiah 57:15). His emergence as God began in the everlasting realms. He then created the spiritual and the natural worlds.

Remember, he created water and fire for the subsistence of humans and spirit beings and divided the natural and spiritual world inside the deep. Both worlds were created from the everlasting realms. You may wonder, "What do I mean by spiritual from everlasting realms?" The spiritual and the natural world are time-bound because they were fundamental concepts of creation – life. In the spiritual realms, God sees the deep, as it were, through this glass crystal device. The sea of glass (crystal) represents the universe we live in. This sea of glass is permeable to angels in heaven in that they descend into this sea of glass and find themselves on earth. It is like someone constructing a massive glass aquarium by which he interfaces between the creatures in the aquarium and his actual environment. But the aquarium being permeable is the deep.

Angels know all things

The deep includes the clouds, galaxies, seas, earth, and planets. It's like placing some fish in an aquarium with the owner of the aquarium watching over the fish and performing the function of changing the waters. Cherubs, angels, and spirit men have access into this aquarium which depicts the earth and our universe. Angels, for example, as light beings, know all things that are in the earth. They know when you will die. They know your tomorrow. They possess the knowledge of all things on the earth. In the book of 2nd Samuel 14:20, the Scripture says. "...According to the wisdom of an angel of God to know all things that are in the earth," is like someone overseeing the aquarium could tell when a particular fish he suspects being sick is likely to die. He can also predict the growth of some fish.

Jesus portrayed the earth as a field of trees in which God is the husbandman, with God's angels as servants performing fieldwork. In one of his parables, Jesus talked about trees – symbolic of humans occupying the earth; but not fulfilling its purpose. Metaphorically he said, "Why is this tree (man or woman) unfruitful but occupying space?" According to the scriptures, "Then said he unto the dresser (angels) of his vineyard, Behold, these three years I come seeking fruit on this fig tree, and find none: cut it down; why cumbereth it the ground earth?" (Luke 13:7). And so, it wasn't by chance, when Jesus walked up to a fig tree in Matthew 21:19- 20 and cursed the fig tree which had been given enough space of three years.

In John 15:1-6, Jesus described his disciples as branches attached to Him, the vine. He was metaphorically seen as the vine, with his Father, the husbandman. Then he said, "Every branch in me that beareth not fruit he taketh away: and every branch that beareth fruit, he purgeth it, that it may bring more fruit." (John 15:2). It is obvious that angels are the servants who discharge the unfruitful branches. Angels also attend to branches which seems productive. The relative depiction of men as trees and branches interconnects the scriptural description of 'men as the fishes of the sea' as seen in Habakkuk 1:14. Therefore, we can see that the earth is like an aquarium or a field of play. Angels and hordes of darkness are seen aiding men belonging to their camps.

One day, while worshipping God, I suddenly began to sense the presence of people around me singing alongside me. But there was no one at home; the neighborhood was calm. I wondered who could have been singing the same song with me, with no one in my room. As I listened intently with my eyes closed, I saw seven angels dancing in time with the rhythms. They could twist all sides as though they had no bones to break. Suddenly, my handset vibrated. It was in silent mode beside my bed. And one of the angels said to me, "Your mom is calling!" But I continued in worship. And when I was through, I checked my handset and discovered it was my mom, despite many contacts in my phone. They then said to me in unison that they know everything on the earth.

Angels often descend into this permeable sea of glass crystal to appear on earth, covering trillions of light years distance in a few seconds. Paul, by revelation, got inspired and wrote thus, "As in a glass (beholding) the glory of the Lord." (2nd Corinthians 3:18). In context, the apostle Paul had a depth of spiritual views of this glass crystal to behold a glimpse of God's glory, but it seems dark. It means whenever one worships God in spirit and truth, being soaked in God, he is trying to access God from inside the sea of glass crystal which might look dark due to the darkness. "For now we see through a glass, darkly; but then face to face..." (1st Corinthians 13:12).

In other words, humans inside the aquarium (dark universe) are trying to behold the face of God from inside the glass crystal in fellowship, longing for God. The Scripture says but then face to face. In other words, light to light. When you get into the light zone universe above, you won't struggle to see God's face anymore. We are currently inside the glass aquarium, striving to behold Him.

I'd like you to picture some fish trying to eat feeds through a glass aquarium in your hands outside the aquarium. The glass aquarium becomes the restriction or barricade between the farmer and the fish. The fish cannot go through the medium since the environment differs. The aquarium is the natural realm where spiritual beings mingle with men and women. As with life, the spiritual realm is a creation of the everlasting realms. The everlasting is superior to the spiritual, while the spiritual is superior to the natural. Things formed in the natural fade off no matter how beautiful they might appear at first.

The everlasting realms

God does interface between the spiritual and the everlasting realms. God sees everything created in the spiritual and natural realms. There is nothing hidden from his eyes, "For neither is there any creature that is not manifest in his sight, but all things are naked unto the eyes of him..." (Hebrews 4:13). Moreover, God kept spirits men (sons of God) as watchers watching over cities and nations of the earth. These watchers perform a function similar to police officers - enforcing the law of righteousness and justice (See Daniel 4:17).

The natural realm is regulated by time, and so is the spiritual realm. Some countries and cities of the world have different time zones. God lives in the everlasting realms uncontrolled by time. The 'time of life' mentioned in the scriptures applies to both realms. The difference is that the spiritual realm is premised upon days, weeks, and years, while the natural is premised upon 24 hours, also making up the days. However, there is a beginning in the everlasting realms initiated by God, which is quite different from the beginning of time in both realms when life began on the earth and the universe.

God predated time and existed in the everlasting realm before he initiated the concept of life and light, which I've touched on elaborately.

Psalms 90:2 says, "Before the mountains were brought forth, or ever before you formed the earth and the universe, you have been from everlasting to everlasting." So, before God's existence in the everlasting realms, there wasn't any self-existing spirit. As it is written, "I am God, and there is none beside me. (Isaiah 45:5). "Is there a God beside me? Yea, there is no God; I know not any" (Isaiah 44:8). So, it all began with God. "I am He, I'm the first, I also am the last" (Isaiah 48:12). As far God is concerned in the everlasting realm, there was none before him, and He went for a search into this everlasting realm, and declared, "I'm the first, and I do not know any." His age is unsearchable. "Thou art God alone, and thy years have no end" (Psalm 86.10 Psalm 102:27 Job 36:26).

The everlasting realm is superior to the natural realm. When God created the concept of life, it birthed the spiritual and natural world as recorded in the book of Hebrews 1:2: "...By whom he made the worlds (the duo-verses)". People who once lived on the earth are in the unseen (spiritual) world, while those alive as humans are in the natural realm of existence. Hence the Scripture used the terms worlds. The worlds also denote the planets, but ancient beings inhabit these planets. Therefore, the natural and the spiritual world summarize the worlds.

The natural world deals with all that the human eyes can see, touch, and feel, such as plants, animals, creeping things, etc., because through faith, we understand that the 'worlds' were framed by the word of God (Hebrews 11:3). He created angels in the spiritual world and made man in the natural world. It's obvious that there are three worlds: the everlasting, spiritual and natural realms. But the English dictionary specified only two realms - the spiritual and natural realms. Whatever seems immaterial is classified as spiritual according to definitions. However, the everlasting realm is quite distinct from the spiritual realm. God formed clouds and waters of the deep in which heaven, earth, and seas are sustained. This I will designate as the spiritual and natural realms. This shouldn't get you confused.

A typical distinction between the everlasting and spiritual realms is seen in the book of Revelation, Chapter 5:1-6. The apostle John, one of the disciples of Jesus, was transported unto the spiritual realm of heaven, in which he saw twenty-four elders and angels round about the throne of God. And there was a proclamation from one of the angels as regards who was qualified to receive a sealed book from the hand of God unveiling the future. And the scriptures recorded that no angel or elder was found worthy in heaven or earth or under the earth to look into the seal until Jesus had to emerge from the 'everlasting realm' into that 'spiritual realm' where angels and elders were seated. So I guess you can now understand the difference clearly. I already told you that the actual everlasting realm is the zone of stones of fire above the light zone universe while we are in the darkness zone.

The elders and angels in heaven know that God does interface between the everlasting and the spiritual realms; men don't know this. Remember, I told you that God is seated upon the floods according to the scriptures." The LORD sitteth upon the flood; yea, the LORD sitteth King forever" (Psalm29:10). In other words, God oversees the spiritual realms where angels thrive including the earth. God lives above the angel's realms. God is in heaven with angels but also interfaces between everlasting realms and the floods upon which he is seated. God lives above the clouds of heaven (paradise) where angels dwell. "I will ascend into heaven, I will exalt my throne above the stars of God (angels in heaven): I will sit also upon the mount of the congregation, in the sides of the north: I will ascend above the heights of the cloud; I will be like the most High" (Isaiah 14:13-14).

The above Scripture indicates God is seated upon the floods (clouds), which we have expounded on earlier. Lucifer knew God's sitting position is above the angels' realm. The 'stone of fire realm' is the 'actual everlasting' from which God came and formed death and life's concept. And of the angels, he saith, Who maketh his angels spirits and his ministers (cherubims) flame of fire. But unto the Son, he saith, Thy throne O God, is forever and ever - everlasting to everlasting" (Hebrews 1:5-8 emphasis mine). The above Scripture dictates God had been in the everlasting realms before forming all things pertaining to life. It is crystal clear that God came from the everlasting realms, and his ways are everlasting (Psalm 93:2, Habakkuk 3:6). The spirit realm has varied dimensions, and not everyone who accesses the spiritual world has access to God.

God being multidimensional, can be on the throne in heaven and at the same time stand on earth and walk in the everlasting realms. I knew this from the scriptures. From His everlasting realms, he does interface with the spiritual and the natural realms. God is the Father of spirit as well as God of all flesh (Hebrews 12:9, Jeremiah 32:27). Psalm113:5-6 says, "Who is like unto the LORD our God, who dwelleth on high, who humbled himself to behold the things that are in heaven, and in earth." This Scripture puts things in proper perspective about the everlasting, spiritual, and natural realm. God humbles himself to behold what is going on in heaven, where angels dwell, and what is going on the earth.

Son from His bosom

God brought his Son Jesus from the spiritual realms into the natural and commanded all angels to worship him. This explains what the scriptures mean when it says, "When he bringeth in his first begotten into the world, he saith let all the angels of God worship him" (Hebrews 1:6). I've already discussed this Scripture before and mentioned that Jesus Christ was once a Star incarnated from the spiritual realms by the name Lord and was made to partake of flesh and blood in our natural realm - hence God commanded all angels to worship him who in human form was lower than angels' nature. As a matter of fact, the angels waited on God the Father to give such orders because Jesus partaking of the inferior nature of man of the dust (beast) was the highest form of humility since angels don't submit to man, but men do worship angels.

Many have been deceived, thinking Jesus was not God. They say, "How can God replicate himself without sex?" Their shallow minds assumed that since humans copulate to reproduce, it must be the same with God. That is ignorance gone too far! Such notions of copulation mentality to reproduce are elementary and childish as far as the spirit realm is concerned. The Son proceeded out of the Father, and Jesus confirmed this when he saith, "For I proceeded forth and came from (inside) God." Hence, he was a Son - from the essence or bosom of the Father (John 8:42).

When you study the scriptures saying, "Without controversy, great is the mystery of godliness, God was manifest in the flesh...seen of angels..." (1st Timothy 3:16). One would be wondering, "What does the scripture mean by 'seen of angels,' are they not all the same type spirits?" Yes, they are. The Scripture here isn't talking about Jesus not having pre-existed humanity, nor was he seen for the first time by angels after birth on earth. No. That is not what the Scripture is saying. The Scripture here is giving a double assurance that Jesus Christ, as God who created the world, partook of the flesh and blood nature of men (humans) and was justified in the spirit realm for undertaking such a venture; hence he was seen by angels who witnessed his participation in the inferior human flesh as once regarded as beasts meant to be taken or consumed. Hebrews 2:11 says, "For both he that sanctifieth and they who are sanctified are all of one: for this cause he was not ashamed to call them brethren." The Scripture also said that God himself was not ashamed to be called their God (Hebrews 11:16). God was not ashamed of calling previous irrational man-beast as his children.

For this reason, "every spirit that confesseth not that Jesus Christ is come in the flesh, is not of God: and this is the spirit of antichrist..." (1st John 4:3). It is crystal clear that stars as light beings witnessed Jesus Christ the Son being born into the earth, so every spirit beings that denied the coming of Jesus Christ in the flesh is a lying spirit (1st John 2:22). Because there are "many deceivers (spirit beings that once lived on earth) are entered into the world, who confess not that Jesus Christ is come in the flesh. This is a deceiver and antichrist" (2nd John 1:7). In the flesh means Jesus came in human flesh. God was too big in the natural to have partaken of human flesh. It is like man becoming little ants. God is a great God who created all galaxies in space, including the planets. His cherubs are mightier than the stars. Science tells us that our sun is 109 times the size of the earth, and there are stars much bigger than our sun (star). So imagine what the cherubs would look like.

God's direct ministers

Cherubs are beasts in flaming fire, ministering unto God. They are made of lamps of fire as higher hierarchy star-light-beings (Psalms 104:4). They operate in the throne room of God and know some secrets of the Godhead. Although cherubs also have their spirit subject to wheels, nonetheless, they are much closer to God the Father. "...As for the likeness of the living creatures, their appearance was like burning coals of fire and like the appearance of lamps: it went up and down among the living creatures, and the fire was bright, and out of the fire went forth lightning. And the living creatures ran and returned as the appearance of a flash of lightning" (Ezekiel1:13-14). And Revelation 1:6 says, "...And in the midst of the throne, and round about the throne, were four beasts full of eyes before and behind."

They usually have six wings with four sided-faces, unlike humans with one face having two eyes in front, a back head, and two side ears. Cherubs have several eyes all over their bodies from top to foot, wings inclusive. "And their whole body, and their backs, and their hands, and their wings, and their wheels, were full of eyes round about, even the wheels that they four had...And every one four had four faces: the first face was the face of a cherub (Ox), and the second face was that of a man, and the third the face of a lion, and the fourth the face of an eagle" (Ezekiel 10:12- 14).

We can see that cherubs have so many eyes and four types of faces in their heads but no back heads. Though, they have back parts and a whole body like man. Each cherub has a north side lion's face; east side man's face; south side ox's face; and west side eagle's face. They have six wings, and under their wings, they have hands like that of man (Ezekiel 10:21). Their foot is like a calf's foot. They also can transform into angels, spirit man, and mortal man based because of their ranks. Cherubs often walk in upright positions like men and do interact with humans. Revelation 6:1 says, "...One of the four beasts saying, come and see." This cherub was seen by John, one of the apostles of Jesus Christ, when he was carried to the spiritual realms.

This shows that cherubs can interact with humans and also interact with angels. "And one of the four beasts gave unto the seven angels seven golden vials full of the wrath of God, who liveth forever and ever" (Revelation 15:7). In other words, Cherubs are God's direct ministers in the everlasting realms. We just saw from the Scripture that one of the cherubs gave golden vials unto the seven angels. They have higher hierarchies than archangels and angels. We also saw in the scriptures how one of the sons of God (spirit man as a watcher) went in between the cherubs to obtain coals of fire. "And he spake unto the man clothed in linen, and said, Go, in between the wheels, even under the cherub, and fill thine hand with coals of fire from between the cherubims, and scatter them over the city..." (Ezekiel 10:2).

Cherubs are higher in authority among all of God's creation. As earlier mentioned, the wings of cherubs are as the voice of the Almighty God, and this is the reason why Satan often deceives mortals by speaking like God to humans, of which some cannot discern the voice of God at times, with some claiming God spoke to them. Satan does imitate God in speech. Remember, Satan once deceived king David into carrying out a census of the children of Israel, which resulted in plagues (See 1st Chronicles 21). So cherubs are God's ministers in flaming fire; God moves upon the wings of cherubs. Psalms 18:10 says, "And he rode upon a cherub, and did fly: yea, he did fly upon the wings of the evwind" The activities of cherubs could be synonymous with a king being borne by four men's shoulders.

Cherubs dwell in the holy mountain of God – as direct ministers like a president's aides having access to his office. Their primary function is to worship God before his throne day and night and escort God. And, of course, they also carry out other duties disseminating information to angels and sons of God regarding what God would have them do. That does not mean God does not deal with angels or sons of God directly. They have hands like a man and the face of a man. Lucifer was once a cherub who operated from God's throne room. He was active in God's kingdom after the recreation of the earth in Genesis. As earlier noted, Lucifer wasn't then a dragon serpent in the discourse that ensued with Eve. I will expound on this shortly.

God made angels

Angels respect cherubs and follow orders issued by them. As mentioned earlier, we have archangels which are chief princes. These have higher hierarchies than ordinary angels, as orderliness in God's kingdom is concerned. Despite the fall of Lucifer, the archangel named Michael couldn't dare raise accusing fingers at Lucifer because cherubs are of a higher hierarchy than archangelic beings. "Yet Michael the archangel, when contending with the devil, he disputed about the body of Moses, durst not bring against him a railing accusation, but said, The Lord rebuked thee." (Jude 1:8). Up until date, Michael respects the hierarchy of this cherub Lucifer. Scripture says Michael would dare not rail at Satan, even though he was a fallen cherub, because cherubs are respected in rank.

Although God placed some angels in charge of fire, sun, water, bottomless pit, death, destruction, light, and thunder. (See Revelation 14:18, 16:5, 9:11; Isaiah 54:16. Psalm 78:49). The scripture talked about the Angel of God's presence that appeared unto Moses in the flame of fire (See Exodus 3:2, Isaiah 63:9). The Angel of His presence does introduce God's arrival. The LORD God placed his name on this angel, which means he can speak on behalf of God. God talks through this angel directly. We saw this scenario played out when Moses was at the burning bush. "And the angel of the LORD appeared unto him in a flame of fire out of the midst of a bush: And he looked, and, behold, the bush burned with fire, and the bush was not consumed...And when the LORD saw that he turned aside to see, God called unto him out of the midst of the bush, and said, Moses, Moses, and he said, Here am I" (Exodus 3:2-4).

This angel of God's presence was standing in a bush and what Moses could see was fire, which was a phenomenon that caught Moses's attention until God called unto Moses from the midst of the angel. In order words, this angel's mind is in synchronism with God. When it comes to this angel, God said, "...For my name is in him" (Exodus 23:21). Meaning he can speak on behalf of God. This was the same angel that called unto Abraham out of heaven when Abraham went for a sacrifice of his son Isaac (See Genesis 22:11-17). This same angel disclosed so many things to John, the apostle in the book of Revelation 1:1, about what God would have John write about the future.

The appearance of this Angel of God's presence was seen in the book of Revelation. He was described as almost like God in appearance. Such a mighty angel capable of standing on the sea with one of his foot and the other foot on the earth: "And I saw another mighty angel come down from heaven, clothed with a cloud: and a rainbow was upon his head, and his face was as it were the sun, and his feet as pillars of fire: And he had in his hand a little book open: and he set his right foot upon the sea and his left foot upon the earth. And cried with a loud voice, as when a lion roareth: and when he cried seven thunder utter their voices" (Revelation 10:1-3).

We could see from the scriptures the same features of the rainbow upon God on the throne was also upon this angel of his presence. Therefore, it means Jesus as Lord amongst the angels also had his personal assistant angel, which the scripture identified saying, "he sent and signified it by his angel" (Revelation 1:1). However, I believe the angel named 'Lord' was responsible for transforming into a man who wrestled with Jacob till daybreak; because the scriptures identified him as an angel, hence the angels said, "...For as a prince thou hast power with God and with men, and hast prevailed" (Genesis 32:28). In other words, Jacob you have shown that you have the power to wrestle with your God in the form of man. The book of Hosea further clarified that this was the angel that visited Jacob (See Hosea 4:12).

God made angels to worship and serve him and several activities in God's kingdom. Angels don't lack food and often rejoice and sing before the throne of God. The food is the manna the children of Israel ate in the wilderness for forty years, and none of them was sick. Man did eat angels' food (Psalm 78:25). Angels could also eat man's food, as in the case of Abraham when he received three angels, for which the LORD was amongst two before the destruction of Sodom and Gomorrah. As the scriptures put it, angels often transform into men, "Be not forgetful to entertain strangers: for thereby some have entertained angels unawares" (Hebrews 13:2).

We also read about Daniel, who got an angelic visitation – Gabriel in the form of man (See Daniel 9:21). Manoah's wife, the mother of Samson, had angelic visitation as well (Judges 13:9-19). Peter, an apostle of Jesus, was released from prison by an angel of God (Acts 12:6-13). Joshua also saw an angel in the form of a man drawn with a sword which came to join the battle against Jericho in Joshua 5:13-15. So, we can see that angels or stars turn humans with radiant skin. But angels are quite different from sons of God.

Satan was acknowledged

Generally speaking, spirit men are referred to as sons of God in the scriptures, as earlier noted. The book of Job 38:4-7 made a clear-cut distinction between the sons of God as spirit men and stars of God, which distinguished mortal men from spirit men. Genesis 2:7 says, "And the LORD God formed man of the dust of the ground and breathed into his nostrils the breath of life, and man became a living soul." Going through these scriptures carefully, it would be observed that Adam, in this context, was formed as man of the dust of the ground. Which denotes Adam was not the first man formed by God. We have the 'men of the spirit,' which the scriptures referred to as sons of God that pre-existed Adam of the dust of the ground. We have already discussed some sons of God together with some angels and archangels who sinned against God and were banished into prison – the darkness of the deep.

We saw the presence of these sons of God in the book of Genesis 6:4. And the scripture says that some of these fallen sons of God turned giants, came in unto the daughters of men, resulting in the deliveries of giants (the Emims, Anakims, etc.) upon the earth. Job 1:6 was emphatic about these sons of God: "Now, there was a day when the sons of God came to present themselves before the LORD, and Satan also came among them." Critical meetings are sometimes convened by God with these sons of God in attendance. These meetings are held in the spirit realms over the children of men. Now, the reasons for some meetings may not be unconnected to the Adamic races that are unconcerned about abstract realms matters.

As with the case of Job, a general meeting of the sons of God under the dark universe was convened. This includes sons of God, stars, and most importantly, Satan, who was recognized as the highest attendee. The point of the meeting was directed at Satan, in which a conversation ensued between God and Satan about Job's faithfulness to God on the earth. This was before Abraham was born. In the same vein, a similar meeting was convened when God needed to recompense Ahab's atrocities back to his bosom. And you know the resolution in this meeting led to a fallen spirit volunteering to persuade Ahab's prophets with deception, for which Ahab was finally killed on a battlefield.

Let's look at the narratives: "I saw the LORD sitting on his throne, and all the host of heaven standing by him on his right hand and on his left. And the LORD said, Who shall persuade Ahab, that he may go to Ramoth-Gilead? And one (spirit) said on this manner, and another (spirit) said on that manner. And a spirit came forth and stood before the LORD, and said, I will persuade him. And the LORD said unto him, Wherewith? And he said, I will go forth, and I will be a lying spirit in the mouth of all his prophets. And he said, Thou shalt persuade him, and prevail also: go forth, and do so" (See 1st Kings 22: 19-23, emphasis mine). In another meeting held spiritually, God berated the sons of God, including the stars of heaven, for being unjust on the earth. God expects these spirits to exercise justice, having gained access to the earth and considering that God revisited them in Genesis. They were expected to deal with humans on earth justly, but they supported the wicked people on earth instead. They couldn't judge like God and were unfair in their dealings with the sons of men on the earth. Let's look at the scriptures in Psalms 82:1-7, which says, "God standeth in the congregation of the mighty; he judgeth amongst the gods. How long will you judge unjustly and accept the persons of the wicked? Defend the poor and fatherless...They know not, neither will they understand; they walk on in darkness. All the foundations of the earth are out, of course. I have said, Ye are gods, and all of you are the children of the most High. But you shall die like men and fall like one of the princes. Arise, O God, judge the earth: for thou shalt inherit all nations."

Naturally destined

The scripture here was not addressed to Adam's natural descendants, who were children of men. God couldn't have been talking to children of men that they shall die like men when men are naturally destined to die one day or the other. It would be absolutely out of context to think this scripture was addressed to Adam's descendants. Some preachers misinterpreted these scriptural verses proclaiming God says men will die because they lack knowledge, which is a wrong interpretation of the scriptures. Does it mean those who have knowledge don't die as well? That is not what the scripture is saying here. God, standing in the congregation of the mighty, implies fallen stars of heaven and sons of God. He judgeth amongst gods (spirit beings). It means the mighty were also gods as rulers in this context. The mighty denotes fallen stars of heaven and sons of God, who became rulers on earth amongst the children of men as presidents of nations, kings, governors, high priests, priests, religious leaders, mayors, monarchs, etc.

God berated them when he said, "How long will you judge unjustly, and accept the person of the wicked?" Of course, these spirits already had access to the earth. So, the LORD was criticizing them on the need to do justice instead. They should defend the poor and the fatherless. They should deliver the poor out of the hand of the wicked sons of men. God further said that these spirits know not, neither will they understand; they walk on in darkness. Therefore, all the foundations of the earth are out. In other words, these fallen stars of heaven and sons of God no more understand the pathway of justice and righteousness, having perverted their ways under darkness, which they cannot change. Therefore, all the foundations of the earth are out, of course.

This means they have deviated off course to falsehood, wickedness, and oppression. The foundation of the earth was laid on truth but has been perverted into deception. They walk on in dark ways of life (lies, wickedness, injustice, and oppression) and have impacted humans with their unjust ways; hence the foundations of the earth are out of the course of equity, justice, righteousness, and peace. In conclusion, God said, "You are gods (fallen spirits that rule among men), and all of you are the children of the most High. But you shall die like men (natural Adam's descendant humans) and fall like one of the princes". The 'children of the most high' implies sons of God. You shall die like men, denotes God was saying these spirits beings shall die like children of men on earth and fall like one of the princes, implying they will undergo the natural death of men. Remember, I told you those spirit men who turned flesh or incarnate into the earth also die like humans. The difference is that they don't die in their actual spirit beings. They incarnate to other places, like John the Baptist, who immediately he died returned to his son's ship (Elijah) status and joined Moses to appear unto Jesus at the mount of transfiguration. This shows the 'congregation of mighty' implied the gathering of the stars and sons of God, as sons of God dwelling on the earth as rulers of the people by oppression and injustice. Of course, God expects that they would do justice like the stars of heaven once did, transforming into humans to fight against Israel's enemies when ancient people turned into humans supporting Sisera, which we have discussed earlier.

So, God said, "they shall die like men and fall like one of the princes." Who are these princes, and how did they fall? The princes refer to fallen archangels that were thrust with a sword into the pit. "Thus saith the LORD God, in the day when he went down to the grave, I caused a mourning: I covered the deep for him, and I restrained the floods thereof, and I caused Lebanon to mourn for him, and all the trees of the field fainted for him. I made the nations shake at the sound of his fall when I cast him down to hell with them that descend into the pit…they also went down into hell with him unto them that be slain with the sword; and they were his arm, that dwell under his shadow in the midst of the heathen" (Ezekiel 31:15-17).

The above scripture talked about the king of Assyrian, who was a principality in the spiritual realms, dwelling among the children of men as a physical king. He was thrust through with a sword, with other spirits shut into the dark universe. Let's look at other scriptures indicating spirit men reign as kings on earth dwelling amongst us. Daniel 7:17 says, "These great beasts, which are four, are four kings, which shall arise out of the earth." These beasts in the spiritual realms would reign as kings, presidents, governors, and religious rulers on earth. Some do incarnate, while others surface among men, telling lies to communities that they came from a so-called village or town which the communities may not search out. You know we have people who are ghosts amongst us in human flesh. Not all leaders are descendants of Adam, which is the reason why they rule without mercy, wasting human lives as soon as they assume leadership positions, as opposed to righteousness and peaceful living.

Some humans are principalities, as we have seen from the scriptures. Don't expect sons of God to incarnate as giants anymore as in the days of Noah's flood. Princes mean an archangel status in the spiritual realm (See Daniel 10:12-13).

Therefore, they shall die like men and fall (die) like one of the princes, which implies spirit beings dwelling among us in human flesh as rulers, kings, governors, presidents, religious leaders, etc., will die like men. In conclusion, Psalms 82:7 says, "...For thou shalt inherit all nations." In other words, Jesus Christ will inherit all nations. Meaning Jesus Christ will rule over all nations of the earth when he returns and in the life to come. Similarly, Psalms 2:8 was addressed to Jesus Christ to have the entire earth for his possession at last. "Ask of me, and I shall give thee the heathen for thine inheritance and the uttermost parts of the earth for thine possession."

Held in high esteem

I know that Psalms 82:6 made a scripture reference to John 10:34-35 in some Bibles. But Jesus wasn't reciting Psalms 82:6 when he addressed the Jews of his days. Let's take a look at the scriptures. "The Jews answered him, saying, for a good work we stone thee not; but for blasphemy; and because that thou, being a man, makest thyself, God. Jesus answered them, Is it not written in your law? I said Ye are gods? If he called them gods, unto whom the word of God came, and the scripture cannot be broken; Say you of him, whom the Father hath sanctified, and sent into the world, Thou blasphemest; because I said, I am the son of God?" (John 10:33-36). When you carefully study this passage of the scriptures, you realize that Jesus said, "Was it not written in your law?" But Psalms 82:6 was not the law handed to the Israelites. Psalms 82:1-6 was a prophetic declaration of what transpired in the spiritual realms between God and the spirit beings, which have just been explained.

So, it is absolutely incorrect and entirely out of context to have someone reference John 10:34 with Psalms 82:6. Jesus also said, "If he called them gods, unto whom the word came." What word? The laws, status, and ordinances, which were the commandments of God handed down to the Israelites. This means Jesus was talking about Exodus 22:28, which says, "Thou shalt not revile the gods, nor curse the ruler of thy people." And we understand the rulers among the people here refer to the high priest, according to Acts 23:5, of which Paul was assaulted and corrected for reviling. It means Jesus reminded the Jews about the law inscribed in Exodus 22:28 when he said, "Was it not written in your law that you are gods?" In essence, the 'gods' as used in John 10:34 denotes that Jesus should have been held in high esteemed or sacred as a high priest, which is the term "gods" or "rulers" among the Jews in his time.

Hence, he said, if God called them gods (sacred rulers of the people or the high priest) unto whom the word of God came (i.e., the law was handed to as custodians), the scripture cannot be broken. In other words, you cannot change the law in this respect. Hence, Jesus subsequently rebuked the Pharisees and said," Say of him, whom Father hath sanctified (appointed and anointed), and sent into the world, Thou blasphemest; because I said, I am the son of God?" (John 10:36, emphasis mine). In other words, dare you to say of him, whom God the Father has chosen, that I blasphemed because I told you the truth that I am the son of God? (Paraphrased)

It denotes Jesus was rebuking the Jews for reviling his priesthood's office. He should have been held in high esteem as a ruler (gods) among the Jews according to the law. Instead, he never denied being the Son of God. Clearly, Jesus was not reciting Psalms 82:6 as referenced in some Bible reference pages.

Chapter 10

Sons of God on Earthly Missions

Now let us take a few more examples of the presence of these sons of God from the universe above. Zachariah 1:8 says, "And I saw by night, and a man riding upon a red horse, and he stood among the myrtle trees that were in the bottom; and behind him were three red horses, speckled and white." Connecting the above scripture to Ezekiel 40:2-3, which says, "In the visions of God brought he me into the land of Israel, and set me upon a very high mountain, by which was as a frame of a city on the south. And he brought me hither, and behold there was a man whose appearance was like the appearance of brass, with a measuring reed, and he stood in the gate."

Both scriptures indicate the presence of the sons of God as seen by prophets Zachariah and Ezekiel in the spiritual realms. These spirit men were seen actively engaged in certain activities. For example, Ezekiel 10:2 says, "And he spake unto the man clothed with linen, and said, Go in between the wheels, even under the cherub, and fill thine hand with coals of fire from between the cherubims..." (Ezekiel 10:2). Spirit men in conjunction with stars of God are engaged in certain activities such as measuring lines, spiritual warfare, errands, acting as representatives of God in churches, watching over cities or nations, and giving feedbacks to God over the earth. The activities of the sons of God as 'watchers' over mortals began with Lucifer, who was once a cherub assigned to watch over Adam and Eve in the Garden of Eden, but Lucifer screwed up, betraying God.

Though I'll come back on what transpired at the Garden of Eden, let's zoom in on a few sons of God who have walked upon the earth after the floods of Noah. However, time will fail me to talk about Daniel as one of the sons of God on an earthly mission, which is evident in the scriptures with God comparing Lucifer's spiritual wisdom to Daniel's. We read how God addressed Lucifer when he said, "Behold, thou art wiser than Daniel, there is no secret they hide from thee" (Ezekiel 28:3). Which shows Daniel was a higher rank son of God incarnated as a young man while Lucifer was a cherub possessing higher wisdom than Daniel in their spiritual profiles. Daniel wasn't yet born on earth when God said these words to Lucifer. Of course, the parents of Daniel were still unknown in the scriptures, which calls for concern. Yet, he was seen as having an excellent spirit (Daniel

5:12). It is also worthy of note to have an angel informed Daniel that he would die maintaining his spiritual position in the end of the days (Daniel 12:13). In other words, Daniel will reincarnate to earth in the latter days.

One might ask, "If that was true, how come Daniel was still praying for interpretations or revelations?" Simple! I'd come to that shortly. First, however, I'd like to touch on other sons of God that came on earthly missions. For example, Melchizedek, a priest of the most High, accosted Abraham when Abraham returned from a battlefield - having recovered his nephew Lot, the King of Sodom, and their goods. "And Melchizedek, King of Salem brought forth bread and wine: and he was the priest of the most high God" (Genesis 14:18).

Reference was made to the sudden appearance of this son of God in human flesh. "For this Melchizedek, King of the Salem, priest of the most high God, who met Abraham returning from the slaughter of the kings, and blessed him; To whom Abraham gave a tenth part of all; first being by interpretation King of righteousness, and after that also King of Salem, which is King of peace. Without father, mother, descendant, having neither beginning of days, nor of life; but made like unto the Son of God; abideth a priest continually. Now, consider how great this man was..." (Hebrews 7:1-4).

If you extract the clause: 'consider how great this man was, it shows Melchizedek preexisted Adam. Scripture says, "Without father, mother, descendants, and having neither beginning of days, nor of life. It shows he was not born on earth and had no beginning of life. There was no trace of his biological father or mother. He preexisted Adam of the dust recreated in Genesis. "And Melchizedek king of Salem brought forth bread and wine: and he was a priest of the most high God. And he blessed him, and said, Blessed be Abram of the most high God, possessor of heaven and earth: And blessed be the most high God, which hath delivered thine enemies into thy hand. And he gave him tithes of all." (Genesis 14:18- 20).

Scripture says Melchizedek blessed Abraham, the father of faith. Melchizedek offered bread and wine to Abraham because he (Melchizedek) was a priest of the most high God. In the Old Testament, Melchizedek was a figure of Jesus Christ to come, who would also give bread and wine to his disciples. As soon as Abraham took the bread and wine, his eyes were immediately opened, and Abraham knew what to do - pay his tithe. If you contrast Jesus, who broke bread and gave it to his disciples, and their eyes were opened, it dictates that the communion opened Abraham's eyes (understanding) (Luke 24:30-31). Melchizedek was one of the sons of God – one of the ancient person in the pre-Adamic earth who walked upon this earth. This was precisely what the apostle Paul was trying to demystify about the personality of Melchizedek to the Hebrew Christians.

If we expound on this, it means Melchizedek had been a priest unto God during the pre-Adamic ages because Salem was never a kingdom on earth in the days of Abraham but a dwelling place of God's tabernacle according to the book of Psalms 76:2. Just like the river Kishon was identified as an ancient river which preexisted Adam. If you'd recollect, I told you earlier that some ancient men who once occupied the earth were saved and translated to the light zone universe above. It means Melchizedek had been a priest who interceded for the saved pre-Adamic men like Moses and Elijah, amongst others. Melchizedek was a priest of the most High in the pre-Adamic times and would have to continue his priestly office in the Adamic dispensations; hence he was a priest that abideth continually. Hebrews 7:3 says, "...Made like unto the Son of God (Jesus Christ); abideth a priest continually." In essence, Melchizedek was made like Jesus Christ, our high priest whose priesthood is unchangeable. So when God said unto the son, "Thou art a priest forever after the order of Melchizedek," it implies Jesus Christ is to continue in his order or pattern of unchangeable priesthood office, of whom he was known as Melchizedek in the pre-Adamic earth, serving bread and wine, hence his sudden appearance on earth without descents. In context, Melchizedek was Jesus Christ to whom Abraham gave a tithe, as King of Righteousness and, at the same time King of Peace; hence he had no beginning of days nor end of life. Let's break down what the book of Hebrews meant by the King of righteousness and the King of peace.

Psalms 45:6-7 says, "Thy throne O God is forever and ever: Thou the scepter of thy kingdom is a right scepter. Thou lovest righteousness, and hatest wickedness..." This scripture talks about Jesus Christ as King of righteousness, which I've touched on that he was the most peaceful amongst the stars of God. The scepter of thy kingdom is a right scepter. In other words, your rulership speaks of righteousness living because Jesus delights in righteousness. Psalms 45:4 says, "And in thy majesty ride prosperously because of truth, meekness, and righteousness..." This also talked about righteousness, peace, and truth often exhibited by Jesus. Revelation 19:11 says, "And I saw heaven opened, and behold a white horse, and he that sat upon it was called Faithful and True, and in righteousness, he doth judge and make war." The word 'prosperously' used in Psalms 45:4 means 'faithfully' as used in the book of Revelation.

All three scriptures point to Jesus Christ, the King of Righteousness. How about King of Peace? Isaiah 9:6 talked about Jesus Christ being born as 'Prince of peace. But let's look at the word King. Luke 2:8-14 talks about shepherds in the field who were visited by the angels of God that heralded Jesus's birth, saying, "Glory to God in the highest, and on earth peace, goodwill toward men" We saw the account of Matthew that when the wise men came to king Herod, they said, "Where is he that is born King of the Jews? For we have seen his star in the east and are come to worship him." (Matthew 2:2).

Shallow minds

These points to the King of Salem unveiled by Paul in the book of Hebrews. Paul had an in-depth revelation of the person of Melchizedek to have been Jesus Christ. That was why he paused and said Jesus Christ was "called of God after the order of Melchizedek, of whom we have many things to say, and hard to be uttered, seeing you are dull of hearing." He was invariably saying the revelations he had about Melchizedek were hard to utter because the Hebrew Christians may not comprehend the mysteries (Hebrews 5:10-11). Paul said that the Hebrew believers were babes in the LORD and that strong meat was meant for mature believers. (See Hebrews 5:12-14). In context, he was careful about shallow minds, just like someone would argue blindly about the truths revealed in this book because of their shallow understanding, perhaps religious traditions. Melchizedek was Jesus Christ, who undoubtedly appeared in the flesh to bless Abraham.

Let's see further proofs from the scriptures in which Jesus clandestinely corroborated his appearance as Melchizedek in disguise. John 8:56 says, "Your father Abraham rejoiced to see my day: and he saw it, and was glad." Take note of the phrase 'see my day' used by Jesus Christ. It means Melchizedek appeared unto Abraham that day. He surfaced as a king in the company of his entourage (angels) in human flesh. Kings don't move alone. He (Jesus) came with some heavenly host (angels) and accosted Abraham that day to bless him. Jesus further told the Jews that "before Abraham, he was," but they couldn't grasp the mystery. He was dealing with little minds, which the apostle Paul called babes in the LORD.

John 8:58 says, "Jesus said unto them, Verily, verily, I say unto you, before Abraham, I am." In other words, I existed before and appeared as King of Salem and blessed Abraham, your Father. But such secrets were hidden from the children of men. Jesus didn't unveil such secrets because it is the glory of a king to conceal secrets, but it is the honor of men to unravel mysteries. Abraham immediately honored him with a tithe. The tithe is a sign of honor unto God because God shielded Abraham in the battle and gave him the ability to get wealth. Why would Jesus come as Melchizedek before being incarnated? Simple! It is because the LORD foreknew Abraham as part of his agenda on the earth. However, the same hypothetical question was asked by Paul. I would show you in the scriptures where the apostle Paul posted this same question as we progress.

God wanted a people for himself since the world was lost to the devils through idolatry. So, God chose Abraham among the seed of men and blessed him. "Look unto Abraham, your father, and unto Sarah that bare you: For I called him alone, and blessed him, and increased him" (Isaiah 51:2). Abraham was such a privileged man whom the LORD visited in the form of man to deliberate issues affecting the overthrow of Sodom and Gomorrah. God's reasoning with mortal man before passing judgment on the earth; sounds profound! Of course, no one heard anything about Melchizedek anymore. It was obvious that Melchizedek left back to heaven unannounced. He featured to bless Abraham that day, and that was all! So, we can see that spirits often infiltrate the earth dwelling amongst us.

I should anticipate that someone might put up an argument citing John 1:18 in the scripture, which says, "No man hath seen God at any time, the only begotten Son, which is in the bosom of the Father, he hath declared him." John the apostle here had no understanding of the mystery of Melchizedek like the apostle Paul. Hence he wrote that scripture. Although John was not saying that no man can see God, instead he said, no man hath seen Jesus who was declared. Perhaps, it could be that when Melchizedek appeared unto Abraham, he appeared as a King of Salem, whose face may differ from Jesus Christ. Like Elijah's reincarnation in the form of John the Baptist, bearing a different name and face but the same spirit of Elijah because the scriptures confirmed that John the Baptist would come in the same spirit as Elijah.

Even the Jews at that time never knew Elijah had come until Jesus told them that Elijah had come and he had been martyred, having fulfilled his assignment. "But I say unto you, that Elias (Elijah) has come already, and they knew him not, but have done unto him whatsoever they listed. Likewise, shall also the Son of man suffer of them" (Matthew17:12). I must confess here that I have never believed in incarnation all my life until God opened my eyes to the truth of the scriptures. The truth remains that incarnation is meant for spirit beings, as you will understand. Jesus Christ talked about John the Baptist being Elijah incarnated. So, either you believe Jesus Christ, or you remain in your little shallow mind of accepting one side of the scriptures, discarding the other.

Hierarchy pursuits

Ancient saved men in the pre-adamic world who departed to God's kingdom above are regarded as watchers on earth (in the spiritual realm), just like the unsaved ancient men act as demons on earth. For example, we saw a watcher issuing orders to bring down

King Nebuchadnezzar. "And whereas the king saw a watcher and a holy one coming down from heaven, and saying, how the tree down, and destroy it..." (Daniel 4:23). King Nebuchadnezzar in his dream (abstract realm) saw a watcher and a holy one which implied a spirit man as sons of God. We already talked about watchers in the book of Zachariah, who walked through the earth in the spiritual realm giving feedback to the Lord.

God sometimes assign these watchers into families to accomplish specific assignment on earth. And once Satan perceived such a move, he would instigate humans on earth to oppose their earthly incarnation and have them killed. He does this by prompting governments or kings to make unrighteous degrees at such times. This was obvious in the time of Moses and Jesus, in which laws were promulgated to eliminate male children in Egypt and Judaea, respectively. The devil knew about their incarnation into the earth. And, because Satan's greatest pleasure is to have men and women weep and suffer on earth. God would have to intervene by sending deliverers to planet earth to rescue his people until the devil's time is up. But, of course, you are already aware Satan and his hordes of darkness have hijacked this earth.

Moses was also one of the sons of God sent to rescue the Israelites from the cruel bondage of slavery in Egypt. This explained what the scriptures meant by Moses being a good or proper child (Exodus 2:2, Hebrews 11:23). And because Satan enjoyed their sufferings in Egypt, he instigated Pharaoh to eliminate all male children of Israel, having seen what God was about to do, sending deliverer to rescue the Israelites from bondage.

Having accomplished his first earthly assignment, Moses would need to return to planet earth for the second time in these last days. What do I mean? The scripture says that Moses and Elijah will be reassigned to feature again in the last days during the great tribulation representing the two olive trees and candlesticks standing by the LORD God of the earth. "And I will give power unto my two witnesses, and they shall prophesy a thousand two hundred and three score days, clothed in sackcloth...These are two olive trees and the two candlesticks standing before the God of the earth...These have power to shut heaven, that it rain not in the days of their prophecy: and have powers over waters to turn them to blood, and smite the earth with all plagues, as often as they will" (Revelation 11: 3-6).

The scripture was explicit about these two men: Moses and Elijah are the two olive trees in the spiritual realms standing before the LORD of the earth. Let's look at the book of Zechariah 4:11-14, which says, "What are these two olive trees upon the right side of the candlestick and upon the left side thereof? And I answered again, and said unto him...Then said he, These are the two anointed ones that stand by the LORD of the whole earth." And that is why we saw Moses and Elijah appear unto Jesus Christ at the mount of transfiguration. If you correctly studied the scriptures, you would agree with me that Elijah's parents remained unknown in the scriptures. Elijah suddenly surfaced like Melchizedek and immediately declared his actual function in the spiritual realm as a man standing before the LORD.'

Elijah didn't access planet earth by birth during his first entry in the Old Testament. He was one of the sons of God whose appearance on earth was like Melchizedek. Elijah dwelled among the inhabitants of Gilead, of which no one could trace his genealogy. Scripture says, "And Elijah the Tishbite, who was of the inhabitants of Gilead, said unto Ahab, As the LORD God of Israel liveth, before whom I stand, there shall not be dew nor rain these three years, but according to my word" (1st Kings 17:1). The scriptures never told us about his parents at any time.

He came and declared his identity as one standing before the LORD God of the earth.'

We've got some phony authors alluding to greater glory in Jesus Christ, arrogating superiority to themselves as being greater than Moses and Elijah. Unknown to them, both men are the sons of God who pre-existed Adam. The simple fact that Paul wrote a greater glory in Christ doesn't cancel out the same God who worked all things according to the counsel of his will from the Old Testament. Many who read and wrote about greater glory in Christ as written by Paul in 2nd Corinthians 3:1-18 are currently quoting the scriptures out of context, alleging that they are greater than all the prophets of the Old Testament. Which is ignorance gone too far! People who claimed to be greater than these prophets of old haven't been able to comprehend the Old Testament scriptures, much less capable of writing inspired texts that could stand the test of time.

Many who have the gifts of miracles, healing, deliverance, and prophetic often pride themselves, forgetting that not everyone needs miracles by which they manipulate so many gullible minds. Some people don't believe in miracles but in a thoughtful process of achieving things. Miracles don't define God. Some people say, 'Without miracles, God does not exist.' What an insult! Such people think they are superior being used by God, but they talk to babes as their congregants. Miracles are simply acts of God. I believe in miracles and have been used by God in that capacity, but God is too big to be confined to the pursuit of earthly miracles. The earth's daily rotation is by far evidence of God's awesomeness, not miracles of pains, blind eyes, cripples, sickness, or bread and butter. Yes, the miraculous distinguishes the interplay of powers in the spiritual realms, but God is much bigger than ordinary acts of miracles. We've got so many believers who think power pursuit is the ultimate, who often quote scriptures out of context, not being mature. They might quote scripture that says, "That your faith should not stand in the wisdom of men, but in the power of God" (1t Corinthians 2:6). Thinking charisma is what defines Christianity, but these same people fail to read the next verse in which Paul wrote; howbeit we speak wisdom among them that are perfect..." (1st Corinthians 2:7). The word perfect expresses maturity in the scriptures.

Some authors erroneously interpret the scriptures in manners to suit their pride, being entirely out of context. And guess what? Many believers who do not have the depth knowledge of the scriptures, having read such books without researching and praying about such scripts, join the bandwagon. They err by not knowing the scriptures. It is inappropriate for us to arrogate greatness to ourselves over the sons of God who incarnated to earth because we got born again as New Testament believers. Some say, 'We are greater than Moses and Elijah' - citing Matthew 11:11, which some authors have explained out of context, misconstruing what Jesus implied. We are born again as adopted sons of God from the natural men of the dust to join the group of the sons of God who pre-existed Adam. John 1:12-13 says, "For as many as received him, to them gave he power to become the sons of God, even unto them that believe on his name: Which were born, not of blood, nor the will of the flesh, nor of the will of man, but of God."

This means those born of flesh and blood or the will of man are not yet classified as sons of God, but only when they become born of God are adopted sons of God, awaiting transformation from dust-matter materials into a glorious body. In context, they will be adopted from among the children of men (as a man of the dust) and would be made perfect after death. Hebrews 12:22-23 says, "...and to the spirits of the just (or justified) men made perfect (with substances of precious stones and light of fire)." To be made perfect means to be recreated with the same substances used in forming the sons and stars of God, currently in the light zone universe above.

We are the adopted sons of God. As it is written, "Having predestinated us unto the adoption of children by Jesus Christ to himself, according to the good pleasure of his will...that in the dispensation of the fullness of times, he might gather together in one all things (all sons of God) in Christ, both which are heaven, and which are on earth, even in him" (Ephesians 1:5 and 10). We are preordained unto the adoption of children. Meaning being earmarked to become children, given that we were made with inferior materials of beasts endowed with consciousness to join the sons of God in the light zone.

Let me give a vivid picture of what I'm trying to share with you. Suppose you made an artificial robot and tried to teach the robot about consciousness. And if this robot eventually gains consciousness and behaves in manners you love, perhaps playing and giving you pleasures, you would wish to change the material used in forming the robot to the same material component you possess so that the robot looks exactly like you and become your friend who does what pleases you. We are made of dust in our beautiful and intelligent state and are still subject to diseases, sickness, stress, aging, and fear of death and destruction.

Adamic descendants are the things on earth – as people predestined by adoption, while the spirit men (sons of God) who existed before Adam are the things in heaven. God will gather them together in one. So, we should be careful of our prideful utterances, saying what we don't know about because we read someone else's book that interprets scriptures out of context. Jesus told his disciples that it is not of him to decide who sits by his right or left hand but the Father when they were carried away in pride of hierarchy pursuits (Mark 10:40). Moses and Elijah are sons of God in the spiritual realms who incarnated. Let's stop speaking in pride because we were born again and begin to say what we know nothing about in ignorance, just because prayer and miracles take place. Moses or Elijah interrupts nature at will.

My servant Moses

Moses was born in Egypt approximately 3,800 years ago (at the time of writing) to the descendants of the sons of Levi. He was made to incarnate into planet earth as one of the sons of God. The LORD of all commended Moses, saying, "My servant Moses is faithful in all my house. With him will I speak mouth to mouth, even apparently (plainly), and the similitude (image, likeness, shape) of the LORD shall he behold..." Numbers 12:7-8. Moses was the only man after Adam who saw God literally. Moses saw God's back parts in the flesh. Other prophets only saw God through visions.

One time, when studying the scriptures, I wept over how Moses was overly concerned about the Israelites, putting his spiritual sonship position on the line. He told God to delete his sonship status out of God's book of life. I mean, I can't imagine such a sacrifice. Yes, it is true that God deleted Satan and other fallen sons of God, but Moses was God's own. So for the sake of the children of Israel, Moses had to put his life on the line. What a love! "And Moses returned unto the LORD, and said, Oh, this people have sinned a great sin, and have made them gods of gold. Yet now, if thou wilt forgive their sin--; and if not, blot me, I pray thee, out of thy book which thou hast written" (Exodus 32:31-32).

Moses referenced God's book in heaven, where his actual sonship was recorded, not an earthly book. He knew what he was saying when he prayed to God to forgive the Israelites or delete his name from the book of life in the universe above. The scripture captured Moses as the meekest (not being vindictive and being God-dependent) above all men on all the earth. He carried out his duties diligently to the end, and never imagined anything against the LORD, even when he was denied entry to the promised land, having pleaded with God severally, knowing his filiation as one of the sons of God. The book of Deuteronomy 3:26 says, "But the LORD was wroth with me for your sakes, and would not hear me: And the LORD said to me, Let it suffice thee; speak no more unto me of this matter."

Moses was not wrath with God in his earthly walk. Hence, God commended and testified about Moses being "faithful in his entire house for a testimony of those things which were to be spoken after" (Hebrews 3:5). In other words, Moses didn't revolt against God's decision even when the children of Israel were to be blamed, unlike Lucifer who revolted over certain decisions God took which resulted in Lucifer's departure from God. I'd come to this shortly. You already read how ancient people exhibited pride in asking God to depart from them, and you also saw how four principalities over the heavens departed from God's camp. So when scripture says Moses's faithfulness to God speaks volumes amongst the sons of God even in the face of pain, it shows Moses was truly humble. It means interactions between God and his creatures might sometimes lead to altercations.

For this reason, the scriptures said, "Take heed, brethren, lest let there in any of you, an evil heart of unbelief in departing from the living God" (Hebrews 3:12). Moses was not objectional to God's decision of not entering the promised land. But the scriptures recorded that the Israelites were provoked during the conversation between them and Moses (a representative of God). Scriptures say that they took up stones attempting to stone Moses had God not shown up (Numbers 14:10). Moses was still interceding for them despite their skepticism about God's capability to see them through. "For some when they had heard, did provoke: howbeit not all that came out of Egypt by Moses" (Hebrews 3:16). Many who were provoked perished along the way. They were hardened in heart, and their "carcasses fell in the wilderness" (Hebrews 3:17).

Moses maintained a humble and quiet spirit which is a great price in the sight of God despite realizing his heavenly filiation while on earth. He would be an icon to be spoken of after that in humility, quietness, and submissive manners he displayed on earth. Moses was overwhelmed by the stiff-necked Israelites of his time but continued his meekness until the end. God buried Moses himself, and no man knew where he was buried to date (Deuteronomy 34:6). So when the scripture says that Moses was a testimony of the things to be spoken after, it means Jesus Christ had to learn by obedience (humility) in the things he suffered. However, Jesus knew he was a Son clothed with flesh. "Though he were a Son, yet learn he obedient by the things which he suffered" (Hebrews 5:8). Jesus learned obedience even to the death of the cross. Do you know what it is to allow people you created to humiliate and kill you? Jesus had to despise the shame and submit unto death.

Unusual on the earth

Moses invented an unusual phenomenon on earth when a company of men provoked him. God honored his words, and the earth opened up - an instant earthquake swept off the company of Koran, Dathan, Abiram, and their families. "So they gat them up from the tabernacle of Korah, Dathan, and Abiram, on every side: Datham and Abiram came out and stood in the door of their tents, and their wives, and their sons, and their little children. And Moses said, Hereby you shall know that the LORD hath sent me to do these works; for I have not done them of mine own mind. If these men die the common death of all men, or if they are visited by the visitation of all men, then the LORD hath not sent me. But if the LORD make a new thing, and the earth opens her mouth, and swallow them up, with all that appertain unto them, and they go down quick into the pit; then you shall understand that these men have provoked the LORD. And it came to pass, as he had made an end of speaking all these words, that the ground clave asunder that was under them: And the earth opened up her mouth and swallowed them up, and their houses, and all the men that appertained unto Korah and all their goods" (Numbers 16:27-32).

God sent Moses from the spiritual realms to deliver the Israelites from bondage, so he performed incredible miracles on earth in his days. Moses and Elijah were sons of God with such unusual stupendous power displayed on earth. "...These have the power to shut heaven, that it rain not in the days of their prophecy: and have powers over waters to turn them to blood, and smite the earth with all plagues, as often as they will" (Revelation 11: 3-6). And if you recall, according to his word, Elijah was a prophet who locked up the heavens from rainfall for three and half years. These are unusual phenomena on the earth. Imagine the dryness caused in the land of Israel in those days. He was sought everywhere in Israel to unlock the heavens.

"And Elijah the Tishbite, who was of the inhabitants of Gilead, said unto Ahab, As the LORD God of Israel liveth, before whom I stand, there shall not be dew nor rain these years, but according to my word" (1st Kings 17:1). Elijah said, "According to my word." This means he was an important son of God (incarnated spirit being) who interfered with nature at will, just like Moses commanded an earthquake at one spot alone where those families stood. He suspended and interrupted seasons by his word. When Elijah was translated into heaven by a whirlwind, the scriptures recorded that fifty men of the sons of the prophets went and stood afar off to view the event. They knew chariots of fire and horses would carry Elijah into heaven without seeing death. (See 2nd Kings 2:1-18). These are unusual phenomena on the earth.

This same Elijah reincarnated to planet earth as John the Baptist. For this reason, the book of John says, "There was a man 'sent from God, whose name was John (the Baptist), the same came for a witness to bear witness of the Light..." (John 1:6-7, emphasis mine). John the Baptist was sent from God as one of the sons of God. John the Baptist walked in the same spirit (spirit beings – as sons of God) and power of Elijah (See Luke 1:17, emphasis mine). Jesus acknowledged the presence of Elijah's reincarnation on earth for a specific assignment; being a forerunner to Jesus. Jesus specifically said, "And if you will receive it, this is the Elias, which was for to come" (Matthew 11:14). In other words, if you would understand it, this is the Elijah, who was carried by chariots of fire into heaven, that you have heard will return according to the prophets. The then Israelites knew Elijah was expected, so they were expectant, not knowing he came as John the Baptist.

Interplay of powers

Moses, as well as Elijah, one time on an earthly mission, failed at their wit's end when confronted with the power of death. One time, Elijah was confronted with pressure and threats from the forces of death acting through Jezebel, King Ahab's wife. Elijah gave up and demanded to exit planet earth because death was stirring at him. Of course, he accessed planet earth by infiltrating the Israelites dwelling amongst them as one of the sons of God who pre-existed Adam. Despite his superiority as one of the sons of God who incarnated, when there was the interplay of powers against him through Jezebel, his consciousness of humanity caused him to flee for his life. Elijah cried out unto God and said, "...I have been very jealous for the LORD God of hosts: because the children of Israel have forsaken thy covenant, throw down thy altars, and slain thy prophets with the sword; and I, even I only, am left, and they seek my life to take it away". And God told Elijah to go ahead and hand over his assignment to Elisha (1st Kings 19:16- 21).

Elisha had to complete Elijah's first assignment with a double portion anointing. Elisha was Adam's descendant naturally, and he received a double portion anointing and did exploits unhindered. Elijah was not used to the violent world under the forces of death, but Elisha was as natural Adam's descendant. When Elisha died, Scripture recorded that the anointing was so strong in his dead bones at his graveyard. The anointing on Elisha was so strong that a corpse in a procession that came in contact with Elisha's graveyard brought about resurrection. "And it came to pass, as they were burying a man, that, behold, they spied a band of men, and they cast the man into the sepulcher (grave) of Elisha: and when the man was let down and touched the bones of Elisha, he revived, and stood on his feet" (2nd Kings 13:21).

Elijah was reassigned, designated as John the Baptist, and also failed at his wit's end when the forces of death confronted him the second time after his reincarnation to earth. When I mean to fail at his wit's end, I mean spontaneous utterances at trying moments due to the wickedness and violence on earth. The people of this earth are used to falsehood, flattery, deception, violence, etc., always hating those who are truthful. John was locked up for being outright with the truth, and the forces of death stirred up again against him through King Herod. John expected Jesus to have him released from prison. It was unknown to John that Jesus was not sent to be a crown king of Israel in his first entry but would return as King his second time. So, John took offense; having suffered in prison for a long time, unknown to him, he had accomplished his assignment, awaiting death.

When a given assignment is accomplished, many who are sensitive often exit planet earth. Like Paul and Peter, they knew their departure times were at hand. The people of the world may not understand this. John heralded and prepared the people's hearts for Jesus's entering and told two of his disciples that this was the lamb of God that taketh away the sins of the world. He was expectant that Jesus would come and rescue him, for which he asked a sarcastic question, which he posted to Jesus, saying, "Art thou he that should come or do we look for another?" (Matthew 11:3). He was at his wit's end; unknown to him, his life was a script accomplished. Jesus said, "But I say unto you, That Elias (Elijah) is indeed come and they have done unto him whatsoever they listed, as it is written of him" (Mark 9:13). John was unaware of what was written concerning him. So he posted a sarcastic question at his wit's end.

This expression of doubt during the trying moments of John the Baptist elicited a response from Jesus, who said, "Blessed is he, whosoever that shall not be offended in me" (Matthew 11:6). In other words, be careful of uttering words because of trying moments.

John the Baptist was at his wit's end, being human. And Jesus said, "For this is he of whom it is written, behold I send my messenger before thy face, which shall prepare thy way before thee. Verily I say unto you, among them that are born of women, there hath not risen a greater than John the Baptist: notwithstanding he that is least in the kingdom of heaven is greater than he; And from the days of John the Baptist until now the kingdom of heaven suffereth violence and the violent (violated ones) take it by force" (Matthew 11:10-12, emphasis mine).

The clause: 'Notwithstanding he that is least in the kingdom of heaven is greater than many teachers and preachers have misconstrued him to date. Many have erroneously dissected this statement and presupposed that Jesus had already demeaned John's placement in the kingdom of heaven for posting such doubtful remarks. Jesus never said John the Baptist was demeaned less than every son of God in the kingdom of heaven. He was not comparing John the Baptist based on John's heavenly sonship. Rather, he was mourning how humans have been so hardened to destroy the greatest prophet ever born. John was more than a prophet being the forerunner of Jesus because all the prophets prophesied until John (Matthew 11:9 and 12). In the words of Jesus: "But what went you out for to see? A prophet? Yea, I say unto you, and more than a prophet" (Matthew 11:9). He was more than a prophet in that he was the beginning of a new chapter. He was the climax of the Old Testament prophets, ushering in the arrival of Jesus Christ, the Savior.

Jesus crystallized the distinction between the supremacy of the sons of God who came from the kingdom of heaven and earthly prophets born of women. It shows that in so far as John the Baptist became his forerunner, he was by that privilege higher than all prophets born of women. In other words, in the natural realm, John the Baptist was higher in rank than all earthly prophets of the law. But with such earthly placement above other prophets, the least person in the kingdom of heaven is greater than he. This implied the least in the kingdom of heaven - son(s) of God is greater than the highest ranked earthly prophet on earth. Because "He that is from above is above all: he that of the earth is earthly, and speaketh of the earth: he that cometh from heaven is above all" (John 3:31).

One spirit being in the kingdom of heaven had greater powers over earthly prophets. We saw a similar scenario played out when Archangel Gabriel visited Zachariah, the priest in Luke 1:20. Angel Gabriel, who came from heaven, exercised his superiority over an earthly priest Zachariah. So, Jesus meant that the least (sons of God) are greater than the highest-ranked prophet born of women on earth in context.

Satanic onslaught

And if John the Baptist who by placement among them that are born of women, and forerunner of Jesus was martyred, then from the days of John the Baptist until now - after Jesus's death, and beyond, the kingdom of heaven (sons of God who came from the kingdom of heaven) will go through violence - Satanic onslaught and the violent (violated ones) shall take it by force - accomplished it at all cost (Matthew 11:12).

In other words, John the Baptist's filiation as one from the kingdom of heaven was greater than his earthly prophetic ministry; hence he was more than a prophet, though he was ranked the greatest prophet on earth. And from his days and beyond - sons of God from the kingdom of heaven - martyred will go through Satan's violence on earth. In context, from the days of John the Baptist, including Jesus myself, talking to you, those who came from the kingdom of heaven would have to be killed, and those who came from heaven as sons of God would have to accomplish it at the cost of their lives. That is why Jesus used the term 'until now, present tense continuous. He further corroborated this in Matthew 17:11- 12, when he said, "... Elias truly first came, and restore all things, "But I say unto you, that Elias (Elijah) has come already, and they knew him not, but have done unto him whatsoever they listed. So likewise shall also the Son of man suffer of them" (Matthew 17:12).

If men could kill the greatest prophet who lived among those born of women, then I, Jesus, would have no choice but to accomplish my mission by force; what he meant by 'violent one taketh it by force. Jesus didn't relegate or demean John's heavenly position as one of the sons of God who came from the kingdom of heaven. He was simply talking to men on earth that John was the greatest prophet sent and was ranked the greatest among them that are born of women. He was lamenting how men could be so used to the devil to such an extent. That was why immediately after this expression, he rebuked the Jews saying, "John the Baptist came not eating nor drinking, they said he (John) hath a devil, and Jesus came eating and drinking, they say he is a glutton and winebibber, then he began to upbraid the cities where his mighty works were done..." (Matthew 11:17-24).

Jesus was lamenting how the Jews had been so hardened in killing prophets sent unto them, and Jesus continued lamenting this wickedness in Matthew 23:2-37, in which he said, "O Jerusalem, Jerusalem, thou that killest the prophets and stone them that are sent unto thee, how often would I have gathered thy children together, even as a hen gathereth her chickens under her wings, and you would not!"

The book of Revelation revealed how these two witnesses - Elijah and Moses from the kingdom of heaven would be killed again in these last days since both have been scheduled to incarnate back to this earth. Of course, they will bear different names and faces (See Revelations 11:7). From the days of John the Baptist, the kingdom of heaven must go through violence until the end of the age.

However, Elijah still retained his heavenly position –as one of the sons of God standing by the LORD of the earth in the spiritual realms; hence he will come the third time to planet earth. It was clear that John (Elijah), having accomplished his assignment, and being beheaded, immediately joined Moses in the spiritual realm, and both appeared unto Jesus at the mount of transfiguration. The death of John did not demean his placement in God's kingdom since he met Jesus again on the mount of transfiguration. So many people who are ignorant of this truth in the scripture have misinterpreted the scriptures to suit their earthly relevance. You know there is this pride in mortals always seeking for hierarchy on who is the greatest as though they are competing with someone. We often show off self for a simple manifestation of the power God gave unto us for his own glory, not our glory, since no flesh shall glory in his presence.

The disciples of Jesus Christ exhibited the same prideful behaviors while with Jesus. Just for the simple reason of casting out demons, they began to pursue hierarchy over God's kingdom in heaven, contending who is the greatest among them (Matthew 18:1). Such arrogant behaviors often manifest in humans who, by privilege, manifested God's gift on earth with some saying, "They are greater than John the Baptist" It is really unfortunate and inappropriate.

We also saw James and John - the sons of Zebedee, came to Jesus, requesting a higher placement in the kingdom of heaven. As a matter of fact, the scripture said they disputed hierarchy. "And they held their peace: for by the way, they had disputed among themselves, who should be the greatest" (Mark 9:34). But Jesus knowing their pride, simply told them that such positions are reserved for those it is prepared for. In other words, stop pursuing positions that have been preoccupied. I knew from the scriptures that such positions had been occupied by Moses and Elijah - two olive trees standing by the LORD of the earth. Instead, Jesus told

his disciples to learn humility in their daily lives. (See Mark 10:35-44). "Whosoever, therefore, shall humble himself as this little child, the same is the greatest in the kingdom of heaven" (Matthew 18:4).

Disputed with Satan.

Now, let's look at the case of Moses, who was judged faithful amongst the sons of God during his earthly mission. At his wit's end, Moses also came under pressure of life through the forces of death operating through humans - the Israelites rose against Moses with murmurings and complaints. Moses failed at this point by stroking the rock instead of speaking. God was, at this point, displeased with Moses. Moses's action was tantamount to unbelief, like that of John the Baptist. God said to Moses, "...Because you believe me not to sanctify me in the eyes of the children of Israel, therefore you shall not bring this congregation into the land which I have given them" (Numbers 20:12).

This singular act in Moses's life permitted the accusers of the brethren to remind God that Moses - one of the sons of God, had failed. This brought about a dispute between Archangel Michael and Satan over Moses' soul in the spiritual realms. "Yet Michael the archangel, when contending with the devil he disputed about the body of Moses, first not bring against him a railing accusation, but said, The LORD rebuke thee" (Jude1:9).

The devil had to contend because other sons of God who failed God were banished into the deep in previous earth and knowing fully well that Moses was one of the sons of God who came on this earthly mission had failed by such act of unbelief - striking the rock twice instead of speaking. And we know the sin of unbelief is the greatest sin committed by man since Adam's sin was categorized under 'unbelief' in that he exhibited unbelief to God's command. So also, Moses's action was classified under unbelief and pride. However, Moses pleaded for mercy, unlike Adam, who defended his actions (See Job 31:33). Moses prayed for forgiveness and continued in fellowship with God, and his mistake was covered. The sin of unbelief or pride is the greatest sin. It isn't the only sin, but it is the greatest. That is why scripture says that those who do not believe in Jesus Christ or his name are condemned already because they did not believe in the only Son of God (John 3:18).

We can see that whenever these sons of God incarnate or reincarnate on the earth, they almost find it difficult to complete their assignments without defaulting. Perhaps, each of them who came to this earth was scared of the power of death and destruction prevalent in this dark universe. As a consequence, certain utterances or actions performed could be classified as failures or imperfections on their part, which could be traceable to imperfections inherited via Adam's seed mingled in them during conception or simply because none of the sons of God could achieve 100% perfection on an earthy mission under the dark universe, except Jesus. I presumed that the proportion of semen (DNA) from Adamic males, which formed some of these incarnated sons of God (Moses and Elijah as a case study) in the womb, interfered with the actual spiritual nature (perfection) they carried.

Levitical priesthood

We have established from the scriptures that sons of God also make mistakes under the dark universe, much less the natural descendants of Adam. Of course, Moses and Elijah –as sons of God who came through Adam's seed mixed or unmixed in them exhibited imperfections. It shows that there is an imperfection in all male seed of Adam, and therefore, there must be a change in the priesthood from the descendants of Abraham if perfection exists. The imperfection that existed in Adam could not make man perfect. "If therefore perfection were by the Levitical priesthood (for under it the people received the law), what further need was there that another priest to rise after the order of Melchizedek, and not after the order of Aaron? For the priesthood being changed, there is made of necessity a change of the law...And it is yet far more evident: for that after the similitude of Melchizedek there ariseth another priest, who is made not after the law of a carnal commandment, but after the power of an endless life" (Hebrews 7:11-16).

Before expounding on the above scriptures, I would like to draw your attention to what the scripture meant when it says, "The LORD hath sworn, and will not repent, Thou art a priest forever after the order of Melchizedek" (Psalms 110:4). Firstly, Melchizedek had been a priest in ancient times before Adam was created. On the second, it means Jesus would follow the same pattern of serving the communion of bread and wine to his disciples as Melchizedek did to Abraham. This pattern of the communion of bread and wine would transcend earthly communion. For this reason, Jesus said he would repeat the communion again in his Father's kingdom in heaven (See Matthew 26:29). Thirdly, Melchizedek did not die on earth. Nobody witnessed the death of Melchizedek. He showed up for a day and disappeared. Melchizedek came with the power of endless life.

So Jesus would have to be a high priest who could not die; hence he was resurrected. Lastly, Melchizedek was a priest of the most High God, and being a priest, he offered sacrifices unto God. Therefore, Abraham gave a tithe so Melchizedek could offer those to God - the Father. It goes to show that Melchizedek appeared unto Abraham as a king as well as a priest like King Solomon, who had a dual function - kingship and priestly role offering sacrifices.

Now, let's get back to the scriptures Hebrews 7:11-16 just read. What apostle Paul was saying, in essence, is that Melchizedek came as a priest of the most high God to bless Abraham. Then under Abraham's lineage, Aaron's priesthood sprung up, and the law was given. So the question posed by the apostle Paul is: if Melchizedek, the high priest of God, came and blessed Abraham, and from Abraham's seed, the law sprung up, as in Aaron and other earthly high priests that followed. What further need was there for Jesus

Christ to rise up again as a high priest? And if perfection (a state of guiltlessness or justification) were to be attained by Levitical priesthood, then there shouldn't have been necessities of change of priesthood under Aaron's. This is a technical question based on reason and curiosity.

Many people get scared of asking questions when it comes to sacred books. They feel it is sinful to query what needs to be queried. Some so-called teachers or professors get irritated and often persecute some students who query the rationale behind certain ambiguities in religious books. And guess what? The 'professor' or 'religious leader' who isn't vast would rather victimize the student(s) for asking questions that sort of dithers their age-long ideology. It shows how religious and stereotypical such professors seem to be. They may be shallow in reasoning and analyzing difficult concepts, perhaps, just bearing the title academically.

I believe questions should not be avoided. You can't stop the critical and reasoning minds. And then we have gullible students who cannot challenge the norms, cannot think outside the box, and always take in things hook, line, and sinker even when they are unclear. Suppose there are omissions or errors in one's script due to myopic views or levels of understanding. In that case, it becomes pertinent for the future generation who might have studied those scripts to critically and constructively correct errors. Just like John Dalton's theory of the atom has been corrected and modified by various scientists as it relates to the atom. So also, errors made by Paul and John the apostles have been corrected in this book. Only the religious, traditional, and dogmatic minds would stick to the status quo without researching further.

The apostle Paul posted a critical question demanding the rationale behind the appearance of Jesus Christ repeating as high priest after his first entry as Melchizedek to bless Abraham, from which the law sprung. Then, Paul attempted to explain that it was because the law was weak and unprofitable; and that those priests came not by oath, and finally, the priesthood from Aaron and other priests may not continue their priestly offices due to human nature of being subject to death; and that because God had sworn Jesus would be a priest forever after the order of Melchizedek; so there was the need for a change as well. (See Hebrews 7:12-28).

In my opinion - in addition to Paul's explanations is that the priesthood under the law couldn't bring about perfection since Adamic nature had faulted the entire process. Even if Abraham had been blessed, he was still a descendant of Adam; hence Jesus had to come as a second Adam in the rank of Melchizedek; he was as a priest of the most high in the pre-Adamic earth. In other words, Jesus had to establish a new nature different from

Adam that would align with his high priestly function. Of course, God set the covenant with Abraham's seed, not Adam, but some traceable elements of Adam would make the priesthood under the law imperfect.

Under the lineage of Abraham, Moses and the children of Israel received the law. But the law was faulty under Adamic nature due to the defiled spirit in man, which was weak to carry out the righteousness of the laws ordained to life. I will expound more on this when we touched on the spirit in man as we progress. Secondly, those priests (Aaron et al.) often meet with death during their priestly office. And that means once a high priest dies, the process would have to be suspended until another high priest was appointed who would stand in the gap to plead for the sins of the people.

Established under imperfection

Now, in between a deceased high priest and a newly ordained high priest, what happens to the sins of the people? Would God release his wrath? So there was the need for a priesthood that would continue uninterrupted and endlessly - order of Melchizedek. In other words, an unchangeable priest who cannot die anymore. That is what the scriptures meant by Melchizedek 'abideth a priest continually (Hebrews 7:3). In other words, Melchizedek is continuing his priesthood office unstoppably in the person of Jesus Christ.

For this reason, John wrote: "...If any man sin, we have an advocate (standby high priest) with the Father, which is Jesus Christ the righteous" (1st John 2: 1, emphasis mine). That is why it is appropriate to confess your sins when you sin as a believer because Jesus still plays the role of high priest for us in heaven as the earthly high priest did in those days. Ignoring to confess your sins is pride.

Jesus, who was Melchizedek on earth for a day to bless Abraham, would have to replicate the same procedure of bread and wine and then offer tithes, and offerings as sacrifices unto God, being a high priest forever with endless life. It is clear that due to imperfections in the office of the high priests ordained by the law, Jesus couldn't have towed the line of Aaron's priestly imperfections that were connected to Adam since "death reign from Adam to Moses, even over them that had not sinned after the similitude of Adam's transgression, there was the need for the second Adam who is the figure of him that was to come" (Romans 5:14 emphasis mine). There was a need to change the laws (Old Testament) established under imperfection: "For there is verily a disannulling of the commandment going before for the weakness (less than perfection) and unprofitableness thereof. For the law made nothing perfect, but the bringing in of a better hope did; by which we draw nigh unto God" (Hebrews 7:18- 19, emphasis mine).

The law made nothing perfect, implying you cannot keep the law and obtain justification before God because "by the deeds of the law, shall no flesh be justified" (Galatians 2:16). The law was derived under the Adamic nature of imperfections. Therefore, if there must be perfection, there must be a change of the law. If there is a change of the law, then there must be a change of root to make the root and the branches align in their new priestly functions. The new root in man would then become priests submitting to their high priest – Jesus Christ.

Melchizedek was once a priest in the pre-Adamic times, but in our dispensation, there are priesthood ordinations with one high priest at a given point in time. Priests don't perform the function of the high priest because the high priest is authorized to enter into the holies of holy. Jesus Christ, a rebranded name of Melchizedek, was the high priest ordained to lead in the order or pattern of Melchizedek. Jesus was to follow in the footsteps of Melchizedek implies Melchizedek also died for ancient people in the pre-Adamic era and was resurrected to an endless life. The word endless life means a life that cannot be stopped by death. In other words, death cannot take hold of him, nor can he be retained by death. This is in anticipation of someone asking, "But Melchizedek did not die, and how come Jesus died?" The simple response to that question is that Melchizedek was not born on earth when he appeared to Abraham, so he was at liberty to disappear. Melchizedek died on earth in the pre-Adamic era as a priest. But he had obtained a new name Jesus, then died and rose again to his continuous life. He couldn't have left planet without going through death, which was the purpose of his coming to have his blood shed for the remission of sins and to retrieve what the devil stole at the Garden of Eden. He then resurrected to his endless life calling as a high priest forever and would return as a King in his second appearance on this earth physically (See Act 1:9, Luke 24:51, Hebrews 5:4,9, Revelation 19:6).

Visualized the agony

Amongst the sons of God who came from the Kingdom of heaven, it was written concerning Jesus that he would not fail nor be discouraged. Scripture said, "He shall not fail, nor be discouraged..." (Isaiah 42:4). So, at his wit's end, he was extremely careful with his words in prayers. This implied that the sons of God on earthly missions were surrounded by weakness in the flesh. What the scripture meant by "compass with infirmity or feelings of infirmities." (Hebrews 4:15). Let's read what Jesus encountered when faced with the forces of death through men: "Then saith he unto them, My soul is exceeding sorrowful, even unto death: tarry you here, and watch with me. And he went a little further, and fell on his face, and prayed, saying, O my Father, if it be possible, let this cup pass from me: nevertheless, not as I will but as thou wilt" (Matthew 26:38-39).

Jesus was sorrowful to death, having visualized the agony of being humiliated, tortured, and killed. However, meticulously, he chose his utterance, which is very important to his assignment. For this reason, the book of Hebrews says, "Who in the days of his flesh, when he had offered up prayers and supplications unto him that was able to save him from death, and was heard in that he feared; Though he were a Son, yet he learned obedience by the things which he suffered, and being made perfect (100%), he became the author of eternal salvation unto all them that obey him" (Hebrews 5:7-9, Emphasis mine).

Jesus being in the flesh, depended upon the Father to see him through the land of darkness where fallen angels of death and destruction are fierce. In the flesh, he feared, but when he eventually died, his God nature surfaced as LORD. He learned obedience in the flesh, being the Son of the most High God. The tendency to exercise his supremacy arose over mortals, but he despised the shame and humbled himself to death. He said, "Thinkest thou that I cannot pray the Father, and he shall presently (right now) give me more than twelve legions of angels?" (Matthew 26:53). And when he was threatened by Pilate, the sitting governor in Judah, Jesus told him that his Kingdom is not of this world. If his Kingdom was of this world, then his servants would fight. (See John 18:36).

It takes a humble lifestyle to sail through such a trying moment, being subjugated to your own creature, making a mockery of you. So, the scripture says that he will not fail nor be discouraged. Even when he was almost giving up, he meticulously chose his words saying, "Nevertheless not my will but thine will, but thine, be done" (Luke 22:42). He was on an assignment that needed to be fulfilled. He was on a specific assignment on earth and would need to finish the task at hand.

Chapter 11

Clothed in Flesh

The frame of the natural man is weak compared to the sons of God, formed with skeletons of precious stones or iron and clothed in flesh of brass. The substances used in the formation of the natural man came from this old earth, which the scripture referred to as the 'dust of death' since it remains the same earth where fallen spirit beings once lived and were imprisoned under death. Psalms 22:15 talks about the dust of death. It shows the substances used in forming Adam were taken from the dust of death. That is exactly what the book of Psalms 22:15 is talking about. Given that it was once polluted earth, God could not have put trust in man, made of the dust of death but would only show him mercy. Job 4:17-19 says, "Shall mortal man be more just than his maker? Behold he put no trust in his servants (sons of God); and his angels he charged with folly: How much less in them that dwell in houses of clay, whose foundation is in the dust, which are crushed before the moth?" Did you notice the word, 'whose foundation is in the dust?' Which dust? Dust of death. In other words, the man of the dust was created with substance of imperfections since his formation was under death.

The substance of imperfections couldn't have been perfect before God unless a constant fellowship with God is maintained through mercy unto perfection. Perfection, therefore, can only be obtained in heaven for those whose spirit successfully passed from the death of dust to paradise, having been clothed with substance of perfection. This means perfection, in a literal sense, implies being clothed with the heavenly substance of holiness. Hebrews 12:13 expressly told us that 'perfection' is only complete in heaven, not earth: "...to the spirits of the justified (by faith) men made perfect" (Emphasis mine). For this reason, angels in heaven are holy, and that is the reason why whenever angels in those days stand upon the earth (dust of death), they often instruct mortals to pull off shoes to enable mortals temporally align with their holiness invasion then. We read about such invasions when Moses and Joshua were asked to pull off their shoes.

The scriptures didn't say God made man perfect at the beginning but upright. Lo, this only have I found, that God hath made man upright...." (Eccl 7:29). Man was created upright from the beginning but clothed with substance of imperfections. Even

Lucifer, made with substance of perfection, failed when he began to traffic the dust of death because God foreknew him. Some religious writers often quote scriptures out of context. They teach in their ignorance, citing Job to have been a perfect and upright man, which they misconstrued as a sinless state. (Job 1:1). So they try to carry out the burdens of trying to be perfect like Job. The Scriptures never said Job was a sinless man. Let me quickly correct such assumptions for those who think Job was sinless from the same book of Job in which Job prayed to God and said, "...Thou makest me to possess the iniquities of my youth" (Job 13:26).

Job prayed unto God not to remember the sins of his youth, which means Job often sinned. By the way, how did Job know his children were cursing God in their hearts? He must have had such experiences because demons often instigate humans (on earth) to curse or speak against God in their hearts. That was why Job pleaded for mercy, sacrificing unto God continually for himself and his children. When the scripture says Job was a perfect man, it means he was mature or trustworthy in his resolution - serving God continually; by consciously seeking God for mercy due to his intimate relationship with God. Perfection is only obtained in God. Uprightness means to be straightforward or truthful in dealings. It means sincerity and not being crafty or hypocritical in behavior.

One time, God rebuked Abraham, admonishing him to be perfect because Abraham had a child with Hagar, trying to help God fulfill His promise about an expected child from Abraham's loins. When Abraham consulted Sarai about what God had told him, Sarah suggested Hagar, who was her handmaid. And for 13 years, God kept mute, watching Abraham's resolve to have a child through Hagar. Finally, God came to Abraham and rebuked him, saying, "Walk before me, and be thou perfect" (Genesis 17:1). In other words, follow my lead, mastering my ways of doing things. God rebuked Abraham because he had waivered or staggered in faith for deviating off course, thinking he was trying to fulfill God's promise of having a seed from his loins. Scripture said, "Abram fell on his face." (Genesis 17:3). This showed he was ashamed to look up because it was almost 13 years since he communicated with Abraham.

Body of Christ

Some religious people would perhaps say, "No. The Bible says that Abraham didn't stagger in faith," citing Romans 4:19-20. If he didn't stagger, why would he succumb to having Ishmael, for which God rebuked him? Abraham was the first to laugh in his heart when God told him he would have a child at his old age despite Ishmael's birth. Let me quickly show you that Abraham was not perfect either. "What shall we say then that

Abraham our father, as pertaining to the flesh, hath found? for if Abraham were justified by works, he hath whereof to glory; but not before God" (Romans 4:1-2). Abraham cannot boast before God that he was perfect, nor can Job. So stop putting on the burdens of self-righteousness. Instead, trust God's mercy and maintain a close relationship with Christ. Never defend your sins or attempt to show a holier-than-thou attitude to another since you will be judged with the measure you judged others.

As always anticipated, a religious mind would immediately quote, "Jesus said we should be perfect as our heavenly father is perfect," citing Matthew 5:48. But the word perfect used by Jesus here implies perfect in love, not self-righteousness. Let's look at the scriptures to understand what culminated in the words used by Jesus Christ: Matthew 5: 43 – 48 says, "You have heard that it had been said, Thou shalt love thy neighbor, and hate thine enemy. But I say unto you, love your enemies, bless them that curse, do good to them that hate you, and pray for them which despitefully used you, and persecute you. That you may be the children of your Father in heaven: for he maketh the sun to rise on the evil and the good, and sendeth rain on the just and the unjust...be you perfect even as your heavenly Father is perfect."

In other words, be good at or adept at showing love as is your heavenly Father. We can interchange the word 'perfect' with 'good at.' God is good at showing love. Job was found 'good at' his continual fellowship and sincere confession of sins before God. Abraham was rebuked for not being 'good in his walk before God - derailing off course in faith.

Furthermore, Jesus used the word perfect in connection to the church at Sardis in Revelation 3:2, which says, "Be watchful, and strengthen the things which remain that are ready to die: for I have not found thy works perfect before God." It is crystal clear that the word perfect means to be good at or adept. I have not found thy works perfect or proficient before God, especially for religious minds who think they are working towards perfection in the flesh made from the dust of death of imperfection. You can never attain perfection, but you can obtain mercy through the righteousness of faith in Jesus Christ. Perfection is only found when you are in Christ daily, overcoming by the blood of the lamb.

In the spiritual realms, God does not put 100% trust in his servants, so he charged them with acts of foolishness, much less man made of dust. For this reason, flesh and blood cannot inherit the kingdom of God; neither doth corruption inherit incorruption" (1st Corinthians 15:50). You can see that the scripture says corruption (imperfection) does not inherit incorruption. In other words, you cannot access heaven where holy angels dwell with your physical body made from the dust of death. That does not mean your new born-again spirit can not access heaven. The physical body made from imperfection cannot inherit the kingdom of heaven. Even when Adam hadn't sinned, he couldn't have had access to heaven with his human body. So long you are clothed with flesh and blood, you have got to learn to put your trust in the mercy of God and not your perfection in the flesh.

Your physical body will return to the earth from which it was taken. It was taken from the dust of death. In my usual style of anticipating public questions, one might ask, "How about Elijah and Jesus Christ, who went into heaven?" Simple, both bodies were changed in the cloud. 1 Corinthians 15:52 talks about the exchange of this body with the heavenly body in the cloud. Jesus, on ascending into heaven, had to drop off his earthy body (flesh and bones) with which he resurrected from the grave. Therefore, the body is called the "body of Christ," which was found sinless. Christ's body is hanging in space (above the darkness) in the spiritual realms, just as we can see the sun. Ephesians 2:21 talked about this body in which "all the building fitly framed together groweth unto a holy temple in the Lord." The current body with which Jesus is clothed in heaven is not flesh, blood, and bones. This was confirmed by John, the beloved apostle of Jesus Christ in the book of Revelations 1:13-17, who saw Jesus had been transformed back into his star-light body for which John fell as one dead before him. This does not suggest he can't make use of his earthly body at will. He used it for people he permitted to return to earth after death or whenever he accessed this earth every morning in the spiritual realm.

He took on him the form of a man of the dust because the human body was the approved body that suits the earth. It is like one being recruited to join the army. One would need to dress in the same uniform as other soldiers to be accepted or to infiltrate the camp so that one is not conspicuously seen as an alien. Now, if every soldier had taken some liquor and a particular soldier refused to take in some liquor, that does not make him an enemy. The uniform and identity card remains his validity about his recruitment into the combat team, but the liquor was not found in his blood when tested.

His seed was a special breed; he didn't drink the liquor other soldiers drank. He didn't sin, but he took on human nature. So that having put on the body of death, he might through the body of death destroy him that had the power of death; that is the devil (Hebrews 2:14). In other words, he destroyed the power of death in the body of his flesh hence his body could cross the death zone universe, though was exchanged. He was the Son of God clothed in human flesh. So let's get back on track with our discourse about the sons of God.

Aware of his sonship

It is worthy of note that not all sons of God sent on an earthly mission had clues of their incarnation into the earth as soon as they arrived here. As with John the Baptist and Daniel, they were completely unaware of their incarnation on earth. For this reason, every son of God on an earthly mission would have to depend upon God the Father as they also rely upon him in the spiritual realms before incarnation. This shows why Daniel prayed unto God. When John the Baptist was asked by some priests and Levites whom he was, he responded in oblivion, saying he was neither Elijah nor one of the prophets, but he was only on assignment to herald the coming of the Messiah. "And they asked him, What then art thou? Art thou Elias? And he saith, I'm not. Art thou that prophet? And he said, No." (John 1:21). Someone who isn't vast in the scriptures might contend religiously having read this scripture about incarnation.

Being incarnated as John the Baptist, Elijah had no clue of his previous existence on earth to have been named Elijah. It was Jesus who knew all things and decided to reveal this secret to the people that John was Elijah incarnated. Are you wondering why I chose not to use reincarnation instead incarnated? Elijah was not previously birthed on earth, so I wouldn't call it reincarnation. No wonder scripture said, "The former things shall not come to mind" (Isaiah 65:17). This implied that at the resurrection of the righteous or in the new earth to come, the present earthly experience will not be remembered. You won't remember that you once had children on this earth, nor will you remember that you existed and went through such terrible things.

All sorrows, death, pains, diseases, sickness, and terrible experiences will be lost from your memory. You won't have any clue of your previous existence on earth, just like John the Baptist had no clue of his first entrance as Elijah. He knew his assignment as the voice of one crying in the wilderness to prepare the way of the LORD. This shows the power of God to recreate something out of nothing. God had in the scripture displayed this capability causing King Nebuchadnezzar to forget his throne for seven solid years and, after that, brought him back to his senses. John the Baptist was dropped inside a case suit which transformed and processed his mind from the spirit realm to become conscious of the universe he found himself, completely forgetting who he was.

John couldn't even recognize Jesus, whom he stood by in the spirit realm; instead, he relied on spiritual perception to know Jesus was the Messiah. John's consciousness had changed from spirit realms into planet earth's consciousness. During John's fellowship with God on earth, God told John that whosoever the Holy Spirit lighted upon was the one to distinguish Jesus Christ from other men. Hence John said, "I knew him not, but he that sent me to baptize with water, the same said unto me, Upon whom thou shalt see the Spirit descending and remaining on him, the same is he which baptizeth with the Holy Ghost" (John 1:33). It means not all sons of God would know of their incarnation to planet earth. God made it so, except when they become too intimate with God, as in the case of Moses, they understand their mission on earth but are still subject to death.

Moses was unaware of his sonship as one of the sons of God in an earthly mission until God appeared to him, then Moses drew nigh to God. At first, he rejected his assignment, giving an alibi to God. It is natural for humans to fear the powers of death and destruction. It was until God showed forth His power against the forces of darkness then Moses had the courage. On realizing his sonship position in the spiritual realm, Moses told God to delete his filiation if God was not ready to pardon the sins of the Israelites. How did he know about the secret book in heaven? He became aware of his sonship as he became intimate with God on the earth. When you get so close to God, he will show the purpose of your existence. This is a proven fact.

Some sons of God may become full-grown men before realizing themselves, as with Moses, while others may not all through their lifetime realize. What is common is that they were men of like passions like you and I, and they felt what we felt in the flesh. They were tempted as we are. "Elias (Elijah) was a man subject to like passions as we are, and he prayed earnestly that it might not rain: and it rained not on the earth by the space of three years and six months" (James 5:16). Like passion means he had the same propensity like every other human to be indulged in immorality, craftiness, lies, pride, drunkenness, and cheating.

Let's look at the case of Jesus, who was God in the flesh who knew all things. He knew from childhood who he was. At 12, he told his earthly mother about his concerns - the Father's business. "And he said unto them, How is it that you sought me? wist you not that I must be about my Father's business?" (Luke2:49). The mother was wondering what the child Jesus meant by such statement, not knowing she was just a medium the Lord came through to planet earth. The same Jesus created her. The child she birthed knows more than she does.

Fear of death

The devil knew Jesus Christ wasn't Adam's descendant; hence he instigated Herod to commit homicide in an attempt to decimate Jesus. But God protected His Son from untimely death. And Satan couldn't do anything through humanity until Jesus was ready to fulfill his assignment. So when the time came for Jesus to wrap up his earthly mission, he agonized in prayers unto God the Father to save him from that hour. In His words, "Now is my soul troubled; and what shall I say? Father, save me from this hour: but for this cause came I unto this hour" (John 12:27).

This implied the human flesh had been made subject to the fear of death. Nobody wants to die except ignorant people who are deceived as terrorists in our dispensation. They are enticed with the false belief of marrying demonic virgins if they agree to blow themselves up. At the same time, those who sent them remain alive. This is the highest level of deception ever seen on earth. There are no virgins out there in the spirit world to marry. There is no marriage after death. Only the living can marry and procreate. "For when they shall rise from the dead, they shall neither marry nor are they given in marriage..." (Mark 12:25).

Humanity has always been subject to this bondage - the fear of death, and that was why Satan said that a man would do everything or give all his savings for his life (Job 2:4, Paraphrase). Death to humans is an unpleasant experience because God's breath (as spirit), which activates the soul, causes the souls in men to desire the everlasting nature impacted at the beginning. Even animals, birds, fish, and creeping things fear death because life which is the spirit in them came from the undying (everlasting) God.

The human soul is made eternal within the body, and it tends to flee death at all cost except when the body is overly sick or old to carry out its functions. Of course, we've got people who make personal decisions to die, due to hopelessness, while others easily give in to death, having heard God's voice. The former might have passed out unfulfilled, while the latter might have accomplished the purpose of existence on the earth.

Those who have their assignments fulfilled seem to align their soul with the voice of the Creator, as with Jesus, whose soul was sorrowful unto death at 33 years, knowing fully well that paying the ultimate price of redemption was one of his purposes, while the unfulfilled ones who commit suicides move straight to hell a reservoir planet of the unrighteous dead.

We have seen so many people castigate Jesus, who left planet earth at 33 years, and these people will say all manner of accusations. I'm not perturbed by the fallacies of men who often talk carelessly about the person of Jesus Christ since I know some men of the ancient world came in amongst us to discredit Jesus and say all manner of things because they are demons in human flesh or are the lineage of fallen spirits men, being celebrities in our societies. I already told you that they were used to blaspheming God. They "despise dominion, and speak evil of dignities" (Jude 1:8). In other words, they often insult the person of Jesus or behave in insouciance manners about God.

Jesus himself knew such persons - fallen spirits in human flesh existed among men of his days; hence he warned his disciples to "beware of false prophets, which come to you in sheep's clothing, but inwardly (spiritually) ravening wolves." (Matthew 7:15). They are humans in the flesh but wolves in their spirit beings. I've been privileged by God to see the spirit indwelling some people I've come across, and it is obvious they are demons in human flesh. We already talked about this.

Jude, the apostle of Jesus, also forewarned us about fallen sons of God who live amongst us as humans to date. "For there are certain men crept in (to planet earth) unawares, who before old ordained to this condemnation, ungodly men (fallen sons of God), turning the grace of God into lasciviousness, and denying the only Lord God, and our Lord Jesus" (Jude 1:4, emphasis mine). The scriptures acknowledged that these fallen sons of God speak against God directly and talk carelessly of the person of Jesus to deceive mortals who seem ignorant. This is because they are pre-Adamic men as a spirit who turned the grace of God into sexual promiscuity. And because demons often produce voluptuous emotions infiltrating dreams and defiling people sexually. Hence the scripture called them filthy dreamers – flesh-defiling spirits.

Filthy dreamers

Fallen spirit men and women sometimes defile the Adamic human race in dreams or hypnotic states, leading to ejaculation or orgasm on regaining consciousness. Many who experience sexual defilements with spirits beings in dreams don't know what to do. Of course, a simple solution to such a level of bewitchment is by the word of God or prayers. However, some people derive pleasure in these experiences, such that male-to-male or female-to-female sexuality is practiced in a hypnotic or dream state. Adamic descendants who indulge in lesbianism and homosexualism will not escape God's wrath unless they repent. Many are under the chains of darkness being addicted to these devices, and they seek to support such evil habits with scriptural backings.

Many have taken to these vices, which began with fallen spirit men in human flesh who also seek to convince gullible minds by quoting scriptures out of context, citing "Jonathan and David made a covenant because he loved his love as his own soul" (See 1st Samuel 18:3). They tell you it means David had sexual intercourse with Jonathan as homosexuals. What a perversion of scriptures to make fools of the children of men? This is a very high-level deception and misinterpretation of the scriptures to suit carnal desires. The scriptures noted David loved Jonathan because they were friends with the same passion for fighting their enemies. They were both bold men who could take up challenges.

Jonathan single-handedly smote the garrison of the Philistines, while David also took out Goliath single-handedly. The courage and boldness exhibited by both friends brought them together as close allies, not on immoral grounds. So attributing Jonathan's love of David to homosexuality is a gross deception. The origin of homosexuality and lesbianism began with fallen spirits of old who dwell amongst us practicing such detestable acts. And so, when the men of Sodom and Gomorrah began to practice it, God swept them off the earth with fire as an example to those who would follow in their footsteps.

Witches, wizards, and occults are usually responsible for arts of forceful sexual invasions in dreams or hypnotic states. It, however, began with these filthy dreamers - flesh-defiling spirits in human forms. The art of defiling someone from a distant point in a hypnotic state is demonic. Such hypnotic or dream-state sexual defilements might occur between nephews, cousins, neighbors, and associates. Truthfully, it means someone as a friend, relative, or associate is involved in voodoo practice unknown to the other who is being defiled. Frequent sexual intercourse in dreams or hypnotic states results in sicknesses, diseases or barrenness, and complications in the human body as they are exchanged for diseases in the womb of women and, in some cases, robbed men's financial fortunes.

I'm not saying any dream in which sex occurred implies demons. However, some do. A married man or woman whose partner travels and is often not home at night may experience such dreams, indicating the sexual needs of the body. However, witches, wizards, and occult people take advantage of the dream world. In most cases, spirit beings (dwarves shape) often hag men, women, and children in a dream or hypnotic state. People often say they were trying to wake up from a dream and found it difficult. They remain conscious of their surroundings, but a force tends to make them hypnotic. Demons in the form of dwarfs or witches create a magnetic force around humans to oppress them.

Many have gone through such experiences over and over. Those are the activities of witches and wizards who often hag people. Whenever you experience such form of hags, you should watch out for voodoo in that vicinity or someone coming from afar to oppress you. Only the power of God is capable of destroying such evil powers. Scriptures also referred to these spirits as 'filthy dreamers' because they defile humans through intercourse. Having accomplished a given task, these spirits in human flesh reincarnate in other countries, cities, or towns.

The skin of a leopard

In some cases, fallen spirits reincarnate to persuade an entire community to form a belief system of reincarnation after death. For instance, Satan could afflict a male child through sickness for which the child may die. The dead child's mother may give birth to another male child, similar to the first child who died. She may be persuaded to ensure a scar is placed on the second male child in the event he dies. And in the event the second male child dies, the mother, on re-conception for the third male child, would find the scar on the exact spot where the second deceased male child was marked.

This whole circle of events is Satan's ploy to have men believe in reincarnation after death always, which may not be true of Adam's descendants, but fallen spirits and their descendants or sons of God as spirit beings. The devil would convince the children of men to form a philosophy about his powers because he will assign his agent who will tell such families to bring certain sacrifices to retain the child alive. In the long run, that child would survive, get old, die, and move to another town. The devil had then succeeded in persuading and perpetuating such belief systems, enslaving an entire community to worship him or form a tradition and leading men out of the way of truth.

The LORD revealed to me on two occasions two persons I knew who died and were buried but are currently walking on the earth as humans again. They are demonic persons who migrate to other villages or cities where nobody knows them, and they continue their existence, and the circle goes on and on. The contention amongst theologians has been, but the scripture says that 'it is appointed unto men once to die, after this the judgment' (Hebrews 9:27). Yes, the children of men as Adam's natural descendants die once, and after that, the judgment. But fallen spirits beings (perhaps their descendants) can continue existence or reincarnation, procreating the earth until their time is up. These fallen spirits have the capacity through Satan to even change the sex of children in the womb of women.

The scriptures described these spirits as "twice dead" according to the scriptures (Jude 1:12). They can get buried in one town or move to another, while the circle continues over so many generations, forming such traditions and religious belief systems in men and women who believe that they will also reincarnate when they die. However, someone who has attained the age of accountability before God that dies prematurely on earth will go straight to hell. It is also possible for God to permit children who are less than the accountability stage to be re-born if they die prematurely. But I haven't found that in the scriptures. There are mysteries on earth beyond our senses.

The LORD once showed me a brother who died and got stuck in the clouds. Within a year after his death, this brother told me several secrets he never mentioned to me while he was alive. A member of his family he left behind confirmed those secrets the deceased brother (hanging in the cloud) revealed to me were absolute truth because he was a party to such secrets. Religious fanatics might discard these mysteries, calling them heresies, but they are truths about our universe. We saw Moses and Elijah appear to Jesus Christ and discussed Jesus's crucifixion, both having died several thousand years back, and Peter, James, and John witnessed their appearance.

Not all humans are descendants of Adam. Some are descendants of fallen spirit men of old who turned flesh. That was why Jesus talked about the parable of the tares and wheat, to distinguish between humans whose descendants are from fallen spirits' lineage and Adam's natural descendants. It is the duty of the angels of God to separate them (Matthew 13:24-31). So many offspring of fallen spirits are on the earth already in their millions. The devils do not procreate giant descendants anymore but have infiltrated humans with average size males and females. Psalms 21:9 talks about the descendants of fallen spirits who will be cast into hell. "Thine shall find out all thine enemies: thine right hand shall find out those that hate thee. Thou shalt make them as a fiery oven in the time of thine anger: the LORD shall swallow them up in his wrath, and the fire shall devour them. Their fruit (descendants) shalt thou destroy from the earth, and their seed from among the children of men - natural Adam's descendants" (Psalms 21:8-10, emphasis mine). Notice the clause: their seed from among the children of men.

Natural Adam's descendants will be separated from fallen spirits men descendants by the angels of God on the last day, and they will be cast into a lake of fire, even if not their fault for having been born into this world. God will not spare the offspring of the fallen sons of God. He will sort them all out! You cannot change the skin of a leopard. That does not mean that the natural descendants of Adam who refused the free gift of salvation would be spared. It is important to establish this hard truth untold in the body of Christ that God will not spare the descendants of fallen sons of God, no matter the genealogical records from Genesis to date - raw truth untold by many people. The question is: 'Why will God do that?' It's simply because the seed of the wicked will eventually manifest itself even in the land of uprightness. Isaiah 26:10 says, "Let favor be shown unto the wicked, yet will he not learn righteousness: in the land of uprightness will he deal unjustly, and will not behold the majesty of the LORD."

It shows that the seed of the wicked will always produce elements of wickedness, even in the land of uprightness; they will imagine evil against the LORD. That was why Jesus gave a parable about a king who invited several guests to his party. "And when all the guests were seated, the king came in to see the guests, he saw there a man which had not the wedding garment: And he said unto him, Friend, how camest thou in hither not having a wedding garment? And he was speechless. Then said the king to the servants, Bind him hand and foot, and take him away, and cast him into outer darkness; there shall be weeping and gnashing of teeth. For many are called, but few are chosen." (Matthew 22:11-14). The king will not permit any form of infiltration into his kingdom because the seed of the wicked will only manipulate things for themselves, not that they genuinely love God wholeheartedly. I will expound more about the seed of the wicked as we progress.

Out of the way of truth

Some people have been deceived, believing they will reincarnate when they die. It is a false belief for the natural descendants of Adam to reincarnate. People who didn't make it to paradise die and move straight to hell awaiting judgment because it is appointed unto (Adam's descendant) men once to die, after this the judgment (Hebrews 9:27). Fallen spirits men who infiltrated the earth came to deceive men into joining their rebellious living, and promise humans reincarnation. Natural descendants of Adam as children of men and women, whose genealogy is not traceable to fallen spirits seed don't reincarnate. For example, the rich man and Lazarus were Adam's natural descendants. We were told Lazarus went straight to Abraham's bosom while the rich man went straight to hell awaiting judgment (Luke 16:19-31).

You have seen from the scriptures that we have spirit men who crept into planet earth to teach men false doctrines and to turn them away from God, promising them reincarnation. "Likewise, these filthy dreamers defile the flesh, despise dominion, and speak evil of dignities. These are spots in your feasts of charity, when they feast with you...twice dead plucked up by the roots" (Jude 1:8 and 12). Their prime objectives are to lead men out of the way of truth. They speak evil of God and Jesus at will, mocking God among the children of men without fear.

Gullible Adamic descendants, men and women, would be wondering how someone could speak against God in such a sarcastic manner and remain alive. They make nonsense of God and even speak against men of God. Some came in unto the daughters of men in Genesis chapter six and began to procreate with women. They have changed the pattern of procreation. They still exist among us to date. They are in churches and among us till the end of the age.

Some ignorant people would tell you that you don't need to say these things. They tell you God loves everyone. God didn't wish any to perish, but that all should come to repentance. The scriptures cannot be broken because we want to suit people's emotions to retain church membership. Is it not written in your scriptures that many are called, but few are chosen, and not every one that saith unto me Lord, Lord, shall enter into the kingdom of heaven? See Matthew 22:14 and 7:21. I must admit that these are hard truths, but we have to save people who are also deceived by these fallen spirit men of old. They, alongside their offsprings, are vessels of wrath fitted for destruction already written in Romans 9:22. Spirit men and their offsprings will not inherit the kingdom of God.

They could be in churches for as much as 60 years but remain evil, even attempting to attack the leaders in God's house. It takes the spirit of God to discern them. ""...Even as there shall be false teachers among you, who privily shall bring in damnable heresies, even denying the Lord that bought them, and bring upon themselves swift destruction. And many shall follow their pernicious (destructive) way, by reason of whom the truth (Jesus) shall be evil spoken of. And through covetousness shall they with feigned words make merchandise of you: whose judgment now of a long time lingereth not, and their damnation slumbereth not...But these as natural brute beasts, made to be taken and destroyed, speak evil of things they understood not, and shall utterly perish in their corruption" (2nd Peter 2:1-3).

They mock Jesus without fear and even accuse Jesus of marrying in secret. They know they are condemned already, seeking many to follow their deceitful way into destruction. They boast and tell you, "Is it not hell? They are ready to go." Some crept into schools or churches pretending to be intellectuals or teachers in churches, but Jesus said, "By their fruit, you shall know them." They are inwardly ghost wolfs. Matthew 7:15 says, "Beware of false prophets which come to you in sheep's clothing, but inwardly are ravening wolves." They have eyes full of adultery and cannot cease from sin to deceive the unstable souls" (2nd Peter 2:14).

So, let's be mindful of whom we keep company with. John, the apostle of Jesus, wrote: "Little children, it is the last time: and as you have heard that the antichrist shall come, even now are many antichrists; whereby we know that it is the last time" (1st John 2:18). Many antichrists imply those against Christ inwardly. Imagine Judas Iscariot influencing Peter or John when they were with Jesus. And Peter had no idea that Judas Iscariot was not supposed to be among them. Had Peter been deceived by Judas's lifestyle, what would have been the end of Peter? Food for thought!

Chapter 12

The Theory of Evolution

As previously discussed, pre-Adamic men are current 'sons of God who once ran the activities of the earth, while other animals such as dinosaurs, gorillas, man of the dust of the ground, etc., existed as beasts before the lockdowns and subsequent Genesis of recreation. The scripture in the book Genesis 2:7 says, 'And the LORD God formed man of the dust of the ground and breathed into his nostrils the breath of life, and man became a living soul.' It is crystal clear that God formed (recreated) 'man of the dust of the ground....' In other words, there was the 'man of the dust of the ground' already in the chaos, whose skeleton was utilized during the recreation. The man of the dust was simply reformed and shaped to look like God. Let me expound from the book of Genesis 1:24-27: "And God said, Let the earth bring forth living creature after his kind, cattle, and creeping thing, and beast of the earth after his kind: and it was so. And God made the beast of the earth after his kind, cattle after his kind, and everything that creepeth upon the earth after his kind: God saw that it was good. And God said, 'Let us make man (of the dust of the ground) in our image, after our likeness: and let them have dominion over the fish of the sea, and over the cattle, and over all the earth, and over every thing that creepeth upon the earth. So God created man in his own image, in the image of God created he him, male and female created he them."

Notice the clause: Let the earth bring forth living creatures after his kind, cattle and creeping things, and beast of the earth. In other words, the earth of old should bring alive creeping things and beasts of the earth using the fossil remains of decayed cattle. It shows what God did was to command the ground to bring forth what already existed in it. The scriptures gave us a typical event of the recreation process when you consider new breed men formed with existing dry bones upon a valley (earth) in Ezekiel chapter 37. The event in Ezekiel 37 was an allegory of what took place in the recreation in Genesis. Although, I know the valley of bones speaks of the future resurrection of the Israelites and Christians in the world to come. It typically denotes waste substances being converted into usefulness.

Fossil remains of pre-Adamic earth were utilized for recreation during Genesis. God made the beast of the earth after his kind and cattle. The phrase 'God made' implies God' reshaped' or 'recreated' the beast, cattle, and creeping things. Previous earth's beasts, cattle, and creeping things would differ from the current Adamic human race in size. When you inject Genesis 2:7 into Genesis 1:26, it will make much sense. So God created man of the dust in his own image, in the image of God created he him, male and female created he them." Because Genesis 2:7 tells us how God formed the existing man of the dust.

One can as thus write: 'Let us make man (of the dust of the ground) in our image, after our likeness. However, it is pertinent to note the skeleton or fossil remains of the particular male and female beasts reshaped to form Adam and Eve in Genesis were also offspring of the (pre-Adamic parent male and female as ancestors) beasts which were once consumed as food by pre-Adamic people before the chaos took place under darkness. The ancestors were referred to as brute beasts or irrational beasts, as man of the dust. They were breeding their kind in the pre-Adamic earth just like cows also breed in this current earth.

Of course, it is practically impossible to have one man and woman beasts fossil remains upon the earth so that you would find male and female beasts with long fingers reshaped into the current human races. Archeological records of male and female humans date back several million years. They are irrational human beasts in the pre-Adamic era, which served as food. God inserted consciousness into the man-beast, having clothed him with sinews and flesh in his resemblance, and then breathed into this reshaped man. It shows man didn't evolve as postulated by Charles Darwin's theory of evolution. Therefore, the concept of several species evolving into man after several thousand years is null and void, or instead, were theoretical presumptions that have formed our school curriculums over several decades. Gorillas, chimpanzees, dinosaurs, Apes, or man-beasts, as it were, were regarded as prey in the pre-Adamic earth.

The book of Jude corroborated that the "man of the dust" was once an irrational beast known to the pre-Adamic men. Jude 1:10-11 says, "But these speak evil of those things which they know not: but what they know naturally, as brute beasts, in those things they corrupt themselves. Woe unto them! For they have gone in the way of Cain...." Notice the clause: "but what they know naturally, as brute beasts, in those things they corrupt themselves." The scripture revealed that ancient men knew that the current Adamic human races were irrational or brute beasts which they once consumed, but they have resorted to corrupting themselves (sexually) with the same beasts they once disregarded. It is like a man having sex with a cow or horse or a woman having sex with dogs or horses they once knew on earth whose skeletons were utilized for recreation in man.

Hence scripture says, Woe unto them for they have gone in the way of Cain. In other words, Cain slept with an ancient woman procreating the earth. In context, they (pre-Adamic men) have corrupted themselves in sexual crossbreeding, which is a perversion. Pre-Adamic men and women as sons of God, made of the flesh of brass, have turned into humans to corrupt themselves with once irrational beast kind of flesh. If you studied the scriptures, it talked about angels who left their habitation (their natural dwelling places in heaven) corrupting themselves with pre-Adamic women and men, for which God cast down and reserved such angels under chains of darkness, the dark universe.

Similarly, Sodom and Gomorrah were set forth in vengeance of eternal fire as an example of people going after strange flesh forcing their way to defile two angels who came to visit Lot. Sodom and Gomorrah people were filled with homosexuals and lesbians who were unrestrained in their lust for sexual uncleanness. The scripture says, Woe unto them because they have gone in the way of Cain - who went after strange flesh of pre-Adamic woman in the land of Nod procreating with strange flesh (pre-Adamic people turned flesh after the fall of Adam to access the earth).

The man of the dust of the ground as previous beasts was coined to form the Adamic human races. God wanted to ensure the human race proceeded from one source and decided to combine both bones together, taking the rib of the man and inserting it into a woman's rib. "And the LORD God caused a deep sleep to fall upon Adam, and he slept: and he took one of his ribs, and closed up the flesh thereof, and the rib, which the LORD had taken from man, made he a woman, and brought her unto the man" (Genesis 2:21-22). God took the rib from the man and inserted it into a woman (beast) so that both should have resemblance and called their names Adam as a set of male and female before he blessed them to be fruitful and multiply and replenished the earth.

And because the newly formed (supplied with flesh, blood, sinews, and tendons) man Adam was coined from previous ancestral beasts in the pre-Adamic world, the scripture said, "Therefore shall a man leave his father and his mother (ancestral lineage of pre-Adamic beasts) and cleave unto his wife (new breed woman recreated with Adam's rib using the same flesh type), and they shall be one flesh - one kind of flesh" (Genesis 2:24, emphasis mine). God took one of the ribs (bone) in man and inserted the same bone into a formed woman on the ground so that attraction would exist. Man searching for his missing rib would find the rib at the breast of the woman protruding to cause a cleaving or attraction to his bones and flesh of the same kind. Hence, Adam said, this is now the bone of my bones and flesh of my flesh.

Therefore, the evolution theory is not correct. Man didn't evolve but left his ancestral father and mother beasts (who begat them in the pre-Adamic world before the lockdowns). Over time, Adam and Eve's descendants would no longer have similarities with other beasts of the earth. Man was reshaped and endowed with consciousness to reason with God, his maker.

And, because man was coined from his ancestral (beasts), God had to teach the newly formed man development. God had to closely monitor the man he formed, relating with him in the garden to ensure he understood life and development. So God would bring forth living creatures and see what Adam will call them, and whatsoever Adam calls any living thing, that was the name thereof. Just like man teaching artificial intelligence some form of consciousness and close-monitoring the robots. I already hinted that the antichrist would be empowered to give consciousness to robots in our dispensation. The robot will function without electricity or a battery capable of speaking and reasoning like a man. This will take place on this earth.

The scriptures gave us clues about every developmental stage man had attained, such as making bricks and using mortar to build houses of clay, including the pyramids of Egypt. I know this might sound weird to someone reading about the great pyramid of Egypt. Let me digress a little: The great pyramid was built in the land of Shinar, which implies Babylon. Before Egypt was founded, that region was called the land of Shinar in Genesis 10:10. It was after several decades that Egypt was carved out from the land of Shinar. And that is the reason why if you measure the distance between Babylon and Egypt may not be more than approximately 2500km.

The Pyramids were built before Abraham was. The book of Genesis 11 talked about men burning bricks thoroughly and applying mortar to build the 'tower of babel,' which are the pyramids. It was clear from the scriptures that when God confounded the language of men and women, the scriptures said they stopped building the city. In other words, they stopped the pyramids. In context, the tower of Babel means the highest pyramid among other pyramids built in the city.

The Pyramids were built with the efforts of giant men in conjunction with Adam's descendants in those days, which God instructed the Israelites to eliminate these giants because they shouldn't have in the first place infiltrated the earth since their era had passed (the pre-Adamic era). Giants in those days were able to lift heavy-weight stones, unlike Adam's descendants. Egypt then became the first civilization on the earth. I'd discuss the infiltration of these giants after the floods of Noah much later. Now, let's get back on track. Adam was formed without the knowledge of the gods. His ancestors were once food to pre-Adamic people. God was comfortable excluding such knowledge about what had transpired between pre-Adamic men and angels.

Replicated abstract

The man of the dust became a living soul or living consciousness. We can also use the term - existing consciousness. It means the man of the dust was at the same time of recreation in Genesis formed as an immaterial conscious being. From the above scriptures, it is obvious that Adam was coined to obtain consciousness (reasoning like the gods). He was breathed upon and became a living soul – a prototype abstract man. In other words, we have the flesh covering the bones and sinews - the outer man. We have the spirit, which is the breath as light vapor. Lastly, the soul formed from the mixture of the formed body made of dust and water breathed upon by passing light energy through the formed body, which produced a 'living abstract man' in man capable of exiting the human body.

There was an illumination upon the formed body on the ground, duplicating an abstract personality called the soul; hence it is called 'an activated conscious being.' The soul is a separate entity in man activated by breath (spirit as in light energy) from God. The entrance of breath from God created a prototype man of the dust with consciousness infused with spirit or light energy. This light energy (spirit) in man explains the reason why external naked current source clashes with the light energy of your body, producing electrocution. The light energy powers the soul and the body. Animals don't have souls, they have spirits, which is the breath, but their spirits have an inbuilt awareness, unlike man with a soul entity.

When animals die, their spirits go down to the earth. They possess the breath of life only. Ecclesiastic 3:19-21 says, "For that which befalleth the sons of men befalleth beasts; even one thing befalleth them: as the one dieth, so the other; yea, they have one breath (spirit) so that a man has no preeminence above beasts: for all is vanity. All go unto one place; all are of the dust, and all turn to dust again. Who knoweth the spirit of man that goeth upward, the spirit of beast that goeth downward to the earth?" Man is flesh consisting of spirit and soul; hence his spirit moves together with the soul towards his maker for judgment or rewards.

The soul is seen in a dream state or after death, looking exactly like the human flesh being a prototype abstract man. It is a replicated abstract personality in man of the dust. Personality here implies it can stand alone from the physical body. Hence in the dream state, it can perform similar activities to the human body as though it were conscious. The Psalmist said, "Thou wilt not leave my soul in hell" (Psalms 16:10). This means the soul often comes out of the body at death while the carcass is buried. Psalms 22:20 says, "Deliver my soul from the sword...." In context, the soul is seen by fallen spirits or witches as a personality to deal with. This abstract will-powered man possesses the seat of consciousness in every human as a separate being inside us. This means the soul, which houses the heart, can immediately detect or sense the impulses from the body's or spirit's mind.

The soul is not the same as the spirit, as wrongly taught in some quarters—the spirit powers both the soul and the body. "...Without the spirit, the body is dead." (James 2:26). Some people call it the subconscious man. The conscious man is the outward man because the soul is spontaneously consistent with the mind of the body. The soul is an exact image of self as an abstract man formed from a mixture of body and spirit. The soul looks exactly like your real flesh but operates in the abstract realms, and that is why you can see yourself in a dream state, sleeping and at the same time running somewhere. The soul can respond to bothering issues and even consult higher realms for solutions to problems while the body is asleep. The activities performed by the body are accounted for after death because the soul functions within the body.

What God duplicated from the formed man of the dust was the abstract consciousness man or shadow-type man. That is why God would often address men as souls in the scriptures. "Behold, all souls are mine; as the soul of the father, so the soul of the son is mine: the soul that sinneth, it shall die" (Ezekiel 18:4). The book of Isaiah 57:16 predicted souls of men failing God before Adam was created. "...For the spirit should fail before me, and the souls which I have made." God identified the spirit beings from the souls of men.

You must have come across the scripture which read, "My soul doth magnify the LORD, and my spirit hath rejoiced in God my Savior (Luke 1:46-47). At other times, you read, "Bless the LORD O my soul and all that is within me bless his holy name" (Psalms 103:1). This shows the spirit and the soul are not the same. God has a soul in him, so also God created the pre-Adamic people or stars with souls. But their souls, as it were, were made of spirit substances as in light substances or precious stones materials which were not weak like the mixtures of substances of Adamic souls.

And that is why the scripture described us as weak things of this world. So when God submerged the pre-Adamic people, their souls, as in spirit substances which I would designate spirit (as depicted in the scripture), remained active since activities of the body are impressed upon the soul. Whenever the spirit of pre-Adamic people comes in contact with the souls of men, the spirit of pre-Adamic people overshadows the souls of men being made of flesh of brass. Jesus had to come and empower the mortal man's spirit to cast out these spirits' invasion of men because God gave the dominion of the earth to Adamic men, but these fallen spirits have already intruded our planet earth, leaving the dry planets. They are spirits without bones but can turn into humans, given the fact that they are higher.

For example, angels don't have bones, but they have force in the spiritual realm to fight like men. And I have been privileged to see angels during worship, and I discovered that they are capable of twisting either way they wish. They have no bones to break, no matter how they twist. They could spiral and as well permeate walls as spirit beings. They can sing like us. Angels also can transform into a human with flesh. Nevertheless, they are spirit beings, for which they can disappear whenever they turn into humans.

Humans were formed with fossil remains; hence the scripture says, "For dust thou art, and dust shalt thou return" (Genesis 3:19). This implies that your skeleton was taken from the ground and will be returned to the ground from where it was taken. The bones and the flesh must be returned to the earth from whence it was taken. "Then shall dust return to Earth as it was: and the spirit shall return unto God who gave it" (Ecclesiastic 12:7). This dictates man was formed with existing fossils, but man didn't evolve. That is why humans turn to sand after burial. The spirit return means the spirit would join the soul. I'd expound more on the soul and spirit as we progress.

Man is flesh which comprises the soul and spirit. But man is more of a soulish realm. In other words, man is inclined to the material and immaterial realms. Man is controlled by what he can see, touch, smell, hear, and taste in the material realm and responds to the thoughts emanating from his heart, the immaterial organ of the soul. People often say, "Man is a spirit, has a soul, and lives in a body." However, man was never a created spirit being. Man is flesh. The formed man became a living soul via the introduction of spirit as breath, an entity conscious of thoughts, signals, and spirit talk, capable of responding by reasoning.

The soul is the conscious personality in man that causes him to understand every material and abstract environment in which a man finds himself; heaven or hell or planet earth or space. If you have a dream, you undergo a subconscious experience, responding as though you were conscious. God never created man a spirit. Angels were created spirits. Man is flesh with soul personality powered by the spirit. If you say angels are spirits, that will be fine because angels were created spirits with beryl, clouds, and precious stones, but Adam was formed with bones and flesh. Jesus said a spirit does not have flesh and bones (See Luke 24:39), indicating that spirit beings are not made of human flesh and bones. God is a spirit.

Empowered to replenish

God wasn't referring to himself alone when he said, 'Let us make man in our image.' God was referring to the sons of God in general. He was addressing the sons of God. And until I had my understanding enlightened by the Holy Spirit, I had the notion that the clause: "Let us make man in our image, after our likeness" implied God was referring to the Holy Ghost and Word as popularly being thought in some quarters to date. That is not what the scriptures meant. God was talking to his teams which are the sons of God, since the sons of God were rejoicing together when God re-visited the darkness, as earlier mentioned.

When God speaks, he speaks alone as God; when he needed something done, he uses the first-person pronoun 'I' to represent the Godhead. So the phrase, 'Let us,' as used in Genesis 1:26 and Genesis 11:7, referred to the spirit beings who worked with him as a team. Sorry, I'm not saying he is subject to take permission, but they are servants and messengers whose minds have been synchronized with God as his elect angels. The scriptures talked about angels who were elect of God just as Israelites were God's elect, indicating that God selected some angels.

Angels have power over mortals. That is why the voice of an angel of God to a man of the dust, when neglected, has a justified, deserved punishment. "For if the word spoken by angels was steadfast, and every transgression and disobedience received a just recompense of reward" (Hebrews 2:2). God has a team he worked with whose minds are synchronized with him. Satan also has a team he worked with. Satan is not everywhere. He has demons who manipulate the human minds to do his bidding because spirit beings often easily manipulate the human hearts, especially into immorality, lies, drunkenness, craftiness, violence, etc.

"And God said, Let us make man in our image, after our likeness...So God created man in his own image, in the image of God created he him; male and female created he them" (Genesis 1: 26-27). Man was made in the same configuration of his maker. It then means it was for the purpose of a relationship or friendship. Even if man was made of weak materials – bones and dust, this zeroes in on the essence of first forming man with dust to observe their preferences, having deposited the soul personality in them. The physical body is used to walk, subdue and replenish the earth, but most important is the immaterial substances.

God formed Adam and Eve. And "Eve was the mother of all living" (Genesis 3:20). God blessed Adam and Eve to be fruitful and multiply; hence human race keeps multiplying by one voice of God to date. That's profound! The first formed male and female were empowered to replenish the earth. When the scripture says "male and female created he them" in Genesis chapter 1, it means Genesis chapter 1 was a synopsis of creation, while Genesis chapter 2 further detailed how creation took place in Genesis chapter 1. Trust you can understand that for those confused with Genesis 1:28, which says, "...And God blessed them..."

Potentials in men

The man of the dust of the ground was primarily formed to co-create, procreate, and fellowship with God. Authority and dominion over the earth were handed over to Adam (Psalm102:18, Isaiah 43:21, Genesis1:28). God specializes in forming things because 'he is former of all things' (Jeremiah10:16). God's nature of forming things was also impacted by Adam, which explains the creative nature in humans. Man is capable of formulating things because he was created like God, who is the creator of all things (Jeremiah10:16). Man invented many things and is exploring the moon and other planets because he was made like God to co-create and explore his world in this realm of existence.

Man has delved into research of things formed before Genesis, such as planets and fossils, which proves the existence of the first earth sunk into the deep waters under darkness. The creative nature of the reformed man of the dust is explosive in our dispensations. Whether some people believe in God or not, the creative nature of God has been impacted in man so long as he engages his mind to think. Man is creative because of the breath of life, the spirit, which inspires the imagination to form things like God. Creativity is part of man before the fall. "For there is a spirit in man, and the inspiration of Almighty gaveth him understanding" (Job 32:8). It is the spirit that inspires men, which is why dead humans cannot formulate things.

God gave the earth to man to take charge of things like plants, fishes, creeping things, and beasts. In other words, man was made lord over the earth with the potential to create things like God and fellowship with his creator. Individual potentials become a function of the creative nature of God in men. For this reason, scripture says, "For every house is built by some man, but he that built all things is God. (Hebrews 3:4). As a matter of fact, God's creative potentials in men are inexhaustive in one's lifetime. Nevertheless, creativity is exclusive to those who engage the power of their imaginations.

In the early days after the recreation in Genesis, the potential in men was put to use, and the scriptures captured God came down to see what the children of men were building. It means their instinct which generated inquisitively about their creator, causes them to gravitate to his assumed location and compels them to explore available resources in that direction. Even the earth, where God is spiritually seated, attracts fallen spirits and stars from various planets and space into it. Man would always long for his maker, just as children move toward their parents.

And so the whole earth began to build a tower which could reach heaven so they could meet God. Their adventures attracted the attention of God. Then God had to distort their plans by confounding their languages across the earth; so that they would fulfill the replenishment purpose on earth first, as initiated from the beginning (Genesis11:1-8 and 1:28).

Creation of God

Man was made to be at par with the Godhead for habitation. God wants to live in men as a person through the habitation of the spirit to spirit (Ephesians 2:22). God wants to take possession of some men completely; hence man was configured in the image of God since the Godhead showed up in human flesh amongst men being witnessed by people in the flesh. God showed up in the person of Jesus Christ in the flesh. This might be confusing for someone who does not believe in the person of Jesus as God in the flesh. Jesus is "the express image of the invisible God and the firstborn of every creature. For by him were all things created, that are in heaven, and are in earth, visible and invisible, whether they be thrones, or dominions, or principalities, or powers: all things were created by him and for him. And he is before all things, and by him, all things consist...For in him dwelleth all the fullness of the Godhead bodily" (Colossians 1: 15-17; 2:9).

What the scriptures meant by 'firstborn of every creature is that God replicated himself as a person from His core state (fiery rock) at the very beginning to form an angelic being named the Lord or the Word by whom he created all things. So everything about God the Father is inside God the Son, which means the Son can infuse back into God the Father and maintain the same shape of the Father. The Father has the seven Spirits of God, so also the Son has the seven Spirits of God. "And I beheld, and, lo, amid the throne and of the four beasts, and in the midst of the elders, stood a Lamb as it had been slain, having seven horns and seven eyes, which are the seven Spirits of God sent forth into all the earth" (Revelation 5:6).

Jesus was known as the Word of God. The Holy Spirit told me the meaning of the term 'Word,' which the Hebrew or Greek Bible references couldn't deliver. They defined the Word as the Rhema or revealed word, and so forth. But the Holy Spirit told me that the Word of God means the 'Creation of God.' Jesus was the beginning of the creation of God. Revelation 3:14 was direct to the point which described Jesus as "the beginning of the creation of God." It means the Godhead hasn't produced anything before other than life and death concepts.

He must have existed for several billion years and later dreamt of forming life (things) as a self-concept which becomes the beginning of the creation of God. For this reason, the scripture says, "In the beginning was the Word, and the Word was with God, and the Word was God." Let me paraphrase the scripture here: In the beginning, was (past tense) the creation, and the creation was with God, and the creation was God himself" I've earlier proven this from the scriptures.

The book of Psalms 33:6 says, "By the word of the LORD were the heavens made; and all the host of them by the breath of his mouth." Interchangeably, by the creation of the LORD were the heavens made... It corroborates the book of Colossians 1:15-17, which says, "By him were all things created, that are in heaven, and are in earth, visible and invisible, whether they be thrones, or dominions, or principalities, or powers: all things were created by him, and for him." The Word as a personality was God who created all things - material or immaterial. He made all things, and without him was not anything made that was made" (John 1:1-3). He was the God we read about in the book of Genesis 1:1. God the Father is addressed as the Lord God, so also the Son is known as Lord God. He is one God in three forms or persons.

The Word as a person was revealed in the book of Revelation 19:11-13, which says, "And I saw heaven opened, and behold a white horse, and he that sat upon him is called Faithful and True, and in righteousness, he doth judge and make war...and his name is called the Word of God. Jesus, who is the creation of God, was seen riding on a white horse. So you can see that the Word, which is now Jesus Christ in the flesh, created everything visible and invisible beings. He was the Word, who had borne different names such as Melchizedek, Prince, LORD, Jesus Christ, and perhaps another name after now, because we saw from the Scriptures that the same Jesus Christ "had a name written that no man knew but himself" (Revelation 19:12).

Jesus also confirmed that he would bear a new name after that in the new world to come. Revelation 3:12 says, "...And I will write upon him my new name." The Word is the same God known as "The mighty God, The everlasting Father, The Prince of peace" (Isaiah 9:6). In contexts, God is inseparable. This should not be confused with mortal man giving birth to a child with a different mindset or views. This was a perfect synchronization of thoughts, reasoning, and voice. It is like a man dreaming and seeing himself.

The Word is God the Son as a spirit person who carried out the activities of creation when there were no water, planets, mountains, sand, rocks, plants, angels, spirit men, etc. This Word, as the 'Creation of God,' was the one who rested, having recreated the heaven (firmament) and the earth in the book of Genesis unknown to many people. He proceedeth out from God with the same content. That is why the scripture substantiates by saying, "...even his Son Jesus Christ. That is the true God and eternal life.' (1st John 5:20).

The same God

Jesus is the true God replicated self of God in the everlasting realm before creating the spiritual and natural world. That is why he would say, "I am in the Father, and the Father is in me..." (John 14:10). Some people teach in error that Jesus used our tithes and offering to worship God the Father. Consequently, they teach gullible congregations that Jesus is God in his class but never God the Father. The scriptures never said Jesus used our offerings to worship God. It is absolute ignorant teaching of men. The scripture says, "For every high priest taken from among men is ordained for men in the things pertaining to God, that he may offer both gifts and sacrifices for sins" (Hebrew 5:1).

Jesus' sacrificial offering is not worshipping himself as God. His participation amongst his creatures (stars, ancient and current men) was to direct men to God, but he was the same God in the spirit. He offered his own body (flesh) as well unto God does not mean he is not God in the spiritual realms. He offers our gifts and sacrifices because they were presented to him as the only qualified flesh on earth that didn't fail on his earthly mission. Isaiah 53:10-11 says, "Yet it pleased the LORD to bruise him; he hath put to grief when thou shalt make his soul an offering for sin...he shall see the travail of his soul, and shall be satisfied."

God was satisfied when Jesus offered his body for the sins of the world, not that Jesus worshiped God himself. You will never find where Jesus or Holy Ghost worshipped God the Father anywhere in the scriptures. Yes, Jesus can pray, which is communication, but the word worship is not. How can you worship yourself? Jesus would say, Father, I thank you. Jesus can say, 'My God' or 'O God' or 'Father,' so God the Father can also call the Son, 'O God.' It is the same God in three dimensions. He came to reconcile between God and man by sacrificing himself, functioning as a high priest who offered his body to God satisfactorily.

Jesus receives our tithes in heaven. Hebrews 7:8 says, "But there he receiveth them, of whom it is witnessed that he liveth." The scripture admonished that all men should honor the Son, even as they honor the Father. He that honoureth, not the Son honoureth not the Father...." (John 5:23). If you ignore Jesus claiming to worship God, you've got no alibi for doing that! This is also applicable to the Holy Spirit. The Holy Spirit is the Spirit functioning inside the Father and Son.

Hebrews 3:7-10 says, "Wherefore as the Holy Ghost saith, To day if you will hear his voice, Harden not your hearts, as in the provocation, in the day of temptation in the wilderness: When your fathers tempted me and saw my works, forty years. Wherefore I was grieved with that generation and said, they do always err in their heart and have not known my ways." As you can see, God the Holy Ghost was the one speaking in the Old Testament in which he saith, I was grieved with that generation. And guess what? Many ignorant people will tell you the Holy Ghost is the third person in Trinity. They erred in not knowing the scriptures and interpreting them out of context with their little minds.

Many assumed that because they have charisma, it automatically meant they had the knowledge of God. No. Charisma is not knowledge. Charisma is simply fasting, praying, and evangelizing after new birth with Holy Ghost baptism, which is accompanied by the power available to every true believer in Christ Jesus. Knowledge involves diligent research, and it is time-consuming. Study to show thyself approve unto God. Studying means soaking oneself in comprehending, analyzing, and cross-checking facts back and forth. If someone prays for the sick and God performs a miracle, it does not mean he has the depth of the scriptures.

He might teach the scriptures incorrectly based on his capacity to think. Many are susceptible to believing errors due to signs, wonders, and miracles, which are the manifestations of the spirit. Yes, there are genuine men of God, but not all miracles are from God. Of course, many people obtain powers from the marine world and perform signs and wonders, enslaving the souls of men and women in the name of the Lord. The LORD has revealed so many churches that practice deception using the name of the Lord Jesus to perform signs and wonders. Let's get back on track.

The scripture talked about the rock which followed the children of Israel during the time of Moses. The book of 1st Corinthians 10:4 says, "And did all drink of the same spiritual drink: for they drank of that spiritual Rock that followed them: and that Rock was Christ." We can see the interchangeability of the Godhead in the scriptures. Only mortal men try to use their little brains to separate God from their own confusion. But the Godhead is the same. Whether you worship Jesus, the Holy Ghost, or God the Father, it does not separate the Godhead. I will discuss the Godhead in more detail later in this book.

If you recall, man was created in God's image. The scripture says that Jesus Christ is the image of the invisible God. If you place Jesus side by side with God the Father, you will have a perfect image of one God, and I have already explained the reason for the concept of life. Every man from planet earth who will access the kingdom of heaven would meet Jesus Christ as God, not in human flesh and blood, but as a person with a body that looks very similar because he obtained our fleshly body. And sometimes, Jesus often changes shape into a very tall person exhibiting his angelic being. So we have God the Father and God the Son. God the Father is massive and does not move about because he is so great. That is why Jesus said, "My Father is greater than I" (John 14:28). Though he came down in person during the time of Moses and was seen by Moses in a rocky body.

The person of Jesus

If you choose to worship God, you are worshipping Jesus, and if you choose to worship Jesus, you are worshipping God. But you must worship in truth and in spirit. One might contend by quoting Matthew 12:32, which says, "And whosoever speaketh against a word against the son of man, it shall be forgiven him: but whosoever speaketh against the Holy Ghost, it shall not be forgiven him, neither in this world, neither in the world to come." Yes, Jesus permitted such because he was seen as human, so he forgave the ignorance of men who related with him as human. And so, he said, "Father, forgive them; for they know not what they do" (Luke 23:34).

In the pre-Adamic times, ancient men rejected him, saying, "Depart from us. What can the Almighty do for us?" But when he came unto Adam's descendant, some believed, and others rejected him. Whatever men have spoken to Jesus is the thing spoken unto God. God the Son has accomplished all things on earth, moved to the throne of God, sitting at the right hand of the Father. For this reason, the scripture says, "Ought not Christ to have suffered these things, and enter into his glory." (Luke 24:26). At the end of this earth, Jesus as the Lamb will remain on the throne of God to be worship by all.

Revelation 21:23 says, "And the city had no need of the sun, neither of the moon, to shine in it: for the glory of God did lighten it, and the Lamb is the light thereof." The scripture says," the glory of God did lighten it, and the Lamb is the light thereof." This shows the light (glory) from God's body is Jesus Christ the Lamb. "And when all things shall be subdued unto him, then shall the Son also himself be subject unto him that put all things under him, that God may be all in all" (1st Corinthians 15:28). Jesus, having moved into his Father's throne continues to interface with the universe under darkness to date – relating with mortals.

An amateur teacher often tries to separate God the Father from Jesus, thinking they are separate entities with different reasonings. You will get your fuses blown up trying that. If you heard Jesus speak to you, you've automatically heard God the Father or God the Holy Spirit, the same God in all. But why would Jesus say, "There is none good, but God" (Matthew 19:17). It is simply because he wants men to look up to one God. He was very careful, disguising himself as an ordinary man so that men would not immediately stop worshipping God in the spirit in faith; since men are fond of worshipping what they could see.

The scripture says, "Jesus did not commit himself unto men, because he knew all men. And needeth not that any should testify of man: for he knew what was in man" (John 2:24-25). Men love seeing what they worship, which is one reason why Jesus will be present on earth as God in the world to come. Some humans worship stars, the moon, Jupiter, stones, snakes, rivers, etc., which are visible. The devils knew that men love to worship images, so they took advantage of them.

Jesus' being in the form of God, thought it not robbery to be equal with God, but made himself of no reputation, and took upon him the form of a servant, and was made in the likeness of men: And being found as a man (of the dust) he humbled himself, and became obedient unto death, even the death of the cross. Wherefore God also highly exalted him and gave him a name which is above every name (Philippians 2:6-9). Jesus was a perfect example of humility. He ensured that men focused on God alone, exalting God so that men would always look up unto God. The essence is for men to know God and depend upon God.

Jesus's thoughts were 100% synchronized with the God the Father of whom he was. He didn't come to planet earth to separate the Godhead, unlike humans who are confused about God in different forms or names. "Then answered Jesus and said unto them, Verily, verily, I say unto you, The Son can do nothing of himself, but what he seeth the Father do: for what things soever he (the Father) doeth, these also doeth the Son likewise...I can of mine own self do nothing: as I hear, I judge: and my judgment is just; because I seek not mine own will, but the will of the Father which hath sent me" (John 5:19,30). Every thought, word, and action of Jesus Christ was premised upon what God the Father does in the spirit.

Shew us the Father

He was the same Father in the spiritual realms praying even if he begot himself as the creation of life. When his disciple got so confused, he asked, "Lord shew us the Father, and it sufficeth us. Jesus said unto him, Have I been so long with you, and yet thou hast not known me, Philip? He that seen me hath seen the Father; and saith thou then, Shew us the Father? Believe thou not that I am in the Father, and the Father is in me? The words that I speak to you speak not of myself: but the Father that dwelleth in me, he doeth the works" (John 14:8-10). The works: the healings and miracles were done by the Father, which was the Holy Ghost. "How God anointed Jesus of Nazareth with the Holy Ghost and with power who went about doing good and healing all that were oppressed of the devil...." (Acts 10:38). The Star named Lord was deposited by the same Holy Ghost into the womb of a virgin and received an outpouring by the same Holy Ghost.

Colossians 2:9 says, "For in him dwelleth the fullness of the Godhead bodily." The word bodily can be interchanged 'fleshly' or rather in the flesh. In other words, Jesus is your God in the flesh, but you needn't worship an image. When it comes to the natural realm, your God is known as Jesus. The fullness of the Godhead, as used in Colossians, substantiates what Jesus said to Philip that he who hath seen him had seen the Father who is in the spirit. The difference is God in the spiritual realm is not made of fleshly materials, even though he became flesh. He was also one of the ancient men who existed as Melchizedek, who finally became Jesus amongst men.

Don't be fooled into thinking that you are worshipping three Gods. The Father, Son, and Holy Spirit are one God! It would be foolishness for men to reject Jesus Christ if they thought he was only a human. If you reject Jesus, you are doomed after death. Godhead dwelt in human flesh in the person of Jesus. It is foolishness for some people to reason, "How can God be seen?" It is like asking how can the stars be seen? You have just been exposed to know that the stars you see in space are spirit beings made of light substances. However, God isn't hiding from men either! God is not scared of being seen by his creatures. Even if he appeared as starlight from the universe above or a rock in space, you wouldn't know him because you are a natural man. So many are confused studying the scriptures regarding God's visitation of Abraham. Some people think God cannot or should never be seen, which has short-circuited their reasoning.

The fullness of the Spirit of God can infest and operate in men. "...As God hath said, I will dwell in them, and walk in them; and I will be their God, and they shall be my people" (2nd Corinthians 6:16). God as a Spirit walking through the spirit of man to influence the body to act in the direction of his will. As it is written, "...I will pour of my

Spirit upon all flesh: and your sons and your daughters shall prophesy, and your young men shall see visions, and your old men shall dream dreams" (Acts 2:17).

This implies an exchange between the supernatural and the natural for the natural to become supernatural. The natural exhibits the supernatural a little on earth and eventually becomes supernatural. This explains why the angels were puzzled about how this exchange would play out on earth. "...Which things the angels desire to look into" (1st Peter 1:12). The Holy Ghost dominates the recreated spirit inside of man to display the supernatural power of God, while "the earnest expectation of the creature waiteth for the manifestation of the sons of God" (Romans 8:19). The manifestation of the sons of God is the expected exchange of the human body into celestial bodies as sons and stars of God.

Believers in Jesus Christ are the adopted sons of God awaiting the complete transformation into celestial beings. They are adopted children of men from the natural (earth) realm into the supernatural - to become sons of God - spirit men and angels who are the servants of God. If you would recall, Jesus said, "...You know not the power of God, For in the resurrection of the dead, they...are as angels of God in heaven" (Matthew 22:29-30). Man was created to be at par to dominate and fellowship with God through the habitation of the spirit. However, things went south. Man was deceived and began to seek his own ways. The distortions brought about carnal thinking in men seeking to understand God by their imagination, resulting in "their foolish heart being darkened" (Romans 1:21). Some could not comprehend the things of the spirit as they are fools.

God foreknew the complexities involved that the natural man would attempt to unravel things in the universe disregarding the God factor and giving room for pride exhibition in the future because many will be confused as already predicted in the scriptures trying to figure out the mystery of the universe we live in. For this reason, God took precautions in forming man with dust so that he could select those who, having not seen him yet, believed in him: As it is written, "Whom you have not seen...yet you believe" (1st Peter 1:8). Those who believed have passed from death unto life, while those who believed not are condemned already.

Chapter 13

Adam Was Made to Rule

Although the knowledge of death was made known to Adam, the angel of death seems inoperative without sin, offense, or disobedience to God. Sin did not originate with Adam. Many think 'sin' originated with Adam. No. The law of sin and death had been operational in the pre-Adamic world before Adam was formed. The difference is that ancient people weren't cut short per generation like the Adamic human races but spanned over several million or billion years before they were cut out of time. We already read from the scriptures that ancient people were cut out of time and submerged before the recreation in Genesis. God knows none of his creatures measured perfectly up to his standard of holiness; hence no man in heaven, on earth, or under the earth was qualified to look in the book God presented when the roll call was made in the spiritual realm (See Revelations 5:1-14).

I believe that someone might contend, saying, "But the scripture used man, not the angels." Yes, that includes all servants of God. The truth is angels are men with wings already described. Angels in heaven were made to confess the name of Jesus for a testimony, just like men confess the name of Jesus, not necessarily for the remission of their sins, but for the new order of things in heaven. Revelation 22:8-9 says, "...And I fell to worship before the feet of the angel which shewed me these things. Then saith he unto me, See thou do it not: for I am thy fellow servant, and of thy brethren the prophets and of them which keep the sayings of this book: worship God." The angel said unto John, the apostle of Jesus Christ, that he does observe the sayings of the Scriptures. It denotes angels also confessed Jesus as Lord.

The book of Revelation 19:10 substantiate this when it says, "And I fell at his feet to worship him. And he said unto me, See thou do it not: I am thy fellow servant and of thy brethren that have the testimony of Jesus...." All angels in heaven professed Jesus as LORD. If you would recall, Archangel Michael said to Satan: "The Lord rebuked thee" (Jude 1:9). It implies angels can now say, "In the name of Jesus, Satan, you are rebuked as well. This is scripturally supported as the heavenly pattern of things changed when the scriptures said, "That at the name of Jesus, every knee should bow, of things in heaven, and things in the earth, things under the earth; And that every tongue should confess that Jesus is Lord to the glory of God the Father" (Philippians 2:10-11). Every tongue should confess excludes no creature. Even Satan, alongside other spirits of death, bowed and declared - Jesus is Lord!

We saw this played out in the book of Revelation 5:13-14, in which every creature in all realms of existence sang unto God and the Lamb Jesus Christ. "And every creature which in heaven, and on the earth, and under the earth, and such as are in the sea, and all that are in them, heard I saying Blessing, and honor, and glory, and power, be unto him that sitteth upon the throne, and unto the Lamb (Jesus Christ) forever and ever." Satan was created by Jesus Christ, and he knew it. He is only deceiving humans to speak against Jesus and God. Satan, demons, death, destruction, and all souls in hell, including spirit beings in heaven, will sing this song unto God in the future. As it is written: "I have sworn by myself, the word is gone out of my mouth in righteousness, and shall not return, that every knee shall bow, every tongue shall swear (confess) that Jesus is Lord forever" (Isaiah 45:23, emphasis mine). Every knee shall bow, and every tongue confesses, excludes no soul or spirit.

Aide the camp

Satan was one of the sons of God who showed up when God convened a meeting of the mighty. Lucifer has much strength when compared to 1,000,000 dead human souls in hell. The strength of his material composition is much stronger than all fallen principalities under darkness. He was once perfect, having walked with God (in the everlasting realm) until Adam was formed.

Lucifer was like a secret service agent in the company of the US President. He was an aide-de-camp; hence the scripture captured his presence in the Garden of Eden. Having refurbished the earth, God gave absolute authority to Adam to dominate other beasts of the fields. And by extension, it means Adam was placed in charge of every living thing except God. Even angels were made to minister unto the man of the dust. God didn't disclose to the angels his underlying motive of forming the man of the dust Adam with weak substances. "...Thou hast put all things under his feet" (Psalms 8:6). Angels were made subject under Adam at first. This didn't go down well with some angels as they were stunned. Lucifer was stunned that God would put the man of the dust in charge of everything after several billion years of existence.

This was God's ultimate plan about the person of Jesus Christ, who would become ruler over all things and would also go through the formed man of the dust. If you studied the scriptures correctly, you would understand that this was why God instructed the angels to worship Jesus Christ as soon as he was clothed with flesh like Adam of the dust. Since the angels knew the man of the dust of the ground was coined from fossil remains of the earth, which were inferior to the angels. So, they wondered if they would bow to Jesus Christ as soon as he was clothed with the same inferior materials.

Man was used to bowing down to angels all through the old testaments with some entertaining fears of death for seeing angels. However, when John, the apostle of Jesus, was transported into the light zone universe above, the angel he spoke with told him not to bow down anymore but rather worship God. "... And he said unto me, See thou do it not: I am thy fellow-servant, and of thine brethren that have the testimony of Jesus: Worship God..." (Revelation 19: 10). Man's dignity was restored in Christ.

It depicts that God subjected the angels to minister unto man at recreation, and this decision seems diametrically opposite to Lucifer's opinion. The scriptures confirmed this mystery in the book of Psalms 8:5-8, which says, "For thou hast made him a little lower than the angels, and hast crowned him with glory and honor. Thou hast made him to have dominion over the works of thy hands; thou hast put all things under his feet: All sheep and oxen, yea, and all the beasts of the field; the fowl of the air, and the fish of the sea, and whatsoever passeth through the paths of the seas."

Implicitly the man of the dust was made a little lower than the angels but was crowned with glory and honor. What glory and honor? Everything created except God. All the works of thine hands implies every created thing. You can see from the scriptures that angels were subject to the man of the dust from the beginning in the garden. Lucifer had no clue about God's ultimate plan in transforming the LORD (Morning Star) into inferior flesh like Adam. I believe God foreknew the pride of Lucifer amongst the stars of God, so he wanted to humble him. So God had to form Adam and then placed all things under him. It was a hidden mystery known only to the Godhead then.

God, who has the foreknowledge of the end from the beginning, knew Lucifer, together with some angels, would not take it. He knew some spirits would fail him. "...For the spirit should fail before me..." (Isaiah 57:16). So, God used Adam to test run his plans, given the fact that the man of the dust can be fixed again when he fails. Lucifer being a hierarchical cherub, did not expect that the earth would be handed over to Adam to rule over all things, much more not submitting to the angels. Lucifer thought God would continue with fallen ancient men and stars who sinned, and things would continue as they were before the lockdowns under darkness.

It was a hidden mystery kept from Lucifer. It is "the wisdom of God in a mystery, even the hidden wisdom, which God ordained before the world for the glory of the man of the dust" (1st Corinthians 2:7, emphasis mine). Man was crowned with glory; hence the scriptures used the phrase 'ordained before the world for our glory. In other words, God pre-determined this before the foundation of the world or recreation in Genesis, that God intended to use the weak and foolish things of this world to confound the wise and mighty. God foreknew Adam's failure and His subsequent plan of redemption for humanity according to his will.

Weak substances

God needed a set of creatures with no knowledge of good and evil - violence free with no depth of spiritual manipulations of things - creatures obsessed with God and nature. You know, a baby's mind creature would be okay. When I refer to a baby, I mean to say a naive creature devoid of manipulative spiritual skills; what the scripture meant by 'foolish things of this world. Adam was made like a baby. He was made a little lower than the angels but crowned with glory and honor. Man was created lower in height than angels. In other words, man was made from dust, while angels were made of lamps of fire and precious stones. Man was formed with flesh and bones - weak substances compared to angels.

Angels were called 'the mighty while the man of the dust was called 'the weak things. That was what the scripture meant by "weak things of this world to confound the things that are mighty" (1st Corinthians 1:27). Man was created naive (foolish) at the beginning, oblivious of such things as violence, sexual perversions, sword, cursing, spiritual strength, and had no idea of what transpired in the past between God and fallen angels/ancient men and women.

Adam was a babe in terms of age, knowledge, wisdom, spiritual might, skill, etc. We saw how one angel referred to Zachariah the prophet as a 'young man. "And he said unto him, Run, speak to this young man, saying, Jerusalem shall be inhabited as towns without walls... (Zachariah 2:4). The phrase 'young man' denotes little of age. Jesus knew men as babes in terms of age and knowledge of spiritual things; hence he referred to his disciples and the multitude of men with children, shouting Hosanna praise as 'babes and sucklings.' Jesus called men babes, and the children he called sucklings.

The Hosanna praise in Matthew 21:1-9 was foretold in Psalms 8:2, which says, "Out of the mouth of babes and sucklings hast thou ordained strength because of thine enemies, that thou mightiest still the enemy and avenger." The mouth of babes and sucklings implied men, women, and children of men from Adam's descendants who were predicted and ordained to sing praises unto God. Jesus said, "I thank thee, O Father, Lord of heaven and earth, because thou hast hid these things from the wise and prudent (spirit beings), and hast revealed them unto babes." (Matthew 11:25, Emphasis mine).

Adam's natural descendants are babes in height and age. Adamic human races were fashioned to praise God, which I believe pre-Adamic people weren't doing. Although angels praise God, it is pertinent to know that abundant praise generations were revealed more in the Adamic human race than in ancient men. I believe that is the reason why the scripture says that God formed the Adamic human race for himself who would show forth the praises of God (Isaiah 43:21). We can therefore say in accordance to the scriptures that out of the mouth of babes and sucklings – human race was the instrumentality of praise ordained or perfected.

Often Jesus called his disciples children, even if they were naturally age mates during his walk on earth. Peter and other disciples had wives already as men, but Jesus would call them children. Why? It is simply because he preexisted and created them all. Men's age, when compared to Jesus, is nothing but babes. How do you compare someone who had lived several billion years and incarnated to a mortal of just 120 years? Scripture says, "Man is of a few days." Our age is nothing before God." Psalms 39:5 says, "...My age is nothing before thee..."

God loved this new man created without knowing good, evil, or spiritual depths. Adam, at the initial state, was the center of attraction, like a baby of 2 years old playing and learning how to pronounce or name things among his parents. Adam was the apple of God's eye, and because he was a babe unaware of spiritual dynamics, God was comfortable with him. Why would God form man with weak substances? He was formed naive and weak so that he could be fixed or transformed in the event he failed, unlike spirit beings that cannot be re-fixed.

Adam can be repackaged if he fails and could be transformed into the angelic or brass flesh body that spirit beings possess. However, created spirit beings such as angels and sons of God may not be recreated with inferior dust materials of bones in order to test run their choice of righteousness anymore, having attained the highest awareness of God. Although they possessed the ability to transform into flesh while their internal skeletal structure remained unchanged. They don't truly die, having been created with substances of spirits. Even if they shed off their bodies, their spirit moves on. Once perverted, you can't change ways. This is where Lucifer failed to take precautions; perhaps he might have hurriedly forgotten the fact that he had attained the highest level of knowledge of all things as regards the Godhead, coupled with spiritual understanding of how things work, and may have been blind to realize that he was a creature who takes orders.

Wired to explore nature

Adam having a naïve mind at that time, had no idea of what fundamentally constitutes good and evil. Newborn babies cannot distinguish between good and evil. So when you play with a child of 2 to 3 years, at most 4, you would appreciate how naive Adam's reasonings were. The book of Deuteronomy 1:39 puts things in proper perspective when it says, "...Your children which in that day had no knowledge between good and evil...." So we can say Adam was a child in heart even if he was a man in stature. God excluded the knowledge of good and evil from Adam and Eve when they were created. As with children who do not know good and evil.

This is typical of us loving children in their tender ages, caressing them, and feeling very comfortable with them, but as soon they grow up (knowing left from right), we gradually withdraw such tender love. God showered love upon Adam and taught him how to give names to things of nature at the beginning. I believe that could be why humans would often explore nature unending. Man was created for fellowship and to attend to nature, but Lucifer once regarded man as weak and foolish things (beasts) of this world because they lack spiritual knowledge. Although, Adam was created with a little level of cunning behavior despite being formed like a child. The scriptures record Lucifer as being more cunning than the man of the dust Adam.

Children who are two or three years old often cry to create attention to themselves. And you can tell when the parents decided to ignore such cunning tears forcing the child to adjust over time. For instance, you instructed a child not to touch a toy or something else. He is drawn or attracted to that very thing you have instructed him not to touch, and when he begins to cry, some parents would immediately allow the child to have whatever he needs for peace. But supposed the parents say no and stick to their decision, the child may cry but would, over time, stop because attention was not given. The child would easily adapt to choking the tears of cunning behaviors. Though not knowing good and evil, children are skillful at playing with toys or building. This was typical of the state of Adam and Eve.

Man was created to attend to nature and preserve it. Scriptures say, "God took man and put him in the garden to dress and keep it." (Genesis 2:15). The instincts in us often tend toward the love and study of nature or creating new things. Man is often excited by new discoveries in nature: plants, animals, planets, moon, stars, etc. Man loves exploring nature, and this gives him fulfillment. Science is one of God's ideas of keeping man busy exploring nature until he closes in. Early men sought to explore nature – by building the tower of Babel. They intended to achieve a particular feat in life, which was to explore the heavens. When man lost fellowship with God, thwarted by Lucifer in the garden, he sought nature and constructed things as part of his inherent nature.

God and nature are one since nature is the work of his hands. Man is often fascinated by nature seeking God inside nature as well. In nature, we appreciate God's wonders. God created nature for pleasure, so he commanded man to attend to nature and maintain it. But man was also found to have destroyed the beauty of nature, which in turn threatens man's existence. When we preserve nature, we tend to live much longer. Some third-world countries are careless about preserving nature; they live in slums with their cities littered with wasteful materials and are unmindful of the environment. They seldom think of the beauty of nature. Some people live like animals, unenlightened about maintaining nature. When humans are devoid of education, the nature of their ancestral fathers (beasts) shows up in them. A society of animalistic behaviors is expected from unenlightened minds.

I have discovered that two fundamental traits affect the human race: Man seeking God and man exploring nature. You either seek God or seek nature. Ecclesiastic 3:11 says that God set the world in the heart of men so that no man can find out the work that God maketh from the beginning to the end. Man will keep exploring nature from one level to another endlessly. If man eventually succeeds at exploring the stars, they will face a new phenomenon of life. The void created in man's hearts having lost contact with God causes them to seek carnal things to fill the void. If you reject God, you will be filled with love for science or the pursuit of things, as recorded in Romans 1:28-32. You are either obsessed with studying nature/pursuit of vanity or seek God - no middle ground.

Peace of mind

The knowledge of good and evil was excluded from Adam at the formation stage because it might distort his focus relating with his Maker or exploring nature. All angels, including Lucifer, knew that Adam was naive. Adam had no idea of the previous violent world that pre-existed him because he was formed with a baby's mind, which requires cognitive learning stages. The keys of death and hell were placed inside the forbidden tree unknown to Adam, but Lucifer, by his wisdom, knew what God kept inside the tree of knowledge of good and evil.

Lucifer, a cherub, had a perfect knowledge of spiritual things working with God: he knew everything God was up to, and no secret was hidden from him over the reasons God asked Adam not to eat the fruit. Moreso, the earth had been handed over to Adam with authority from God, yet Adam was unaware of spiritual knowledge of the keys of death and hell placed under him right in the forbidden tree. Such a sensitive material kept under Adam? Could God be blamed for keeping the keys of hell and death under Adam? No. Why? It is simply because God needed man to have peace of mind without delving into things that would distort his peace and focus. "For thou will keep him in perfect peace whose mind is stayed on thee..." (Isaiah 26:3).

Certain information disturbs our peace of mind, causing us to lose peace and tranquility – and sometimes throws us into an apprehensive or depressed state of mind. God wanted Adam to focus on relationships through worship, praise, exploring nature, and naming things. Don't get involved with sinful matters you are not supposed to be concerned about. This was the order of things in the Garden of Eden before the fall of Adam. God needed a creature man he would love and play with as a friend, devoid of violence and knowledge of what had transpired in the past between God and fallen spirits beings which were banished from his kingdom. At the beginning, God prevented Adam from attaining such knowledge of violence, sexual perversions, and ungovernable behavior exhibited by ancient people and stars of heaven.

The fellowship between God and Adam got so excited, such that it sparked envy among angels, with one spirit beings saying, "When I consider the heavens, the work of thy fingers, the moon, and the stars, which thou hast ordained; What is man (of the dust) that thou art mindful of him? (Psalms 8:4, emphasis mine). The scriptures talked about God's love towards man with such an enormous authority over the works of his hands. As mentioned earlier, God would come to Adam and present birds, cattle, and creeping things before him and wait for Adam to name them. This shows there was a fellowship devoid of suspicion or acrimony whatsoever. It was a sweet fellowship, free of violence, pains, sickness, sin, lack, fear, death, etc.

Adam was relating to God directly as well as the cherubs. This is where so many people missed it, thinking God only dealt with Adam by voice. They erred, not knowing the scriptures. If God was dealing with Adam verbally, how come the scripture says that God brought things unto Adam to see what Adam would call them? The Lord God was in person visiting Adam like he visited Abraham as LORD. Many people are confused about God the Father and God the Son. I know someone is irritated, saying God cannot be seen. God is not running from men. No worries, I'll come to this as we progress.

Adam relating to God directly in the land of the living and God Almighty in the light zone universe above implies Adam was made lord on earth. At the same time, God would be LORD in heaven, with the angels ministering to Adam (man on earth) was crowned with honor and glory despite being a little lower than the angels. This was intended so that the LORD would become flesh to rule over the earth in the long term, even though man was temporally given authority to rule as a test. I believe God also wants to remove certain things that are shaken so that the things which are unshaken would remain in his kingdom. The placement of Adam over the earth and all the things sparked jealousy, though the angels couldn't protest. But Lucifer reacted against it.

In addition, Lucifer innately loved being worshipped for two reasons: Firstly, it had been his primary duty in the holy mountain of God, worshipping God in the third zone universe, which is above the light zone universe. And you know, most people often resort and stick to their expertise after losing their occupational jobs, as this has been the norm. Secondly, the majority of the angels had been submitting to his hierarchy as a cherub. However, as soon as God handed over the earth to man, Lucifer, became envious of man to have been in charge of all the earth with such authority. He coveted the earth and sought to have Adam, God's beloved creation, chased out.

God had by his authority given charge that angels should submit unto man instead, which was a build-up into God's mysterious plan of his Son to inherit all things who would become a man of dust as well. Lucifer had no clue of God's mystery plan, so he couldn't take it; he was proud and diametrically opposed to God's decision here. Lucifer already knew some secrets of the Godhead as a cherub in God's holy mountain, being much closer to God in that capacity. He then decided to betray God by swindling Adam and Eve to take charge in an attempt to reverse God's choice of Adam, given how things were playing out. He had no clue about the plan of God at this stage but reacted and rebelled against God's orders by quickly obtaining the available resources at Adam's disposal.

He would need the support of some angels to gain his ambition which means one of the options available to explore is to have fallen angels and sons of God, who are locked up in the darkness of the deep, join him in the formation of his kingdom. He was displeased with God's choice of having a weak and naive Adam made of dust to run the affairs of the earth. And that means he will need to take possession of the keys of death and hell kept under Adam (inside the forbidden tree) to enable him to execute his planned objectives; since Adam had no clue of the authority vested in the keys kept in the forbidden tree under his nose (of course, he can't use it either). Adam was only threatened not to touch the forbidden tree, but Lucifer knew what was in there. The keys of death and hell would fall off the tree only when its fruit was consumed by Adam, not necessarily Eve alone. The keys will grant fallen stars and pre-Adamic beings, who were once banished to outer space, to access the earth, which is death, to evade the earth and feed on human flesh and blood in the spiritual realm.

The father's explanation

Lucifer needed to have these fallen sons of God (angels of death and destruction, amongst others) dominate the earth, making him likable to these hordes of darkness. Even the angel of death bought Lucifer's idea. Hence he left standing for the LORD. This was where Satan nursed the idea of being like God, as you would realize shortly. Jesus recognized the fact that Satan has a kingdom; hence Jesus said, "If Satan also be divided against himself, how shall his kingdom stand?" (Luke 11:18). When Lucifer was in the Garden of Eden with Adam and Eve, that was when he conceived the idea of having his kingdom which he nursed to himself because God made the man of the dust ruler over all things displacing fallen sons of God far apart to other planets under the darkness from accessing the earth.

Lucifer had been used to ascending and descending as a cherub dwelling in the holy mountain of God, his usual abode in the third universe above the light zone universe, and also visiting Adam in the garden of Eden at will on the earth (Ezekiel 28:13). "By thy great wisdom and by thy traffic..." (Ezekiel 28:5). You can see, he was full of wisdom trafficking between the fire, light and darkness zones- the multiverse. Little wonder he still moves up and down to date. We have earlier established how Lucifer is still occupying outer space amongst the galaxies and regularly visits the earth. (See Job 1:7, 2:2, 1st Peter 5:8). He was envious of the relationship between God and man. God was mindful of man and often visited man at the cool of the day, which implies early morning or evening hours - sunset.

Lucifer's separation from God began with God creating man. And I'll show you further proofs from the scripture that Lucifer sinned from Genesis. God wanted man to rule over all things, but Lucifer was opposed to it in preference for pre-Adamic people to be banished. Moreover, the man formed looked naive to him, not knowing what was at his disposal - the keys of death and destruction kept inside the forbidden tree; neither could man distinguish between good and evil at that time. God kept all things in subjection to Adam. "...Thou hast put all things under his feet..." (Psalms 8:6). Lucifer communed with some fallen stars as well, and this whole drama culminated in bitter envying against man and God.

The scripture identified this envy that emanated from Lucifer as 'bitter-envying.' "But if you have bitter-envying and strife in your hearts...This wisdom descended not from God, but it is from the devil" (James 3:14-15, emphasis mine). He became bitter and envious; hence scripture identified his 'bitter-envying.' However, being a trusted cherub, God didn't get involved. Like Cain became wroth over God's acceptance of Abel's offering. Lucifer, together with fallen angels, became envious of Adam. Envy often erupts whenever one is treated with love more than the other in any given relationship. If you recollect, the elder brother to the prodigal son envied and protested when the Father decided to welcome his lost brother home, having killed a fat calf. (See Luke 15:25-32).

Thanks to the elder brother, who understood the Father's explanations and cooperated. As mentioned earlier, it seems it always arouses envy whenever one is treated better than the other because the spirit in men tends to envy. "Do you think that the scripture saith in vain, the spirit that dwelleth in us lusted (tended) to envy?" (James 4:5). That is why envying spirit attracts all manner of evil works. And of a truth, Jesus gave the parable of the prodigal son while addressing the mixed feelings between the sons of God in heaven and the man of the dust of the ground. The man of the dust strayed off course, but the angels should not get envious because man had wandered far away, lavishing God's resources with devils.

The elder brother to the prodigal son symbolizes angels and sons of God in the kingdom of heaven, with Adam and his descendants representing the younger son - kept in the Garden of Eden - God's property with no lack of food whatsoever. The sons of God in heaven, as well as Adam, are scripturally recognized as sons. The scripture chronologically traced Adam to have been the son of God (Luke 3:38). So Jesus had to share his blood to redeem the man of the dust as the prodigal son. "And having made peace through the blood of his cross, by him to reconcile all things unto himself; by him, I say, whether be things in earth or things in heaven" (Colossians 1:20). The reconciliation of the prodigal son and those in heaven is very crucial. Jesus had to pay the price of redemption for the lost man of the dust who would subsequently put on celestial bodies like the angels of God to live forever after that.

And that is why one of the angels told John the Revelator, saying, "I am of thy fellow servant and brethren that keep the sayings of this book." Angels are brethren being servants of God. The angel said I am of thy brethren who also obey the scriptures. Jesus predicted men and angels' reconciliation in heaven by that parable of the prodigal son. No need to be envious like Satan got jealous of man. The angels had whatever they needed as elder brothers with the Father always. The man of the dust has had enough experience of what it takes to be freed from God into sickness, pains, tears, diseases, suffering, lack, death, violence, fear, etc.

Lucifer was mindful of the keys hidden in the tree of knowledge of good and evil that could unlock the angels of death and destruction into the earth, given that the earth was refurbished under darkness where fallen spirits were banished. Lucifer couldn't have had access to the forbidden tree since only Adam was mandated by God's word to take charge of all the earth, including the tree of knowledge of good and evil, including the tree of life. He then waited until Eve was formed. The cherub Lucifer, in his ambition, was closely monitoring the daily events. He knew Adam and Eve were naive of the wielded powers placed in the forbidden tree (though restricted) but also lacked knowledge of good and evil besides spiritual things.

Unwittingly submit

Adam and Eve were concerned with activities of seeing beautiful things God created; Lucifer, being a cherub, knew such classified secrets. If he got Eve to influence Adam to eat the forbidden fruit, it would mean he had succeeded in his plans to obtain the keys since Lucifer knew a spiritual law that says, "You are a servant to whom you obey" (Romans 6:16, John 8:34). That means Adam whom God placed in charge of all things, would now submit to Lucifer's voice, which is indirect worship of Lucifer. He was well-informed of what God told Adam - not to eat of the fruits of the tree. That means God was concealing something from man to avoid the knowledge of the gods, who were enemies of man ready to avenge man's occupant of the earth.

So Lucifer then orchestrated how Adam would unwittingly submit his authority to him, granting Lucifer access to the keys that would unlock the angels of death and hell restrained from accessing and inhabiting the earth. If Lucifer's plans go through, Adam would no longer be ruler over all things. And once Lucifer took possession of the keys, his objective was to release other comrades locked up in the prison of darkness and to overthrow God. He wanted his own kingdom, and so the earth would be his last resort if the coup d'etat failed. He could hide under the authority of being in possession of the keys of death and destruction untouched, worst-case scenario. Of course, he couldn't have displaced man whom God loved without hurting God.

It means whatever was done to Adam, by implication, dictates rebellion against God's orders. Lucifer needed these forces of death and destruction to attack and overthrow God. One might ask, "Why would God place the tree of knowledge of good and evil there?" It is simply because it was the earth of old. The tree of knowledge of good and evil grew out of the same dry land of old. "Why didn't God keep it in heaven?" It is because the scripture says God kept all things that passed through the sea under man. This means fallen spirits of death and destruction, including creeping things and birds of the air, were kept under Adam, who seems naive to the angels and Lucifer. Moreover, God foreknew man would fail. It was a free-will test for Adam to exercise his volition.

Chapter 14

At the Garden of Eden

Lucifer must have carefully observed Adam and his wife, knowing Eve was susceptible, unlike Adam, who heard God directly. He must have also observed Eve's influence on Adam being a companion Adam loved. Eve was categorized as someone who loves discussing and finagling things. Eve was finagling around the forbidden tree. I believed the tree of knowledge of good and evil was very attractive, like the tree of life. You know the scriptures describe the tree of life to have 12 different types of fruits bearing its fruit every month (Revelation 22:2). It means the tree of life produces oranges, pawpaw, banana, apple, mango, grapes, berry, pineapples, avocado, etc. hence I assumed the tree of the knowledge of good and evil would also look attractive. I think that was why Eve was fascinated by the forbidden fruit, upon which Lucifer came to her as a man cherub when Adam was busy in the garden.

Lucifer rehearsed what God instructed Adam, evoking Eve's opinion. And then Lucifer began to display the benefits of eating the forbidden fruit by demonstrating the capabilities of the gods (spirits) to change forms which caught Eve's attention. According to the scriptures, the pronoun 'he,' as used in Genesis 3:1, dictates Lucifer was a man cherub when he engaged Eve in the conversation. But given that he could change forms, Eve then described him as a serpent, which actually means a "deceiver." He enticed Eve at the moment by transforming into a lion, eagle, ox, and man. Perhaps, he was displaying his four-sided faces, and Eve wanted to be like the Lucifer having such faces.

Eve wasn't scared of Lucifer's capability to transform from man into these other life forms since there was no fear in life at such a cognitive stage. Just like a baby reaching out to a lion's face without fear. Some babies often play with cobral (venomous elapid snakes) unknown to them. The cognitive levels at this stage were devoid of fears whatsoever. Don't forget that Adam and Eve were 100% full of God's glory and sinless at the initial stage. They weren't restrained from seeing cherubs, men who looked similar to Adam, although cherubs had a different texture of flesh unknown to Adam. Adam and Eve interacted with cherubs and saw the Lord God, that created all things one-on-one. However, they could not see the fallen spirits who were shut out of the earth because of their deeds. Adam and Eve, at this time, could see spirit beings until they ate of the forbidden tree and got their senses upgraded to what is known as good or evil.

It should be noted that fear, shame, and spiritual blindness came when the knowledge of sin (of the pre-Adamic world) entered, which brought man into the natural realm of the limitation of spiritual blindness. Some people think Adam didn't see God directly. We all grew up in our fallen state of Adamic nature and have gotten used to this natural realm of not seeing beyond the physical.

Some might argue that the Bible teaches that "No man can see God," which is an incorrect interpretation of the scriptures that has been taught over the years.

We must shut our minds to this traditional belief that God can't be seen. Matthew 5:8 says, "the pure in heart shall see God."

Whenever I listen to some people teach that God dealt with Adam by voice alone, I wonder how men have been so conditioned in their minds not to seek God and encounter him like Moses. Moses saw God's back part because God gave an open check to his children, saying, "And you shall seek me, and find me when you search for me with all your heart" (Jeremiah 29:13). Adam at creation had a pure heart and was sinless, so God visited Adam one-on-one. Of course, it also depends on whom God shows mercy coupled with the heart's desires. I have had the God experience in a clear trance, which I have shared in this book. Though in a trance experience which is almost real as your physical eyes being opened.

Fascinated and enticed

One thing I have practiced over the years is studying scriptural writings in-depth and criticizing where necessary. And I could tell when a process was skipped. In my critical analysis, I realized Eve couldn't desire to be 'wise like the gods' without any corresponding actions or inactions which might have stimulated her interest in eating the forbidden fruit. How could she tell the fruit would make her wise by mere words and then to become wise as who? Of course, to become wise as the gods like Lucifer, who had the supernatural capability of transforming himself. Lucifer said, "...And your eyes shall be opened, and you shall be as (we) gods knowing good and evil" (Genesis 3:5). Some inducement to become like Lucifer while the phrase 'knowing good and evil' was the essential included into the transformation capabilities. An undisclosed dramatic occurrence was put up by Lucifer, which attracted Eve to desire to be like the gods.

In what transpired at the Garden of Eden, the scriptures depicted the Cherub Lucifer metaphorically as a 'serpent' in Genesis chapter 3:1, which says, "Now, the serpent was more subtle than any beast of the field which the LORD God had made. And he said unto the woman, Yea, hath God said, Ye shall not eat every tree of the garden?" This scripture should read: "Now, the cherub, Lucifer, was more subtle than any beast of the field which the LORD God had made" Many people think Lucifer was already in his fallen state as Satan (in serpentine form) when he engaged Eve. Unfortunately, that is far from the truth.

It does not make sense that God would release his enemy to tempt Adam and, after that, pronounce a curse on that enemy to have succeeded at swindling the one he permitted. What an irony! Such notions have generated a lot of controversies.

If God pronounced a curse, it means he least expected such action from his own trusted cherub assigned as a guardian cherub, though he foreknew all things already. One might contend, "How about the case of Job? Was it not God who permitted Satan?" Yes, but God didn't lay any curse on Satan since Satan had been judged already in the Garden of Eden. The scenario in the garden was a complete betrayal of trust. I believe someone else might contend: "But the scripture says that it was a serpent." The word 'serpent' actually connotes a "deceiver," which is a general description of Lucifer in Genesis 3:1. Lucifer was used to changing forms before Eve - being a god (spirit); hence Eve referred to him as a serpent, which means deceiver. Job 12:16 says, "...the deceived and the deceiver are his." The book of Revelation 12:9 detailed him as a serpent called the Devil and Satan, describing Lucifer as a dragon serpent.

The cherub Lucifer wasn't a dragon serpent before the deception. He was a cherub that usually accompanied the Lord God to the Garden of Eden. We already saw from the scriptures that God confirmed Lucifer was used to visiting the garden in Ezekiel 28:13 according to the scripture: "Thou hast been in Eden the garden of God." Lucifer was in the company of God as a cherub visiting Adam; hence he knew what God told Adam, of which Adam related same to Eve. As I said earlier, man was crowned with glory and honor but a little lower than the angels; hence cherubs were attending to man like a guardian angel. Probably, God doesn't want man corrupt, given the experience of some angels who failed in the pre-Adamic world. So God was comfortable with cherubs watching over man. I believe when man fell, angels were later assigned to watch over man.

The presence of a cherub introduces the presence of God. Throughout the scriptures, prophets and sons of men who saw cherubs would often see God as well. Ezekiel saw cherubs and saw God above the cherubs. "And above the firmament that was over their heads was the likeness of a throne, as the appearance of a sapphire stone: and upon the likeness of the throne was the likeness of a man above upon it" (See Ezekiel 1:26). Isaiah the prophet saw cherubs (seraphim), and also saw God clothed in majesty. "In the year King Uzziah died, I also saw the Lord sitting upon a throne, high and lifted up, and his train filled the temple. And above it stood the seraphim (cherubs): each one had six wings; with twain he did cover his face, and with twain he covered his feet, and with twain he did fly." (Isaiah 6:1-2).

John the Revelator saw God and cherubs in the spiritual realm around God's throne. "And immediately I was in the spirit: and, behold, a throne was set in heaven, and one sat on the throne...and before the throne, there was a sea of glass like unto crystal: and in the midst of the throne, and round about the throne were four beasts full of eyes before and behind" (Revelation 4:2-6). And we saw from the scriptures that one of the beasts (cherub) spoke to John, the apostle. "And when the Lamb had opened the seals, and I heard, as it were thunder, one of the four beasts saying, Come and see...And when he opened the second seal, I heard the second beast say, Come and see" (Revelation 6:1-3).

Cherubs are spirit men with wings like the angels, though they have six wings, while angels have two. So also, Lucifer was a man and could change forms into a lion, ox, and eagle. It means when the scripture says that Lucifer was more "subtle than any beasts which the LORD God had made," Lucifer was more subtle (cunning) than Eve, playing with Eve's mind by changing forms. Lucifer was more subtle than any beast of the field, which implies he was wiser than man, who is recognized in scriptures as the 'beast of the field' which the LORD God had made. Adam and Eve were referred to as the beast of the field here, an indication that man was a beast. Man was a beast endowed with consciousness, recreated in the image of God.

One might contend, "If he was a deceiver, it means he was already a fallen cherub!" No. He was more subtle, wiser by implication, by perverting the truth, thereby inventing the concept of deception/lie into existence. The term 'serpent' was metaphorically used to distinguish his cunning/cleverly inherent nature, which he began to exhibit as soon as God gave Adam authority. In a sinless state, Adam was described as cunning, which I've exemplified by children's ability to play with toys or cry when in need of something despite not attaining the knowledge of good and evil. Don't forget Lucifer was regarded to have been much wiser than Daniel in heaven, much less Adam of the dust, who was a baby recreated in his presence. Lucifer should be much wiser or more subtle than Adam. God knew Lucifer was accumulating bitter envying, but God kept mute, allowing Lucifer to rope himself in. He foreknew Lucifer's reasonings and arrogance being objectional to God's orders. Of course, there are certain decisions the president would take, and his chief of staff may disagree with such an idea, but we saw Moses submit all through. We also saw an angel speak to God humbly in the scriptures.

The formation of Adam and subsequent dominion over all things was the litmus test that produced Lucifer's underlying motives for God's handling of the whole situation regarding fallen stars and sons of God. Lucifer felt he was smarter, not knowing God knew his pride and objection to God's choice of the man of the dust perceived as foolish and weak. Lucifer then devised a plan to swindle man instead. Lucifer's enticement to Eve was: You shall be as gods...." Eve desired to be like the cherub (god) who changed form. Often children show interest in driving cars even at the tender ages of 2 to 3 years. Eve desired to be wise like the gods. Lucifer must have made her think: "If you want to change form and be like the gods, then you need to eat of this tree for God doth know that in the day you eat of it, you will be as gods..."

The conversation ensued between Eve and Lucifer, a man cherub who had been familiar to Eve. For those who are ignorant of this truth, perhaps still contending, let me ask some basic questions: "If he was a serpent before the fall or deception, how come God cursed him into a serpent again? You can say the serpent then had hands and feet. If that was the case, then he was a cherub. How come his food chain was changed to dust if he was a serpent before the conversation that ensued?" So, we can see that Lucifer was still in God's camp before he fell, and he was not a serpent, neither did he enter into any serpent to engage Eve. Could an ordinary crawling serpent know what is on the mind of God than man, whom God created to oversee the earth alongside creeping things?

The scriptures depicted him as a serpent because his actions metaphorically portrayed him as a deceiver. Many people often get confused studying the scriptures to date, not thinking outside the box, and comparing scriptures to scriptures, and this has been a challenge. For instance, some people think Lucifer was an angel, but the scriptures described Lucifer as a cherub, not an angel. Of course, one would hastily quote 1st Corinthians 11:14, which says, "And no marvel; for Satan himself is transformed into an angel of light." We have already established earlier that Lucifer does transform, being a higher star. He could transform into an angel, ancient men, or a man who are all lower grades than he. Similarly, angels can transform into spirit men or man without wings.

This shows Lucifer can change forms, which he used in luring Eve, which Eve was fascinated to become like the gods. The scripture used the word serpent to emphasize his personality and used the subjective pronoun 'he' to distinguish him as a man cherub (beast). As you will understand, the curse from God eventually turned the cherub into a dragon-serpent in the subsequent verses. Please follow on to know the truth. He can transform into a lion, as seen in the book of 1st Peter 5:8, which says, "...Your adversary the devil, as a roaring lion, walketh about seeking whom he may devour."

You can see the changing nature here of the same beast, Lucifer. He was referred to as a roaring lion here. So he does change forms at will. Eve was attracted to this transforming capability of Lucifer; hence the Cherub Lucifer engaged Eve in a conversation as a weaker vessel - an emotional vessel (See 1st Peter 3:7). Weaker vessel doesn't translate into physical weakness, but emotional weakness. This has been a woman's nature from the beginning, not necessarily because of the fall. A companion made to always discuss things and become emotional towards the discourse. Eve was discerned to always be emotional. Lucifer saw this weakness in Eve, who loves things and gets emotional since she came and met Adam, who had been in the garden before she was formed.

Misrepresentation of the serpent

Eve got acquainted with Adam, asking questions about the garden, she loves communicating a lot, and Adam must have informed her of God's instruction about the forbidden tree. But she didn't know Lucifer, a guardian cherub, was envious of man of the dust. She has no idea of what transpired on the previous earth. Lucifer saw man as an impediment, so he internally dislikes man because of the authority God bestowed upon him, whom he perceived as naive. Man was given authority over all things but had no knowledge of the previous earth. He was formed to dominate all things but had no spiritual depth as to what extent. So, he was concerned with nature study (science) and would subsequently fellowship or play with God like children are emotionally attached to their parents. And because Adam was busy out there, fascinated by nature, Lucifer took advantage of Eve. 1st Corinthians 2:11 says, "Lest Satan should get an advantage of us: for we are not ignorant of his devices (cunning craftiness)." And up to date, Lucifer still takes advantage of our thoughts by instigating negative thoughts in our hearts.

He tactically engaged her by asking her a question: "Hath God said, Ye shall not eat of every tree of the garden?" And because she already knew Lucifer as God's trusted aide, a man cherub who was familiar to them, she responded to him by saying, "...We may eat of the fruit of the trees of the garden: But of the fruit of the tree which is in the midst of the garden, God had said, Ye shall not eat of it neither shall you touch it, lest you die." (Genesis 3:2-3) She immediately got emotional and began to disclose all she had ever heard. Obviously, it wasn't a serpent that spoke to Eve in the garden but a man cherub; hence, the scripture used the pronoun he. "And he said unto the woman...."

We saw how God had to send other cherubs of that capacity which Adam and Eve saw protecting the tree of life with a flaming sword after the fall. God sent cherubs of the same ranks, not angels, because angels were lower in rank than cherubs. But so many people are confused, thinking it was a serpent. How could Eve stoop so low to discuss with an ordinary serpent? Where were the other animals then? Why can't a pig or goat counter the serpent's voice? Remember, Adam gave names to animals and birds. There was no account of any creature communicating with Adam while he named them. Scripture would have captured one of the beasts or creeping things greeting Adam in the garden. There was no reference in the Bible to animals or birds speaking to Adam or Eve. I mean, this is logic!

We have had so many misrepresentations of the serpent used in Genesis 3:1. It was never a serpent in Chapter 3:1 before God cursed the serpent to go upon his belly as a serpent again. Someone might say, "It means the serpent had legs and hands before being cursed by God. If it had hands and legs, it means he was a cherub before he became dragon-serpent after the curse, as seen in the book of Revelation 12:3, which puts things in proper perspective that he became a dragon-serpent, not the ordinary serpent we find in the forest or our neighborhoods.

Of course, I should anticipate someone else might contend that an ass spoke to Balaam and that animals and birds were used to talking in those days. That is not true either. However, to set the records straight, let's look at the scriptures in which an ass spoke to Balaam: "And the angel of the LORD went further, and stood in a narrow place, where no way to turn either to the right or to the left. And when the ass saw the angel of the LORD, she fell under Balaam: Balaam's anger was kindled, and he smote the ass with a staff. And the LORD opened the mouth of the ass, and she said unto Balaam, What have I done unto thee, that thou hast smitten me these three times?" (Numbers 22:26-28). Without much ado, it is evident that God opened the mouth of the ass because we never saw the ass speak to Balaam or the angel until her mouth was opened, indicating an unusual phenomenon.

Lucifer was subsequently cursed into a dragon-serpent similar to the dinosaurs but not a dinosaur. Dinosaurs have hands, but this cherub Lucifer was stripped of hands, even if he could still change forms. It is like the scripture referring to Jesus Christ as a 'lamb,' but that doesn't suggest Jesus was a lamb hung on the cross. Far be it forever! It is crystal clear that a physical serpent didn't talk to Eve. Little minds should learn and stop teaching scriptures superficially.

Another school of thought is that the Devil spoke to Eve through the mind. If that were true, why wouldn't God speak to Adam and Eve through the mind as well, since

Lucifer and God are both spirits? Why would God physically search for Adam and Eve if it was a mind talk? Was it mind talk that brought the formed animals for Adam to give names? Responding to your mind does not call for physical hiding among trees. So, we can see that Eve spoke to a cherub named Lucifer as a man, not a serpent or mind, before the cherub was cursed into a serpent, called the old serpent or dragon, as we shall discuss in detail. We have seen from the scriptures how stars turned into humans.

Other misrepresentations of the serpent in Genesis are far from the truth, with some schools of thought portraying the forbidden fruit as representing fornication or intercourse between Adam and Eve. What they call Adam's apple. That isn't true either because Eve was Adam's wife. Such scriptural interpretations are fallacies. Although the knowledge of sexual intercourse entered after eating the forbidden fruits, it does not mean intercourse represents the forbidden fruits. Just like a child would feel free bathing in public without being ashamed. Once they start distinguishing between sexual intercourse, they have clearly crossed into good and evil. Adam and Eve were once naked, unknown to them, so it was easier for Lucifer and the angels to regard them as foolish.

Proud and objectional

If Adam and Eve had produced a child before the fall, then that child would have been a sinless child, which is another race altogether. Others might say, "The serpent had a sexual relationship with Eve first; hence the seed issue arose." That in itself is a complete fallacy, being out of context. There was no record of the cherub being a father of a child Eve delivered. Such insinuations of sexual intercourse to have represented the forbidden fruit are complete carnal misrepresentations of facts - out of context! Lucifer was proud and objectional to God's decision. He felt once he obtained the keys to death and hell, he would succeed in overthrowing God and chasing man out. Overthrow God? An impossible mission! "Woe unto him that strive with his maker" (Isaiah 45:9).

Trying to be what he is not. But since he can't get at God, he would have to dispossess man of his authority. But then, the secrets God kept from Adam were exposed, which was not to allow man of the dust to acquire knowledge of what transpired in the past between God and fallen spirits, who were violent, being imprisoned under darkness. God completely excluded the knowledge of the previous earth's experience from Adam and created Adam with a command warning him, "Of every tree of the garden, thou mayest freely eat, but of the tree of the knowledge of good and evil, thou shalt not eat of it: for in the day thou eat of it, thou shalt surely - eventually die" (Genesis 2:16-17, emphasis mine).

For on the day you eat of it, you shall eventually die, which implies there is a spirit called death in that tree. Often, people conceal things from children, tactically refusing to disclose the underlying motives behind their concealment. Adam only knew about his relationship with God and his love for nature. He had no idea that eating the fruit of the tree (of knowledge of good and evil) would open up those fallen angels of death and destruction locked up in the chains of darkness. But Lucifer knew all these secrets, which he took advantage of. He knew that God wouldn't like Adam to be disobedient and behave like those fallen spirits locked up because they were violent sociopaths.

So Lucifer came to Eve and said, "...You shalt not surely die, for God doth know that in the day you eat of it, your eyes shall be opened and you shall be as gods (spirits) knowing what is good and evil" (Genesis 3:4-5, emphasis mine). This implied you shall be as fallen gods (spirits) to know what God approves or disapproves of. In order words, you have not tasted what we spirits (gods) knew about. You are still a baby! There is what we gods know that you have not known yet! He enticed her emotions to have her think that she could possess the same ability to change forms like the gods (spirit beings) and then stylishly introduced knowing good and evil experiences.

But Eve was unaware of Lucifer's bitter envy against man God put in charge of all things. Lucifer presented the situation to Eve, insinuating that God was hiding something from her. God knows that when you eat of it, your eyes shall be opened, and you shall be wise like the gods. And of a truth, spirit beings do change form to a man of the dust at will, just as men or women practicing witchcraft transform into animals or fowls through the power of Satan.

Someone might ask: "How did he sneak in to engage Eve in the garden without God being aware? Jesus gave us some clues as to what transpired. Jesus said, "Verily, verily I say unto you, He that entered not by the door into the sheepfold, but climbeth up another way, the same is a thief and a robber." (John 10:1). Take note of Jesus's comment using the pronoun 'he.' This means Lucifer, the cherub that covereth (protected), sneaked out from the holy mountain in heaven as though he was heading for his usual assignment of guardian cherub and applied other ways. What other ways? Deception, or perverted truth, which Lucifer explored in robbing Adam of his glory.

But he couldn't have done that without being familiar with Adam and Eve. As we shall soon find out that the scripture referred to Lucifer's trafficking between heaven and earth was what corrupted his thinking. He leveraged the opportunity to have traffic between the Garden of Eden and heaven. And during his visit to this prison realm under darkness, since the earth was recreated under darkness, Lucifer saw fallen stars banished under darkness. And discovered that their colors had changed from pure white to brown, red, yellow, blue, green, black, etc. hence the scriptures say that even the stars of heaven are not pure in God's eyes. That doesn't imply the seven colors of the rainbow are impure light.

Take note!

Perhaps, Lucifer felt for those fallen principalities spirits whom he knew for several billion years but hated man of the dust who was naive. He knew the keys to unlock them were in the hands of Adam and Eve, right in the forbidden tree. So in trafficking between heaven and earth, he was reasoning things out. Remember, God said Lucifer was corrupt because of the multitude of his trafficking. "Thou hast defiled thy sanctuaries by the multitude of thine iniquities, by the iniquity of thy traffick...." Ezekiel 28:18. I will come back to this in detail. Nevertheless, it is evident that Lucifer was opposed to God's choice of forming man of the dust.

I believe he felt pitied for them, perhaps, he had some close allies angels or archangels imprisoned under the darkness for several thousand years. Of course, there were other principalities (beasts) locked up as well as seen in the book of Daniel and Revelation. So he was in a dilemma but hated man of the dust so much. He then sneaked out to visit Eve and disclosed the secrets kept from Adam and Eve kept to obtain the keys to death and hell, which would enable him to release fallen angels and overthrow God. The best option is to deceive Eve, who had much influence over Adam. Adam was always preoccupied with his work. Eve was emotional and susceptible.

Judgment time

Lucifer must have immediately moved back into his position and returned with God, or he remained in the garden as a guardian cherub. Hence he was present when God queried Adam and Eve. The question is, "Was God not aware when all this took place?" Yes, he was aware. But as his usual style, he would often wait until judgment time – his style of allowing his creatures to do whatever they wanted cannot be overruled as free morals. God would often allow us to choose and act in our own ways before passing his judgment. The first time God interfered in a matter between Cain and Abel didn't yield any result in stopping Cain's choice of fulfilling his desire to have Abel killed. God passed his judgment at last.

Jesus waited for Judas to kiss him as though he cared for Jesus, even when Jesus knew

Judas Iscariot would betray him. He allowed him to kiss before Jesus passed judgment on Judas Iscariot. King David also had his way when he committed adultery with Uriah's wife and had Uriah killed. God waited for him to have accomplished his ways before passing judgment through Nathan, the prophet. Check the entire scriptures. God would always allow us to do what we wanted before passing judgment. Lucifer was also allowed to deceive Adam and Eve and was judged with a severe curse.

Whenever I hear people sing or say that God should take their entire 'human will' to become God's will while they are still alive, I wonder what kind of statement or song is that? There is nothing like God completely taking over your will when he already created you as a free moral agent. God will not tell you to brush your teeth, eat, work, or study your scriptures. You are trying to subject your desire to His occasionally. But it doesn't imply he will completely take over your desires or will. Only Jesus, who became flesh as God, is perfectly synchronized with the Father. One time in the Garden of Gethsemene, his earthly environment (flesh) clouded his will, but when he realized it, he said, "Not my will but Thine be done." Let's not lose track of our discussions about Lucifer and Adam.

God came to judge Adam as his usual pattern of dealing with his creatures. One thing I have learned about God over the years is that he would watch you carry out your ways without talking to you, but he will always come and show you where you went wrong. This is where we all should fear and tremble. The scripture says we should work out our salvation with fear and trembling because we can derail off course, and God may not respond until judgment time. Jeremiah 9:24 says, "...I am the LORD who exercises lovingkindness, judgment, and righteousness, in the earth, for these things I delight, saith the LORD." God takes pleasure in rewarding us according to our ways (his judgment style) on earth. And he does that in righteousness.

This speaks volumes of his nature, judging right - justice. He is fair in judgment. He will never contend with you when you are acting in your own ways, but he will at last judge you in righteousness. Our thoughts, actions, and inactions may be right in our eyes, but God is wiser than our sense of judgment. So, God judged Adam and Eve after the whole exercise wound up. Lucifer presented an enticing knowledge acquisition to Eve, which was half truth confirmed by God, but his motive was deceptive. Lucifer's motive was to obtain the keys of death and hell hidden in the forbidden tree unknown to Adam. He knew God kept all things (power of death and destruction) under Adam's feet inside that forbidden tree. That is what the scriptures meant by "...Thou hast put all things under his feet" (Psalms 8:6).

Lucifer was very crafty. No wonder scripture says, "Lucifer was more subtle." He was the Father of lies or deceit. John 8:44 says, "...for he is a liar and the father of it." In order words, he was the first spirit to invent deceit (lie), saying something craftily with a hidden motive, which is the characteristic common to his followers. So Jesus said Lucifer used other ways of deceit or lies to deceive Adam and Eve. You know we've got people who are subtle like Satan. They wait until you are excited or happy and take advantage of your mood. Or they sometimes spoil your mood by making unnecessary demands to satisfy their selfish aims and keep you in an uncomfortable position. That is craftiness! You are free to disregard whoever makes you uncomfortable, taking advantage of your happy mood.

We saw this scenario play out when King Herod observed his birthday party. During Herod's state of ecstasy, Herodias took advantage, requesting the head of John the Baptist, and the scripture says that King Herod was sorry for being in an inconvenient position. He felt terrible, but because he had bound himself with an oath, he had to keep to his words (See Matthew 14:1-11). Similarly, Lucifer took advantage of Eve's emotions. He presented the secrets as though God was concealing an important secret from Adam and Eve, not knowing God doesn't want man corrupt and eventually die. Lucifer was a liar here.

That is why Jesus said, "He was a liar and a murderer from the beginning" (John 8:44). He lied to Eve because he wanted man to eat of the tree, which would grant him (Lucifer) access to the keys of death and hell, and in so doing, he would plot the coup d'etat of the Godhead. This was the meaning of 'murderer' Jesus referred to here. Of course, Lucifer's words were embellished to underscore points in the eyes of Eve. Lucifer was indirectly plotting how to overthrow God because he obtained the power of death and destruction. The retrieval of the keys of hell and death were the primary reasons Jesus came to planet earth, besides shedding his blood for the souls of men. But before I proceed, I would holistically take a critical analysis of what transpired in the Garden of Eden.

Purpose of analysis

Now, let's analyze the conversation that ensued between Lucifer and Eve. The scripture confirmed God excluded the knowledge of good and evil from man at the formation stage, which Lucifer later exposed, and God confirmed Lucifer's words. God said, "Man is become as one of us, to know good and evil: and now lest he put forth his hand, and take also of the tree of life, and eat, and live forever." (Genesis 3:22) Then let us see what Satan said to Eve. "...You shalt not surely die, for God doth know that in the day you eat thereof, then your eyes shall be opened, and you shall be as gods (spirits) knowing good and evil" (Genesis 3:4-5).

The first comment here by Lucifer was, "You shall not surely die." Let's assume here that Lucifer was correct in his words. Not because Adam didn't die that day, but because Lucifer didn't know the actual composition of the new man formed to die, since his knowledge was limited to previous spirits beings recreated by God that did not eternally die but rather were banished into the darkness of the deep. So he knew that created beings could be shut out in darkness, not that they eternally perished. Am I saying God is lying? God forbid! What Lucifer said was half-truths in disguise because his underlying motive was aiming at something else - the key to hell and death, which was unknown to Eve.

Lucifer was not a Creator, he was created, so he never knew God meant what he said in that God could terminate the human body out of planet earth and remove the soul of man. His knowledge was limited as a cherub created by God, so he assumed God was concealing something from man. Lucifer is not God and cannot create humans. Then one might ask: "If that is the case, in what area did he lie then?" He lied to deceive or fool Eve because he had an ulterior motive to get Adam and Eve to eat the fruit while he obtained the keys of death and destruction unknown to them.

To deceive is to craftily obtain by pretext. Lucifer was the first spirit to invent lies or deceit, as we have discussed earlier. Man is used to the concept of deception invented by Satan in several ways. Abraham used it to get himself saved from being killed by the Egyptians on approaching the land of Egypt in Genesis 12:11-20. The sons of Jacob used this invention on Shechem and Hamor when their sister Dinah was defiled in Genesis 34:1-31. Pharaoh of Egypt used it on Moses when Pharoah discovered that there was respite in Exodus 8:8-15.

A woman named Rahab used it to dissuade the king of Jericho, thereby securing the two spies who visited her house. (Joshua 2:1-11). The Gibeonites used it on Joshua to secure their lives from destruction (Joshua 9:1-24). Here are a few examples: Samuel, a one-time prophet in Israel, used this invention when he wanted to anoint David to avoid Saul coming after him (1st Samuel 16:1-3). One might contend, "But it was God that told Samuel what to do," Yes. God saw that this invention works for men who inherited it from Lucifer, a fallen cherub. It was observed that men love this invention more than raw truth. When you tell certain people the truth, it causes them to hate and think evil of you, especially those the scriptures classified as fools.

Proverbs 9:7-8 says, "He that reproveth a scorner getteth to himself shame: and he that rebuketh a wicked man getteth to himself a blot. Reprove not a scorner, lest he hate thee: rebuke a wise man, and he will love thee." There's a maxim that says truth is bitter. Many people hate those who tell them the truth; instead, they love flatteries that work for humanity. Jesus observed that humans love deceit; hence he was quoted as saying that men love darkness rather than light because their deeds were evil. For every one that doeth evil hateth the light, neither cometh to the light, lest his deeds should be reproved. But that doeth truth cometh to the light...." (John 3:19-21).

We also saw from the scriptures that Herodias Philip's wife, who King Herod, the tetrarch, confiscated, hated John the Baptist for telling the truth about their affairs. So men inherently love the concepts of deception invented by Lucifer in our universe, which we are all used to in politics, families, business, etc. David utilized this invention on Uriah, urging him to go home, eat and sleep with his wife. So deception seems to thrive in the human race world all over. Some religions have approved lying or deception as the norm, adducing that so long it is just to achieve a given objective. They are ignorant that this is Lucifer's invention and that they will move from life to death zone. Hence the scripture says all liars shall have their part in the lake which burneth with fire and brimstone (Revelation 21:8).

God also permitted this invention through the instrumentality of fallen spirits for humans in the scripture because many people don't like truth. They prefer flatteries that suit their emotions. Sorry, I'm just being straightforward here, analyzing the scriptures. God permitted a spirit to apply this invention when deliberating the destruction of Ahab. In the near future, God will use this invention for people who hate the truth in these last days.

Let's see this from the scripture: 1st Thessalonians 2:7-12 says, "For the mystery of iniquity doth already work: only he who now letteth will let until he is taken out of the way. And then shall the Wicked be revealed, whom the Lord shall consume with the spirit of his mouth, and shall destroy with the brightness of his coming: Even him, whose coming is after the work of Satan with all power and signs and lying wonders, And with all deceivableness of unrighteousness in them (people) that perish; because they received not the love of the truth, that they might be saved. And for this cause, God shall send them strong delusion, that they should believe a lie: That they all might be damned who believe not the truth, but had pleasure in unrighteousness."

God shall send them strong deception or misleading minds because they don't love truth since they prefer unrighteousness – deception. That is, humans do not like raw truth. So how else would you convince someone who has concluded what they want to do in their mind but just seeking your opinion? You take sides for their happiness and destruction because you cannot change them as free moral agents. God foreknew many people would perish because they did not love the truth, so God would have no choice but make them believe in lies. The strong delusion will cause them to be deceived by the same Satan they love to follow.

I could remember a prophet named Balaam who was enticed by the promotional offers by the King of Moab Balak in Numbers 22 and 23. Balaam kept pressurizing God on whether to follow Balak's men despite God's initial warning not to do so. God saw Balaam's desire for promotions offered by Balak, so God permitted Balaam to go with them. But it wasn't God's original intention, what we call permissive will. So we can see that God used this invention for the simple fact that mortals love it. Mortals dislike anyone who tells them the raw truth. They see it as opposition. And I believe some people would resist the truths presented in this book. Now, let's get back to our critical analysis regarding Lucifer's underlying motives.

Reason for countering

On the other hand, let's say Lucifer lied in his words, "You shall not surely die." In this case, he countered God's word and added a reason for disagreeing. He twisted the story and made Eve see what God was hiding from them. He said, "You shall not surely die, for God doth know that in the day you eat thereof then your eyes shall be opened, and you shall be as gods (spirits) knowing good and evil" (Genesis 3:4- 5). In other words, he lied and backed up his reasons with convincing points. He introduced new points that God confirmed to be true. And guess what? The scripture was fair enough to report the truth by saying, "And their eyes were opened," which aligns with Lucifer's suggestion. The scriptures recorded that their eyes were opened, and they realized they were naked.

Now, this tells you that God is not a manipulator of things. He is a just and fair God. One of the reasons I believe in the scriptures 100 percent is that I have found out that God was fair in all of the scriptures. What do I mean? The evil and good deeds of men, including what God did or any other spirit, were all reported as they occurred; they were reported in truth. There was no bias reporting in the scriptures. Some authors would suit themselves alone like some so-called 'books' that support only one side of the coin. When such books are challenged by their followers, they tell their followers, "Nobody has the right to question what has been written. "The Bible is not like that! It tells you the good and bad sides of life - fairly! And if you have some questions unanswered in the Bible, it is simply because you don't know or your teacher in your location is ignorant.

I know someone might even condemn me for saying, "Let me assume here that Lucifer was correct in his words, "You shall not surely die." Well, I'm not writing as a fanatic or dogma, but being open-minded about truth. Religious people don't question things. They are often dogmatic! They cannot philosophize, holding unto religious traditions for years. Any religion that persecutes its followers for asking a question is bogus. For crying out loud, we are made to think! Humans are not peacocks! If your religion cannot answer questions, you think we're wrong, get out from it! You are in bondage! That is why I'm writing to make everyone know the truth and decide for themselves.

The scriptures reported God confirmed some words Lucifer told Eve in the scriptures. Someone once said, "We are already made like God, created in his image. Why would Lucifer say we should be like God?" Anyway, such notions that we are already made like God are out of scriptural context because it is just amateur and biased reasoning. What do I mean? God himself confirmed that Adam is become as a god. "And the LORD God said, Behold man is become as one of us, to know good and evil" (Genesis 3:22). In other words, Adam and Eve had acquired the knowledge of the gods (spirit beings). Take note of the word become. Man had just moved from childishness or a baby state to join the knowledge of the gods, which means becoming like the spirits who already know good and evil. Although, it's just one aspect of spirit beings acquired by man of the dust, Adam.

Lucifer said that you shall be as gods, knowing good and evil. But Eve didn't obtain such capability to change forms as displayed by Lucifer when he enticed her. You shall be as gods (we spirit beings). Take note that the scripture used the continuous tense 'knowing.' This means man had acquired the nature of discerning or knowing good and evil. There was an acquisition of the knowledge of the gods (spirit beings) who already knew violence, cursing, rebellion, war, sex, etc., as I will expound on shortly.

Chapter 15

Consciousness that Kills

We discussed earlier that the phrase "Let us make man," as used in Genesis 1:26, talked about God addressing his team of spirit beings. God was referring to the sons of God when he said, 'Let us make man in our own image and likeness.' And it was after Adam ate the forbidden fruit then God said, "Man is become as one of us, to know good and evil and lest he put forth his hand...and live forever." The objective case pronoun 'us' used here was generic. Man has attained the knowledge of spirit beings. That means man had upgraded to the status of the gods, which includes God, Lucifer, and spirit beings that pre-existed Adam.

The tree of life was right in the middle of the garden, and Adam was carefree, indicating Adam was like a baby, unconcerned with complex matters. And, of course, Adam was initially formed with a baby's mind whose parents could strip naked in his presence, knowing full well that the baby could not tell the difference. But as soon as Adam tasted of the fruit of the tree, God had to dispatch a team of cherubs who deprived Adam of acquiring the additional "spirit's status" of eternal life. If man had acquired the forever-living nature of the gods, it would have been disastrous for the human race.

Of a truth, all created spirit beings live forever. Are we now saying that Lucifer was right when he said, "You shall not surely die" because spirit beings don't eternally die? Lucifer was never a creator, so he must have assumed man wouldn't die eternally since he saw fallen angels, once dead, still alive, shut off under darkness. He never knew God meant that man would physically die at last. However, his motive was to obtain the keys of death and hell to overthrow God, being in confederation with fallen spirits that supported his course.

God couldn't have allowed man to obtain the forever-living nature of the gods because ancient men, once submerged in flood under darkness, exhibited some arrogancy because they were created with elements of the gods. Man, on the acquisition of the knowledge of the gods, also got influenced and was found to have delighted in violence and wickedness, which brought about God's recourse to repentance of the man of the dust and eventual reduction of man's life span to 120 years. This limit was placed on men (spirit men in human flesh and Adamic descendants). Had God not limited man's lifetime, you can imagine the level of wickedness perpetuated by some people in authority ruthlessly dealing with their fellow humans on earth.

And what would have become of life if such a level of wickedness had continued unabated? And, if man had succeeded in eating the tree of life in sin, imagine someone who got a cancerous disease and was in pain forever without coming out of such pain. You can agree that God is good and much wiser, inventing the concept of death so that certain pains, sufferings, and deviant behaviors can be set aside from life.

Although death pre-existed Adam, God indicated that he never wanted Adam to die; hence, he initially excluded such knowledge from Adam. The reason is that acquiring the knowledge of good and evil would certainly result in sin consciousness, which in turn would obstruct Adam's free flow of fellowship to God since sin consciousness deadens one's love of God which in turn is death to the soul or weakness. Man, having acquired the consciousness of violence, cursing, abuses, wars, sexual immorality, etc., and eating of the forbidden fruit of the tree, had obtained the nature of fallen spirits whose nature has pervaded the entire human race. One of the acquired natures is the violence being practiced by humanity.

The natural tendency to kill infiltrated the human race. Had man acquired the tree of life in addition, it would mean God lost all to Lucifer. God was right when he forewarned Adam, "...For in the day thou eat of it, thou shalt surely—eventually die" (Genesis 2:17, emphasis mine). God was the Creator, so he knew exactly what he was talking about. He cannot lie, but he did keep secrets from Adam. His words are always true. Someone might ask, "But man didn't die that very day what happened?" I'll come to that shortly. Remember, we are criticizing scriptural accounts based on hypothetical viewpoints.

The bottom line

Let's take a critical look at the third point of view: Let's assume Lucifer knew Adam would actually die, and because he hated man for being in charge of the earth or being loved by God that much, he then lied to Eve, persuading her to believe in a lie. This means he was envious that man quickly perished out of the earth. The tree of life was right in the garden, and Lucifer never suggested to Eve that the tree of life was much better; instead he suggested what would quickly destroy man. Think about that! Let's also assume Lucifer didn't get all the gist of what God told Adam. He must have observed Eve's actions, always grabbing things while playing around the forbidden tree.

Therefore, Lucifer could psychologically decode her lust/desire though exhibiting restrictions about the tree. He then asked: Yea, hath God said, You shall not eat of every tree of the garden? And as soon as she saw the benefits of eating as presented by Lucifer (capable of transforming), she screwed up. Lucifer knew the keys of death, and hell was right in there. He had to cunningly present a twist of the story, evoking her suppressed interest in eating of the tree. She had the propensity to disobey before being tempted. Deception works best on an individual's tendency to gain the support of their intended course of action.

But then Lucifer needed Adam to perish in his preference for fallen sons of God. I believe God saw this enmity; hence God said, "I will put enmity (for the bitter envying you had towards man) between you and the woman, and between your seed and her seed, and you both will have a polarized relationship for life; with her seed toppling your authority, and you Lucifer persecuting the seed of the woman." In other words, Lucifer's hatred against man is extreme. Now, both of you become enemies forever! Perhaps, Lucifer wanted to lure her to his side, so God had to split the friendship.

Let's criticize from the fourth point of view: Lucifer was envious of the sweet fellowship and how God was overly concerned and comfortable with Adam, who knew nothing about what had transpired on earth before. So Lucifer thought to himself and said, "Is it not because Man had no knowledge of the gods, that is why you loved him and care for him more than the angels and cherub? Let me make man acquire what we know, and let's see the outcome". Just like he contended about Job saying, "...Doth Job fear God for nothing? Hast thou not made a hedge about him, and about his house..." (Job 1:9-10). So, Lucifer introduced a disconnection in the relationship by deception so that the preferential treatment of Adam and Eve would cease.

He tactically introduced another version of the story through deceit. In all of these four critical analyses, the bottom line remains Lucifer saw the keys of death and hell hidden in the forbidden tree – indisputable! God recognized these stolen keys (as authority); hence he said, "...The seed of the woman shall bruise thy head (authority), and thou shalt bruise his heel (persecute and attack). That is to say, Lucifer, you had bitter envy against Eve, whom you swindled who knew nothing regarding previous issues won't end here, but the seed of Eve shall debase you at last.

I imagine someone saying, "God would have informed Adam about everything in advance." Not so. You don't discuss certain information with kids of 1 or 2 years. It would make no sense to them at that stage because their minds cannot comprehend such classified information. And guess what? The impact of Adam's disobedience was felt years later when the entire earth was filled with violence.

The truth remains that Lucifer was envious of Adam; hence the scriptures state, "What is man that thou art mindful of him or the son of man that thou visited him?" So there was envy towards man of the dust of the ground Adam created.

Remember, Joseph's brothers hated Joseph because he was loved of God, who gave him a great future. Saul attacked David because he was God's choice. Daniel was thrown into Lion's den simply because he was praying to God always and was beloved of God. It shows that those who God loves become the envy of others, even among believers. For this reason, Jesus gave the parable of the prodigal son in advance for angels not to envy the party (The Lord's supper and wedding) that would be organized in heaven over the sons of men who were once 'dead' but now alive. The angels of God understood the parable more than the children of men. The Lord opened my eyes to this parable.

Approved and disapproved

An amateur would think the devil was supporting humans by revealing to Eve that they were naked. "...You shall not surely die; for God doth know that in the day you eat thereof, then your eyes shall be opened, you shall be as gods, knowing good and evil" (Genesis3:4-5). That wasn't the point here. Lucifer didn't say, "Your eyes shall be opened, and you shall know that you are naked." That wasn't what he said. He was specific when he said, "And you shall be as gods (spirits), knowing good and evil."

You shall be as spirits knowing what God approved and disapproved of or knowing between what is right and wrong. It was an introduction to another consciousness which is sin consciousness as well. Adam and Eve were introduced into the violent world of death and destruction. They were now conscious of such things and could discern good or evil actions. The nudity awareness wasn't the objective, but it was to acquire the keys of hell and death in order to wipe out humans and overthrow God. Adam was exposed to the world of violence which pre-existed him. For the first time, God would thrust them out of the Garden of Eden with the use of the sword, which indicates man had been exposed to the 'sin of violence, and this is where the manifestation of the world of violence began.

Man acquired the violent nature of fallen spirits banished into the darkness of the deep. This violent nature was evident in the life of Cain, the first descendant of Adam. Violence erupted in man's world. Adam was deceived into committing sin, meaning man chose to join the fallen spirits' camp. Like the prodigal son who wanted to taste the power of freedom from the father, he went out and tasted the 'sin of violence, in which his friends plundered his resources, and he began to be in want. Adam sinned and, by his actions, had joined the camp of the devil. That is what the scripture meant when it said, "He (Adam) that sinned is of (belongs to) the devil, for the devil sinneth from the beginning (in the Garden of Eden). For this purpose, the Son of God (the seed of the woman- Jesus Christ as second Adam) was manifested so that he might destroy (reverse) the works (retrieve the keys of death and destruction, including healing the sick caused) of the devil" (1st John 3:8. emphasis mine).

Adam had, by his actions, submitted his heart and authority to the devil who lured him into sin, the sin of a violent world. Sin originated before Adam. I knew from the scripture that some of the angels, who muttered secretly against man to have been made ruler over all things after several billions of years of being with God, joined Lucifer. So they were opposed to man of the dust ruling over all things. They planned it all. They were blind to God's ultimate plan of the person of Jesus, their Lord, who would also become man of the dust. Lucifer robbed Adam of his authority and took over the keys of death and destruction to kill and destroy. The scripture referred to him as a "thief that cometh not, but to steal, kill and destroy. (John 10:10). He stole the keys kept under Adam and took Adam's authority over all things.

Lucifer was the thief who stole the keys of death and hell, having released the fallen spirits of death and destruction to cause sickness, pains, lack, diseases, destruction, and death. An anticipated question might be: "Why would God place the keys of death and destruction (hell) under a naive man? Is there no other place to hide the keys?" It is because God would ultimately become man in the flesh, in the person of Jesus Christ, who will have all things subdued under him. So man would have all things subdued under him at last. That is why scripture says, "...All things are yours. Whether the world, or life, or death, or things present or things to come; all are yours." (1st Corinthians 3:21-22).

Death was included here. In other words, everything will be reversed as at the beginning planned by God. Death will be kept under man. Sure, Jesus had already obtained the keys of death and hell, which was once in the hands of Satan, because the devil obtained, or had the power (keys) of death and hell he stole at the garden. And when Jesus arose, he declared that all power is given unto him, in heaven and earth. And he reiterated the same to John, the apostle saying, "...I have (recovered) the keys of hell and death" (Revelations 1:18, emphasis mine). However, we shall soon discover that God made the devil marvel about his love for man beyond Lucifer's wildest dream and that his purpose must stand. God does whatsoever he pleased, and no man would dare ask him why (Psalm 135:6). Having holistically criticized the event in the garden, let's roll back the ball to what transpired between Lucifer and Eve.

Pursuit of knowledge

Eve desired something that would make her wise like Lucifer. What kind of wisdom? It is the wisdom to transform like Lucifer, a created spirit being who already possessed such abilities. Lucifer enticed her with such capabilities and then introduced her to what had transpired in the previous earth's experience of the sin of immorality and violence. She craved knowledge of the gods to be like Lucifer. She was fascinated, and so she desired such wisdom of the gods. She exhibited the pursuit of knowledge.

Similarly, humans are still searching for more knowledge to date. Man cannot be tamed in ignorance. She saw that the tree would make her wise. She went for it. Isn't this typical of women's craving for things?

She wouldn't have craved for it if there was no corresponding display of the benefit of Lucifer's beguiling nature and enticing words; hence she called Lucifer a deceiver (serpent). "And when the woman saw that the tree was good for food, and it was pleasant to the eyes, and a tree to be desired to make one wise, she took of the fruit thereof, and did eat, and also gave unto her husband with her, and they did eat. And the eyes of them both were opened, and they knew that they were naked, and they sewed fig leaves together and made them aprons" (Genesis3:6-7). She went for it so that she could be wise like the gods. "And the LORD God said, Behold man is become as one of us, to know good and evil: and now, lest he put forth his hand, and take also of the tree of life, and eat and live forever." (Genesis 3:22).

However, the knowledge obtained became their undoing. The knowledge brought worries and anxiety. The knowledge brought death, misery, violence, sickness, diseases, pain, etc. Without Adam, the story is incomplete. She influenced Adam to eat before both had their eyes opened. Eve's eyes were not opened until Adam ate because God's word to Adam placed him in a position above Eve; in addition to having been created first, hence God first addressed Adam, whom he commanded by his word. God went for his word in Adam and found out that the word was contaminated by influence. Eve was the closest to Adam as his helpmate. Their intimacy brought about the influence. She was the bone of Adam's bones and flesh of Adam's flesh. They were of the same kind of flesh and were attracted to each other as companions. You know, just like two children at ages 2 or 3 running after each other playing. If the first child climbs a table, the other will mimic them.

Lucifer knew that the easiest way to have Adam disobey God was through his wife, who was his intimate. Adam had been obedient until an external force acted on his thoughts. Adam said, "The woman whom thou givest to be with me, she gave me of the tree, and I did eat" (Genesis 3:12). Sorry, I'm not criticizing women, just that Satan also uses the same tactics to date. External forces often influence us from what God told us to do. Peter suggested to Jesus not to die; Jezebel influenced Ahab; Eve influenced Adam; Job's wife tried to influence Job; Sarai influenced Abram to have Haggai, to mention a few.

But after God sternly warned Abraham, Abraham was resolute in his decision not to be influenced by Sarah anymore; hence he didn't inform Sarah when he wanted to offer Isaac. God saw this resolved and dogged determination to obey God, so God said, "For I know Abraham that he will be in command of his children and his households..." (Genesis 18:19, emphasis mine). Eve emotionally influenced Adam to eat of the fruit. "For Adam was first formed, then Eve. And Adam was not deceived, but the woman being deceived was in the transgression" (1 Timothy 2:13-14). Well, whether Eve was in transgression or not, Adam was first called upon by God as the authority figure. God didn't give a commandment to Eve but to Adam. So God went straight to Adam, saying, "...Hast you eaten of the tree, whereof I commanded thee, that thou shouldest not eat?" (Genesis 3:11). You can see that God was direct to point questioning Adam.

Lucifer wouldn't have succeeded if he got Eve alone to eat of the forbidden tree; he needed Adam, who was the head. So he waited patiently for Adam to have partaken of the fruit of the tree. Adam's submission to Lucifer's deception means opposing God's simple instruction, which made Adam a servant to Lucifer. God did not spare Adam any way for listening to Eve, though he later showed mercy by being a Father.

God said that man has become as one of us. Man, in his childish state, who is less than a thousand years old, has obtained the knowledge of the gods. However, their eyes were opened to another phase of fear, shame, sickness, lack, pain, violence, and death. They became slaves instead of rulers over all things. Fear and shame set into their conscious mind. Man immediately began to fear animals and creeping things. Everything under Adam came under aggression and violence. The lion became enemies with man. The violent world pervaded man and the animal kingdom. Lions began to eat goats. Animals also began to eat one another. The violent world permeated the earth.

Flaming sword

Having obtained the knowledge of good and evil from the tree made them aware that they were naked, which brought shame upon them. Lucifer stole the keys unknown to Adam and Eve but used the same stolen keys to release the angels of death and hell locked up in the darkness of the deep alongside many other fallen spirits who immediately turned into human flesh to enjoy the land of the living. So Adam hid, having gained the consciousness of what God approves or disapproves of. Of course, only God originated the concept of good and evil before the formation of spirit men, angels, and cherubs who preexisted Adam.

The knowledge to understand that the tree of life is better, which, if he ate of it, would make him live forever. God had to immediately assign cherubims with a flaming sword to keep him from the tree of life. (Genesis 3:24). Adam and Eve were shocked about the outcome of their actions. God was upset with man by placing a sword that turned every way around the tree of life. Man had been manipulated and deceived into the world of violence once exclusive to spirit beings that preexisted Adam. For the first time, God showed Adam the sword.

"So he drove out the man, and he placed at the east of the garden of Eden Cherubims, and a flaming sword which turned every way, to keep the way of the tree of life" (Genesis3:24). Adam and Eve saw sword turning every way. The sword is a weapon or instrument invented by ancient men of old who lived on this earth before Genesis. God was displeased despite the warnings. Man had unwittingly chosen violence which would fastrack death, having forwarned Adam. Adam and Eve feared the sword and fled for their lives.

Shut out

Scripture recorded that Adam and Eve heard the voice of the LORD God, and they hid amongst the trees of the garden, meaning they knew God was heading in their direction. "And they heard the voice of the LORD God walking in the garden in the cool of the day, and Adam and his wife hid themselves from the presence of the LORD God amongst the trees of the garden. And the LORD called unto Adam, and said unto him, Where art thou? And he said, I heard thy voice in the garden, and I was afraid because I was naked; and I hid myself" (Genesis 3:8-10). They were used to seeing God in their sinless state. Why hide among the trees if they weren't used to seeing God? If God was dealing with Adam by voice, how else could they hide from God among trees?

If someone called you on your cell phone while in the bathroom, does that mean you cannot answer the phone call right there in your nudeness? Hearing a voice from the cloud doesn't call for hiding. God was used to visiting them one-on-one. If it was only God's voice, why would God search for them? Asking, "Where art thou?" The LORD was right in the garden in person, like he visited Abraham. But all of a sudden, Adam and Eve became afraid and hid amongst the trees of the garden. That tells us that they were used to seeing God. They were thrust out of seeing spirit realms into the natural world only. Their eyes were shut out from accessing God, unlike when they were in their sinless state. Scripture assured us that those who are redeemed and make it to heaven shall see God's face again (Revelation 22:4). Adam and Eve, in their pure state of heart, saw God one-on-one since the day they were created.

They heard the voice of the LORD God (who was) walking in the garden towards their direction. God asked Adam, "Where are you?" They hid physically, but Adam and Eve could no longer see God because of sin. A cloud or veil had come between man and God. The veil covered Adam, who thought he could still see God as usual, while hiding himself as soon as he became conscious of his nakedness. He never knew he had been thrust out from seeing God literally. A veil had come between God and man. The veil or covering cast is over all people and nations on the earth from the time of Adam and was referent in the scripture of truth which says, "And he will destroy in this mountain, the face of the covering over all people, and the veil that is spread over all nations." (Isaiah 25:7).

This explains why men cannot see God, who is their Creator. If fallen archangels, angels of death and destruction who sinned, were shut out in the darkness from seeing God, man would also be shut out from seeing God. The cloud of sin which came between resulted in the invisibility to the spirit realms. No more seeing God, but the voice of God. No more seeing the spiritual world, but only by hearing his voice. So God was heading in their direction. They couldn't see God anymore; hence the scripture says they heard the voice of the LORD God (who was) walking in the garden in the cool of the day. The Lord God was in the garden in person. Man was shut off from accessing the spiritual world. He is now concerned about the natural world.

Controlled by spirits talk

I believed the LORD God was approaching while singing His usual song to see his beloved creatures. But Adam hid himself being ashamed that he was naked. Lucifer had succeeded in destroying the relationship, and he is still doing that to date, not wanting man to have fellowship with God. God lost the first Adam to Lucifer. Adam fell short of the glory of God. This means Adam's descendants, over time, would no longer see God, angels, or cherubs. And from that moment, Satan also controlled man through spirit talk. Adam, on hearing a voice in the spiritual realm, is compelled to act. For this reason, Prophet Jeremiah cried out, saying, "O LORD, I know that way of man is not himself: it is not in man that walketh to direct his steps" (Jeremiah 10:23).

Man is being controlled by spirits talk. Some people hear voices of suicides mission. Others hear the voice of stealing, rapping, killing, hatred, cursing, envying, anger, lusting, etc. A voice suggesting to a leader to commence war with another country, and the leader would then sought out avenues of creating tensions unnecessarily. Man is being controlled by spirit voices to do the right or wrong things in life. Everyone is controlled by an inner voice. No matter who you are, you are controlled by one voice or the other. God talks to you, and also Satan and his demons. Even your spirit talks to you, and your soul immediately pick such signals.

Man stepped out of God's glory. However, whenever man steps back into God's glory, to an extent, man could once in a while experience angelic beings. Like Peter, James and John saw Elijah and Moses, who had lived on earth thousands of years back, standing with Jesus Christ (See Mark 9:1-9). Whenever man gets back into the glory of God, the veil could be seen through just that it is darkly, which I have touched on regarding the sea of glass. But because man had fallen short of glory, man would remain blind to the spiritual world. Some prophets of God see angels directly whenever their eyes are opened. Man is being controlled by voices that often compel him to obey much of the time. Adam was oblivious of pre-Adamic history coupled with being formed with a childish mind, so he was deceived. I believe that is why God showed Adam and Eve mercy, despite the unrepentant attitude of Adam. And this has been the problem of Adam – giving an alibi! God does not tolerate anyone who justifies his shortcomings. God said, "He dwells on high with the humble and contrite spirit."

And Jesus gave a narrative of two persons who went to pray, in which one of them was sincere in his prayers unto God, acknowledging his weakness and confessing sins truthfully. And there was this other guy, probably a religious Pharisee who always claimed 'holy than thou attitude condemning others, but has his weakness as well. He had a log of wood or beam, according to Matthew 7:4. After both have ended their prayers unto God, Jesus being God himself, who knew what they had prayed, made a clear statement about the outcome of their prayers. And Jesus said the one who was sincere (truthful and humble) went home more justified than the other who seemed to show self-righteousness but was hypocritical. (See Luke 18: 10-14).

You would do yourself a lot of disfavor, being proud, and remain unchanging to God. God held Adam accountable for his choice, irrespective of the excuse about his wife,

Eve. Those who claim self-righteousness and defend themselves over their wrongs are disregarded in the sight of God. However, God, in infinite mercy, clothed Adam and Eve, which shows nakedness would have been taken care of if they hadn't sinned anyway. But an amateur would think that God wanted man uncovered. Some think Lucifer's suggestion was in order. If not, man would have remained nude. That is childish thinking, far from the truth. Was it not the same God who clothed them at last? Lucifer coveted the kingdom of this world. He wanted Adam to worship him as the God of this world. He envied Adam. These are the essential points of what transpired in the Garden of Eden.

Chapter 16

Lucifer's Deposition

God couldn't have permitted the Cherub – Lucifer to tempt Adam and, after that, curse him. It doesn't make sense! God isn't a schizophrenic! The truth is Lucifer betrayed God after several billion years in the Garden of Eden. God was provoked; hence he cursed him, and the curse deformed Lucifer on the spot into a dragon serpent for the betrayal of trust. Lucifer forgot his placement that he was in the class of God as God's direct minister. He was cursed above every cattle and every beast of the field. In other words, he was stripped of his royalty as a cherub and became a dragon similar to a serpent that crawls, though still with two feet to stand, like the dinosaurs or penguins. Penguins have feathers, but Lucifer lost his hands completely even when he transforms himself. This implied his hands were plucked off immediately when God spoke.

He deserved it because he betrayed God. He had underlying motives of perverting truth and revealing secrets known to spirit beings in the pretext of telling the truth. "And the LORD God said unto the serpent; because thou has done this, thou art cursed above all cattle and above every beast of the field; upon thy belly shalt thou go, and dust shalt thou eat all the days of thy life" (Genesis 3:14). In other words, the Lord God said unto the 'cherub' is what should have been written, because God couldn't have cursed a serpent to become a serpent again. As earlier stated, the word serpent was a metaphor for being a deceiver, which portrays a general description of Satan in the scriptures. Lucifer's betrayal provoked God; hence he cursed him to become a dragon-serpent looking terrific or horrible.

Lucifer was a trusted cherub in that hierarchy and capacity who envied ordinary man and then imagined a coup against God. Lucifer's action of disclosing such secrets to Eve was tantamount to child abuse. It is like someone teaching your young children certain deviant behaviors which might corrupt their minds at such cognitive stages. He was envious of man being given attention more than anything else. Adam being devoid of the knowledge of good and evil makes God laugh and happy, just like some parents enjoy their young toddlers playing at home. Children at this stage make the home enjoyable; hence the scripture says children are the heritage of the LORD. God enjoys children so much. Lucifer was envious of this relationship.

Lucifer was cursed into a serpent for thwarting God's love and happiness for man. Many still think the serpent referred to in Genesis implies the usual snake. No. That isn't what the scripture says. Many are just assuming things. Snakes generally don't possess hands and legs. But this serpent has feet like the penguins walking on their feet. Let's see an accurate description of the serpent used: "After this, I saw in the night visions, and behold a fourth beast, dreadful and terrible, and strong exceedingly; and it had great iron teeth: it devoured and brake in pieces, and stamped the residue with the feet of it: and it was diverse from all the beasts that were before it; and it had ten horns...whose teeth were iron, and his tail of brass; which devoured, brake in pieces, and stamped the residue with his feet" (Daniel 7:7 and 19). And in Revelation 12:3-4, the scripture says, "And there appeared another wonder in heaven; and behold a red dragon, having seven heads and ten horns, and seven crowns upon his heads. And his tail drew the third part of the stars of heaven, and did cast them to the earth: and the dragon stood before the woman which was ready to be delivered..."

In context, he became a dragon with a tail moving like a serpent creeping upon his belly. He was seen stamping upon other beasts with his feet. You can see from the scriptures that after the curse from God, his feet were retained, which did not enable him to stand in an upright position; instead, he crawls on his belly, moving with his feet. He is known as the old serpent in the book of Revelation, which is actually a dragon-serpent. God couldn't have cursed a serpent to become a serpent again if he was a physical serpent before the curse. However, he retained his ability to transform into a man, being a spirit.

Nails of brass

Being a dragon, he retained certain features such as iron teeth, a tail, nails of brass, ten horns, eyes all over, and exceedingly dreadful. This serpentine shape, after the curse from God, made him fierce and horrible. Hence the scripture referred to him as the King of Terror (Job 18:14). If stretched, he is more than 20ft long, a black and shining dragon serpent with two legs. This is based on the vision I had of this shining black dragon-serpent along the tunnels to hell, of which I knew in that vision he was. His mouth always speaks great things against God in blasphemy (Daniel 7:8 and 19). Often he speaks against God because he has bitter envying against man and God. His deformation into a serpentine shape still hurts him. People resent their enemies often by speaking against them.

The book of Revelation 12:15-16 puts things in proper perspective regarding the word serpent used in scriptures. It says, "And the serpent cast out of his mouth water as a flood after the woman, that he might cause her to be carried away of the flood. And the earth helped the woman, and the earth opened her mouth and swallowed up the flood the dragon had cast out of his mouth." We can see the scriptures used serpent or dragon interchangeably. And the third person pronoun subjective case 'he' was also used, indicating a man cherub. We can see that he is capable of casting out a flood from his mouth. Lucifer retained certain spiritual powers as a spirit with which he could manipulate humans to follow his ways. He's got the majority of followers in the world of men who believe in his powers to achieve fame, riches, and the ability to oppress others. Lucifer had been with God for so long, and it's expected that he learned certain secrets by which he could transform into different creatures.

Such powers were not withdrawn from him despite his hands being cut off. Some ignorant folks say Satan has no more power. But the scriptures never said so. Jesus said, "I give unto you power to tread on serpents and scorpions and over all the powers of your enemies..." (Luke 10:19). Jesus said he gave us (believers) power over... And even after Jesus rose from the dead, he said Satan would be responsible for the death of some disciples of the church of Smyrna (Revelation 2:8- 10). God also cut off Lucifer's food chain from heaven. God said, "Dust shall thou eat." The curse placed upon Lucifer, coupled with the change in his food chain, points to the fact that Lucifer was separated from God in the Garden of Eden.

We saw from the scriptures that Lucifer could still stand to his feet. One time, Satan stood against Joshua, the high priest. And he showed me Joshua the high priest standing before the angel of the LORD, and Satan standing at his right hand to resist him" (Zachariah 3:1). This shows Satan retained his foot to stand. Unlike typical snakes in the forests that have no feet. You could recollect earlier the scripture said Satan often walked up and down, to and fro, upon the earth in the spiritual realm, indicating that he retained his feet (See Job 1:7). His greatest force lies in his hands; hence they were cut off. However, parts of his body remain useful by which he causes havoc, given that he retained his spiritual powers.

The devil can cause fire to fall from the sky, and he can also cause a flood of rain waters upon the earth. As a spirit, he exercises power over elements of nature, to an extent, having perverted his wisdom in manipulating things as far as performing miracles on earth. The manifestation of the powers of darkness is witnessed in our world every day, with a good chunk of the world's population practicing enchantments, star gazing, sorcery, etc. Lucifer is a high-ranking cherub who knows much more than most angels and archangels. He hasn't been seen by so many people who claimed to have seen him. He's a very high rank being in the class of God. Daniel, in the scriptures, saw him in a clear vision and accurately described him. He's got many departments in his kingdom, categorized as principalities, powers, and wickedness in high places under him who would stop at nothing but deceive humans.

Perpetual enmity

It was observed that as soon as Lucifer succeeded in swindling Adam and Eve, God told him that he already had a plan B. God immediately told Lucifer his plan B - the second Adam – the person of Jesus Christ as in a mystery hidden from Lucifer. Lucifer was perplexed that God was dogged to have man dominate all things as he had spoken. However, at this point, Lucifer had already succeeded in his plot over the first Adam. Lucifer was never willing to have man rule over all things. He was so proud and opposed to the idea of the man formed, so he rebelled. It wasn't because he was a very beautiful angel as a light-bearer and became proud of his beauty as purported in some quarters. Those are unfounded theories taught as being "scriptural" that result from many being superficial in studying the scriptures.

Someone might say, "But the scripture talked about beauty as one of the reasons for Lucifer's disposition," citing Ezekiel 28:17. You need to listen to the Holy Ghost, who inspires and teaches. He told me these truths, and I just wrote them down and then scoured the scriptures to substantiate what I was told. I don't mean to denigrate anyone who might have wrongly taught about the scriptures based on their level of understanding. One time, I read a translated scriptural version that erroneously interchanged Lucifer as 'the Morning Star, which is entirely out of scriptural context; men erring in translations not knowing the scriptures. I don't fancy translated versions because they can be interpreted without the Holy Spirit speaking; they are just vocabularies to embellish and amplify words. More so, I have been privileged to read a few verses of the angel's scriptures in a vision, which were written in typical King James Versions. I'm not against anyone translating the scriptures for easier understanding, just that I comprehend the original King James Version, which sticks more to memory than the translated versions.

Lucifer hated the man of the dust with bitter envy. God said, "I will put enmity between you and the woman and between thy seed and her seed." In other words, I will put a perpetual enmity between you, Satan, and the woman and between your descendants and her descendants. Satan tricked her to topple Adam. So God had to put enmity between Satan and the woman. "The seed of the woman shall bruise thy head (authority or power), and thou shalt bruise his heel (persecute, attack, and kill)" (emphasis mine). God knew Satan's envy and hatred towards the man he made to rule over all things of which Eve was unaware. Eve thought Satan was a nicety divulging such secrets against God. Even Adam was unaware of his authority over the angels, so Lucifer swindled and toppled him.

God had already foreordained his Son, who would eventually restore all things to the status quo - a hidden mystery kept from Lucifer and the angels before the foundation of the world. The second Adam was predicted to emerge from the bloodline of the woman. Why the bloodline of the woman? It is because the weaker vessel, which Satan disdained, would produce a seed (man) that would topple Satan's spiritual dominance over the earth. Jesus Christ was the second Adam born of the Virgin Mary, while the devil's seed is the antichrist. The first Adam submitted the keys of death and hell to Satan unwittingly, but the second Adam retrieved the keys. Why the use of the second Adam? It is simply because the second Adam birthed a new breed of people called born again or sons of God who weren't born of the will of man nor the will of the flesh but were spiritually begotten of the Spirit.

Moreover, God saw Lucifer's intention to take possession of the earth in the same manner ancient people acted in the pre-Adamic world, which was why the seed issue arose in Genesis 3. God knew that the cherub Lucifer wanted his compatriots to unite and chase humans out of the earth. Lucifer wanted fallen spirits and their descendants to replenish the earth so that they would re- possessed the land of the living instead of Adam, whom they regarded as foolish, weak things and based things of this world. God had foreknowledge of Lucifer's intention to procreate his own seed upon the earth. God sees the end from the beginning (Isaiah 46:10).

God created the earth for Adam's dominance, not the giant fallen spirits. However, since man had unwittingly submitted his authority to Lucifer, God would still need the man of the dust to continue the earth and topple the enemy and avenger. The avenger used in Psalms 8:2 speak of ancient people who intended to avenge man of the dust. An avenger means someone who wants to take vengeance. Spirit beings, in conjunction with the enemy Satan are the avengers intending to re-possess the earth instead of man. This was the earth they once occupied for several billion years. They were phased out for Adam and his descendants to populate; hence the scripture used the word replenish the earth in Genesis.

God used a typical 'man of the dust' whom Satan despised to topple Satan's authority. That was the reason why God said, "The seed of the woman shall bruise thy head." When the scriptures say, "Jesus Christ didn't take on him the nature of an angel, but the seed of Abraham," it means the man of the dust whom Satan despised and hated, as weak or foolish things of this world were hidden in Jesus who came to topple the devil without an angelic body (See Hebrews 2:16). Man was called foolish things or naive things of this world because he is got no spiritual dynamics at manipulating things.

The Son of Man, as the seed of the woman, took the keys of death and hell from Satan. Herein lies the sayings that if the prince of this world "had known it, they would not have crucified the Lord of glory" (1st Corinthians 2:8). This was the undoing of Satan by the same human he called foolish things. Satan opposed God's choice of forming man of the dust Adam. In his pride of opposing God's choice, he lost his hierarchy, and God disposed him to join the prison darkness under the deep. God proved to the devil that he is the Almighty God and that his word can never fail. God said that His counsel shall stand and that he will do all his pleasures (Isaiah 46:10). I believe Satan should have been regretting his actions by now, though, too late!

Thoughts of overthrowing God

God would always declare his Word before executing them since there is a spiritual law that suggests words go before God for anything to be formed or created. Scripture indicates that God does enunciate words before things spoken come into manifestation. "For he spake, and it was done; he commanded, and it stood fast" (Psalms 33:9). He spake, then it was carried out, he commanded, it stood fast. And in the book of Isaiah 55:11 says, "So shall my word be that goeth forth out of my mouth: it shall not return unto me void, but it shall accomplish that which I please, and it shall prosper in that thing where I sent it." In other words, the Godhead is known for words. All things were formed by the Word.

For Jesus to become a high priest, a spoken word consecrated as declared by the Godhead. "...the word of the oath... maketh the Son who is consecrated forevermore" (Hebrews 7:28). In a similar vein, God had to declare the deposition of Lucifer to effect changes in the everlasting realms. God went on to say, "...I will cast thee as a profane (outrage) out of the mountain of God: I will destroy thee O covering cherub from the midst of the stones of fire. Thine heart was lifted because of thy beauty; thou hast corrupted thy wisdom because of thy brightness: I will cast thee to the ground, I will lay thee before kings (fallen stars and sons of God who fell before Lucifer in the darkness of the deep), and they shall behold thee. Thou hast defiled thy sanctuaries by the multitude of thine iniquities, by the iniquity of thy traffic, therefore will I bring forth a fire from the midst of thee, it shall devour thee, and I will bring thee to the ashes upon the earth in the sight of all them that behold thee" (Ezekiel28). The iniquity of thy traffic will be expounded shortly.

So, we can see that the cherub was deposited by a spoken word from God. God brought fire out of the exact spot where Lucifer's seat had been in God's holy mountain and threw it down to the deep (hell). "But thou art cast out of thy grave (plain) like an abominable branch, and as the raiment of those that are slain, thrust through with a sword, that go down to the stones of the pit; as a carcass trodden under feet" (Isaiah 14:19). When the scripture says, "cast out of thy grave, or plain, or position like an abominable branch" it means Lucifer lost his seat or place of authority in the holy mountain of God as a cherub who was once part of the kingdom of God to join his comrades who had been in the prison of darkness (our dark universe), hence the scriptures used the phrase 'as the remnant of those that are slain, thrust through with a sword.'

Other comrades or hordes of darkness were already thrust through with swords before Lucifer was cast out to join the stars in space. Lucifer formed an alliance with the principalities of death and hell, releasing them to occupy the earth. And because he was the one who released them, they welcomed his ideology that Lucifer wanted them freed, so the rebellion to overthrow the Godhead and repossess the earth once more. Lucifer's actions here could also connect to the parable Jesus gave about an unjust steward whose authority was about to be taken from him, and he had to craftily take sides with the master's debtors so that when he failed, they may receive him into an everlasting habitation (See Luke 16:1-13). Although God decreed him to rule over the fallen stars of heaven and all sons of God under the darkness, he had to seek support in his bid to overthrow God.

Lucifer defiled his sanctuary (his office), and his seat was thrown out. He was trashed out to hell (an ever-expanding planet(s) under the darkness), prepared for deviant spirits. That was how Lucifer lost his hierarchy and joined other fallen spirits of death and destruction shut out in the prison of darkness – in this universe. It was never by war in heaven which we have been taught over the years, which many have erroneously referenced to the book of Revelation 12:7, which says, "And there was war in heaven...." God is too big for a small creature like Satan to be displaced. There was never war in the very throne room of heaven where the angels dwell, much more the stones of fire where God lives. I know this might sound weird against popular religious beliefs and teachings over several hundred decades which portrayed war taking place in heaven for Lucifer to have been evicted from God's kingdom. No worries, I'd come to these proofs from the scriptures and correct these aged long teachings, which you will realize scriptural truths for yourself.

Unfortunately, the scriptures never said that some 'stars of God' were influenced by Lucifer's propaganda opposing God's idea of the man of the dust to rule over all things. You know we have had some wrong theological teachings over the years: Lucifer took one-third of heaven's angels during the war that broke out in heaven. I can tell you that most theologians have erred in not knowing the scriptures. Challenging such notions over the years might seem weird, but I can tell you such assumptions are entirely wrong. I'd come to all this as we progress. Lucifer was acting on his own and was only thrown out to meet other deviant spirits already shut out in this dark universe.

As said, Lucifer could be likened to the unjust steward whose lord would have his account of his stewardship. Because he would be displaced, he quickly allied with his lord's debtors so that they could receive him into an 'everlasting habitation' (Luke 16:1-9). Lucifer knew he would be stripped of his authority; having betrayed God immediately joined the stars of heaven, including the angels of death and hell. Satan had been stripped of his authority in the throne room of God forever. In the nearest future, it would require one archangel to grab and lock up Satan, according to Revelation 20:1-2.

Now, you must understand that the word 'devil' isn't ascribed to Lucifer alone. The scripture used 'devils' in place of demons as well. So demons are referred to as devils. (See Leviticus 17:7, Psalms 106:37, Matthew 8:16, etc.) However, Lucifer, the highest fallen cherub amongst the devil, was distinguished as Devil because he was the first spirit to think of overthrowing God – designated as a murderer. The Lord God trusted him as a guardian cherub before he subtly stole the keys of death and hell kept under Adam. Jesus called him the Thief. Lucifer betrayed the trust reposed on him by stealing. And God said, "How art thou fallen from heaven (lose your hierarchy as Cherub), O Lucifer, son of the morning. How art thou cut down to the ground which did weaken (cause men to sin, sick or die) the nations! For thou said in thine heart, I will ascend into heaven, I will exalt my throne above the stars (angels) of God: I will sit also upon the mount of the congregation, in the side of the north: I will ascend above the heights of the clouds, I will be like the most High" (Isaiah 14:12-14, Emphasis mine)

God was lamenting the fall of Lucifer, who was such a high-ranking cherub, and still, he deviated from God's ways because of envy, which led to pride and ultimately challenging God's orders. Lucifer's pride, referred to in the scripture, was his opposition to God, not his beauty per se. I would come to the scriptural context of the word 'beauty.' However, let's look at the proper behavior expected of every human being. In Zachariah 1:13, an angel was found to have approached God in humility, pleading with God regarding the children of Israel, asking, "How long will God keep his indignation against Israel after seventy years of captivity?" And the scripture captured, The LORD answered the angel with good and comfortable words. Moses, as earlier explained, was found faithful in God's entire house for a testimony because even when Moses realized that he had a filiation with God in the spirit realm as one of the sons of God, he was still humble even though God denied him the Promised Land even after he pleaded severally with God.

But in the case of Lucifer, he was reactive and became violent, and the Spirit of God departed from him. He would have humbled himself as a cherub and approached God by presenting his opinion. Still, he felt God took the wrong step in appointing man to run the earth instead of fallen angels and ancient people. More so, crowning man with such honor and glory when the man formed was weak and naive, unknown to him, and God had a plan for why he chose to make man a little lower than the angels and at the same time crown him with glory and honor. God had Jesus Christ in mind. Lucifer failed since he didn't display any form of humility in the dispute. God dwells with the contrite and humble spirit but resists the proud.

So, Lucifer felt he had what he wanted - the keys to death and destruction, which made him proud, thinking he was untouchable. He gained a kingdom for himself. He's got the earth for himself. His next move was to overthrow God. He felt with the fallen angels of death and destruction that, he could utilize that support to overthrow God. Unfortunately for him, God was not created, he created death himself.

Orchestrated rebellion

It was obvious Lucifer thought of undertaking an ascension risk back into his position in the holy mountain of God, the place of the stones of fire where he had been before he fell into Eden. Like I told you, he was in the garden when God delivered his judgment against him for his betrayal. Lucifer had mapped out his plans to overthrow God; hence he said he would ascend to heaven to be like God, having obtained the keys of death and destruction stolen from Adam, but he forgot that he was only a creature, not God. His knowledge was still limited. Jesus referred to him as a murderer from the beginning. John 8:44 says, "He was a murderer from the beginning..." Meaning that he orchestrated rebellion with the forces of death and destruction with the intent to overthrow the Godhead - an impossible adventure.

God saw his thoughts and had his hands cut off by the voice alone, which says, "Upon thy belly shall thou go." Having walked up and down in the holy mountain of God, Lucifer could have posed a more serious challenge, but God knew where his greatest strength lies, and God stripped him of it. God stripped his hands as a cherub so that his hands could not perform his enterprise. As it is written, "He disappointed the devices of the crafty, so that their hands cannot perform their enterprise. He taketh the wise in their craftiness..." (Job 5:12-13). God stripped him of his plans to use his hands, so his hands could not perform his intended overthrow. He then knew his Maker could cut off his hands without a sword, just by voice. What a mighty God! Lucifer intended to carry out a coup against God.

In the book of Revelation, this form of rebellion will be permitted on this earth once again in the nearest future to satisfy the devil's ambition. Lucifer will gather a multitude of people (spirit beings) in human flesh to battle against God on earth (Jerusalem, the capital of Israel) with the intent to overthrow, but God himself is a consuming fire. The scripture referred to this final battle in which the principalities, namely, Gog and Magog, as fallen princes, will influence a multitude of people to battle against Jesus Christ and the saints of God, which is the battle to overthrow Almighty God (Jesus Christ). Revelation 16:14 says, "For they are the spirits of the devils, working miracles, which go forth unto the kings of the earth and the whole world to gather them to the battle of that great day of Almighty God." Lucifer wanted the throne of God. A creature battling his Maker sounds funny anyway!

And we already saw that this battle will be wrapped up as written in Revelation 20:7-9, which says, "...Satan shall be loosed out of his prison, and shall go out to deceive the nations which are in the four quarters of the earth, Gog and Magog, to gather together to battle: the number of whom is as the sand of the sea. And they went up on the breath of the earth and compassed the camp of the saints about, and the beloved city: fire came down from God out of heaven and devoured them." The beloved city is Jerusalem. Let's get back on track.

So the LORD said to Lucifer, "With thine wisdom and thine understanding, thou hast gotten thee riches gold and silver into thine treasures. By thine great wisdom and by thy trafficking, hast thou increased thy riches (power of death, and control of the earth), and thine heart is lifted up because of thine riches" (Ezekiel 4-5, emphasis mine). He stole the treasures of the earth, the gold and silver. He stole man's glory and took the keys of death kept in the forbidden tree. So Lucifer increased his riches as soon as he obtained the keys of death and hell. This also made him set his heart in pride, thinking he was powerful, and felt he needed not to submit to God anymore.

Unfortunately, his treason failed. Hence, God said unto Satan, "Wilt thou yet say before him that slayeth thee, I am God? But thou shalt be a man and no God, in the hand of him that slayeth thee and thou shalt be brought down to hell the side of the pit" (Ezekiel 28:9, Isaiah 14:15). In other words, Lucifer was in the class of God. So he would have said to the cherub or archangel assigned to cast him out of the Garden of Eden that he is God. He already had this superiority mindset as God. God chased him out of the garden down to hell through the instrumentality of other cherubs or principal angels in heaven to the side of the pit. This implies hell as a pit that pre-existed Lucifer's eviction. Like I told you, there were fallen spirits imprisoned in darkness before Lucifer fell.

God also told Lucifer that Lucifer has limits as a man and that he is not God. Lucifer being a cherub, was also a man. The book of Isaiah 14:16 says, "...Is this the man that makes the earth to tremble, and did shake the kingdoms?" This speaks of the future, which states that people in hell will be shocked when they eventually behold Satan in man's shape and would be wondering, "Is this the man that makes the whole earth shake?" He was a creature and could never become God in any capacity.

Become weak

Moreover, God said to Lucifer, "Thou sealest up the sum (perfect of my creation that understands all mysteries) full of wisdom and perfect in beauty. Thou hast been in Eden the garden of God ...thou art the anointed cherub that covereth, and I have set thee so: Thou was upon the holy mountain of God, thou hast walked amid the stones of fire. Thou was perfect in thy beauty (of holiness) from the day thou wast created till iniquity was found in thee. By the multitude of they merchandise (exchange of earthly wealth with man by deception), they have filled the midst of thee with violence (treasonable thoughts), and thou hast sinned". "Therefore, I will cast thee as a profane out of the mountain of God: I will destroy you O covering cherub, from the midst of the stones of fire. Thine heart was lifted because of thy beauty (placement), thou hast corrupted thy wisdom because of thy brightness (starlight): I will cast thee to the ground (universe under darkness), I will lay thee before kings, and they shall behold thee...thou shalt be a terror (King of Terror) and never shall thou be anymore (will cease as the king of terror after a while)" (Ezekiel 28:12-19, Emphasis mine).

Which beauty was God referring to? The beauty of being a holy cherub placed in such an enormous authority, having walked on the stones of fire with God. Not just physical beauty. There is a spiritual beauty of holiness, which God only has. He once told me: "You will behold my holiness when you come into my kingdom." In other words, God is so pure. Lucifer was described perfectly in beauty (holy), having been with God in the very stones of fire realms. But now stands in opposition to God over Adam, who was made to be in charge of all things. He suddenly became proud in opposition to God's choice of Adam, as though he had become God because he obtained the keys to death and hell.

God further said, "Hell from beneath is moved for thee to meet thee at thy coming: it is stirred up the dead (fallen angels) for thee, even all the chief ones (chief prince angels) of the earth; it hath raised up from their thrones all the kings of the nations. All they (fallen princes and angels) shall speak and say unto thee, Art thou also become weak as we? Art thou become like unto us? Thy pomp (magnificence) is brought down to the grave (hell), and the noise of thy viols (sweet voice): the worm is spread under thee, and the worms cover thee. How art thou fallen from heaven, O Lucifer, son of the morning! How art thou cut to the ground which did weaken the nations!" (Isaiah 14: 9-12, emphasis mine).

In other words, Lucifer's place of authority was removed out of the mountain of God to meet with fallen angels of death and destruction in hell. Scripture says hell from beneath is moved to meet with thee. Meaning fallen angels of death and destruction will welcome you, Lucifer. The principalities and powers of darkness shall surrender their thrones or lordship for you, Lucifer, to lead them, and that was how Satan became the King of terror. He became the head of those principalities and all fallen spirits. God also said, and they shall say unto you, "Art thou become weak as we? Art thou become like unto us? That is, have you anointed cherub come to join us? You great commander in heaven has come to join us and become like us?"

Lucifer joined fallen spirits who were already in our dark universe as soon as he beguiled Adam and Eve.

God said, "Behold, therefore I will bring strangers upon thee, the terrible of the nations: and they shall draw their sword against the beauty of thy wisdom, and they shall defile thy brightness. They shall bring thee down to the pit, and thou shalt die the death of them that are slain in the midst of the seas" (Ezekiel 28:8). We can see that the beauty of Lucifer refers to his rank, not just physical attraction. That is, as a cherub having such authority in God's kingdom. Then God declared that he would bring fallen princes who are already in darkness upon Lucifer to defile his brightness and send him to the pit of hell, and he shall die the death of them slain in the midst of the seas. The midst of the seas talked about the universe under darkness. Thou shalt die the death of them slain in the midst of the seas means Lucifer will fall like one of the princes. He will experience death just like ancient people or stars of heaven perished in their bodies.

Chapter 17

Bessom of Destruction

Lucifer intended to populate the earth, but God saw his imagination. He desired the earth to have been his kingdom, where he would rule over instead of Adam. Don't forget this was the earth the fallen sons of God once occupied. On seeing the woman (and future women) capable of replicating, Lucifer immediately purposed in his heart to influence fallen sons of God to have intercourse with the daughters of men, which might result in procreating giants upon the earth. Lucifer saw the possibility of replicating through women in the future since he knew spirit beings were also flesh. The fallen sons of God who once lived on this earth were flesh of brass, not made of bones in their skeletons. But it could turn into flesh like a man. It was a window of opportunity for Lucifer and his comrades. But God had foreknowledge of Lucifer's dream in a split second.

Lucifer's dream came to fruition when fallen sons of God began to rape women to populate the earth with their offspring, and this led to the violence on the earth then. Genesis 6:1-2 says, "And it came to pass, when men began to multiply upon the face of the earth, and daughters were born unto them, that the sons of God saw the daughters of men that were fair; and they took them wives of all which they chose." The scripture was emphatic that they took them wives of all which they chose" In other words, they forcefully raped women and killed the men because they were giants. But the natural Adam's descendants also possess the might to have these giants killed, just as Lamech slew one of the giants. Lucifer intended to eliminate Adams' desendants and have the earth populated through the fallen sons of God instead. That was why the seed issue arose in Genesis when God talked about the seed of the devil and the seed of the woman.

When the violence of giants raping women erupted, God had to step in because these fallen spirits who turned flesh had already gained access to the earth. They introduced violence and corrupted the natural Adam's descendants, teaching them violence and rape. So imagine a scenario in which Adam's natural descendant was killed and his wife taken. Of course, he will fight back. And that was how the earth learned the violence of killing one another with no government. And suppose these giants had succeeded in occupying the earth without any corresponding challenge from God. In that case, man would have been chased out forever, and God's purpose of recreation was defeated.

God had foreknowledge of Lucifer's resolve and said, "Thou shalt not be joined with them in burial, because thou hast destroyed thy land, and slain thy people: the seed of the evil-doer shall not be renowned. Prepare slaughter for his children for the iniquity of their fathers; that they do not rise, possess the land, or fill the world's face with cities. For I will rise up against them saith the LORD of hosts, and cut off from Babylon the name, and remnant, and son, and nephew, saith the LORD. I will also make it a possession for the bittern and pools of water: I will sweep it with the besom of destruction, saith the LORD of hosts. The LORD of host hath sworn, saying, Surely, as I have thought, so shall it come to pass; and as I have purposed, so shall it stand" (Isaiah 14:20-24)

God foresaw Lucifer came to kill and destroy the human race (thy people), who are natural Adam's descendants, so God also prepared slaughter for the seed of the fallen sons of God (evil-doers). What the scripture implies by "They shall not be joined unto men in burial" is that the flood of Noah would sweep the giants away, including their seeds, who were also giants born of women. God hates seeing spirit beings as giants and their offsprings being joined in burial with Adam's descendants. All seeds of the devil as giants born on earth during Noah's days were swept off the earth by the flood. God had foreknowledge of Lucifer's thoughts that if Lucifer and his comrades were unsuccessful in their coup against God, then Lucifer would resort to procreating the earth with his seed to advance his kingdom on earth. So God said, "Prepare slaughter for his children for the iniquity of their fathers, that they do not rise, nor possess the land, nor fill the world with cities." What slaughter was God talking about? God was talking about using a flood of waters as a vehicle of destruction.

God responded to Lucifer's intention by saying that his children, who would be giants amongst men, would be swept off the earth with a besom of destruction, which is the great flood in Genesis 7:11. God had to counteract Lucifer's plans. "For I will rise up against them saith the LORD of hosts…I will also make it a possession for the bittern, and pools of water: and I will sweep it with the besom of destruction, saith the LORD of hosts". (Isaiah 14:23). Remember Genesis 6:4, it talks about the seed born by women were men of renown. God already said, "…The seed of the evil-doer shall not be renowned." The renowned seed of the giants was upon this refurbished earth. God was mindful of saving mankind from being displaced out of the earth by these giants. I will expound on the giants as we progress on how they were eventually eliminated even after the flood of Noah.

Lucifer introduced witchcraft, cultism, secret societies, stargazing, necromancy, idolatry, etc., through his comrades after the flood so that mankind would associate and worship him. He has advanced his work amongst humans, raising men and women that would implement his programs through secret societies, promising them fame, long life, power, wealth, etc. But those who haven't spent time ruminating about an after-life experience often fall prey to his antics. In our societies, the men of renown or celebrities (as currently used) were once the seed of the devils. The terminology men of renown emanated from 'men of old' or 'ancient people.' Fallen spirits no more procreate giants, but average humans and they have infiltrated the earth.

The first promise Satan gives to his followers is fame and wealth. That is, to be popular and celebrated by all men. The scripture says, "For that which highly esteemed among men, is abomination in the sight of God" (Luke 16:15). Someone might hastily quote saying, "But the scripture says we shall reign on the earth." That scripture talked about the reign of the righteous in the new world after this world is over. The scripture has forewarned that the seed of the devils will not be established upon the earth. God would sweep off the entire lineage of fallen spirits, including their remnants as sons or nephews, etc. No seed of the devil will have access to the kingdom of God (the New Jerusalem) in the earth to come.

Multitude of iniquities

Moreover, God said to Lucifer, "Thou hast defiled thy sanctuaries by the multitude of thine iniquities, by the iniquity of thy traffick" (Ezekiel 28:18). In other words, whenever Lucifer left the very everlasting realms (stones of fire) to visit Adam and Eve in the Garden of Eden, he would often see fallen archangels, angels and ancient people shut under darkness. He was trafficking through the darkness covering space to the earth. It was this movement that got him thinking and corrupted his heart. There is no way he could have brought evil into the throne room of God because the concept of evil was excluded from the light zone universe. Lucifer got contaminated during his visit to this darkness zone. Sin or evil cannot cross into the throne room of God for whatsoever reason. Lucifer's repugnant thoughts defiled his sanctuary (seat), or his thoughts were seen in the very throne of God from afar. His heart was x-rayed while planning his revolution on earth while in the Garden of Eden.

The word "multitude of thine iniquities" implies unrighteousness or violent disposition attributed to Lucifer during his trafficking up and down. The scripture was emphatic on Lucifer's iniquities, which I would like to enumerate: The number one sin of Satan was pride. His placement in God's kingdom as a wise and trusted cherub made him proud to the extent that he objected to God's decision to have man rule over all things. Although his drive to worship was a function of his usual duty over several billion years in the holy mountain of God, he also loved being worshipped. He already had the mindset of God dwelling in the everlasting realms with God. God must have probably seen Lucifer's discontentment over Adam's ordainment to run the affairs of the earth. God knew his pride, so God immediately had to inform Lucifer that he (God) would bring seed from the same woman to inherit the earth - the person of Jesus Christ, despite Lucifer's toppling of the first Adam's authority.

If we connect the dots, we see this in Psalms 82:8, which says, Arise, O God, judge the earth: for thou shalt inherit all nations. This scripture perfectly described Jesus Christ, who would inherit all the earth, as the second Adam (Man). God knew Lucifer and his comrades would also oppose the second Adam (Jesus Christ) as a man of the dust. Lucifer organized a strong resistance against God's decision to have the second Adam rule over the earth as well after the fall of the first Adam. But God said to Lucifer with his comrades, "Yet have I set my king upon my holy hill of Zion" (Psalms 2:6).

Lucifer and his comrades in the spiritual realms formed a formidable resistance towards God's choice of His Son Jesus to come to the earth and have all things subdued under him. But these hordes of darkness, referred to as kings and rulers of the earth, took counsel together against the LORD and his anointed (Jesus Christ), saying, "Let us break their bands asunder, and cast away their cords from us" (Psalms 2:2-3). However, God gave a double assurance to his word that Man (the second Adam) will rule over the earth, and he will be the one to be worshipped - Jesus Christ. To be doubly sure, God said unto his Son, "Ask of me, and I will give thee the heathen for thine inheritance, and the uttermost parts of the earth for thine possession" (Psalm 2:8). God's word is infallible.

The number two iniquity of Satan is betrayal. Satan subtlety disclosed to Eve what God was preventing man from attaining - violence and sin consciousness. Satan is never to be trusted. God trusted him so much to have him visit Adam and Eve, and he knew what God forewarned Adam. He capitalized on and hijacked the opportunity against God. Little wonder God said, "...by the iniquity of thy traffic," showing his freedom of movement between heaven and earth corrupted his thoughts. When people are allowed to have access to classified information, they might have different views in the process of analyzing the situation.

The number three iniquity of Satan is lies or deception. He concealed his underlying motives from Eve during the conversation that ensued. He presented the idea to Eve of seeing God as her enemy who was hiding something good from her. He lied to Eve that she would be wise like the gods because Eve observed Lucifer's ability to transform into Lion, Ox, Eagle, and Man. But Eve was never able to transform. Instead, Lucifer subtly introduced the immoral and violent world, which was a complete perversion. Lucifer wanted the keys to death and hell. God wanted Adam to avoid the tree of the knowledge of good and evil, but Satan tricked Eve, promising she would be as wise as the gods who know good and evil.

He didn't tell Eve about the death. Instead, he denied the death threat and presented another terminology of knowing good and evil. That was a twist, folks! He was truly subtle! Don't you ever trust Lucifer, even if he promised you something; he's got a target - your soul after death. There are people in the Wicca world he had promised his seat, telling them to kill more humans; then he would make them sit as queens and kings in his kingdom, and you know, he is just after their soul when they eventually die; often end up in hell. Satan is the father of lies.

The iniquity of Satan is treason, which Jesus implied is murder (John 8:44). God said, "By the multitude of thy merchandise, they have filled the midst of thee with violence, and thou hast sinned..." (Ezekiel 28:16). As earlier explained, he became violent with treasonable thoughts that filled his heart so that he could obtain the keys of death and hell. And because he loved violence, attempting a coup against God, God then cursed him, saying, "Thou shalt be a terror for a while, and never shall thou be any more" (Ezekiel 28:19, emphasis mine).

The number five iniquity of Satan is stealing. When Lucifer was in the garden, he knew how naive Adam was to spiritual things. So Lucifer thought about how to rob Adam and Eve of the keys and subtly obtained their authority, and that was the reason Jesus said, "The thief cometh not, but for to steal, kill and to destroy..." (John 10:10). What did he steal? Man's authority as given by God. He succeeded in tricking Adam and Eve and took their glory.

During the temptation of Jesus, Satan claimed that the glory was delivered to him. But we all know he stole them by tricking Adam and Eve. "And the devil took him up into an exceeding High Mountain and showed him all the kingdoms of this world, and the glory of them. And saith unto him, I will give you all these things if you fall down and worship me. For they were delivered to me (by Adam) and whomsoever I will I give it "(Matthew 4: 8-9, Luke 4:6, Emphasis mine). The devil stole Adam's dominion, and the devil is trading it for fame, wealth, and power. You must have read from the scriptures that Satan said, whosoever he will, he gives. His human agents are working for him on the earth, with some of them in secret societies.

Became a terrorist.

Satan was cursed to be a terror because he loved violence. He hated Adam and, in addition, plotted a coup against God. For you to plan a coup, you will require forces backing you up. Satan saw the keys to unlock thousands of fallen angels of death and destruction to overthrow God, but since the coup failed, he then took control of the earth from Adam. His plot failed, and God cursed him to be a terror, and he is now crowned the King of terrors (Job 18:14). "Thou shalt be terror (for a while), and never shalt thou be any more" (Ezekiel 28:19, Emphasis mine). Lucifer was cursed to become a terrorist.

I have seen many people cry out in ignorance, saying, "Why would God allow this to happen to me? God is wicked! God killed my child, brother, wife, husband, etc. Why would God allow people to be sick and die in pain? They yelled everything at God in their ignorance. Even some ignorant ones teach everything they experience is God's will. That is completely ignorant teaching. God isn't the problem. Man acquired the sin of violence, which brought sickness, death, and lack through deception. But many would say, "But God allowed Satan." No, God didn't allow Satan. Satan betrayed God. Satan is steering the world's pains, sufferings, and death. Someone would immediately quote the book of Job that God permitted Satan. That was after Lucifer had already betrayed God and gained access into the earth. So Satan, in a bid to show off to God that all humans on the earth were under Satan, God had to showcase Job. It was an isolated case study.

Your pains and tears are Satan's glory. Whenever you are in tears, Satan rejoices and gets strengthened spiritually. Satan and his demons took control of the world from Adam as soon as his coup to overthrow God failed. He resorted to the earth because he didn't want man to be in charge of the earth. Remember, Luke 8:31 says the devils were begging Jesus not to send them back to the deep darkness, probably because they love staying on the earth, their previous abode. They have gained access into the land of the living. And that is why whenever idol worshippers pray, these spirits answer their prayers. They already gained access into the earth when Adam sinned.

Satan dominated the earth and became the God or prince of this world, which we know is for a while. (See 2nd Corinthians 4:4). His dominance over the hearts of men produces sinful thoughts, which translate into sickness, death, pain, lack, etc. However, he instigates men to point accusing figures at God. He is lying to people that God caused them their pains and sicknesses. He prompts humans in their hearts to curse God, but he has never suggested to anyone the need to investigate his activities. It's all about apportioning blame to God, even if he (the devil) was responsible. How about his betrayal of God? Don't trust Satan. He is always a liar.

Satan is busy out there buffeting the world, and he tells humans God is responsible for all their calamities, but he has never admitted that he released death and destruction into our world from the darkness of the deep, having deceived Adam and Eve. He had the power of death and destruction. He often tells lies that it was Adam who sinned. He deceived Eve to transgress against God. He impacted his nature of violence against God and man upon the human race, which is the sin of violence. This is what the scripture meant when it said Jesus came to "take away the sin of the world" (John 1:29). The sin of the world is violence which manifested in the form of killing, stealing, lies, deception, idolatry, hatred, envying, adultery, oppression, backbiting, evil speaking, malice, etc. The sin of the world is violence, and that was why the first time God mentioned sin in the scripture was in the book of Genesis, chapter 4:7, which we shall expound on shortly.

The spirits of death and destruction released by Satan pervaded the human race and influenced humans to kill one another. Fallen spirit beings once loved violence, having invented swords, arrows, darts, etc. They permeated the earth with violence, manifest in various forms abusive words, cursing, envy, strife, oppression, wars, etc. We have all witnessed violence all over the earth from the time of Cain to date: Governments killing their citizens to remain in power, wars amongst nations, and communal clashes - all forms of violence. Violence permeated humanity, with people dying every day. No one seems to understand the reasons they are acting violently. Men have acquired the nature of the gods (fallen spirit of old).

We can conclude that Satan and his cohorts became terrorists to human lives. This explains why we have terrorists on earth. The tendency to kill and destroy entered the human race. All over the world, it is all about wars, conflicts, and violence. The slightest provocation often tends to eliminate the opponent. Our social media, newspapers, and television networks are always on alert to the nature of destruction and death daily. Humans are used to the violence and destruction they inherited from Satan and fallen spirits. So also the creeping things, fowl of the air, and animals adapted to violent living.

Mankind has further developed mass weapons of destruction due to this nature of violence that pre-existed Adam. Satan knew that violence could be intensified amongst humans if their spouses were touched. He then strengthened his comrades to forcefully take women belonging to another man to increase the violence amongst them. Chemical and nuclear weapons are being developed to increase the violence on earth. Men are in constant search and modifications to destroy one another, unknowingly to them that they are manifesting the nature of fallen spirits who once occupied the earth.

Sin also means violence

God told Satan that he had sinned because Satan was filled with violence: "By the multitude of thine merchandise, they have filled the midst of thee with violence, and thou hast sinned: therefore, I will cast thee as a profane out of the mountain of God: and I will destroy thee, O covering cherub, from the midst of the stones of fire." (Ezekiel 28:16). To be profane means to be outraged or to violate the sacred order of a place, to become intemperate. Lucifer violated the sacred rule of peaceful coexistence. God is a peaceful God, and he abhorred violent living. Satan became envious and bittered and began to imagine plotting a coup. But while meditating on it, God saw his resolve, and he got a curse for it. He betrayed God, so God said Satan had sinned or transgressed.

The word sin here actually means the sin of violence. The word sin was first used when God warned Cain. God said unto Cain, "...Sin (of violence) lieth at thy door...." In other words, Cain watched it, and you are about to commit the sin of violence. Violence is coming close to you. You are about to exhibit the nature of Satan, who came to kill and destroy. God saw this nature of violence in Cain. So the original word for sin or iniquity also means violence. The ten commandments advised the Israelites to live harmoniously as angels do in heaven. For instance, thou shalt not steal, thou shalt not kill, thou shalt not commit adultery, and so forth, all dictate how men should avoid violence living among themselves on the earth.

Let's take a look at the 10 Commandments. God said thou shalt not worship other gods (spirit beings) or make graven images to serve them. Why? They will teach you the ways of violence. That is why nations that serve other gods often kill their children or massacre human lives without recourse to peaceful living. Nations that engage in worshipping idols sacrifice humans or eat humans and have no regard for human lives. They can oppress and violently take what does not belong to them. The Devil taught them how to enjoy human suffering and pains without feelings. Those who consult mediums often search for the blood of humans to gain powers. We can go on and on.

God said, "Honor thy father and thy mother." In other words, don't be violent to your parents. Don't insult them. Respect them that it may be well with you. Next, is thou shalt not covet thy neighbor's wife or property, etc. The same thing, Do no violence. Don't desire someone else's property because if you desire it, it will lead to envy, wrath, anger, stealing, and possibly looking for a way to collect it secretly, which might end up in bloodshed or using mediums to terminate them.

How about stealing, killing, and adultery? They all speak of the same sin of violence. The only exemption in the ten commandments is that man should rest as God rested. So we can see that the sin of the world is violence. Violence entails envy, anger, wrath, malice, evil speaking, attacking, cursing, abusive language, evil thinking, fornication, adultery, etc. Immorality is taking someone's property without paying for it, which is stealing. Once it is paid for, it is no more stealing, which we have traced to the sin of violence.

Satan came to steal, kill and destroy, which all boils down to violent living. Man cooperated with Satan, and there cannot be an end to stealing, accidents, fires, hurricanes, or death on the earth until God removes the sins of the world. So when scripture says Jesus is the lamb that taketh away the sin of the world, it also means Jesus will eventually remove violence from the world. Did you get that?

The manifestation of the violent world began with Cain, who slew his brother Abel. God knew that as soon as Adam ate the forbidden fruit, his descendants, Cain, would manifest this violent nature. Scripture says, "...And Cain was very wroth, and his countenance fell...And Cain talked with Abel, his brother: and it came to pass, when they were in the field, that Cain rose against Abel, his brother, and slew him" (Genesis 4:5-8). Cain talked subtly with his brother with a hidden motive like Satan did. Cain spoke as though there wasn't any problem, but God saw his wrath or bitter envy against Abel. Then the thought of killing accumulated. Cain fulfilled Satan's mission.

Cain didn't yield the warnings from God but went ahead and slew his brother. These were Adam's first descendants, manifesting the world's violent sin. Cain couldn't control his wrath because the spirits of death and destruction had taken over him. So people began to kill themselves on the earth daily, and they point fingers at God. Such accusation at God is a function of ignorance in men. Nobody wants to take responsibility for their actions. Some say it all boils down to God, who gave man free will. God allowed it. God should not make us with free will. Man is a free moral agent to act in his own ways. But I discovered that many don't blame the devil or themselves. They often speak against God and are ignorant that Satan released these spirits of death and destruction into this world, so please hold the devil responsible.

The next character in the scripture was a man named Lamech, who also toed the same line of violence. The Scriptures say, "I have slain a man to my wounding and a young man to my hurt. (Genesis 4:23). In other words, "I have killed someone who wounded me" You can see the violent nature of these enemies of mankind manifesting in humans. Lucifer said in his twisted words, "You shall be as gods (spirits), knowing good and evil (violence) that will destroy you eventually" (Genesis 3:3-4). Man has become "gods," knowing violent aspects of spirits of destruction and death, which he used against man.

It is all about the tendency to kill or hate one another through evil speaking, envy, aggression, backbiting, gossip, malice, clamor, hatred, maligning, etc.

But too late

All forms of violence could be traceable to the root of envy and strife. Of course, we cannot rule out selfishness which is the reason for envy. So many people in the world are engrossed in envy, which stems from selfishness. The scripture says, "Do you think that the scripture saith in vain, the spirit that dwelleth in us (men and women) tendeth to envy? (James 4:5). Once there is an envy spirit, there must be pride because where envy and strife are, there is confusion and every evil work (James 3:16). Envy and strife indicate the manifest presence of the spirits of death and destruction in the hearts of people. Cain began with envy. Saul envied David. Joseph's brothers envied his dream. Satan envied Adam. Strife means being contentious, often leading to evil speaking, conspiracy, oppression, murder, and evil thoughts. And we know that strife and envy lead to violence in the heart.

Once you are envious, you are destructive because other people's progress irritates you; even if you didn't say it out loud, your heart did, and God saw it. Even pastors envied themselves for the anointing in the life of another who had the calling of God. They manifest the spirit of envy, which springs out of selfishness. Envious people are selfish and proud. Pride means inwardly opposing the person you envy. Satan's pride was against God, who ordained Adam. Many people attacked the president of the United States of America because he was envied. Perhaps, he was rich before becoming the president. Envy is destructive because it is violence in the heart against someone.

Satan obtained the power of death and destruction, which he used to destroy Job's children in one day because he envied Job. Satan, in his envy of Job, said to God, "Hast thou not made an hedge about him, and about his house, and about all that he had on every side? Thou hast blessed the work of his hands, and his substance is increased in the land" (Job 1:10). He plagued Job with sicknesses and diseases (Job chapter 1 and 2). He was envious of Moses's body because Moses submitted to God despite being denied the Promised Land. Lucifer contested for the body of Moses because he was envious. Lucifer is still envious of man entering the light zone universe; hence he accuses them before God day and night. Lucifer envied Jesus' ministry and plotted to have him killed by one of his own disciples.

Having entered into Judas Iscariot's heart, he instigated him to betray Jesus and made

Judas feel worthless, influencing him to commit suicide (Luke 22:3, Matthew 27:5). Suicidal thoughts dominate many people because Satan influenced their hearts to their own destruction. These evil spirits speak and encourage humans to go ahead and commit suicide or drink poison. The devil presents the negative side of life to them, encouraging them to commit suicide. The devil won't stop until their victims fall prey to suicidal pressure. Those who have a personal relationship with Jesus Christ can overcome such unwanted pressure of evil thoughts. Every thought which tells you to commit suicide is of the devil.

Sometimes, these spirits often instigate people to kill at will. Imagine someone who held a knife in the kitchen, an evil spirit of destruction will whisper to them to go ahead and stab their neighbor. But when you are mature, you tell him to shut up and get out! Of course, those who commit manslaughter would be punished for it. In the military, these spirits motivate them to spill blood or rape women. And you know what? Humans who participate in these things feel proud and laugh over their atrocities, not knowing that a day will come when they cannot laugh forever. A day will come when they cry for forgiveness but too late. They will join the devils influencing them in the lake of fire. Of course, Satan knew men love violence.

Chapter 18

The Violence on Earth

Although the nature of violence was distilled in humans through fallen spirits, it is observed that some humans also delight in violence. Adam's descendants loved the power to terminate someone's life with ease. And so the entire earth then was corrupt and filled with violence but for Noah and his family. Adam's descendants participated in raping women and maiming others. The scripture says, "...When men began to multiply upon the face of the earth, and daughters were born unto them that the sons of God saw the daughters of men that they were fair (beautiful), and they took them wives of all which they chose...And God looked upon the earth, and behold, it was corrupt; for all flesh (fallen sons of God including natural Adam's descendant) had corrupted his way upon the earth. And God said unto Noah, the end of all flesh is come before me; for all the earth is filled with violence through them; and behold I will destroy them with the earth" (Genesis 6:1,12-13).

In other words, the nature of immorality and violence permeated and multiplied across Adam's natural descendants together with the offspring of the giants. This is precisely what the scripture meant when it says 'all flesh' had corrupted his way upon the earth.' Humans, who were Adam's descendants, adapted to the violence of raping women of their choice but unknown to them, these giants weren't part of them. They infiltrated the earth as soon as Adam's sin was known to them. "There were giants in the earth in those days, and also after that when the sons of God came in unto the daughters of men, and they bare children to them, the same became mighty men, which were of old, men of renown. (Genesis 6:4). Fallen spirits as giants procreated the earth and still intend to populate the earth to have natural Adam's descendants chased out. This underlying motive was foreseen by God when he addressed Lucifer in the Garden of Eden.

Children born unto these fallen sons of God were also mighty men of old – a replica of their fathers. They were men of the pre-Adamic world popular amongst Adam's descendants on earth. As you are already aware, they infiltrated the earth when Adam tasted of the food that led to death in the garden. Similarly, some forms of initiation come through food and drink being consumed, and they spiritually opened us up to other realms. Dining and eating food sacrificed to idols could open us up to spiritual contamination. Food and sexual intercourse are avenues by which our spirits can sometimes be contaminated spiritually. We saw the Israelites rise up to eat, drink, and play (openly displaying their nakedness). The food of death (knowledge of good and evil) was responsible for Adam and Eve's awareness of sexual drive, violence, diseases, death, etc. Through the food of death, man gained the knowledge of the gods and became violent in bloodshed and cursing. The food of life produces eternal life in man. Jesus had to introduce the communion of life once used in the pre-Adamic world to mitigate the effect of the food of death in us.

The nature of violence has permeated the nations of the world; hence Jesus said that nations would rise against nations and kingdom against kingdom until the end of the world. It is a falling world of violence, and so the chain of events associated with the destruction of the earth, such as wars, earthquakes, landslides, hurricanes, tornadoes, volcanos, extreme weather conditions, diseases, pestilences (covid 19 or flu), famine, accidents, etc. which are detrimental to humanity will continue unabated (See Matthew 24:1-51). So long as hierarchy cherub Lucifer had gained spiritual control of the earth, there must be a complete overhaul of the earth again. The question often asked is, "Why didn't God destroy the devil immediately?" I will come to this as we progress.

End to violence

When violence erupted among men to an alarming proportion, God had to put an end to it in the days of Noah. He told Noah and his sons that violence was the reason for the destruction of the first (Adamic) world with a flood of waters (See Genesis 6:1-22, 7:1-24). It is obvious God was fulfilling his word of promised and told Lucifer that he would sweep out the seed of the renown with a besom of destruction as written in Isaiah 14:26. This shows God was not primarily targetting Adam's descendant's humans (flesh), but then Adam's descendant were found corrupt as well. The scriptures captured God regretting his actions of sweeping alongside the Adamic descendants who toed the path of violence and sexual immorality.

He was referring to Adam's descendant men (Noah), not the giants and their offspring. That is precisely what the scripture meant when God said, he will no more curse the ground for man's sake, nor will he any more smite every living thing because Noah, as Adam's descendant, had offered him a sacrifice of uncontaminated beasts and fowl (Genesis 8:21). God specifically told Noah and his family that "whoso sheddeth man's blood, by man shall his blood be shed: for in the image of God made he man" (Genesis

9:5-6). In other words, God hates violent living. He desired peace amongst us. Not the abusive lifestyle initiated by these fallen spirits. You know, we've got people who may not be involved in immorality, drinking, or smoking, but are very good at cursing, keeping malice, envying, jealousy, quarreling, backbiting, selfish, speaking evil of one another, etc., which unknown to them are the true nature of fallen spirits.

God wants us to be at peace in our hearts. God abhors hearts prone to violence while speaking peace with their lips. Psalms 28:3 talks about "the wicked and workers of iniquity which speak peace to their neighbors, but mischief is in their hearts." God wants us to be at peace with one another on earth. "Thy kingdom come" actually means "Your peaceful reign comes." There can never be an end to violence in families, kingdoms, and nations until the kingdom of God comes on the earth. So when Jesus said, "Thy kingdom come; Thy will be done in earth, as it is in heaven" (Matthew 6:9). It means he wants the earth to become like heaven where only peace and love exist.

For this reason, Jesus came and preached peace unto men - heralding the threshold of the kingdom of God on earth. He needed to let men know that this nature of violence on the earth is not God's will for the man of the dust. He introduced the true nature of God when he said, "...Love your enemies, bless them that curse you, do good to them that hate you and pray for them that despitefully use, and persecute you". (See Matthew 5: 39, 44). When Jesus saw his disciples exhibit this nature of envy, strife, and contention among themselves, Jesus told them to forgive endless times and stop exercising prideful lordship over one another. This is precisely what he meant when he said forgiveness should be seventy times seven, no matter the offense (See Matthew 18: 21-22, Luke 22:24-30). They have got to adopt a new lifestyle of peaceful living despite the nature of the violence they inherited.

The law of heaven is to love God and to love your neighbor as yourselves (Matthew 22:37-39). And that means living in peace and harmony. That is why Jesus would say, "...My peace I give unto you, not as the world giveth..." (John 14:27). His peace was given in your spirit; therefore, let not your heart be troubled. One might say, "But God asked the Israelites to kill and take possessions by the conquest of some specific area of lands in the scriptures." Yes, God did that because humanity had already acquired the nature of violence pending when God's kingdom or rulership will manifest on the earth. However, God asked the children of Israel in those days to eliminate the heathen nations because giants were found among them, which were offsprings of fallen spirit beings in human flesh that infiltrated the earth from the days of Adam to Noah and beyond.

Fallen spirits taught men idol worship by appearing to mortals who go about carving images and worshipping the hosts of heaven. So their idolatrous life spurred God to abhor them. God would have no choice but allow all those who worship idols to join fallen spirits in the land of darkness at last, not the earth where life exists. This also explains why people go to hell. God allows people to go to hell because they choose these spirits as their gods; therefore, joining their gods in hell is justified before God. That is why the scriptures say," The wicked shall be turned into hell, and all nations that forget God" (Psalms 9:17). All those who claim not to believe in God will have their part in hell, joining the god they worship. However, after Jesus came, there was an open door for those who believed to come and receive the free gift of eternal life.

"For God so loved the world, and gave his only begotten Son that whosoever believed in him should not perish, but have everlasting life" (John 3:16).

Jesus came and preached peace to the Jews - the need to love their enemies. He went as far as correcting the notions that Moses permitted divorce because of the hardness of the people's hearts, but from the beginning, it was not so (Matthew 19:8). Implying things often go southward in marriages as a result of violence and immorality. So also, the violent law of an eye for an eye, tooth for a tooth was permitted in the law until the reformation of all things. "What then is the purpose of the law? The law was added to mitigate the excesses of the transgressions - the acquired sin nature of violence in humans until the kingdom of Christ is made manifest…wherefore the law was a schoolmaster to bring us unto Christ…." (Galatians 3:19 and 24) (emphasis is mine). God knew violence could not be removed entirely from the earth until his kingdom came physically. This means Lucifer, the King of Terror, would have to be displaced from space – the height of the stars of heaven for violence to end.

And of a truth, there's no violence in the kingdom of God – the light zone Jesus came from. Angels coexist in heaven by love, joy, peace, and righteousness. Although there are angels of war drawn with swords, known as armies of heaven, assigned to clean-sweep the wicked who delight in violence on the earth, nonetheless, God is still patient with the wicked peradventure they will repent (See Revelation 19:14). God by His word had promised us his kingdom to come, there shall be no more war or violence among men: "…Nation shall not lift a sword against nation, neither shall they learn war anymore…and none shall make them afraid…" (Micah 4:3-4, Isaiah 2:4). The wolf and the lamb shall feed together. The lion shall eat straw like the bullock: and dust shall be serpent's meat. "They shall not hurt nor destroy…" (Isaiah 65:25).

In other words, animals will no more eat one another. Lions will not eat goats anymore, neither shall jaguars eat crocodiles. Animals will live in harmony in the new world to come. It will be a kingdom of peace and righteousness. No more violence and abusive language. No more rape, fighting, war, and bloodshed. When God eventually brings His kingdom on this earth, the scripture shall be fulfilled, saying, "Come, behold the works of the LORD, what desolations he hath made in the earth. He maketh wars to cease unto the end of the earth; he breaketh the bow, and cutteth the spear in sunder; he burned the chariot in the fire" (Psalms 46:8-9). The book of Hosea 2:18 further substantiates this. It says, "In that day will I make a covenant for them with beasts of the field, and with the fowls of heaven, and with the creeping things of the ground; and I will break the bow and the sword and the battle out of the earth, and will make them lie down safely."

This implies no more violence, as in serpent striking man, nor ants or scorpions stinging man. Animals and creeping things will no more eat one another. No more destruction of lives and property. No more hurricanes, tornados, earthquakes, fire disasters, etc. People will not build and another inhabit; neither will they plant and another eat, instead they shall enjoy the work of their hands (Isaiah 65:22). The true lifestyle of God's kingdom was introduced by Jesus to his disciples and followers when he told them to love their enemies, do good to them that hate you, curse not, neither be angry without a reasonable cause and avoid the use of abusive language. In the kingdom of heaven, there is no abusive language or fighting: just love, peace, and joy.

This was the lifestyle Jesus introduced on earth; hence he told us to pray that the will of God be done on the earth as it is in heaven. Jesus's teachings permeated his followers, who heeded his doctrines, which is why Christians are being killed in most parts of the world. It isn't that they cannot fight back as Peter did in retaliation, but because they have received a new spirit, which took out of them the nature of violence (Matthew 5:1-46). The scripture substantiates this when it says,"...He came and preached peace to you which were afar off, and to them that were nigh" (Ephesians 2:17).

Effect of righteousness

Jesus came to preach peace to all mankind. He demonstrated this heavenly lifestyle when he engaged a Samaritan woman at a well of water, who immediately expressed to herself that she had nothing to do with the Jewish people. She told Jesus that the Jews and the Samaritans have no dealings (John 4:9). In other words, we are enemies. Why are you asking me to give you water? He was trying to introduce the actual lifestyle of the kingdom of heaven where there is no quarrel, abusive words, stealing, fighting, etc., just peaceful coexistence in love and joy. God wants heaven's lifestyle on earth as well. What is this kingdom of God all about? The scripture says, "For the kingdom of God is not meat and drink, but righteousness, and peace, and joy in the Holy Ghost" (Romans 14:17).

Now, let us look at the scriptures to see the effect of righteousness that characterizes the kingdom of God. In Isaiah 32:17-18, the scriptures say, "The work of righteousness shall be peace, and the effect of righteousness, quietness, and assurance forever. And my people shall dwell in a peaceable habitation, a sure dwelling, and a quiet resting place." Peace will be abundant in the new heaven and earth. This substantiates what the scripture meant when it said, "The fruit of righteousness is sown in peace of them that make peace." (James 3:18). Take note of the effect of righteousness, quietness, and assurance forever. The result of righteousness is peaceful coexistence forever. Corroborating James 3:18 that the fruit of righteousness is sown in peace. In other words, the manifestation of righteousness is peaceful living seen in them that makes peace.

Invariably, the righteous are known for peaceful living. This is one of the characteristics of the righteous person. This has nothing to do with a hypocrite who looks pious but possesses a heart that gathers evil thoughts or someone who deliberately hurts and hypocritically apologizes, knowing fully well what they have done was deliberate. You know we have people cunning like serpent-looking pious but are dangerous like Satan who comes as an angel of light. The fruit of righteousness is sown in them that make peace, and the effect of righteousness is quietness and assurance forever. This also means meekness becomes the watchword for such righteous people. You can see that righteousness here means peaceful living in the world to come. Being passionate about your neighbors' feelings and caring for one another is the hallmark of the meek. Peace will be abundant during the millennium reign of Christ on this earth and in the world to come.

Jesus' teachings on the mount indicate peaceful living is the lifestyle of the kingdom of God - a violence-free world in the universe above. He said, "Blessed are the peacemakers for they shall be called the children of God" Matthew 5:9. Jesus came to preach peace, and one of the reasons the kingdom of darkness had him killed was because he did no violence to men as a Son of God. The kingdom of darkness saw Jesus as an alien in the flesh and had to attack and kill him because he didn't deceive or commit any form of violence on the earth during his earthly ministry. The hordes of darkness were utterly blind to his redemptive purpose - the souls of humanity. Instead, they saw him as an alien who refused to participate in violence like them.

As far as the kingdom of darkness was concerned, violence, oppression, evil speaking, abusive words, war, attacks, and destruction were the norms. The souls of the peaceful ones of the earth are their primary target for the onslaught. The powers of darkness had Jesus killed because he committed no sin of violence, nor was deceit found in his mouth. Scripture says, "...Because he had done no violence, neither any deceit in his mouth." (Isaiah 53:9). He did not conform to the world pattern of violence and deceit.

And the book of Peter corroborated this in 1st Peter 2:22, which says, "Who did no sin (of violence), neither was guile found in his mouth" (Emphasis mine). He was the Son of God incarnated in the flesh and did no violence, nor did he lie or deceive any man. Jesus said that the prince of this world cometh, and had nothing in him" (John 14:30). The prince of this world discovered that Jesus did not commit any form of violence, nor did he deceive any man. He was straightforward and truthful.

I guess someone might contend that Jesus said that he didn't come to send peace on the earth quoting Matthew 10:34-35, which says, "Think not that I am come to send peace on earth: I came not to send peace, but a sword. For I am come to set a man at variance against his father, and the daughter against her mother, and the daughter-in-law against her mother-in-law." An amateur in the word may take this scripture at face value contending that Jesus came to set sword, not peace. No. That is not what the scriptures implied here. Jesus said his arrival on earth 2000 years ago was not the time for his peaceful earthly reign. Instead, it would create family divisions because some people will believe in him while others may not, resulting in family conflicts.

For instance, Jesus teaching the Jews to love the Samaritans would certainly create divisions amongst those accustomed to the enmity between them. Some families may reject such a move for peace, while others may not. A father may disagree with the wife, children, or father-in-law because believing in Jesus and his teachings could set family members against one another. If you take a look at the preceding scripture properly, it says, "Whosoever shall deny me before men, him will I deny before my Father which is in heaven." (Matthew 10:32). To be precise, he said 'Think not that I am come, is present tense. Indicating this period of my coming was to set family members against family themselves just because some will believe in me.

Someone else might contend that Jesus said, "Woe unto the Pharisees of his days." Yes. Jesus was forthright with the truth, declaring the troubles (woes) that await the Pharisees and Sadducees in the future. He didn't flatter them in his words. You know, some people flatter others, being insincere in their hearts. Jesus does not talk with double mouths; he tells you the truth undilutedly.

Someone else might say Jesus calls some people fools, citing Matthew 23:17. Yes, when people lack understanding hearts, they are termed fools. Fools are people who hate truth and lack understanding at heart (See Proverbs 1:22, 8:5). There are reasons why Jesus designates people as fools in the scriptures, despite the warnings in Matthew 5:22, which says, "Whosoever is angry with his brother without a cause (reason) shall be in the danger of the judgment.

So, there were reasons why Jesus uttered the word fool. Moreso, he is your God anyway! Someone might say, "How about Jesus's secrecy to his disciples," citing John 7:1-11? I looked up those scriptures and found that Jesus was 100% correct in what he told his disciples. He was specific when he said, "Go you up unto this feast: I go not up yet unto this feast; for my time is not yet full come. When he had said these words unto them, he abode still in Galilee. But when his brethren were gone up, then went he also up unto the feast, not openly, but as it were secret" (John 7:8-10). Of course, in expounding these scriptures, Jesus said he was not going yet. In other words, he is not going with them immediately; hence he abodes in Galilee for a while before he eventually went.

Some other person might say, "How about taking a whip on money changers and overturning their tables?" That is no violence but correction as it relates to doing the right thing. The money changers broke the law by turning the synagogue into a marketplace. Governments of the world often do that to citizens who constitute a nuisance at certain event centers. Clearly, Jesus acted in accordance with peaceful coexistence, and no life was lost in the process. The money changers in the temple did not revolt because they knew they were wrong selling at those spots. So, it is evident that Jesus did not commit the sin of violence inherited by all humans from Adam; hence he was gentle and peaceful. Satan could find no fault in him. Even Pilates said that Jesus was faultless in his assessment of his peaceful lifestyle.

He was gentle to a fault; hence the scripture wrote, "A bruised reed shall he not break, and the smoking flax shall he not quench...till he has set judgment (justice) in the earth: and the isles shall wait for his law." (Isaiah 42:3-4). He will not destroy any life until he has established his purpose of incarnation on the earth. The isle shall wait for his law. What law? It is the law of peace, love, and righteousness. Jesus rebuked his disciples when he was prompted to send fire like Elijah to destroy the lives of those who opposed Jesus in Jerusalem. "But he turned, rebuked them, and said, you know not what manner of spirit you are made up of" (Luke 9:55-56). In other words, you, my disciples, are now Christians and have been transformed or made up of the spirit of love and peace. You are no more made up of the violent nature you were used to. Christians lead a peaceful life all over the world. It is never a sign of weakness to be peaceful.

Appropriate time

Jesus created the world, but a bruised reed shall he not break. As sons of God, Moses and Elijah did violence during their days. They wasted human lives where necessary in the Old Testament, but Jesus said, "The son of man is not come to destroy lives but to save. (Luke 9:55). The kingdom of darkness saw Jesus was too gentle and didn't use his power to destroy any life. They were wondering why Jesus didn't behave like them. God made them view things from a different perspective.

However, the same Jesus Christ who preached peace now will, at his return, sweep out all the wicked and violent humans who oppressed, especially the spirit men living among us in human flesh on this earth right now. That is what the scripture meant when it said, "as in the days of Noah, they were eating and drinking, marrying and giving in marriage until Noah entered into the Ark" (Luke 17:26-27). We have had fallen spirits procreating this earth in average human flesh since the days of Moses, as earlier explained. They are recruited from all walks of life. Some specialized in committing violence of raping, ritual killing, shooting children or people, or even suicide bombing. Jesus, alongside his hosts of angels as men, will kill with the sword all humans who refused the free gift of salvation and all the seed of the wicked on this earth. Jesus created the earth, and he owns it.

Those who said Jesus should not rule over them shall be slain with the sword on his arrival and sent to the land of the dead. Fallen spirit men in human flesh who once said the man of the dust should not rule over all things will meet Jesus Christ at his second coming, and they will be slain by the sword. Jesus, the second Adam as a man of the dust, was ordained to reign and inherit all things according to God's mystery plan for the earth. That is what the scripture means when it says, "But those mine enemies, which would not that I should reign over them, bring hither, and slay them before me" (Luke 19:27).

Remember, the kings of the earth stood in opposition to Jesus as God's anointed to reign over the earth in Psalms 2:2-3. The wicked and violent people on this earth who wouldn't want a peaceful reign of Jesus will have their flesh given unto the birds of the air to eat their flesh because they love violence. You can't serve God and love violence. Jesus came to preach peace. The Lord Jesus will sweep out all forms of violence exhibited by humans from the earth at the appropriate time. "The LORD shall break in pieces the oppressor...and his days shall the righteous flourish; and abundance of peace so long as the moon endureth." (Psalms 72: 4,8).

However, before ending the violence on earth, God would need to chase out completely the devils out of the heavenly realms they currently occupy. These spirits, which influenced wickedness on the earth through spiritual wickedness in high places, will be chased out. If violence must stop physically on the earth at last, then the spiritual forces responsible would need to be curtailed and cast out of the heavenly realms in space. It will be a fierce battle between God's angels and Satan's. This war will take place in the future in the spiritual realm before Jesus will physically resurface on this earth at his second coming. Without his return, violence cannot come to an end.

Remember, the violent nature of Satan and his comrades was predicted by God would come to an end, according to the scriptures. God said unto Satan,"...Thou shalt be a terror, and never shall thou be any more" (Ezekiel 28:19). God has a time frame to put an end to violence and destruction going on the earth. He will completely banish Satan alongside hordes of darkness in the lake of fire under darkness. God said, "He will not contend forever with these spirits" (Isaiah 57:16). This corroborates what we read in Genesis 6:3, which says, "And the LORD said, My Spirit shall not always strive with man..." God would not continue to strive with fallen spirits, men in human flesh, nor will his angels continue to confront demons forever.

God prevented Adam and Eve from eating of 'the tree of life after Adam had tasted of the tree of knowledge of good and evil. If Adam had tasted of the tree of life immediately, it would have meant his fate would have been sealed like the fallen spirits that cannot be remedied, unlike the man of the dust, which God could fix again with atonement and recreation. You can see that God is good in preventing Adam from eating of the tree of life. One of the reasons Jesus said that only God is good is because he saved the human race from perishing forever, unlike spirit beings who have no hope of repentance. God has a plan to put an end to the violence of these spirits once and for all.

Of course, some humans love the violent life of killing, stealing, raping, and drinking blood. At the appropriate time, God will cut off all who oppress on the earth by violence or wickedness and send their souls to the eternal lake of fire forever and ever. Like I told you, God is selecting souls from the earth. He won't permit such deviant behaviors of fallen stars, ancient people, or Lucifer anymore. Lucifer, who left his kingdom, succeeded in impacting his nature in humans. Individual characters or ways in eternity to come are being x-rayed and observed while on the earth before passing to perfection. Our experiences in leadership positions, wealth opportunities, adversities, pains, sicknesses, resistance to God's instructions, and other behaviors are observed while we go through the earth.

It may surprise you to know that other angels also observe the angels of God in heaven, who come into this darkness universe due to the past experience of Lucifer. If Lucifer, a cherub who had walked in the stones of fire realms, could fall, then all other angels are monitored to this date to see if they also might fall. That doesn't mean they are suspected, just that God is being doubly sure. Angels are holy, coming from the light zone universe. The darkness zone universe is where Lucifer rules over his own people.

The second heaven

The curse upon Lucifer made him king of terror over other spirits of death and destruction. Going through the book of Revelation, it was revealed that the devil would instigate men to persecute and attack Christians. In chapter 12, Satan would attack the remnant of Israel. In chapter 16, he will gather men into a great battle of Armageddon. It is all about violence and a violent world. God will put an end to the violence on earth. However, ending the violence on earth will not be feasible until the powers responsible are dealt with and overthrown. There will be a fierce battle between 'stars of God' and 'stars of heaven' currently occupying space. And this is what the scriptures meant by war in heaven.

You know, there has been this misconception amongst the Christain community that war took place in heaven from the beginning before Satan was cast out of heaven into the earth. It does not matter if any have been teaching such erroneous messages over the hundreds of decades. I don't mean to condemn any. Many who claim to have attended a certain level of biblical education are susceptible to errors because they equate charisma to knowledge. Charisma is a manifestation of the power of God for the unbelieving to believe, but the depth of the knowledge of God is superior. There's a complete difference between the depth of knowledge and charisma. Moses had charisma, but his father-in-law had to counsel him because he lacked administrative knowledge. Hosea 6:6 says that God desires us to obtain the knowledge of God more than receiving our burnt offerings.' And of a truth, signs are for the unbelievers, and this speaks volumes about why Peter could heal the sick and perform miracles, but when it comes to the depths and revelations of the scriptures, he confessed that the writings of Paul were hard to understand. "…Even as our beloved brother Paul also according to the wisdom given unto him hath written unto you; As also in all his epistles, speaking in them of things; in which are some things hard to be understood, which they are unlearned and unstable wrest, as they do also the other scriptures…" (2 Peter 3: 15-16).

I have listened to many teachings that are entirely out of scriptural context. The apostle Peter acknowledged that many are grappling with Paul's writings. The unlearned and unstable are confused with the mysteries of the depth of knowledge Paul had about the scriptures. But that doesn't imply Paul was 100% correct in all his write-ups. What do I mean? Paul, in his days, discarded scientific views and wrote that God brought light out of darkness. But we are in a better position to study and articulate his epistles, possibly making necessary corrections as led by the Holy Ghost, having compared scriptures to scriptures relevant to our times. Some religious fanatics would react to this remark, but I'm not perturbed. I'm of God who told me the truth.

Now, the book of Revelation specifically talks about things that will shortly come to pass (Revelation 1:1). Scripture says Jesus took the book out of the hand of the Father, unveiling God's mysteries. And whenever a seal was loosed, a dramatic effect was displayed as written by God on how it will all be wrapped up (Revelation 5:8, 6:1). The book of Revelation isn't an extra-ordinary book which differs from previous scripts of the Old or New Testaments it was simply a conglomerate of the chain of events about predictions that are articulated in their order of occurrences. The prophecies written in the book of Revelation were all about the future.

For instance, the book of Daniel captured the war predicted to take place in space between Archangel Michael with his angels versus Satan and his angels, which have been typified by stars of God and stars of heaven. Daniel 12:1 says, "At that time shall Michael stand up, the great Prince, which stand up for the children of thy people: and there shall be time of trouble, such as never was since there was a nation even to that same time: and at that time, thy people shall be delivered every one that shall be found written in the book of life." Expounding on these scriptures shows this event is futuristic. It talks about the great tribulation to come when it predicts Michael's confrontation with Satan in the book of Revelation.

As you are aware, Satan has a kingdom made up of different departments, which the scriptures referred to as principalities, powers, and spiritual wickedness in high places, etc., which at the moment are in space as galaxies of stars. And this is where Satan operates from, though he moves up and down the earth, as earlier expounded. These spirits influenced so many things going on in the earth. That is, fallen spirits are in space, influencing the human hearts. Remember, they had access to the earth. As earlier explained, these spirits, including Satan, often walk freely on the earth whenever they descend as stars leaving their domain in space. And this speaks volumes about why charms work for many people because fallen spirits beings are responding to their prayers from space. Witches and wizards are aided to assail through the air by the devil's powers.

Psalms 17:11 says, "...They have set their eyes bowing down to the earth." In other words, they operate from the heavenly realms – the realms of the galaxies and planets above and beneath. Scripture talks about how people worship the queen of heaven by pouring out drink offerings: "The children gather wood, and the fathers kindle the fire, and women knead their dough, to make cakes to the queen of heaven, and to pour out drink offerings unto other gods..." (See Jeremiah 7:18). The people of this world are used to worshipping Satan through idolatry. Some people attend meetings in the underworld inside waters, and some in the Wicca world. Many believed in the powers of their gods, using charms for survival and contracts or positions which some communities, cities, and nations recognized and observed holidays to gods of the moon, rivers, mountains, planets, stones, stars, and queen of heaven, etc.

The children of Israel, in those days, refuted prophet Jeremiah's counsel from the LORD God, who created all things. The Israelites vehemently told Jeremiah, "...We will not hearken unto thee. But we will certainly do whatsoever thing that goeth forth out of own mouth, to burn incense unto the queen of heaven, and to pour out drink offerings unto her, as we have done, we and our fathers, our kings, and our princes in the cities of Judah, and in the street of Jerusalem: for then had we plenty of victuals, and were well, and saw no evil" (Jeremiah 44:17). Many believe that they cannot do away with cultism or idol worship because it would mean they cannot survive this world. They strongly believe in the queen of heaven to give them food and whatsoever they need, which is a perversion because every good and perfect gift comes from God, who allows both the sun and rain on good and evil people of the earth (Matthew 5:45).

Many are unaware that God shows them mercy by protecting and blessing them, attributing their fortunes to their gods or charms. Like the one-time king of Persia named Cyrus, who was conquering nations by the hand of God upon him, but he never knew it was the God of heaven and earth who prospered him on the earth, which he attributed to his gods unknowingly. Isaiah 45:1-4 says, Thus saith the LORD to his anointed, to Cyrus, whose right hand I have holden to subdue nations before him...I will give thee treasures of darkness and hidden riches in secret places...though thou hast not known me." The majority of the world's population worship these fallen spirits to date. They make sacrifices to these spirits, who also provide stolen fortunes to their worshippers from the treasures of darkness.

It shows not everyone who enchants or prays by stretching hands to the sky prays to God Almighty. We have expounded earlier that the several planets and stars under the darkness are the domain of fallen spirits. Often, the term second heaven (which speaks of space) was derived from apostle Paul's third heavens experience which as written in the

Scripture in 2nd Corinthians 12:2. The Scripture substantiates the occupation of the second heaven by fallen spirits when it spoke of the Prince of Persia, a principality with other stars over Persia who withstood the angel of God for 21 days in the heavenly realms, thereby preventing the errand angel from accessing Daniel who had been fasting and waiting for answers to prayers.

The book of Daniel 10:12-13 says, "...Fear not Daniel: for from the first day that thou set thine heart to understand and to chasten thyself before thy God, thy words were heard, and I am come for thy words. But the prince of the kingdom of Persia withstood me one and twenty days: but lo Michael, one of the chief princes, came to help me; and I remained there with the kings of Persia." Take note of the word "kings of Persia." In other words, the principalities over Persia held the angel of God for 21 days before Archangel Michael came to the rescue. Satan is known as the prince of the power of the air (Ephesians 2:2).

In other words, Satan is the lord over these fallen spirits. And that is why some people still worship the sun, moon, and stars and make incantations to the heavens. In their ignorance, so long as their prayers were answered, God Almighty has answered them. No, they worship what they know not. Of course, many are aware of these spirits and boast of their powers. The true living God does not support evil, falsehood, and oppression. His ways are pure, and his works are wrought in truth and righteousness – the distinguishing factors.

The book of Ephesians 6:12 talks about spiritual wickedness in high places. In other words, spiritual wickedness exists in heavenly places. Demons operate above the earth with a wicked and oppressive mindset over humans. Sometimes worldly music is made to saturate the airwaves, and this suddenly pops up in people's hearts over a given geographical location on the earth. Some people can't resist singing such worldly songs in their hearts, even when there are no sounds of such music around their vicinity. Satan is the prince of the power of the air. And so these scriptures point to where Satan currently occupies in the second heavens with some fallen archangels and angels. Of course, some fallen spirits are in the seas, oceans, rivers, and under the earth - dry places or dry planets beneath. The book of Revelation 5:13 talks about creatures under the earth - those in the seas and oceans of the earth.

War in heaven

Having established that the second heaven and hell is the domain where fallen spirits operate and influence humans, we can refer to the prophecies of Daniel about the war scheduled to take place in the heavenly realms recorded in the book of Revelations 12:7-8. The prediction of this war in heaven was also revealed to John, the beloved apostle of Jesus Christ. "And there was war in heaven (heavenly places): Michael and his angels fought against the dragon, and the dragon fought and his angels. And the dragon prevailed not; neither was their place found in heaven (the second heaven)."

Many theologians erroneously think and teach that there was war in heaven where God's actual throne is resident with the angels in heaven and that Satan, in the course of his rebellion, was chased out by the war in heaven before Genesis. No. That isn't what happened. Several preachers and theologians have not adequately studied the scriptures before jumping to conclusions about this war in heaven written in the book of Revelation 12:1-11. They assumed this war had been fought, which is not true. And as always anticipated, one might say, "What is he talking about? The scripture says there was war in heaven." Of course, that was what I thought growing up in the LORD, but I found out that it was wrong when the LORD opened my eyes to know the truth of the scriptures. The heaven used in the book of Revelation was not the actual heaven where God interfaced with the angels of God in the light zone universe above.

It is like an amateur who is unskillful in the word, reading Genesis 1:1, which says, "In the beginning, God created the heaven and the earth." And he would assume it applies to only the firmament above the earth where rainwater falls from. No. We can see from the scriptures that the actual description 'heavens' was used in Genesis 2:1, which says, Thus the heavens and the earth were finished, and all the host of them. Heavens here implied several planets and the earth, which have established that God formed these planets as already discussed. We have the third heaven, which Paul talked about in 2nd Corinthians 12:2. Paul was referencing the levels of planets and heights of the heavens. So when John says there was war in heaven, he was reporting the event in that revelation shown to him as regards things to come; hence he used the auxiliary verb 'was.' It wasn't that war had already taken place in heaven where God is resident, and then a serious war broke out to bring Satan down. Sorry, I'm correcting so many wrong teachings over hundreds of decades here. Just follow on to know the truth.

If you further study the scriptures properly, you will find that Satan was cast out as the accuser of the brethren. If this war had taken place before the foundation of the earth, where were the believers then? Was the blood of Jesus shed before Adam was created? No. If anyone says 'yes,' such a person contradicts the scriptures. 1st John 4:2-3 says, "...Every spirit that confesseth that Jesus Christ is come in the flesh is of God: And every spirit that confesseth not that Jesus Christ has come in the flesh is not of God: and this is the spirit of the antichrist..." Antichrist implied people, languages, and nations who hate Jesus and often denounced his death, burial, and resurrection. They don't believe that Jesus Christ died physically in this world. They are myopic in their reasonings on how someone could be born without human copulation. They are confounded with the mystery of how someone died and rose from the grave. And so, in a bid to act in denial, they refute reality.

I presumed someone else would hastily quote, saying, "Oh! Jesus died in the spiritual realm before physical manifestation on earth. Hence, the scripture says, "Slain from the foundation of the world" (Revelations 13:8). That is ignorance gone too far! "Every spirit that does not confess Jesus Christ did not come to die in the flesh is the spirit of the Antichrist" (1st John 4:3). Jesus didn't die in the spiritual realm. He died on this earth physically 2,021 years ago (as of this time of writing) and was witnessed by many people. In addition, the scripture emphasized that Jesus died once, not twice. Meaning he didn't die spiritually and physically. Take note! He didn't die spiritually before the foundation of the world, in case you are erroneously quoting 1 Peter 1:20. The scriptures say he was appointed to death before the Genesis of creation.

God appointed Jesus to die before Adam sinned, as in a hidden mystery from Satan and the angels. And as soon as Adam fell, God said to Lucifer, "The seed of the woman shall bruise thy head, and thou shalt bruise his heel." We have already discussed this in detail. So Jesus was slain, which means appointed to die. That is what the scriptures meant when they say Jesus was foreordained (as second Adam) before the foundation of this world but was manifest in these last days for us (1st Peter 1:20). In other words, Jesus was appointed to die, spilling his precious blood, and take over as the second Adam as a man of the dust from the first Adam who would fail God as already foreseen by God that the soul he made would fail as well as the spirits he made. We have seen this in the scriptures as well.

Powers of heavens

The Revelation John saw about the war in heaven referred to what had been predicted when it says that the powers of heavens shall be shaken. We saw this in several scriptures. "For thus saith the LORD of hosts; yet once, it is a little while, and I will shake the heavens, and the earth, and the sea, and the dry land." (Haggai 2:6, Isaiah 13:13). And Jesus corroborated this by saying, that the powers of heavens shall be shaken. (Matthew 24:29). These powers of heavens being shaken referred to the war in heavenly places that was revealed to John the Revelator and Daniel. And the apostle Paul also wrote: "...Yet once more I will shake not the earth only, but also the heaven. And this word, Yet once more, signified the removing of those things that are shaken, as of things that are made, that those things which cannot be shaken may remain" (Hebrews 12:26-27).

In the above scriptures, Archangel Michael would lead God's host against Satan's hosts in space (See Daniel 12:1 and Revelation 12:7-8). Michael and his angels will eventually chase Satan and fallen angels from occupying space. And as you can see from the scriptures, this is the second heaven (under the darkness in space where stars are seen from the earth) where Satan operates. Satan and all stars of heaven will be thrown out of space after the great tribulation before Jesus will eventually come and reign on earth for 1000 years. Jesus confirmed that the stars of heaven shall fall, and the powers that are in heaven shall be shaken (Mark 13:25). And prior to this time, there have been some shakes in the heavens and the earth during Noah's floods and the exodus of the Israelites from Egypt, including the defeat of the Anakims on earth. Past shaking in the heavens was what Paul meant: the things that are shaken were made. In other words, Satan and his host of angels were things made, already shaken by God (as in wars fought in the Old Testament by the LORD as wars of the LORD) which shall be removed.

In the nearest future, God will shake the heavens and earth again, which will be the final onslaught against Satan, his stars, including ancient men and their descendants that belong to Satan's camp on earth. Michael and his angels will handle the powers of darkness in space; after that, Jesus Christ, at his second coming, will physically return with some angels who will turn into men and will dash in pieces humans who obey not the gospel together with all the kings of the earth who are on earth as stars of heaven. Psalms 2:9 says, "Thou shalt break them with a rod of iron; thou shalt dash them in pieces like a potter's vessel." This will be the end of the violence. I already told you that Jesus would slaughter fallen spirits, men in human flesh and their lineage who are wicked rulers on earth.

Jesus, at his second coming to planet earth, will slaughter and give the bodies of fallen spirits and their offspring to birds of the air to eat the flesh of adults, men, and women, children inclusive. This will be after the reign of the Antichrist, who would be a man capable of giving life to an artificial intelligence robot to speak and reason like a human. The people of this world will praise the Antichrist, given his intelligence and ideologies. The Antichrist will speak against God and make a caricature of the person of God because of this ability to give consciousness to a robot (Artificial Intelligence). He would claim to be God himself because of this power granted to him by God to create life in a robot. I have touched on that before.

The world would marvel here because when men shoot this robot, a miracle will occur, which will be automatic recovery (healing) of the physical wounds on this robot. The Antichrist will perform miracles and cause literal fire to fall from heaven in the sight of all that dwell on the earth. He will boast against God. This delusion is meant to attract people of this world to Satan. The Antichrist would be a fallen spirit being incarnate in human flesh and will be destroyed when Jesus Christ returns. Revelation 19:17-21 says, "And I saw an angel standing in the sun; and he cried with a loud voice, saying to all the fowls that fly in the midst of the heaven, Come and gather yourselves together unto the supper of God; That you mayest eat the flesh of kings, and the flesh of captains, and the flesh of mighty men, and the flesh of horses, and them that sit on them, and the flesh of all men, both free and bond, both small and great…and the fowls were filled with their flesh.

The book of Haggai 2:21-22 says, "I will shake the heavens and earth; and I will overthrow the throne of kingdoms, and I will destroy the strength of the kingdoms of the heathen…" Because God would not continue to have devils interfere with his programs. He will not contend forever (Isaiah 57:16).

God has been patient for over 6,000 years with Satan and these fallen spirits of death and destruction who have had sway infiltrating the earth at their whims and caprices. Satan has been judged already in Genesis, awaiting sentencing to an everlasting lake of fire. The outcome of this future war in space was foretold in Revelation 12:9-10, which says, "And the great dragon was cast out, that old serpent, called the Devil, and Satan, which deceiveth the whole world: he was cast out into the earth, and his angels were cast out with him. And I heard a loud voice saying in heaven, "Now is come salvation and strength, and the kingdom of our God, and the power of his Christ: for the accuser of our brethren is cast down, which accused them before our God day and night." This spiritual conflict will displace Satan's control over the heavenly places.

After chasing Satan and his angels out from the heavenly places, Jesus would then reign on earth for a thousand years, and there will not be any form of deception on earth anymore. It will be a period of peace on earth. This means the kingdom of God is about to dominate the earth, which had been under Satan and his comrades. The kingdom of God and the power of his Christ (anointed) actually connect what the scripture says in Psalms 2:2, that the kings of the earth took counsel against the LORD and against his anointed. His anointed will eventually possess the earth at last, as written in Psalms 82:8, which says, "…for thou shalt inherit all nations." Satan and his comrades can only oppose God's agenda on this earth for a while, but ultimately God's purpose will prevail. God is the author of life.

And until Jesus came to planet earth 2000 years ago, died, and rose again to obtain the keys of death and hell from Satan, Satan could not have been curtailed by any mortal man or angel. The death of Jesus created the platform for Satan to be cast out. John 12:31-33 says, "Now is the judgment of this world: now shall the prince of this world be cast out...this he said, signifying what death he should die." The death, burial, and resurrection of Jesus also made provision for the blood of Jesus as an offensive against the prince of this world to be cast out of the heavenly places. Without the blood of Jesus Christ, believers are defenseless in the spiritual realms.

Despite Satan's accusations against the children of God, God showed mercy upon the man of the dust and made a provision of the blood of the Lamb as atonement for sins. Satan accuses believers because he was thrown out of the light zone universe, which is far more beautiful and unfading. I believe Satan is missing the worship songs and the joy of the light zone universe, so he always points accusing fingers at those who also sinned before God so that God would cast them out of his presence as well into hell, a place of suffering and darkness. He is still envious of the man of the dust entering the light zone universe. But scripture says, "And they overcame him by the blood the Lamb, and the word of their testimony; and they loved not their lives unto the death" (Revelation 12:11). Believers in Christ should depend on God's mercy and apply the blood of Jesus as the only provisions for cancellation of sins. Many people who trusted the efficacy of the blood of Jesus were found to have been unafraid of death. Some gave up their lives for the sake of Jesus, the hope of their souls after life's earthly experience.

Chapter 19

The Concept of Good and Evil

The death of the human body is never the cessation of life. Instead, it is a continuation of the eternal life or death concept created by the everlasting God. I told you that created spirits and souls were made to join the everlasting streams of life. That is why Adam was reshaped and formed using fossil remains from the previous earth. As irrational beasts, they became living or eternal souls. Naturally, death is the disposal of the 'body in exchange for another 'earthly' or 'a glorious new celestial' body in the abstract realms. Man was formed from the 'dust of death, so the fundamental concept of death stemmed from the knowledge of good and evil, a concept which pre-existed angels and fallen spirits. The scripture says, "Unto God the LORD belongeth the issues from death" (Psalms 68:20). In context, the concept of death originated with God, which I have touched on earlier. God, who is the author of life, initiated the concept of death from the beginning of all things to subject created spirits and souls. The concept of death originated from the knowledge of good and evil, which we have identified to have pre-existed Adam and Eve as both concepts are interdependent.

There is a correlation between 'the tree of knowledge of good and evil' and 'the preknowledge of death' forwarned in the garden. Deuteronomy 30:15-19 says, "See, I have set before you this day, life and good, death and evil...blessing and cursing: therefore choose life that both thou and thy seed may live." In other words, the preknowledge of evil (sin) is the preknowledge of death. Conversely, the knowledge of good is the knowledge of life, and the knowledge of blessing sets the knowledge of cursing in motion. The wages of sin (as knowledge of evil) lead to death (Romans 6:23, emphasis mine). Having established earlier that the knowledge of good and evil originated from God, not Satan, the issues of death belongeth to God alone, who initiated it. It must be clear that at the beginning, God created life and death, light and darkness, good and evil, cold and heat, male and female, sun and moon, summer and winter, day and night (See Genesis 8:22).

These foundational works of God indicate that the concept of good and evil are the sources from which the universe under darkness is premised before the fall of any spirits or stars. His creations would then interact between both good and evil concepts over time. But some schools of thought have it that the force of good and evil implicitly dictates God and Satan were two equal opposites from the very beginning. Most theologians attribute the concept of good to God and that of evil to Satan. And, of course, I knew such notions stemmed from superficial studies of the scriptures, which often lead to fallacy. Other schools of thought are of the opinion that they need not accept the concept of good and evil, portraying a neutral stance on life. This in itself is living in denial because the entire human race has undoubtedly inherited the knowledge of good and evil through Adam's disobedience.

Those who claim to have dismissed the concepts of good and evil are living in denial because they cannot deny the fact that humanity is daily passing on. Therefore, denying the concepts of good and evil is tantamount to denying the death of humans and the burials we perform for the departed souls. However, in certain quarters, it has been observed that people who claimed to have dismissed the concepts of good and evil were found to exhibit some form of insecurity whenever someone approached their spouse with the intent to woo them away. Now, if these critics who claimed to have dismissed the concepts of good and evil react against someone who attempted to woo their spouse, it is obvious their reactions contradict their antagonisms of the concepts they claimed to have dismissed.

The above analogy depicts a clear-cut situation indicating that the majority portray 'evil' as offensive in every reasonable sense. Nobody wants their spouse to be forcefully taken or have his hard-earned money stolen, but some don't mind – amongst reasonable and unreasonable humans. We live in a world where the good and bad, the lazy and hard working, liars and honest, fools and wise, the educated and uneducated all exist. We were all shaped in iniquity. Psalm 51:5 says, "in sin did our mother conceive us." Once born into this world, you have automatically inherited the consciousness of good and evil, rain and sun, right and wrong, rich and poor, sick and healthy concepts. Even Jesus acknowledged that the poor would always be on the earth (John 12:8). As a matter of fact, God admitted he created the lame, blind, deaf, etc. "And the LORD said unto him, who hath made man's mouth, or maketh the dumb, or deaf, or the seeing, or the blind? Have not I the LORD?" (Exodus 4:11).

This positive and negative experience dictates the duality of existence in our universe under the darkness – the spiritual and natural world. And so, it would be unwise for someone to assume an end to existence at death since there is a life and death experience of the undying soul who received everlasting breath from everlasting God at creation.

The soul transcends beyond the last breath of man. God was straightforward in admonishing Adam that he had the choice of life and death, even if Adam had a baby's heart at that stage. So is everyone who is born into this world automatically acquires good and evil consciousness. Although there is an accountability stage in which a child is expected to attain this knowledge of good and evil, such a cognitive stage is known to the angels of God, who often take records of individual performances and archive them.

The concept of good and evil has saved many lives from destruction, as we have all witnessed. We know most humans don't enjoy war, but some love it. And in a bid to forestall incessant conflicts of wars on the earth, countries of the world came together to form an umbrella body called the United Nations. Its purpose is to curtail and forestall this nature of violence on the earth which had been termed evil. The concept of good and evil births the presence of governments on the earth. The first world destroyed during Noah's flood had no governments in place. Of course, we all know that whenever people are unchecked and ungoverned, they end up in anarchy. Now, we have governments in place to checkmate the excessive behaviors of humans. The book of Romans 13:3 says, "For rulers (governments) are not a terror to good works, but to evil works." Governments were instituted to counter violent (evil) living and promote peaceful (good) coexistence among citizens.

And that means the presence of government does limit the impact of violence in humans. Hence the courts of law were established to try cases of violence such as rape, manslaughter, robbery, murder, etc. Governments also take responsibility in the fight against external aggressions which invades their territories. In general, the government regulates the acquired violent nature in humans, which is what the scripture also meant by rulers are not terror to good behavior. Conversely, we have pockets of governments that are not a terror to evil works but rather a terror to their citizens; nonetheless, such evil governments are usually investigated by subsequent democratic governments. It all depends on the civilization of the countries involved.

Appropriate or inappropriate

It means the concepts of good and evil also have advantages. The essence of the concept of good and evil was set forth by God to test-run individual hearts and obsessions amongst his creatures, whether spirits or humans. And to date, some people still think that evil originated with Satan, implying Satan's opposition to God from the very beginning. They err by not knowing the scriptures. We all experience good and bad things in life because of the knowledge of good and evil, which predates man's existence.

God alone, at the beginning, classified certain behaviors as good or evil, just as man designated certain things harmful or dangerous.

Remember, God is the Father of spirits (Hebrews 12:9). So a father dictates what behaviors are appropriate or inappropriate in a given family.

Let's take a clue from a parent with two kids at age 1 or 2. If either of these children acted foolish, perhaps putting a finger into an electrical outlet, the father might yell at the child to stop. The child begins to understand what is good or evil from parental instruction over time. So also, every creature, whether spirit or human beings, obtained the knowledge of good and evil from God. God planted the tree of knowledge of good and evil in the garden. So, Adam's partaking of the forbidden fruit brought him into the knowledge of good and evil, which God instituted from the beginning of time.

In the previous earth, God expressed his displeasure over certain behaviors exhibited by his angels and spirit men before Adam was formed. We saw a spirit's admission to this fact in the book of Job. This shows Satan is not and has never been the originator of the concept of evil. It all began with God. God said, "I form light and create darkness: I make peace and create evil: I the LORD do all these things" (Isaiah 45:7). Fallen spirits were perpetually on the evil side of killing and destruction, which we have expounded on earlier. They conceive falsehood and oppression and cannot think righteous thoughts, so God was lamenting that these spirits don't have the capacity to judge rightly anymore.

Don't forget the scripture says, "God created the waster to destroy" (Psalms 54:16). This means God created the angel of death and hell to destroy stars or people who would go off course. God created evil also means he classified evil behaviors. He is displeased with certain behaviors and pleased with others. It was observed that whenever God was displeased with the Israelites in those days, the destroyer was permitted to destroy them. 1st Corinthians 10:4-9 says, "But with many of them God was not well pleased: for they were overthrown in the wilderness...and were destroyed of the destroyer." Those whose ways displeased God were destroyed in the wilderness. So when the scripture says that unto God the LORD belongeth the issues of death, it means the angel death was formed by God to subdue creatures who go contrary to his true nature of peace, mercy, justice, love, and uprightness.

Adam had a choice between life and death placed before him, as the tree of the knowledge of good and evil and the tree of life were symbolic of what the scripture meant by life and death set before you. Whatever is pleasant to our eyes is termed good, and unpleasant things are evil. God created things that he termed good, which is why the book of Genesis described what God created as good. "And God saw everything that he had made, and, behold, it was very good" (Genesis 1:32). The sun, plants, planets, beasts, fishes, lights, humans, stars, etc., were classified as very good. The stars which were reignited were touched with the power of his word.

Everything except the darkness was categorized as very good at the beginning because God separated the darkness (evil) but didn't call the darkness good in Genesis. God was satisfied with his works under the darkness but separated the darkness, which is evil. Satan's action in the Garden of Eden was classified as sinful, evil, or disapproved by God. And the darkness covering the entire space was separated from the sun, which was declared good even though our solar sun was a fallen star in the previous world. This tells us that the fundamentals upon which Adam was formed under darkness and light were invariant to the concept of good and evil, which predated him.

When God said that man is become one of us, it implies Adam obtained one aspect of the knowledge of the gods. God exhibited this aspect of the knowledge acquired by cursing and then showed Adam a sword via the cherubs. I told you spirit beings (gods) were used to the violence of cursing and wars in the pre-Adamic world, and this nature was inherited by man, who was once a beast endowed with consciousness. God placed a curse upon Eve, upon Lucifer and the ground was a function of this concept of the knowledge of good and evil initially prevented Adam. The question is: "Why does he still find fault if he also participates in cursing and wars?"

It is because God replicated himself, participating in his own concepts as a star amongst created things. It was God (as LORD) who cursed Lucifer and Eve. He also does good and evil, which I have explained earlier what sorts of evil he does. God declared his counsel to man, urging man to choose life in order to live – indicating his preference. So God's choice for humanity is known irrespective of the darkness. Hence, he said, I place life and good, death and evil before you. In other words, his counsel is not hidden from any creature. Similarly, pre-Adamic people were informed of God's counsel that they ignored, and we have seen from the scriptures that God shall wound the head of him that goeth on still in his ways.

The same God who cursed Adam showed his good side to Abraham by blessing him. So when the scripture says, I placed blessing and cursing before you, it means God exhibits good and evil knowledge by blessing and cursing. While I was writing this aspect of God cursing as spirit beings do, the LORD made me understand that curse means to place an embargo on someone. That is to restrain someone from proceeding further.

No vacuum in life

However, we must understand that there is quite a difference between sin and evil. All forms of sin - transgressions, iniquities, and abominations are evil, but evil is not necessarily sin. Spanking a child who misbehaves is evil (unpleasant) to the child but not a sin to the parent. Evil actions are unpleasant. We saw this played out in the scriptures in which God was provoked by the rebellious attitudes of the Israelites in that they were worshipping idols, and he would punish them for their evil deeds. This doesn't mean God sinned. His "evil actions" are a recompense for a creature's behaviors. "Thus saith the LORD of hosts, the God of Israel; Behold, I will bring evil upon this place...because they have forsaken me..." (Jeremiah 19:3-4). There was a cause for the unpleasant or evil action. And of a truth, God does permit evil to befall his own occasionally.

We saw in the scriptures that the evil spirit was ascribed to God. For example, the scriptures say, "But the Spirit of the LORD departed from Saul, and an evil spirit from the LORD troubled him." (See 1st Samuel 16:14, 19:9). This does not necessarily mean that God sent the spirit to trouble Saul. Of course, God could also send the spirit, as all spirits belong to him. Perhaps, as soon as the Spirit of God departed from Saul, an evil spirit will certainly enter. There is no vacuum in life. It is like someone saying," I don't belong to God's camp or Satan's camp. If you reject the LORD God, it automatically means you have accepted Satan. There is no neutral ground in life.

The spirit of pride or confusion must have influenced you to have you say that you are neither in support of God or Satan. Satan was never the author of the concept of evil. His rebellious thoughts were classified as evil. Lucifer was a victim of this concept, just that his reasonings corrupted him to think about a coup which is wickedness. Some people naturally love wickedness and violence. Lucifer knew God's ways and had once walked in God's way before he fell into his evil ways. "Thou wast perfect in thy ways from the day thou was created, till iniquity was found in thee" (Ezekiel 28:15). His path was classified as evil.

Evil also implies destruction or disaster in a given city."... Shall there be evil in a city, and the LORD hath not done it?" (Amos 3:6). Now, someone might read this and say every bad or good thing comes from God. That is not what the scripture meant. This scripture was directed to the then Israelites with whom God was dealing. God began by saying to the Israelites then: "You have I known of all the families of the earth: therefore, I will punish you for all your iniquities. Can two walk together, except they be agreed...shall there be evil in the city, and the LORD hath not done it?" (Amos 3:2-6)

God was careful to inform the Israelites that his covenant with them was the basis of afflicting them with evil. He couldn't have interfered in their affairs if there wasn't a connection. And that means he is so protective of them, to the extent of ensuring their well-being, and that evil cannot happen in the city of Israel without his foreknowledge. So this was specifically written to the Israelites, not everyone. However, nothing could make God unaware of all realms of existence.

Some people think all evil (unpleasant) occurrences or experiences on earth are permitted by God, which is a partial truth. Such persons are living a delusive life. They have not come to understand that Satan as a personality has a desire just like humans desire to drink or drive. He does execute his own desire on the earth, given the fact that he is on a mission of killing and destroying humanity through sicknesses, diseases, violence, famine, accidents, disasters, and death. And because Satan can desire to afflict someone at his own whims and carprices, does not mean he must take permission from God. There are people Satan afflicts with sickness and diseases, but such persons can become healed after prayers are offered to dispel the powers of Satan and set such persons free in the name of Jesus.

However, God sometimes permits evil to happen to people, whether righteous or sinful. Why? In order to test their faith or perspectives on life and mature them for life, and in turn, strengthen and equip them for life. The more experiences we have, the more we know how to overcome certain life challenges when they surface. Many are praying to stop the challenges of life, some of which are natural, while others are satanically manipulated to distress people. Some people will tell you that failure is just an event. It simply positions you to do well next time. But you know we've got people who may tell you that after praying, all your problems or challenges are over. They are just gimmicks!

Endure hardness

The scriptures admonished us to add patience in our walk with God on the earth. James 1:3 says, "Knowing this, that the trying of your faith worketh (requires) patience. But let patience have her perfect work, that you may be perfect (matured), and entire (thorough), wanting (lacking) nothing" (Emphasis mine). This implies that faith in God does not exclude you from facing challenges. Romans 5:3-4 says, "...But we glory in tribulations also: knowing that tribulation worketh (requires) patience, and patience births experience, and experience births hope" (Emphasis mine).

Some people are just too naive and emotional. They don't want the troubles or challenges of life. They dread the challenges of life and often yell at God. Some would even begin to hate God for the simple fact that someone whom they loved so much had passed on. It may be their best friends or family members they love or depend on. You see them cry, and they don't want to hear anything about God. They get frustrated and angry at life. And this might depress them to the point of hopelessness in life. Some are so emotional to the point of thinking about how to commit suicide because someone they loved cheated on them or died. Someone they trusted failed them, so they gave up hope.

I believe such persons have not come to the reality of their lives. Getting frustrated over someone who jilted you is not the end of life. Let me ask you a question. Suppose you were the one who jilted the other person. What would happen? You have got to grow out of such an emotional situation and face the reality of life under darkness. Jesus said that 'offense must come in this life, no matter how careful you are. The person you trusted today can hurt you tomorrow. So get ready for life's eventualities. Also, many are uninformed of the kingdom of heaven, a better planet where the violence of thieves, economic depression, or death does not exist. Having this view would encourage you instead of getting you frustrated and depressed in life. People who commit suicide don't ever walk into the kingdom of heaven. You must endure hardness as a good soldier of Jesus Christ (2nd Timothy 2:3).

You have got to endure hardness in life. It is all part of life to go through trying times. It is not always rosy! Some say that life is meant to be enjoyed alone, citing 1st Timothy 6:17. Ask such a person to tell you their stories. They have endured their hard times as well. Everyone has a story about how they arrived or succeeded after a given process. In addition, going through the entire passage of the scriptures in 1st Timothy 6:1-17 will prepare you for the kingdom of God that is to come. Life is challenging and stressful for a majority of people. Something would make you cry. Somebody will hurt you no matter how careful you are. A man born into this world is of few days and full of troubles (Job 14:1, emphasis mine).

Many people have not come to terms with the reality of life that this present world will one day come to an end. They have no idea that all humans ever born must leave this planet earth one day at a time, whether they like it or not, and it does not matter if they travel to planet Mars or Jupiter. By rapture or death or tribulations, the earth will be reeled off. No one will remain forever in this present world, though it is not best to die an untimely death. You have got to understand that the death of humans is certain - the reality of life. "For we brought nothing into this world, and it is certain that we carry nothing out." (1st Timothy 6:7).

One might ask, "Why will everyone die?" It is because God already said that all humans born into this world would return back as souls to Him. "Thou turnest man to destruction; and sayest, Return, ye children of men." (Psalms 90:3). This scripture points to the fact all humans would exit planet earth, not necessarily because Adam sinned, but because the earth was formed under darkness. Does that mean we just wait for death without achievement? No. Life goes on. Live your best, make an impact on earth, and create a footprint that affects lives by your inventions in science, your talents, and whatever God deposited in you that will positively affect your world and help humanity. But it would amount to waste if the world celebrates you on earth and you lose your soul to an everlasting lake of fire by rejecting Jesus Christ, your only hope after death. Don't be fooled into thinking you will reincarnate after you have attained the accountability stage for judgment since it is appointed unto men (Adam's descendants) once to die; after this, the judgment (Hebrew 9:27).

The scriptures say, "Their beauty shall be consumed in the grave..." (Psalms 49:14). In other words, no beautiful skin, height, or facial beauty will not be consumed by the grave at last; the most beautiful young man or woman would soon fade away. God has a plan for your entire life and the future world to come. Jesus spoke of the world to come when he said, "...neither in this world, neither in the world to come." (See 12:32). God has a hidden mystery of life, and we are the players in the field.

The hidden mystery

God's initial plans to have the man of the dust rule over all things without the knowledge of the gods (violence and immorality) must come to pass; this was the hidden mystery. The acquisition of the knowledge of good and evil also permitted the presence of the spirits of death and destruction by Lucifer to unleash pains, sickness, diseases, accidents, death, wars, and destruction of lives and property. God had to prove to the devil that the devil's wisdom was foolishness as far as God was concerned. And so, God hid His power in His Son, the man Jesus Christ, and allowed Satan to unleash his ministry of killing and destruction upon him. Satan killed the flesh of Jesus, not the God content in Jesus. Satan and his comrades killed the container, not the content.

One might contend, "But it was humans who killed Jesus Christ, not Satan and his comrades." Earlier, I showed you scriptural proofs that the powers of darkness killed Jesus with some spirit men incarnated in human flesh amongst the soldiers, Pharisees, and Sadducees. But to clarify this, let's look at the book of Psalms 22:16. It says, "For dogs have compassed me: the assemblies of the wicked have inclosed me: they pierced my hands and my feet." And Jesus knew that among the Pharisees and soldiers who killed him, there were fallen spirit men in human forms among them. Hence he said, "...But this is your hour, and the power of darkness" (Luke 22:53).

He knew spirit men, in conjunction with Adam's natural descendants, got him killed to fulfill the scriptures. And because these fallen spirit men often reincarnate at will on the earth to deceive humanity, the scripture says Jesus Christ at his second coming will also meet the same spirit men over two thousand years ago who pierced him in human forms at his second coming, since they live among us unknowingly and often incarnate at will. I know someone might be perplexed to hear this. This is not heresy. It is right in there in the scriptures. Revelation 1:7 points to this fact: "Behold he cometh with clouds (angels), and every eye shall see him (physically), and they also which pierced him (spirit men in human flesh): and all the kindreds of the earth shall wail because of him, even so, Amen" (Emphasis mine). We have dealt with how Satan and his comrades use reincarnation to deceive natural descendants of Adam to live care freely, hoping they will reincarnate.

However, Satan least expects that the death of Jesus would set prisoners free from his own territory in the land of darkness as well. Satan was clueless that the death of Jesus would restore Adam's glory and authority. Adam will certainly rule over all things as planned by God at the beginning without the spirits of death and destruction influencing them. The violent nature impacted in Adam would be excluded from man at the resurrection of the dead.

For this reason, the scriptures admonished the children of men who would partake of that world "to be of one mind, having compassion towards one another, to love as brethren, be pitiful, be courteous: Not rendering evil for evil, or railing for railing, but contrariwise blessing; knowing that you are thereunto called that you should inherit a blessing. For he that will love life and see good days, let him refrain his tongue from evil, and his lips that they speak no guile (flattery or deception): Let him eschew evil and do good; let him seek peace and pursue it" (1st Peter 3:8-11, emphasis mine). Peaceful living and love for one another are the ingredients that will characterize the life to come. You can begin to practice this future world since you have already obtained the nature of that life in you, only if you have accepted Jesus Christ as your LORD and Saviour and are led by the Holy Ghost.

Combat ready

Jesus Christ is the second Adam who will be worshipped in the world to come by all redeemed souls of men and women saved from amongst the Adamic human race of the dust. He was predicted to topple Lucifer's dominion over the first Adam. The second

Adam was tempted at all points as we are, yet without sin (Hebrews 4:15). The scriptures recorded that "when he was reviled, revile not again; when he suffered, he threatened not; but committed himself unto him that judgeth righteously" (1st Peter 2:23). He came for a purpose, and that is, to announce the kingdom of God which is all about love and peaceful living, contrary to the violence men were used to.

This gospel of peace and love was also preached to the departed souls of men who joined and adapted to the violent world in the days of Noah. Jesus's mission of preaching peace to dead souls of men and women in the spiritual realms was captioned in the scriptures of truth, which says, "...By which he went and preached unto the spirits in prison, which were sometimes disobedient when once the longsuffering of God waited in the days of Noah, while the ark was in preparation, wherein few, that is eight souls were saved by water" (1st Peter 3:18-20). Jesus went straight into the spiritual realm as soon as he gave up the ghost and preached the gospel to human souls (which Peter indicated by spirits) who participated in the violence in the days of Noah. Such opportunity will no longer be available to any dead soul leaving Earth.

So many scriptures substantiate the fact that he went straight to the land of darkness (hell), where the forces of darkness operate, holding many departed souls captive because of sin. Psalms 16:10 says, "For thou will not leave my soul in hell...." This shows Jesus visited hell. On his arrival, the kingdom of darkness suddenly heard the voice of someone coming for the keys of death and hell almost 4000 years after Lucifer stole the keys. The voice issued a command saying, "Lift up your heads, O ye gates; and be ye lift up, ye everlasting doors; and the king of glory shall come in" (Psalms 24:7). For which the kingdom of darkness trembled in response, saying, "Who is the King of glory?" And Jesus said, "The LORD strong and mighty, the LORD mighty in battle" (Psalms 24:8).

They were perplexed to have seen the LORD present right there in deep darkness. They thought they were through with the son of God like they dealt with John the Baptist without any corresponding challenge in the spiritual realm. They were perplexed beyond measure that it was the LORD himself hidden in human flesh. Jesus was alone because he was also a warrior - strong and mighty in battle without any angelic backup right in the land of darkness with fallen principalities and powers of darkness in their thousands. This was a clear-cut case of the soul of a man of the dust (in the power of God) versus all the powers of darkness put together. Lucifer can tame more than a million souls of men in hell (the land of darkness), but this very soul of Jesus was superior. It brings to mind the principalities over Persia, who once held the angel of God in space who was sent on an errand to Daniel before Archangel Michael intervened.

But here comes Jesus right in the land of darkness against all the kingdom of darkness in their trillions, and they could not raise any dust at him because his weapons of warfare were sharp two edge swords and arrows proceeding from his mouth, by which the powers of darkness fall under him. Psalms 45:3-5 says, "Gird thy sword upon thy thigh, O most Mighty with thy glory and majesty...thine arrows are sharp in the heart of the king's enemies whereby the people fall under thee." And the book of Revelation 1:16 says, "...Out of his mouth went a sharp two-edged sword...." Jesus was combat-ready in hell beneath, as the man of the dust whom Satan despised as foolish things of this world. Because he was combat ready, his response to the kingdom of darkness when asked who this King of glory was: "The LORD strong and mighty, the LORD mighty in battle" (Psalms 24:8). He is the man of war! Peaceful, but also a warrior as well, which denotes the goodness and severity of God.

Remember, in the book of Genesis, God told Lucifer the seed of the woman shall bruise thy head. To bruise means to box or to fight with fists. But Jesus's arrows and swords proceed from his mouth, and no power can withstand him in all realms of existence. And, of course, this violent aspect of the gods was what Adam became when God said, "Man becomes one of us to know good and evil," which implies the violence world. And so, Satan had no choice but to submit the keys of death and destruction, which he had subtly obtained from Adam in the beginning.

For this reason, the scripture wrote: "And having spoiled principalities and powers, he made a shew of them openly, triumphing over them in it" (Colossians 2:15). For you to triumph, it means you fought a battle. For you to plunder someone's goods in his presence, you must first bind the strong man before plundering his goods (See Matthew 12:29). And so when Jesus arose, he said, "All power is given unto me in heaven and earth" (Matthew 28:18). The power here implied the keys of death and destruction as revealed in Revelation 1:18. It was a hidden mystery to Lucifer.

The second Adam came to restore all things for us to have dominion over all things in the peaceful world to come. Hence, Paul wrote, "Therefore let no man glory in men, but in Christ (the second Adam). For all things are yours...the world, or life, or death, or things present, or things to come; all things are yours" (1st Corinthians 3:21-22, emphasis mine). Christ, who triumphed over principalities and powers, is the last or second Adam referenced in 1st Corinthians 15:45. However, the battle for the souls of the children of men born by women between God and the Devil has been declared. Whoever wins the heart wins the man. Satan knew humans were more concerned with material things, so he entices them from such an angle. Though Jesus had won the battle, Satan is resilient to have more followers.

If God is all-knowing

Many often ask, "If God is all-knowing, why didn't God know that Lucifer would eventually rebel against him?" Another question might be, "Why didn't God destroy the devil as soon as man fell into sin? These are serious questions in the hearts of men. I took out time to search the scriptures to answer these questions as much as I could.

God said unto Jeremiah, "Before I formed you in the belly I knew you, and before you came forth out of the womb, I sanctified you, and I ordained you a prophet unto the nations" (Jeremiah 1:5). In other words, Jeremiah was pre-ordained. Jeremiah's destiny was outlaid in the spiritual realm before birth. Many teachers would say you have lived your life before you were born in the spiritual realms. That is not true. Many erroneously think that Jesus died in the spiritual realms before he died on earth. That is complete ignorance. When the LORD foreknew Jeremiah, it denotes God's ability to see your tomorrow. God always speaks of your future. God sees into your future, and we can deduce from this scripture that God knows the end from the beginning, even as far as things or situations that do not currently exist, as though they already existed. (Isaiah 46:10, Romans 4:17). God who created Lucifer foreknew that he would rebel after several billion years of existence. He knows in advance that life will go through such a phase, and he's never perturbed. God knew that Lucifer would one day become the king of terror. He fashioned him for that purpose.

God is not overly concerned with the devil. He is not perturbed. He alone created a world without end. Remember, there is no end to existence because after this world comes another and another, a world without end (Ephesians 3:21). One phase into another and keep the ball rolling and interesting. He formed all things for his pleasure and can never be displaced forever. He is God alone, who knows the end. Someone might contend, how am I sure God knew Lucifer would become a rebel at last? Hear what God said concerning one of the fallen principalities of the kingdom of darkness named Gog concerning the future. He said, "Thou shalt ascend and come like a storm, thou shalt be like a cloud to cover the land, thou and all thy bands, and as many people with thee. Thus saith the Lord God; It shall also come to pass that at this same time, shall things come into thy mind, and thou shalt think an evil thought" (Ezekiel 38:9-10).

The scripture seems to predict the future performance of this principality named Gog when it says that a time will come when Gog will have a multitude of people as the sand of the seashore under his control and that because Gog would have such a multitude at his disposal, an evil thought will come into his mind. This repugnant thought will prompt Gog to risk a coup de tat against God and the saints on this earth – which is the battle of Armageddon. In other words, being lord over so many people also produces proudful tendencies. One's ability to imagine thoughts from the vast ocean of good and evil is directly proportional to preordainment or individual prideful tendencies.

The principality Gog at the moment may not have conceived such notions but will unwittingly fulfill the scripture at the set time in the future. So in providing an answer to the above question, it is an indication that God knew all things in advance before forming all things that such a pugnacious thought would flood the heart of Lucifer as soon as the man of the dust was formed. This shows that the repugnant thought that flooded Lucifer's heart was a hidden mystery. However, Lucifer loved it. Although we cannot rule out God's purpose overriding your will, it is obvious that Lucifer rose against God's choice of Adam based on predetermination.

And from experience, we all know that you cannot be tempted by things you are not interested in. If someone hates smoking and, by chance, is exposed to an environment of smoking, it might stimulate repulsion, not the desire to smoke. Only on rare occasions is someone coerced into evil vices. However, once an escape route is made available, he would certainly escape from such bondage. Thoughts only test your innermost desires or attractions, but you don't allow them to settle, especially when such thoughts are not in alignment with your values. Lucifer meditated on this pugnacious thought and gave it a voice in his heart, and God saw it. We all go through similar situations daily whenever certain thoughts flow through our minds, and we utter words in response to such thoughts.

Of course, there are no limits to thoughts flow since the power of imagination is active. Spirit beings, as well as humans, generate thoughts through the imaginations of the heart. In so far as there is no end to life, there is no end to the power of imagination. However, God, the Father of flesh and spirit, classifies thoughts into two extremes, good and evil. So his creatures acquired the nature of God – distinguishing between good and evil. Yes, God foreknew Lucifer would be the God of this world, but God wouldn't interfere until Satan personified these thoughts by implementing them. "For every one shall be salted with fire" (Mark 9:49). In other words, everyone shall be tested with the flow of evil thoughts. Hence, "If thy hands offend you cut it off..." (Mark 9:42). No matter how anointed or holier than thou you think you are, currents of evil thoughts are permitted to go through your mind to arouse your innermost obsession.

Jesus counseled us to "take no thought" (Matthew 6:31). Meaning thoughts are permitted to flow through our mind, but you should not take them into your heart. Thoughts are progressive; the longer you hold them, the more they occupy your mind and connect with similar ideas. Without the power of imagination, things cannot be created, and humans potentially create new thoughts daily, of which some imaginations birth realities. Applications such as Microsoft, Zoom, Skype, Facebook, Amazon, and WhatsApp, are functions of the imaginative powers of the mind. We sometimes generate thoughts of cheating on someone or being suspicious of others, even when they are innocent.

Thoughts flow every second-count more than the speed of light. According to the scriptures, the universe is wired and saturated with airwaves of thoughts and words (Psalms 19:4). Thoughts generated from a given heart but not acted upon are someday picked up as a signal by another heart and could be acted on. I remember I once thought of opening a recreational playground for children in a particular city several years back. At this particular time, no one had opened such recreational centers for children in that city, but I abandoned the idea. A few years later, a few people implemented the idea. God often searches hearts to know thoughts generated per time in all of his creatures. And the imaginative heart is the core of life. We shall discuss more on this as we progress.

Why didn't God destroy Satan?

The second question: "Why didn't God destroy Satan as soon as man fell?" This question has been populated in several minds of those who heard of the fall of Adam at the beginning in Eden. I also pondered this question for years until the Holy Spirit enlightened my mind, and I was satisfied with his reasons. One of the reasons God didn't immediately destroy Satan was the fact that man would have been forever lost to Satan. His purpose of recreation would have been lost forever.

It means he wasted his efforts after recreation and then lost man to Satan. Since man unwittingly took sides with Satan, destroying Satan automatically implies destroying man and stopping the earth's replenishment. He created man to inhabit and replenish the earth. He foreknew the deception and had already marshaled out a plan B which he foreordained before the foundation of the world (1st Peter 1:20). He had to be resilient. No victor, no vanquished.

Next is that Satan already had the keys of death and hell in his possession. This means God, at this point in time, may not be able to sentence Satan to the lake of fire, which is the second death, so long as the power of death was still in his possession. A man was needed to retrieve the stolen keys from Satan in hell, given that Satan took them from man (not an angel) on earth. And this was one of the reasons Jesus came to earth as a man, though despised by Satan at the beginning as foolish and weak things of this world. Jesus came as the second Adam to obtain the stolen keys of death and destruction in line with God's counsel to Satan that the same seed of the woman Lucifer despised would retrieve the keys. .

But it has to be a superior personality higher than principalities to topple such a hierarchy cherub. Lucifer was higher than archangels being in the class of God, and could not be displaced by angels unless the keys of death and hell were retrieved from his hands. We saw in the scriptures that in the future heavenly war (in space), Archangel Michael and his company of angels overcame Lucifer by the blood of Jesus. Jesus became flesh to retrieve such sensitive material from Lucifer through his death; hence the scripture says the death of Jesus signifies Satan's defeat. Satan would still have possessed the keys of death and destruction if Jesus hadn't stepped in. And so when Jesus wrote, "Now is the judgment of this world; now shall the prince of this world be cast out (John12:31). It implied Satan could only be defeated after Jesus's death and after many days (perhaps hundreds of years) Satan would be thrown out of space by Michael and his hosts.

Another reason is that Satan was a created cherub who cannot be eternally annihilated but can only be punished (Revelation 20:10). God will have to fulfill his word about the seed of the woman. He is not in a hurry, as eternity is not a billion years. Eternity is not 30 billion years; it is the power of eternal life. Hebrews 7:16 talks about the power of an endless life. There is no end to existence in the spiritual realm. Lucifer cannot be obliterated spiritually but was predicted to die for the first time under second death, just as innumerable stars of heaven who once lost their light bodies having been shut down under death for several thousand years before re-illumination in the recreation in Genesis. According to the scriptures, Lucifer will die the death of those in the midst of the seas.

Chapter 20

The Sin of Adam

So much has been said about sin, and often we hear people talk about sin. Everyone blames Adam's sin. What is sin? A typical definition of sin is disobedience to God. Sin is the transgression of the law, which means to cross a boundary. But sin was in the world before Adam. Pre-Adamic people sinned before Adam was formed, but many are unaware of this fact. The book of Romans 5:13 says, "For until the law, sin was in the world: but sin was not imputed until the law." Before proceeding further, is it true that sin was not imputed until the Mosaic laws were given? No. Sin was imputed before the Mosaic laws. To impute is to hold accountable.

In context, the law here refers to God's instruction to Adam. What law was handed to Adam?"...Thou shalt not covet" (Romans 7:7). Covet what? Don't covet the forbidden fruit. "Thou shalt not eat of the forbidden fruit, for in the day thou eatest thereof thou shalt surely - eventually die (Genesis 2:17, Emphasis mine). In other words, don't covet the forbidden fruit was the commandment given to Adam. I know apostle Paul was talking about the Mosaic laws, but an analogy could be drawn from the same scripture about the sin committed by Adam. Now, if the above scripture was narrowed only to the Mosaic laws before imputing sins committed, then how about the people destroyed by the flood of Noah? What about Sodom and Gomorrah? By what laws were they destroyed?

No law was handed to them prior, but sin was imputed to them, for which they perished before the Mosaic laws came. There was no law given by God to the people of that generation to repent of regarding crossbreeding sexual immorality that resulted in the violence. But then we saw Noah preach to his generation according to 2nd Peter 2:5. Noah may have had no idea that the giants of his days were alien as pre-Adamic people crossbreeding with Adamic descendants humans. Similarly, Lot must have preached to his generation about homosexuality or lesbianism. And your guess is as good as mine that the people would not listen. In either case, the warnings from Noah and Lot were the laws handed to their generation for which sins were imputed to them.

How about Cain?

What law was given to him before he was punished? God had to forewarn Cain that the sin of violence was about to engulf him (sin lieth at the door) - indicating sin was in the world before Adam. Despite the warning, Cain went ahead and killed his brother. How did king Abimelech know adultery was a sin even when Moses was yet born? How did Joseph know adultery was wrong? Adam was given a law, and he was held accountable for breaking the law. Sin was imputed to Adam, so God cast him out of the Garden of Eden. So when scripture says, "Sin was in the world until the law. It also denotes sin pre-dated Adam, not necessarily sins that reigned from Adam to Moses. Sin did not originate with the Adamic human race. Fallen spirits sinned before Adam was created.

God gave free will to all created spirits and human beings alike, and both have free will capability to exhibit certain traits within the boundary limits of love. However, God classified certain behaviors out of bounds. This stepping out of bounds is sin or transgression. The free will granted to his creatures is being taken to an extreme, which some people now crave an autonomous life. A demand for a completely autonomous life is a function of pride and ingratitude on the part of those canvassing for it. Agitating for autonomous life would be possible if one existed and created a separate universe, not designated life or death. Demanding for autonomous life within the universe created by God is foolishness as no one has ever self existed before, nor has what it takes to form lands, life, or planets.

This means such autonomous agitation would lead to an ungovernable and uncontrolled life that can only be granted in eternal damnation. Pride in mortals to obtain freedom from God after being created could be unattributable to fallen spirit's influence over mortals but may be a function of individualistic mindedness, dictating such a group of persons deserved eternal damnation, having benefited from the gift of life, but now demanding the acquisition of things of life, with an unwilling attitude to acknowledge the giver of life. Such a level of autonomous agitation is wickedness that should be judged outrightly.

You cannot agitate for freedom to avoid being unaccountable to God since you don't have what it takes to form the water you drink, which sustains your life, nor do you have what it takes to keep your soul alive forever. The pleasure derived from sin has forced many to demand freedom from God, just like pre-Adamic men did in their days. Sin and its deceitfulness (the evil concept initiated in this universe) seem pleasurable and loved by many when salted.

Sin is acting opposite of God's law of love, righteousness, and peace. An analogy of the scenario in the Garden of Eden would be like a four-month-old baby attempting to put a handset into its mouth. You don't spank the baby because of such attempts. Instead, you take away the handset. But as soon as the child is older and can understand right from wrong, you can show your disapproval of unwanted behaviors. God's disapproval of Adam's action is what we call transgression. In other words, Adam stepped out of his bounds.

The parent of the four-month-old baby should know that the little child would choose to place the handset in their mouth; likewise, God knew that Adam and Eve would make the wrong choice. The tendency of this child to put the handset in his mouth was anticipated because the child had no idea of the effect of its actions. Adam and Eve were warned that the effect of their sin would be death which pre-dated them.

The knowledge of sin

Romans 7:7 says, "…For I had not known sin, but by the law…." Let me expound on this: It implies Adam came to the knowledge of death through the commandment or instruction given to him. Correct? Yes. Genesis 2:17 says, "In the day you eat of it, thou shalt surely die." In other words, on the day you cross your bound, you shall surely (eventually) die. The 'law of sin and death emanated from the 'concept of evil,' which God initiated to test his creature's preferences. Adam avoided the forbidden tree because of the fear of death, which was the preknowledge of sin. This implies the law of death came with the knowledge of sin. Or else, how did Adam know what death looked like, and why did he get scared? The commandment did. Are we saying that the commandment was a sin? God forbid! Every word of God contains its requisite knowledge because out of God's mouth comes knowledge (Proverbs 2:6).

But the knowledge here is the knowledge of death given to man, which instilled the fear of death in him. "But sin, taking occasion (opportunity) by the commandment, wrought (manifested) in me all manner of concupiscence (tendencies). For without the law, sin was dead. For I was alive without the law once: but when the commandment came, sin revived (became conscious of sin), and I died. And the commandment (law) which was ordained to life, I found to be unto death. For sin taking occasion by the commandment, deceived me, and by it slew me" (Romans 7:8-11 Emphasis mine). Adam was once alive before God gave him the commandment. In this case, sin was abstract to Adam's consciousness, even if he was formed with substances taken from the earthly realm.

He was like a baby playing all by himself and fellowshipping with God. During this period, Adam was naive, not knowing what was hidden in the tree and the danger it posed. When the commandment was issued, the awareness of sin (thou shalt not) triggered his consciousness via the knowledge (fear) of death, which is the law of sin and death. Jesus once said that if he had not come and spoken unto them, they would not have sinned: but now they have no covering for their sin." (John 15:22, paraphrase). It means instruction often triggers one's volition to subscribe or not. If God hadn't told Adam about the tree which causes death, it then means Adam wouldn't have sinned so long as there was no law in place. Correct?

What do I mean? Let me first paraphrase the scriptures. "...For I had not known sin, but by the law..." (Romans 7:7). The law here is the commandment from God. "Thou shalt not eat of the forbidden fruit, for in the day thou eatest thereof thou shalt surely - eventually die" (Genesis 2:17, Emphasis mine). So when Adam thought of the tree, he thought of the law of sin and death, which is: 'Thou shalt not eat of it, or else you will die. Suppose the command "thou shalt not" is taken to an extreme. In that case, it limits a free moral agent, who being unguided, would often exhibit his volition in a directionless manner crossing the boundary limits of love into destruction unwittingly. So we have the "out of bound limits" made known to this free moral agent, Adam. Instead of ignorantly walking into the camp of death, whose forces are superior to him, he was warned about the consequences of sin.

In context, the phrase 'thou shalt not is the preknowledge of sin without the act. So long the knowledge of death was passed unto Adam, he had by such knowledge received the preknowledge of sin with it, even if the sin was not committed. The knowledge of death taking opportunity by the commandment (the law) manifested in Adam and Eve all manner of tendencies to sin, giving the exercise of their free will (rights). That is why I know that Adam would have indeed failed. The knowledge of death is the preknowledge of sin because the sting of death is sin, and the strength of sin is the commandment (1st Corinthians 15:55). You can see the connections from the scriptures that the knowledge of death through the law stimulated the tendencies to sin in Adam. The strength of sin is the commandment. The man of the dust couldn't have overcome sin, which came through the knowledge of death.

In essence, the law of sin triggers fear and tendencies to sin, which leads to death, but the law of faith triggers hope of eternal life, producing joy, even though the joyful spirit is caged in a sinful body of death. Faith is the fruit of the Spirit of life, so faith grants us access to the Spirit of life. Someone might be confused when I said, "Sin and death predated Adam." The law of sin and death was also given to fallen sons of God. Let me explain. When fallen spirits sinned, they were shut down in darkness which is death to them. Their flesh of brass was shed off like the natural man of the dust, who drops off his flesh of clay, turning into natural sand, while the soul advances into a dry land under darkness (hell) if such soul was found unjust or ungodly or unclean before God. Fallen sons of God had their spirits moved to the dry places or planets in space.

Similarly, Lucifer, who also sinned at the beginning (in Genesis), would die the death of those that were slain amid the seas. It means Lucifer would shade off his starlight body just like ancient people were once submerged in deep waters before the recreation in Genesis. As I said, Lucifer will, for the first time, experience death in the lake of fire kept in this darkness zone universe. The seas here refer to the universe under darkness. Obtaining the keys of death and hell was necessary for the subjection of the principality angel named death to be subject to a superior death power called the Second Death. This means the first prince in charge of death was darkness, and the second death (a higher prince) is the lake of fire since death and hell will be cast into the lake of fire, as earlier explained.

Adam was surrounded by the forces of death who had already sinned in the past. The knowledge of death that came via the commandment aroused his tendency to exercise his free will. It was a 'free will exercise' versus the commandment. It means the propensity to that was in Adam and Eve had been subjugated until a counter suggestion was readily available, which empowered the exercise of his free will. Despite the deception, both were deemed to have acted on free will volitions, having weighed the available options. Free will implies acting in your own ways when left to chance - acting unrestrictedly. Without the law, free will couldn't have been exercised in a contrary manner. It shows that the law was the only test to prove free moral agent behaviors.

Some people canvassed against the free will concept in an attempt to exonerate man from blame when they say, "Why would God allow man to be freed?" But you will all agree that we cannot think differently without free will. God is not selfish and is never interested in forming creatures that represent his image as zombies. He seeks reasonings from them. Free will has never been the problem. It becomes sin when you blame the game because of your addictions despite the free gift of salvation that is made available.

Gradual aging

Sin is the act of disobedience to God's voice. When God spoke to Adam in the Garden of Eden, his spoken word could only be conveyed directly to Adam's spirit man. God as a

Spirit talks to our spirit man, which vibrates through our soul - awareness, even if you are standing before God. Psalms 62:11 says, "God hath spoken once, twice, have I heard..." The spoken word hits the spirit and vibrates through the soul. God's commandment went through Adam's spirit, even if Adam's ears were opened. Adam's spirit, through his physical body, indulged in disobedience. It showed two things are involved here: First, the setting aside of God's instruction to abstain from the forbidden fruit, and secondly, the sin of Adam permeated his spirit, soul, and body.

The human heart has a department called the conscience. The conscience is not the soul, but the soul conveys the heart's conscience. The conscience of the heart being defiled causes a continuous remembrance of things done by the body. The soul filters impulses from the heart and spirit. Though the conscience is permanently conscious of sins committed, if not washed in the blood of Jesus Christ, the soul remains in a closed compartment with the spirit and heart. I will expound on the differences between the heart, soul, and spirit as we progress, which many wrongly assumed are the same.

The physical body which ate the forbidden fruit actually ate the spiritual substances of death. That is why the body wears out over time, aging unto death. Eating the forbidden fruit causes the human flesh to experience sickness, diseases, pains, aging, wrinkles, etc., eventually leading to death. The chain of events that culminated in the phrase "surely die" or "eventually die" was enumerated by God in the scriptures. Still, many people skipped this later part of the scriptures, which detailed what God meant by "in the day thou eatest thereof, thou shalt surely die."

Many misconstrued it to mean instant death of the body, but the scriptures gave us a proper perspective of the phrase "surely die," in which God detailed the processes involved, saying, "...In sorrow shalt thou eat of it all the days of thy life; thorns and thistles shall it bring forth to thee; and thou shalt eat the herb of the field; In the sweat of thy face shalt thou eat bread, till thou return unto the ground; for out of it wast thou taken: For dust thou art, and unto dust shall thou return" (Genesis 3:17- 19). This implied Adam would toil and experience hardship, sickness, and aging before death. I see no reason why people criticize God other than their lack the understanding of the scriptures. Death impacted Adam's flesh through gradual aging via suffering, sickness, and aging. Adam was shut out from seeing God. He was handed over to death, but his spirit man didn't die. Instead, his spirit became defiled, dormant, and dimmed. He came short of glory. He has shut off fellowship with God, which some have wrongly interpreted to mean Adam died in the spirit.

The phrase 'died spiritually' does not implicitly suggest Adam's spirit died. No. It means Adam was shut off from seeing God. When the Prodigal son seeks freedom from his father, thinking he could survive on his own, he was regarded as one dead. "For this my son was dead, and he is alive again" (Luke 15:24). That does not mean that the prodigal son actually died. So also, Adam didn't die in his spirit man. He was thrown out of God's divine provisions and coverings. He was driven out of God's covering in the Garden of Eden to a place where he would wear out in an attempt to survive life. So God ensures his word, handing Adam over to death, where Adam will be buffeted with sickness, scorching sun, and labor until he physically dies. Though Adam ate the forbidden fruit when he was about 120 years old, he lived on toiling and aging until 930 years.

Exchanged in split seconds

Adam's spirit was defiled and dormant, but his spirit didn't die. The scripture clearly states in James 2:26 that "the body without the spirit is dead." Had the spirit died, the body also would have died. But the body can die without the spirit being dead. The spirit fell short of its initial content of 'glowing' or 'glory' (Romans 3:23). The fullness of God's glowing nature went dimmed in Adam's spirit. The glory of God glowing in the spirit of Adam got dimmed and dormant, which is the meaning of "short of God's glory." We can say, less light. That is why the born-again experience deals with the disobedience of the old man – the spirit in Adam who sinned.

In other words, the spirits of Adam's descendants need to be recreated since God relates with the spirit in man. We discovered that Enoch, Abraham, Samuel, and Moses all walked with God despite Adam's disobedience. Their spirits were revived or reignited, though the conscience was still sin conscious. God had to overhaul the internal recreation exercise of the man of the dust without shutting down the system (without man's death), which I think is an innovation. "...A new spirit will I put within you." (Ezekiel 36:26). Adam's defiled, dormant, and dimmed spirit would have to be changed without necessarily shutting down the human breath. How can that be?

This operation occurred after the death and resurrection of Jesus Christ in humans. This spiritual surgical operation without shutting down the system becomes a miracle in the spiritual perspective in that the scriptures say, "The wind bloweth where it listed, and thou hearest the sound thereof, but canst not tell whence it cometh, and whether it goeth: So is every one that is born of the Spirit" (John 3:8). The ways and workings of the Spirit are mysterious to the children of men. The wind of the Spirit went through that individual without sound and deposited a new spirit in him. The defiled, dimmed, and dormant spirit was exchanged without the body's death during the born-again experience. That makes it a miracle!

One could wonder, "How can your old spirit in you die and a new spirit inserted while breathing?" Such a phenomenon got Nicodemus, who was a religious Pharisee, perplexed. He asked, "...How can a man be born again when he is old? Can he enter into his mother's womb and be reborn?" (John 3:4). The defiled old spirit man died and was exchanged in a split second when confession was made by which the new man obtained the second Adam's life. This means the born-again experience is not only the confession of Jesus alone but an exchange of a new creature (second Adam's life) inserted into the human flesh spiritually while still breathing, and the old Adamic spirit in man dies.

This mystery is an earthy spiritual experience and is only available to those who accepted the sacrifice of Jesus Christ, confessing him as LORD and Saviour. It is an operation carried out by the wind of the spirit, invisible to the human eyes, while the effects are manifest in that individual after that. The question is, "Where is the old spirit man that died?" It was buried when the believer got baptized by immersion because water is the habitat of spirits. The old man was trashed out into the deep. "Know you not that so many of us as were baptized into Jesus Christ were baptized into his death? Therefore, we are buried by baptism into his death...knowing that our old man (the old spirit in man who died when he accepted Jesus Christ at the born-again stage) is crucified with him that the 'body of sin' (old spirit) might be destroyed, henceforth that we should not serve (labor under) sin. For he that is dead (death of the old man) is freed from sin" (Romans 6:4-7, Emphasis Mine).

The "body of sin" actually means the old spirit in Adam, which became defiled, dormant, and diminished in glory, died. The dead spirit in man was washed in water by baptism. The burial of the old man is very crucial, which explains what Jesus meant when he said, "Suffer it to be so now: for thus it becometh us (men) to fulfill all righteousness" (Matthew 3:15). In other words, Jesus dropped the Adamic nature mixed with his body through Mary's blood, his earthly mother's contamination during the baptism at Jordan. This implied your old spirit man (Adamic nature) must be buried through water baptism after declaring Jesus Christ as your LORD and personal savior in fulfillment of all righteousness (John 3:5). Your new spirit has fulfilled all righteousness which makes you complete in him. This shows you obtain the righteousness of God in your new spirit that is now as righteous as Jesus. As earlier said, the old spirit in Adam didn't die. It was defiled, dimmed, and dormant because we discovered that many people in the Old

Testament related to God through their spirit despite Adam's transgression.

Purchased possession

Prophets of old who walked with God - aligning their consciousness with God in fellowship reignited and had their spirit restored to almost full glory status, even if their soul retained sin consciousness. This tells you that if the spirit of Adam died as popularly being masqueraded in some quarters, man would not have been alive anymore in the first place, much more being able to reignite his spirit in God's glory even in the sinful flesh of Adam. But so many people got reignited.

Although the soul sometimes maintains its guilt emanating from the conscience of the heart, which was corrupt, continually having the attendant effect of evil imaginations (Genesis 6:5).

The saving work of Christ at the cross of calvary dealt with the spirit of Adam, which sinned, while the soul of the regenerated Christian is still unsaved. The blood of Jesus purifies the components of the soul since blood makes atonement for the soul in man. It means the blood is needed to cleanse the heart's conscience whenever the soul sins, which is embedded in the soul for restoration. The book of Psalms 23:3 says, "He restoreth my soul...." In other words, God brought back my soul consciousness of his person. The soul being defiled by thoughts, performance, and words of the body was deemed deviated, and this characterizes many who are under the infirmities of the body.

Hebrews 5:2 talks about being off course (deviation), which characterizes the Christian journey since it is anticipated that there is the likelihood to deviate during the journey, just like an airplane sometimes drops in the air while on a journey. This temporary deviation is understandable because allowance was put in place for them that are temporally out of the way or fall into sin but realized and retracted. The apostle Peter deviated in his journey but repented and realigned his focus. That is why it is unhealthy to judge anyone who is weak because he could repent at any moment and be restored. Not one Christain can boast of being sinless after accepting Jesus Christ as LORD and personal savior so long he is in the flesh. However, the world would often criticize and crucify genuine believers or pastors who fell into sin as though they had attained perfection.

No matter how anointed a man of God might be, there was an allowance made for repentance. The soul of every born-again Christian is expected to be saved at the end of their faith. Jesus admonished his disciples to be patient to have their souls salvation at last. He said unto his disciples, "In your patience, possess your souls." (Luke20:19). In another scripture, it says, "Receiving the end of your faith even the salvation of your souls" (1st Peter 1:9). Confidence in Jesus's sacrifice on the cross and absolute faith in his gift of righteousness is required in the heart of every believer at the end of faith.

The sin of Adam was registered in the heart's conscience, and because the spirit is synchronized with the soul, the soul was affected. This implies the soul needs to be changed when we receive our new body in the world to come since an overhauling process has begun on the earth. Had the soul been saved together with the spirit, no Christian would sin anymore after being born again on earth. But you cannot change the soul without changing the body. Since the soul came into being as an extraction of substances coined from the body and spirit during recreation captured in Genesis 2:7. Hence, the body has to die first, making death a necessity for those on earth.

The flesh, bones (fossils), and blood taken from this earth (dust of death) to form man can never inherit the kingdom of God; it must be changed by death or rapture. The flesh profits nothing at last. (John 6:63). It must wear off by aging or death. But the skeletons are preserved after death because they would be used again during the resurrection of the dead. "The hour is coming, and now is, when the dead (chosen believers that are in the grave) shall hear the voice of the Son of God: and they that hear shall live." (John 5:24, emphasis mine).

The skeletons will be used in the resurrection of the dead on earth again for those who will participate in the first resurrection of the dead captured in Revelation 20:4- 5, which says, "...And I saw the souls of them that were beheaded for the witness of Jesus, and for the word of God...they lived and reign with Christ a thousand years...this is the first resurrection." So we would have people in Christ who will be resurrected to life again on this earth. The skeletons are reserved in the grave for the first resurrection, and Jesus promised they should live and reign with him again for a thousand years.

Jesus bought you over from the powers of darkness unto himself when you accepted Him as LORD and Saviour. "For you are bought with a price: therefore, glorify God in your body, and in your spirit, which are God's" (See Ephesians 1:14, 1st Corinthians 6:20). The book of Ephesians 1:13 talks about the redemption of the purchased possession, which deals with Christians waiting until the soul and body are changed. It means a complete takeover of what has been bought by the blood of Jesus. The born-again spirit would not be changed anymore when a child of God departs from planet earth into paradise, but the soul. The spirit will be clothed with a cloudy body, just like the angels and sons of God.

I could remember the death of a sister who passed on during delivery. My eyes were opened to see her soul. She was lamenting, sitting beside her carcass for hours in the spiritual realm, how she had suffered on earth. She said, "I suffered, I suffered on earth from my youth," after that, I saw light, and she walked into glory. That was when I knew she had departed into paradise. Her body was taken for burial, but the spirit, in oneness with the soul, was absorbed in light into the universe above. Prayers at a burial are just ceremonial. They add nothing to the departed souls. And it does not matter who prays.

One time, a friend of mine passed on suddenly, but prior to his demise, the Lord revealed every bit of what he ate that resulted in his death, which was poison. A few days later, I saw his soul move from the earth and hung in the cloud. While I was thinking about how a believer's soul could be suspended in the cloud, the LORD enlightened my mind, and I then understood the cloud of witnesses talked about in Hebrews 12:1. It implies those who were martyred were found under the altar (See Revelation 6:9). The martyrs of Jesus will be re-fixed to a glorious body superior to the earthly body of flesh and blood hence God is not overly perturbed about death, except when such destiny was cut short unfulfilled.

As earlier explained, God will fix the man of the dust (Adam) again, but fallen spirit beings who sinned cannot be fixed anymore, as they cannot return to the light zone universe. That was why Jesus said, "Only God is good," having saved the human race from perishing forever. Your spirit was changed during the born-again encounter, while the soul is constantly cleansed or renewed by God's word and the heart's conscience by the precious blood of Jesus Christ. The flesh profits nothing; only needed to accomplish destiny or individual assignments on earth. And that means man must exit the earth by death for the body and soul to be recreated. It is crystal clear that God will no longer put in any effort regarding sin after the death of Jesus. It is once and for all sacrifice for sin; that is why there remains no more sacrifice for sins if we lose this precious opportunity once saved (Hebrews 10:29).

Sin and wickedness

God had to start all over with man because of the distortion at the beginning. The distortion was sin. I know sin is sin, even the thoughts of the heart. But sins are categories – transgression, iniquity, abomination, etc. We also have what the scriptures referred to as "Wickedness." There is a difference between sin and wickedness. Sin is a general term, but wickedness deals with an inhuman attitude to man or God. Some people may not sin but are categorized as wicked. Wickedness is relational, burn out of selfishness.

A born-again Christian may not sin but can be wicked and selfish. Jesus portrayed his judgment on Christians would be based on wickedness and selfishness.

He gave a typical example when he talked about a man traveling on a journey. This man was accidentally attacked by armed robbers, wounded, and left half-dead. Then it happened that a Levite and priest had passed this man at an interval of time, and both "Christians" seemed unconcerned and uncaring, perhaps due to racial discrimination, tribal or religious difference, selfishness, etc. However, the scriptures recorded that a Samaritan had passed by that way and showed compassion to this man, and he was commended for his compassion for humanity (See Luke 10:25-37). The Samaritan, who was a 'sinner,' acted in love according to heaven's ethics.

Wickedness is what you do against your neighbor in your closest. It is an intentional act to oppress, maltreat, suppress, and be merciless—man's inhuman attitude to man. Wickedness could be in the form of selfishness and pride. The rich man was in hell because he had no compassion for Lazarus, whom he once knew on earth. He was in a position to help Lazarus while on earth but was selfish and wicked (Luke 16:19-31). All for himself alone: "For I was hungry, you gave me no food, sick, you visited me not, thirsty you gave me no water to drink; naked, you clothed me not" (Matthew 25:31-45).

Joseph refused wickedness against Potiphar even when Potiphar was unaware of his wife's move to have Joseph commit adultery. The wife of Potiphar offered her body for sexual pleasure, but Joseph thought good how kind Potiphar had been to him. Potiphar trusted Joseph such that he did not ask Joseph to account for anything in the house as a steward. So Joseph said to Potiphar's wife, "How can I do this great wickedness and sin against God?" (Genesis 39:1-9). He felt he could not repay Portiphar with evil, having trusted him that much. He had his conscience alive.

Once, a wealthy young ruler came to Jesus justifying himself. He claimed to have kept all religious laws blamelessly, for he said, "All these have I kept from my youth." But Jesus replied and said," One thing thou lackest, Go sell all you have and give to the poor, and come and follow me, then thou shalt have eternal life." Scripture recorded that he was sad and went home sorrowful because he was self-centered, not wanting to give to others (See Luke 18:18-23).

Wickedness is watching someone die when you could have helped. It's doing everything within your power to make someone cry and miserable. You are simply glad you oppressed someone without a corresponding challenge. The Judge of all the earth will answer the wicked on the judgment day on the final exit of the earth. "Be not over much wicked, neither be thou foolish: why shouldest thou die before thy time?" (Ecclesiastic 7:17). Because "...the wicked shall be cut off from the earth..." (Proverbs 2:22).

God will cut off all forms of wickedness: ingratitude, unthankfulness, and selfishness, which are categories of wickedness. Wickedness is manifest daily. It will be judged outrightly by God. It is often expressed by suppressing the voice of the conscience, and you could perceive certain hearts being seared with hot iron exhibiting lies in hypocrisy (1st Timothy 3:2). The wicked encounter a strained relationship with the spirit of God because the heart of the wicked tends to resist God.

Chapter 21

Relationship with God

The wicked will be ashamed on the Day of Judgment. To be ashamed is to have one's conscience convicted over a regrettable misdeed. In other words, shame strips you of your defense mechanism. It brings you under guilt. Romans 3:19 says, "...that the world may become guilty before God." Guiltiness torments until mercy is sought. Guilty conscience leads to less confidence. Only the blood of Jesus Christ is capable of cleansing a guilty conscience when sins are confessed before God. Adam became guilty of wrongdoing, and he knew it. Having attained sin consciousness, Adam had unwittingly set himself up against God. The enmity that built up in his mind translated into separation from God. He became an enemy in his mind. And once the mind is against someone, the relationship gets strained. Colossians 1:21 talks about being "...enemies in your mind by wicked works..." Adam and Eve became enemies in their minds and hid themselves because of shame.

The scripture says, "...Adam and his wife hid themselves from the presence of the LORD God in the midst of the trees of the garden" (Genesis 3:8). Shame becomes the resultant effect of a guilty conscience. Shame and fear pervaded their entire beings. Adam came under the bondage of shame and fear. Fear is not necessarily a by-product of sin because the fear of the LORD is the beginning of wisdom. The word of God conveys the fear and knowledge of the LORD. It's expected of a child to respect or fear his parents much more God. The spirit of God instills the fear of God in all creatures of God. Psalms 89:7 says, "God is greatly to be feared in the assembly of the saints, and to be had in reverence of all them that are about him." When you see God in majesty, you will fear and worship. Often the fear of God keeps you from acting contrary to his will.

Job held his mouth when he saw the LORD. Job responded by saying, "I have heard of thee by the hearing of the ear: but now mine eye seeth thee, wherefore I abhor myself repent in dust and ashes." (Job 42:5-6). Job was amazed, having seen the LORD. When Abraham saw the LORD who visited him in the company of two angels in the flesh, Abraham felt inferior and said, his own body is dust and ashes. Similarly, Job saw the LORD and also felt inferior. This tells you the kind of body the LORD has on entering planet earth. Both men feared the LORD in their days. The fear of God in righteousness doesn't torment. It enables us to communicate with him and, over time, reach out to the love side of God. God loves but also disciplines. The scriptures talked about the goodness and severity of God. The goodness of God drives us into God's arms of love. His force of love is stronger than his severity side since he does display his severity with mercy.

Adam once enjoyed this affectionate relationship with the Lord, but when sin penetrated his consciousness, love and confidence were displaced in exchange for the fear of death. Sound mind was substituted with the bondage of death. 2 Timothy 1:7 says, "For God hath not given us the spirit of fear; but of sound mind." Adam fled in fear of God. The fear of death entered the human race, leading to fear of the unknown and bringing men under bondage. Adam was afraid of death throughout his life, and he "was subject to bondage" (Hebrews 2:15). Fear is bondage. Man, animals, creeping things, fishes, fowls, and insects all came under the fear of death, avoiding death at all costs. Adam was in bondage and spent his life fleeing death. "... I heard thy voice, and I was afraid" (Genesis 3:9).

The same voice Adam heard that brought peace of mind became dreadful to him. The voice which taught him the science of naming things formed from the ground became dreadful because of his guilty conscience. Two fears were established: Dread of God and fear of death. Adam was afraid of God and, at the same time, in the bondage of death.

Abusing God

Sin brought the fear of death in man and the fear of being uneasy in approaching God. This strained relationship between God and man degenerated and was further exacerbated by abusing God, which came about by the enmity of the mind. Adam's mind went into enmity by joining fallen spirits of death used to abuse God. And this is why many people abuse God in their hearts from a young age. Many young people find themselves abusing God in their hearts, and they might be wondering how such repugnant thoughts infiltrated their hearts. Humans often find themselves opposing God and apportioning blame to God. There is severe pressure and a tendency to resist God in the human heart, regardless of age. It is a function of the fallen spirit nature that permeates the hearts of men, constantly influencing and corrupting their thoughts at the slightest opportunity.

Some people curse God in their hearts whenever they are overly pleasured by drunkenness, gluttony, or immorality. Many inwardly utter words against God but fail to realize that He also created pleasurable things for us to enjoy. As a matter of fact, people who are indulged in prostitution or sexual immorality, cheating, drinking, and bloodshed have formed the habit of abusing God at will. Of course, evil spirits instigate men; nonetheless, it is our responsibility to reject such thoughts. We should war against these spirit beings influencing our hearts, whose presences are very much on the earth's realm and also ruling from the darkness in space, rivers, and planets.

Such unexpected thoughts of abusing God at heart ought to be rejected as they are initiated by fallen spirits amongst us, who whisper such words in the form of thoughts to us. Scripture says, "Casting down imaginations, and everything that exalteth itself against the knowledge of God, and bringing into captivity every thought to the obedience of Christ." (2nd Corinthians 10:5). You should immediately cast out such evil thoughts from your heart, not meditating on it. Thoughts that abuse God are triggered by Satan and his comrades in the heart of men and women only in this dark universe.

Job realized that his children might have cursed God in their hearts. "...For Job said, It may be my sons have sinned, and cursed God in their hearts..." (Job 1:5). And we saw Job's wife knew such current of evil thoughts of abusing God in her heart that often flowed through her; hence she suggested that Job should curse God and die. I have been wondering how these unexpected satanic currents of abuse towards God permeated the human hearts on the earth. Of course, I know the scripture acknowledges that Satan has access into men's hearts. "The devil having now put into the heart of Judas Iscariot..." (John 13:2). Satan puts thoughts into men's hearts. Satan often injects abusive thoughts against God into men's hearts at the slightest opportunity. This happens to children as well those of the age.

And I also knew from the parable of the seed sower told by Jesus that Satan has access to men's hearts, which is very dangerous because it could lead many to backslide (See Luke 8:12). God has access into men's hearts, so does Satan because, being a spirit, Satan learned things from God. And this means the battle of life is in the heart. The spiritual warfare of this life on earth is about the state of the heart, whether for or against God, regardless of your years on earth. So the scripture admonished us to guide our hearts with all diligence, for out of it are the issues (essence) of life (Proverbs 4:23). I once communed with God about this deception of Satan who is not seen infiltrating men's hearts and how it was not men's fault. But the LORD said," I agree that Satan deceived men, but I will hold men responsible for their choices." This implies that the force of good and evil tests our innermost tendencies, which means we have a choice. But many are enslaved by these forces of darkness, struggling with addictions being unable to overcome for years.

Make caricature

Satan taught fallen stars how to access human hearts. The habit of abusing God could be dated back to the days of old (the pre-Adamic era) when ancient people rose up against God, rejecting God, saying, what can the Almighty do for them? Even in hell, human souls in there often abuse God to date. When Adam fell, the nature of these spirits robbed Adam's descendants, and that is how the heart of men began to curse. It's your duty to cast down every imagination which exalts itself against God, even if it requires you to respond verbally. You didn't initiate such abusive thoughts, but Satan and his hordes of darkness did. Whenever an inadvertent abusive thought pops up, tell the devil that he is a rebel, and he will leave you alone! But I do not say you tell the devil that he is stupid because one time when I did that, God immediately corrected me, saying, "Satan is not stupid!"

According to the scriptures, all such abuses of God will be met with judgment from God. God will cast these spirits beings into the everlasting fire at last, in which they will be tormented. We saw the judgment of these fallen spirits in the book of Daniel, Jude, and Revelation. Daniel 7:11 says, "I beheld then because of the voice of the great words (abuses) which the horn spake: I beheld till the beast was slain, and his body destroyed and given to the burning flame." When the scriptures refer to a beast in this instance, it means a fallen spirit incarnated in human flesh. Revelation 19:20 expressly talks about the beast as a personality. "And the beast was taken, and with him the false prophet that wrought miracles before him, with which he deceived them that received the mark of the beast, and them that worshipped his image. These were both cast alive into the lake of fire burning with brimstone. And the remnants were slain with the sword of him that sat upon the horse, which sword proceeded out of his mouth: and all the fowls were filled with the flesh."

Spirit beings live among us as humans. They are now average humans who dwell on this earth, not giants. The beast represents the antichrist government or a celebrity on this earth who will openly speak against God and abuse God at will. The same antichrist (beast) was spoken of in Revelation 13:4. It says, "Who is like unto the beast? Who is able to make war with him?" And if you read further, he opened his mouth against God. God will respond at the appropriate time. The antichrist as a government would greatly influence the people of this world by issuing defamatory comments about God and Jesus Christ. It would make people see why they don't need God since he (antichrist) can give life to a robot (A.I.) and perform miracles. And because of his deceivable words, many will join his cunning ways.

The scriptures identified the government of the antichrist as murmurers and complainers. Jude 1:16 says, "These are Murmurers, complainers, walking after their own lusts, and their mouth speaketh great swelling words..." He will make a caricature of the person of Jesus. He might begin with a movie alleging that Jesus Christ had a sexual relationship and that Jesus even had children. He will be very bold in his actions, and the world will follow him. He is the very seed of the devil in human form. The Lord once opened my eyes in a vision to see the spirit inside the person of the antichrist, but what I saw was indescribably terrific and horrible to behold. The antichrist will be out to deceive men and women since he is known as the man of sin. Sin is why these devils will be permitted to have their final onslaughts.

Loving relationship

But I found out that despite sin, a relationship was still established. God indicated his disapproval but went ahead with the relationship, which is much more important. His primary purpose in creating man was to have them praise him joyously (Psalms 22:3; Isaiah 43:21). God declared the end from the beginning that the man of the dust must dwell on this earth in peace at last. Although Satan thwarted the relationship between God and man, God still seeks to continue the relationship. The love for man costs him so much. Man could be likened to a missing sheep whose Shepherd went all out seeking to restore him into the fold despite his failures and inadequacies.

For example, in a marriage relationship between a man and woman reared up in different backgrounds, it is expected individual backgrounds would influence their behavioral outcomes, which I'd designate as - likes or dislikes. It is pertinent that if the relationship is prioritized above the designated outcomes which pose the challenges, one might overlook or consider seriously such shortcomings. It all depends on the individual parties involved. Some parties amplify the dislikes, which leads to divorce, while others tolerate and accommodate each other leading to a continuous relationship. If either party endures and tolerates the failures and inadequacies of each other, they might end up nurturing the marriage in the long run.

Similarly, in the beginning, God established a relationship with Adam. But when man sinned, God was angry and pronounced a curse on the ground for man's sake.

The love for man was far more important than the sin committed because man was deceived into sin. God considered the relationship far more important than the sin. God forgave man but had to make true his word that man would eventually die by enumerating the sequences before death occurred. His bowels of mercies poured out, so he made coats of skin and covered their nakedness. "Unto Adam and his wife did the LORD God make coats of skin, and clothed them" (Genesis 3:21). You can see that there was a relaxed mind from God toward man afterward.

The problem with Adam and Eve is that they didn't show any remorse or repentance; instead, they engaged in self-defense which necessitated the provocation to curse. Had they owned up, there would not have been any curse. This is what the LORD told me. Cain, as one of the descendants of Adam, was also cursed by God, but Cain pleaded for a lesser punishment, saying, "My punishment is greater than I can bear" (Genesis 4:13). And God, who is compassionate and merciful, listened to his plea and immediately had to reduce his punishment. God is merciful because of relationship. Relationship is what makes him happy since there is nothing he cannot create. But relationship affects God's soul. Enoch walked with God and was translated due to a relationship with God.

Noah also walked with God in his generation and offered God an offering. Scripture recorded that the LORD smelled a sweet savor. God said in his heart, "I will not again curse the ground any more for man's sake" (Genesis 8: 21). In other words, what God is saying is, "I need to set aside this curse stuff because what I'm seeking for, is my lost relationship." God isn't overly concerned with sin; hence he dealt with sin issues so that man can be reconciled unto God. Simply acknowledge your sins by repentance, and continue in the relationship with God, who is being waited for you. God seeks a man or woman with whom he can relate. Fellowship is God's passion for man because "the Father seeketh such to worship him" (John 4:23). Relationship with God daily overrides sin consciousness in Jesus Christ.

Of course, it's anticipated that someone might contend saying, "Must it be in Jesus Christ alone? Can't someone worship God without accepting Jesus Christ and go to heaven? What about saints of old who worship God and are now in heaven?" Nice questions! Yes, I agree that saints of old, like Job, Moses, Abraham, Elijah, Daniel, etc., are now in heaven. They were servants of God in the Old Testament, and they made it to heaven being in fellowship with God. But then, the same scriptures you read made it clear that God, who at sundry times and in divers manners spake in time past unto the fathers by the prophets, hath in these last days spoken unto us by his Son, whom he hath appointed heir of all things, by whom he also made the worlds" (Hebrews 1:1-2).

And this is the problem. Many religions teach that they can access God without Jesus Christ. They see Jesus as the man they cannot worship or believe in. But Jesus didn't reject any man who worshipped him on earth either since he was God. Scripture says that God dealt with men through the prophets in the past, but in our dispensations (2000 years ago to date), in fulfillment of the mystery of the seed of the woman spoken about in Genesis, God has appointed his Son Jesus Christ. In other words, Jesus is the seed of the woman who will override Satan's powers and eventually possess the earth, as discussed earlier. Jesus created the world as a person. So, refusing to accept Jesus as your LORD and savior and believing that you are the seed of Adam or Abraham is counterproductive. The mysteries of the Godhead have been unveiled in this book.

You may not be privileged to see any other book which explains these mysteries from the scriptures; God revealed these things to me. You are advised to believe and accept Jesus Christ now. For this reason, Jesus said that he is the way to the Father (John 14:6). The Father was in Christ reconciling the world unto himself: "To wit, that God was in Christ, reconciling the world unto himself, not imputing their trespasses unto them; and hath committed unto us the word of reconciliation" (2nd Corinthians 5:20). Reconciliation speaks of getting back to a relationship with God. Relationship with God is everything God is seeking in man. The lost fellowship frustrated by Satan will begin all over again in the world to come, but you should now live as though you are already in the new world, fellowshipping and loving God right now.

Relationship establishment was why God did not rebuke Abraham even when he lied to cover up Sarah, saying Sarah, his wife was his sister to save his life. God had to defend Abraham and deal with Pharaoh and Abimelech (See Genesis 12:11- 20). He weighed Abraham's reasons for lying at that point in time, not that God approved of telling lies since Lucifer invented the concept of lie or deception. Abraham must have repented of his sins and continued fellowship. However, so many are busy out there chasing how to overcome sin and missing out on a relationship with God. Many serve God to escape hell, but no relationship with God. Scripture says, "For if Abraham was justified by his performance, he could not have glory before God" (Romans 4:2, emphasis mine). So long you are in the flesh, don't expect to be 100% perfect, but your daily fellowship with God keeps you on track.

Sins are covered

King David was a typical example of a man who loved the LORD. He understood God's love and knew that a genuine relationship with God canceled his sins. He knew the power of being in love with God, and he wrote, "Blessed is the man whose transgression is forgiven, whose sin is covered. Blessed is the man unto whom the LORD imputeth not iniquity, and in whose spirit there is no guile" (Psalm 32:1-2). When you seek a relationship with Him as in worship, praise, prayers, and walking in love, it cancels out your sins, and your soul is restored. Constant fellowship and walking in love does override sins. That is why there was a provision for repentance to those who realized their sins and asked for forgiveness of sins. 1st John 1:7 says, "But if we walk in the light as he is in the light, we have fellowship with one another, and the blood of Jesus Christ cleanseth us from all sins." To walk in the light is to walk in love which implies your love for God in fellowship, which also translates into love for the brethren.

Jesus sacrificed himself to restore the lost relationship between God and man, which canceled man's sin (Hebrews 9:26). In other words, sin is not the focus anymore, but continuous fellowship with God is what matters. We should acknowledge and confess our sins when we come into fellowship with God. Refusing to confess sin is pride in itself. We are sin polluted conscious and unconsciously daily. The Holy Spirit told me that 'whenever His people are gathered in his presence, they are cleansed, but when they move into the world, they get polluted. However, some people are so engraved in sin consciousness and have lost their relationship with the Holy Spirit. You can never be overly conscious of sin and love God simultaneously. Because anytime you excessively focus on your sins, you become ashamed, which dwindles your confidence. However, when you are conscious of your righteousness, it causes you to trust in his mercy. You must trust in the mercy of Jesus like a son would run into the hands of the Father, not remembering sins.

It brings to memory an experience I once had with one of my sons when he was four years old. He was spanked for wrongdoing. A few minutes later, he dashed into my room and hugged me, completely forgetting all that had happened. Immediately the Holy Spirit spoke to me and said, "This is the way I want you to come into my presence." No wonder Jesus said, "...Whosoever will not receive the kingdom of God as a child cannot enter" (Luke 18:17). It dawned on me that relationship overrides sins. Hence the scripture says, "Let us therefore come boldly to the throne of grace that we may obtain mercy..." God does cancel your sins because of your relationship with him. But when you know you have offended him, be sure you apologize and confess your sins. Don't pretend all is well and cover up your sins.

Of course, you cannot remember all of your sins since there are also presumptuous sins, but love covers the multitudes of sins. For "there is no fear in love, but perfect love casteth out fear: because fear hath torment. He that feareth is not made perfect in love"

(1st John 4:18). God is the Judge and had the prerogative to strike out Satan's accusations at us. He doesn't take orders from Satan. That was why Joshua, the high priest, was vindicated even when Satan stood to resist him. Moses was also vindicated despite Satan's accusation over him. Sin consciousness blocks our flow with God, which could make you deaf to hear God since your mind is filled with fear. You have got to substitute it with righteousness consciousness.

Trying to stop sinning may take you a lifetime, and you may not attain that feat before death. People who tell you they don't sin are liars. They often sin in their hearts and sometimes speak evil, murmur, complain, backbite, gossip, lust, exhibit pride, and use abusive language consciously or unconsciously. Some even distrust God in trying moments. You are not the worst sinner. You can seek God right where you are. He accepts you just as you are. Jesus became sin so that we might obtain his righteousness. Hebrews 2:17 says, "Wherefore in all things it behooved him to be made like unto his brethren, that he might be a merciful and faithful high priest in things pertaining to God, to make reconciliation for the sins of the people."

Jesus came down from heaven as a man to experience what we go through in the flesh, just like he became an angel to understand them. Jesus understands us because he was made flesh to understand our weaknesses. That is why Jesus Christ could weep. Jesus wept when Lazarus died (John 11:35). He understands the pains we endure in this world with sicknesses, lack, and diseases plaguing us. He knows how we feel when we lose our loved ones. He understands our weaknesses. Hence, he was bruised for our iniquities and wounded for our transgressions. Sin is the root cause of our suffering and grief.

Scarlet in color

Many people cannot identify the content of sin. They talk about sin but cannot identify what sin is. Have you ever asked what sin looks like before God? What do you think sin looks like? Some people think sin is a black substance. No, sin is a reddish fog or smoke in the sight of God that looks like crimson or scarlet. It comes between man and God with a repugnant odor. (See Isaiah 1:18, 44:22). Though not all sin produces smoke or fog, some are spots. God's face is inaccessible when sin comes between man and him. As mentioned earlier, some sins are categorized as "iniquity," an implied term for unrighteousness. When the scripture says, "...God will do no iniquity..." it means there is no unrighteousness in God (Zephaniah 3:5, Psalm 92:15).

When Jesus bore all of man's sins on the cross, he cried, "My God, My God, why art thou forsaken me?" (Matthew 27:46). At that moment, there was a huge fog from the sins of the entire human race which came between the Father and the Son. Jesus couldn't see through it to see the Father; hence, he cried out, "Why art thou forsaken me?" You can recall God asking Adam where art thou? The cloud of sin came between God the Father and Jesus the Son, just like it came between God and Adam in the garden.

I have found out that sin is also represented by reddish spots, which stain the spiritual garment of a believer. Such a stain on the spiritual garment is regarded as a filthy garment. A typical example was Joshua the High Priest, who unknowingly was dressed in a filthy garment when he stood before the angel of the LORD in the spiritual realm. Scriptures had it that Satan stood at his right hand, indicating a claim on Joshua's soul due to his stained garment.

However, Joshua was God's chosen vessel, so God had to override Satan's protests and accusations (See Zechariah 3:1-5). You can see the advantage of seeking to please God in fellowship daily, who alone is the Judge of all. When lawsuits are filed at the courts of law, the Judge has the final verdict. And that is why the scripture said, "Who is he that condemned? It is Christ that died..." (Romans 8:34).

Whenever a reddish cloud of sin comes between God and man, he (God) alone has the prerogative to blot out or remove sins far away to a forgetful destination (east from the west) or cast sins into forgetful seas. Sin is forgiven when true repentance comes from a sincere heart. God forgives and overlooks our sins as we seek an intimate relationship with the Holy Spirit. The blood of Jesus Christ takes care of our sins because the place of prayers is the place of confession of sins. The blood of Jesus Christ takes away our sins and permanently deletes them whenever we sincerely confess them.

Efficacy of the blood

Blood is necessary for the atonement of the soul. From the days of Adam, the issue of blood for sins committed was introduced by God. And this is traceable to the very beginning when God accepted the spilling of the blood of animals as atonement for the sins of Adam and then used the coats of skin to clothe Adam and Eve. At first, Adam didn't know how to appease God. God indicated to man that a blood sacrifice was needed to restore the soul. The first skinned animal was the sacrificial lamb for Adam's transgression.

Blood was needed for Adam's sins to be covered. The animal God skinned was a lamb because the same animal's skin was used for clothing. Scriptures state that Adam related with God after the fall, and Eve said, "I have gotten a man from the LORD" (Genesis 4:1). Adam taught his children, Cain and Abel, how to offer sacrifices unto God. God related with Adam after the fall because he was merciful. He will not keep his anger forever.

In the case of Cain and Abel, it is evident that Abel brought animal sacrifice while Cain brought the fruits of the ground (See Genesis 4:3-4).

The firstlings of flock and fat thereof connote the tithe and a quality offering in the book of Proverbs. However, God accepted Abel's offering because of the blood sacrifice of animals but not Cain's offering. Cain did nothing wrong, but God indicated that reconciliation with man would require a blood sacrifice due to the presence of sins. The fruit of the ground offered by Cain wasn't wrong but was ineffectual as it relates to the human soul because without sin being set aside, the fruit of the ground offering cannot atone for the soul.

Leviticus 2:12 says, "As for offering of the first fruits, you shall offer them to the LORD: but they shall not be burnt on the altar for a sweet savor." Only animal sacrifices were offered as sweet-smelling savor unto the LORD (Lev1:17). Abel's sacrifice was accepted as a sweet-smelling savor when God consumed the offering from the altar. The scriptures didn't express the manner of acceptance, but we can take a clue from the sacrifice of a bullock cut in pieces. God accepted sacrifices from Elijah when fire fell from heaven and licked up the sacrifices and wood on the altar (1st Kings18:33-38).

However, Cain was very wroth, and his countenance fell. He didn't understand the proper channels of appeasing God. Was it then his fault? No! That was the reason why God asked him: "Why art thou wroth?" He made his offering in ignorance (See Genesis 4:1-10). He went into violence by murdering his only brother. He became "of the devil" who plotted to overthrow God, having obtained the keys of death and hell. God didn't hate Cain after rejecting his offering. That is why he asked him, "Why are you wroth?"

Next was Noah, who offered a burnt offering on the altar that was acceptable to God as a sweet-smelling savor. God had to reverse the curse placed upon the ground for man's sake. So, we can see that God takes pleasure in blood sacrifices because the life of the flesh is in the blood. Whenever an animal is sacrificed, the life in the blood, which is the spirit in the blood, vapourises and permeates God's throne to pacification. Leviticus 17:11 says, "For the life of the flesh is in the blood: and I have given to you upon the altar to make atonement for your souls: for it is the blood that maketh an atonement for the soul." The blood of animals was meant for a peace and sin offering to appease God on behalf of the souls of men. Can we now say that since man was coined from the dust, dust (flesh, blood, and bones) becomes the atonement for their soul?

It must be a clean beast to appease God, but it cannot take away sins registered in the conscience of the heart. The practice of yearly sacrifices by the Israelites in those days could effectively cleanse the flesh only. After the death of Jesus Christ, the use of the blood of animals was abolished and replaced with the blood of Jesus Christ because the blood of Jesus Christ does cleanse the conscience from dead works. "Neither by the blood of goats and calves, but by His (Jesus Christ's) own blood he entered once into the holy place, having obtained eternal redemption for us. For if the blood of bulls and goats, and ashes of a heifer sprinkled on the unclean, sanctifieth to the purifying of the flesh; how much more shall the blood of Christ, who through the eternal Spirit offered himself without spot unto God, purge your conscience from dead works to serve the living God" (Hebrews 9: 12-14).

We can see that the blood of Jesus Christ goes straight into your conscience to remove sins committed, while the blood of animals was for purifying the flesh. I believe one might ask, "But I still have remembrance of sins committed some time ago, even after confessing sins?" It is simply because such a person is religiously bound in ignorance. Confessing the same sin over and over is a function of ignorance of the efficacy of the blood of Jesus Christ. You need to renew your mind with God's word (Romans 12:2). Some people say that you must confess your sins to a priest for you to have them forgiven. That is ignorance on the part of those who don't have fellowship with the Holy Spirit. People make men their God and lack connectivity with the Holy Spirit. To whom does the priest confess his sins? "Men make God of themselves" was God's voice to me some time ago.

Blood for souls

Someone might ask, "Why does God need blood to forgive sins? Can't God forgive sins without blood?" But we just touched on why dust was needed for dust. Why do you need food to survive? Can you live without food? Why do we need inoculations against Covid 19 and other ailments that require them? However, God does cancel sins without blood sacrifices. We saw this in the dispensation of John the Baptist, in which baptism was the criteria for the cancellation of sins. "John did baptize in the wilderness, and preach the baptism of repentance for the remission of sins." (Mark 1:4). What was required then was just repentance and confession of sins, get baptized by immersion, and your sins are forgiven.

However, such forms of cleansing in the Old Testament, including John's era, were all temporal as both forms did not get to the heart's conscience. Jesus was made of dust (flesh, blood, and bones) for humanity to obtain forgiveness of sins and be reconciled. It would require confessing the blood of Jesus Christ, which was not physically poured on anyone, to have one's sins purged from the conscience in the abstract, and faith is also an abstract concept. Sin is an intangible concept, and so also your conscience.

Certain chemicals are needed to neutralize some substances, just like the Covid 19 would require soap and water or alcohol-based sanitizers to neutralize the virus on contact. Spiritual things answer to spiritual things. If the spirit of the flesh is in the blood, it means the spirit answers to the abstract soul in man. It implies the spirit, which is the life in the blood sustaining the soul, was infused into the soul enabling the soul to live on until the soul ceases; since God breathed into man to become a living soul at creation. In other words, the spirit in the blood sustains the dying soul in men, because sin does weaken the soul personality. The scripture in Isaiah 14:12 says, "Lucifer didst weaken the nations." Lucifer will weaken the souls of men through sin. You are aware that the soul is an abstract personality in man powered by the spirit of man.

The blood of Jesus atones for the soul daily, so when the scripture says, "How much more shall the blood of Christ, who through the eternal Spirit offered himself without spot to God," it means the Holy Ghost activated the blood of Jesus Christ as living blood requiring no yearly sacrifices. But once and for all, sacrificing himself and his blood became active in heaven to date. And we saw this truth in Hebrews 12:22-24, which says, "But you are come unto mount Zion and unto the city of the living God, the heavenly Jerusalem, and to an innumerable company of angels...And to Jesus the mediator of the new covenant, and to the blood of sprinkling...." The blood of Jesus is much active in heaven as it was on the cross of Calvary.

Blood is necessary to purify the conscience of the heart imbedded in the souls to be cleansed since the soul personality is often weakened by sins committed in the flesh. Hence the Psalmist wrote in Psalm 103:2: "Bless the LORD, O my soul, and forget not all his benefits: Who forgiveth all thine iniquities, who healeth all thine diseases." God can forgive without requesting blood, but the truth is that in the spiritual realms, the soul retains its guilt, so God must use life for life, hence the blood for the souls of humanity. "...It is the blood that maketh an atonement for the soul" (Leviticus 17:11). To have your sins forgiven and canceled, you need the blood of Jesus Christ.

Chapter 22

The Abstract Man of Dust

In the scriptures, Lucifer was referred to as man. "...Yet, thou art a man, and not God" (Ezekiel 28:2). The fact that he was created with substances of light and precious stones, he was addressed as a man (Ezekiel28:13). In other words, he was made after nature. Ancient men of the pre-Adamic times formed with elements of nature (precious stones) were also referred to as men. Angels are men as creatures. "...Even the man Gabriel" (Daniel 9:21). In a similar vein, Adam formed with the fossil remains of the ground and clothed with flesh, was also called the man of the dust of the ground. Psalms 9:20 says, 'Put them in fear, O LORD, that the nations may know themselves to be but men.' In other words, stars, sons of God, and humans are men created by God. Adam was recreated with certain substances.

The flesh is the outer layer that covers the sinews, bones, blood, and brain of the recreated man of the dust. As discussed earlier, the soul is the abstract replicated body recreated from the mixture of the existing formed body by the infusion of light to produce a shadow type functional man. The soul is forever living from the moment God carved it out as the subconscious man. It is more active in the dream state or when it exits the human body at death. It is an abstract body that mirrors the flesh. Whatever the body does, the soul is also deemed to have performed.

If I talk to you, I would be talking to your physical body knitted with your soul. But God or Satan speaks to your spirit (of which your soul is synchronized with your spirit); your physical ears may not hear any sound, but you are aware of the voice on the inside. This explains why a true man of God may be talking to you and, at the same time listening to God in the spiritual realms. The soul houses the heart in the abstract realm, so we can say the heart is also the subconscious (Luke2:35). The body is closely knitted to the soul in man by a thin line of silver cords (Ecclesiastes 12:6). When a man steals, the soul is deemed to have stolen, because the performances of the body are impressed upon the soul.

The rich man, who died in Luke 16, had his soul (body) carried to hell. He was unaware of his soul personality until he died and came to realize that the spiritual realm does exist, for which he requested for to cool off his tongue. When people die, their soul is a replica body they had while on earth because the soul is an extract mixture of the spirit and the flesh. Souls that didn't make it to heaven descend down to hell. When the soul eventually goes for judgment, the spirit becomes a shadow since the body's performance is ultimately impressed upon the soul.

One time, a prophet in Israel named Habakkuk wept concerning a king who delighted in genocide. Habakkuk cried unto God concerning the level of destruction, as in the number of people massacred so far, but God replied to Habakkuk, saying, "Behold his soul which is lifted up is not upright in him..." (Habakkuk 2:4). In other words, the king's soul was deemed perverse inside the body. The king was proud, and his soul was deemed to have acted in unrighteousness and wickedness. This king was busy destroying lives that would be required of him in judgment. After death, this king will remember his murderous acts while on earth. Of course, he will be very weak at that time, having put off the flesh. Fortunately, we are the most privileged generation to have witnessed people who died and returned from the dead educating us about their experiences in hell or heaven.

Soul is weak

Multitudes of human souls go straight to hell, a reserved planet of the dead. I could vividly recall my trance experience. I heard a loud voice that spoke from the black cloud over hell that the lady I saw had just come from planet earth. Job 17:16 says, "They shall go down to the bars of the pit when our rest together is in the dust." It dictates innumerable souls of men and women and children held in cells (bars) weeping and gnashing teeth who couldn't make it to paradise. Hell is a place of darkness reserved for departed souls judged unrepented or who have refused the free gift of salvation offered by Jesus Christ. Job 33:30 says, "To bring back his soul from the pit, to be enlightened with the light of the living." The light of the living speaks of the earth.

Those in hell are in deep darkness where no trees, water, animals, or mountains exist. Just dry land. Psalms 22:29 says, "All they that be fat upon the earth shall eat and worship: all they that go down to the dust shall bow before him: and none can keep alive his own soul." No mortal can say he will not die, and at death, all human souls must bow before God. Whenever humans depart planet earth through death, they are 100% more conscious of their performances while on earth. They are faced with their past actions while on earth because all activities of the body impact the soul. It is not enough to die or commit suicide, but the soul's destination becomes a concern. You can escape hell by accepting the free gift of God.

In the spiritual realm, the human soul is weak and weightless as a sheet of paper without strength compared to angels or demons formed with spiritual substances. The soul being a prototype man made of skeletons and clothed with flesh on departing planet earth, cannot be compared to fallen spirits already made with precious internal stones. So long man was made of dust matter from which the soul was also coined, it means the human souls would be weak, except when such souls live in righteousness and love and therefore go straight to paradise.

In the spiritual realms, demons seek to afflict the human soul with sickness, darts, arrows, etc., which causes the soul to be weak, and when a soul is wounded, it can become too weak, forcing the body to disconnect the knitted silver line cord. The soul can be stabbed or wounded spiritually. That is why you read scriptures saying, "those that seek after my soul to destroy it" (Psalms 63:9, Psalms 35:4-9). Forces of darkness operating through humans often chase the souls of men in the spiritual realms to have the poor in spirit killed. The afflicted and defenseless souls are referred to as poor in spirit. That is precisely what the scripture meant by "poor in spirit" (Matthew 5:3). This implies they are not indulged in manipulating their spirits to unite with demons to commit violence against any.

And you know, when a conscious being goes after a soul, using mediums, the assailing spirit is more aggressive because demons are aiding it, but God, in his mercy, would always send his angels to rescue the oppressed souls of men who trust in him. This oppression also necessitated the empowerment of the believers to trample upon demons in the name of the LORD Jesus Christ. When a child of God who is energized in the spiritual realms by the Spirit of God confronts a human spirit under demonic influence, demons would bow to the energized spirit of the Christian who exercises his right on the earth at the mention of the name of Jesus Christ in prayers. One such way is building up the spirit man by praying in tongues, which energizes the spirit of the born-again child of God. The believer could also build his spirit by praying, living uprightly, studying God's word, fasting, communion, and evangelizing (Jude 1:20).

Continuous re-alignment

The soul of man of the dust who is already born again is yet saved. Therefore, it requires continuous re-alignment processes with the regenerated spirit in him. Romans 12:1-2 says, "I beseech you therefore brethren, by the mercies of God, that you present your bodies a living sacrifice, holy, acceptable unto God, which is your reasonable service. And be not conformed to this world: but be transformed by the renewing of your mind that you may prove what is that good, acceptable, and perfect, will of God." The scripture was emphatic about renewing the mind (soul consciousness), which goes to the root, counteracting the impression of the body in favor of the regenerated spirit so that the soul would not conform to the systems of the world.

The book of Hebrews 10:39 says that "we are not of them that draw back unto perdition, but of them that believe to the saving of the soul." Notice the phrase: 'the saving of the soul,' an indication that the final 'salvation of the soul' together with the new spirit is what counts. It's expected that the believer's soul aligns with the new regenerated spirit in him much of the time, which enables him to walk in the consciousness of his new life since the flesh and the regenerated spirit always have conflicting drives. "This I say walk (align your consciousnesses or soul) in the Spirit, and you shall not fulfill the lustful desires of the flesh. For the flesh wars against the spirit and the spirit against the flesh, and these are contrary to one another so that you cannot do the things you would" (Galatians 5:12-17).

In other words, the battle is between the flesh and the recreated spirit in man, the dilemma of the soul. And this was Apostle Paul's frustrations when he wrote the book of Romans about the flesh and the new spirit conflicting desires in which the soul is switching between both ends. Paul said he delights in the things of God inwardly (based on his spirit drive), but the flesh would often express its Adamic nature contrary to the regenerated spirit. "For that which I do, I allow not: for I what I would, that I do not; but what I hate, that I do" (Romans 7:15). Indicating an inward battle every believer goes through only when on the earth realm irrespective of his position in faith.

The soul of every born-again believer has been used to the Adamic sinful nature, but on receiving the recreated spirit, which is the second Adam's nature, the desires of the flesh and the new recreated spirit seem to conflict with each other. The fight for supremacy over the soul by the spirit and fleshly desires in the Christian journey compelled apostle Paul to cry out, saying, "O wretched man that I am! Who shall deliver me from this body of death?" (Romans 7:26). In other words, it is either you are spiritual or carnal sometimes. That is, the soul acts in awareness of the recreated spirit or fleshly impulses all the time. It becomes a spiritual battle subduing the fleshly desires; if not, it can override the new spirit's desires and cause the believer to walk carnally (Romans 7:7-18).

The natural man is made of material and immaterial consciousness, but he is often conscious of the material realm. Hence he is dominated by his senses much of the time, except when he chooses to engage in the immaterial consciousness. Some people seldom yield to spiritual dominance. When a believer in Christ walks in material consciousness, he might fall into sin following the dictates of the flesh, which an unbeliever might see and be amazed why the born again also sins.

However, the natural man who has not experienced this recreated spirit is unconcerned about these things because it makes no sense to him. For "the natural man received not the things of the Spirit of God: for they are foolishness unto him: neither can he know them, because they are spiritually discerned" (1st Corinthians 2:14). The natural man thinks of food, clothing, parties, drinking, and all forms of pleasure until he suddenly departs planet earth and discovers this (present) life is not all there is.

Spirit of man

God breathed into the formed man of the dust of the ground - the breath of life, which we understand is the spirit, energized the flesh without which man couldn't have functioned in awareness or reasoning because "If God gathers unto himself his spirit and breath, all flesh shall perish together, and man shall turn into dust" (Job 34:14-15). This implied that the breath of life (light energy) replicated a newly formed soul and, at the same time, kick-started the heartbeat, leading to blood circulation to all body parts. Genesis 2:7 says, "And the LORD God formed man of the dust of the ground, and breathed into his nostrils, the breath of life; and man became a living soul."

Adam could recognize God in his immediate environment as soon as he was impacted by this breath of life from God. The spirit from God, which is the breath, as a vapor in the form of candlelight, on being introduced into the formed man (body) on the ground, replicated a soul personality with consciousness and gave life to the body since the spirit came from an everlasting source. The breath (spirit) that was breathed into Adam has no flesh, bones, or blood but took the shape of the man as a vapor. Just like gas taking the form of its container. The impacted breath from God was the life (energy) entity from the everlasting realms, which bears witness to God inside Adam. It came from God; therefore, it bears witness to God on the inside of every created thing.

Everything created and made bears witness to God. The scripture talked about floods clapping hands to God. "Let the floods clap their hands: and let the hills be joyful together" (Psalms 98:8). The trees of the field also clap before God (See Isaiah 55:12). The deep, which includes all planets, have hands and utter voice. Habakkuk 3:10 says, "...the deep uttered his voice, and lifted up his hands on high." An indication that things formed have life in the spiritual realm. Psalms 148:7-13 talked about fire, hail, storms, snow, vapor, etc., all taking directives from God. I have touched on lightning, giving feedback to God about its location already. Once, I saw a cloud that looked like a man's hand, just like the one Elijah saw when he prayed to God. Another time, God asked Moses to speak to a rock to bring forth water for the Israelites to drink (See Numbers 20:8). Even now, the mantle (rock) at the earth's center communicates with God, but science cannot understand the mode of communication.

You naturally don't get springs of water from a rock in the wilderness. So we can see that everything created, including the sun, moon, and stars, understand the voice of the Creator. Living things, such as birds, fishes, animals, humans, etc., were made and breathed upon by the life of God. The spirit in man is like a vapor, according to the scripture. James 4:14 says, "For what is your life? It is even a vapor..." It is like a candlelight with which God searches the imaginations of the heart. I told you earlier that light came from life and is the sign of life. Proverbs 20:27 says, "The spirit (as life) of man is the candle of the LORD, searching all the inward parts of the belly." It means the breath God passed into man is a vapor in the form of light energy. This shows the spirit glows at the initial state of creation. God impacted it and communicates words to that living light energy in man.

But dead bodies don't talk because the life in them has departed into the abstract world. However, their souls could communicate with the living (in dream or trance) since their spirit is synchronized with their souls, and both depart as one entity. Many have witnessed departed souls communicating certain secrets to the living in dreams which I've cited some examples. When light was infused into Adam, it caused Adam to be conscious of God, enabling him to relate with God. It inspired Adam to sing songs of praise unto God. The spirit in Adam caused Adam to have God's consciousness at all times. It became the connection by which Adam could relate to God. It was infused into Adam to make him walk upon the earth and caused his brain to function in reasoning.

Adam was able to worship or serve God with his spirit. Romans 1:9 says, "God...whom I serve with my spirit". Jesus said, "God is a Spirit and they that must worship him, must worship him in spirit and truth" (John 4:24). Your spirit within your body is the medium through which you can pray or worship God. You connect to God via your spirit man inside of you. We can take a clue from a car battery that causes the entire mechanical and electrical systems to function when infused. The spirit in man was transfused to the heart via the nostrils.

For this reason, everyone breathes through the nostril for survival. Those unable to do so are supported through the mouth or pipe with oxygen. But you must breathe to live. The spirit is like vapor which science refers to as oxygen in the blood, corresponding to scriptural writings that "The life of the flesh is in the blood" (Leviticus 17:11, Genesis 9:4).

This means every living thing in the earth's realm has some form of gas to survive. Oxygen is a form of vapor gas. Gases are vapors. Oxygen runs in the blood, and once there is no oxygen in the blood, life is at risk. The spirit is the inner man because it resides in the blood like oxygen gas, thereby taking the body's shape. Therefore, the spirit will resemble the body without flesh and bones since spirits don't have bones and flesh according to Luke 24:39, which says, "...a spirit hath not flesh and bones".

Constant opposition

Adam's spirit glowed at the initial state of sinlessness. But as soon as Adam sinned, the glowing spirit became dimmed, defiled, and dormant, which the scripture referred to as falling short of glory or light, as already discussed.

Now, given that the heart organ was the first recipient of the breath of God through the nostrils in man, which energizes the blood circulation process, it is obvious that words (speech) would come from the same spirit in the heart through the lungs (vocal cords). This dictates that whatever affected the spirit has an associated impact on the heart from which sound is produced from the heart, but the heart was corrupt when the spirit of Adam got defiled (Genesis 6:5). The soul, which houses the heart, being synchronized with the mind of the body was also corrupt resulting in the enmity against God. And that is the reason why the scripture says that "the carnal mind is enmity against God, not being subject to the laws of God; neither can it be" (Romans 8:6, emphasis mine).

Little wonder many hearts are against God and are heading to hell, the planet of the dead. The hearts and minds of men often rise against God, refusing to be subject to God in pride, having been bought over by the opposing forces of darkness. This constant opposition to God in the human heart is the only earthly experience under darkness where good and evil concepts exist. Angels in heaven don't have such opposing thoughts in their hearts, but they only have pure thoughts and words. What compels us to speak against God are manipulative spirits of darkness or, let's say, the interplay of the forces of good and evil found only in this universe under the darkness.

Notwithstanding, we must take our stands in God. We don't have to give in. "Fight the good fight of faith, and lay hold on eternal life, whereunto thou art called, and hast professed a good profession before many witnesses" (1st Timothy 6:12). It is a spiritual battle! We have seen many people who once knew God fall away. Many gospel musicians who once knew God ended up living an immoral life, drunkenness, drugs, gamblings, or vices, which portrayed an end to their Christain journey. Many have renounced the faith due to the forces pulling their hearts apart to sinful pleasures or idol worship. Evil spirits don't rest unless they cause someone to fall (Proverbs 4:16). They attack our hearts daily. When you overcome today, Satan will wait for you tomorrow. Satan is not afraid of the anointing upon you. He's permitted to tempt you at all times. Even Jesus was left for a season by Satan.

The mind of the spirit

Although Adam was formed as a free moral agent to dominate the earth, it is worthy of note that the spirit man in Adam also possessed its own mind, which tends toward God, and bears witness to its source. The human spirit has its own mind, which differs from the mind of the body. Ephesians 4:23 talks about "the spirit of the mind." In other words, we can appreciably say the spirit man has his own faculty of thoughts, which vary from the mind of the body. You use the mind of the spirit to contact or hear God, while the mind of the body is meant for physical things. Both minds are versatile in exploring things, with the mind of the spirit for spiritual things and the mind of the body for earthly things.

Your recreated spirit is dominated by the Holy Ghost's thoughts, in what the scripture meant by the mind of Christ (1st Corinthians 2:16). Your spirit mind does pray, praise, worship, think scriptures, and listen to God's voice. But your conscious mind is dominated by natural things. The mind of the body cannot be tamed for a day without switching all directions. Two conflicting minds - one is spiritual, the other carnal. The carnal mind of the body is set at enmity against God, and it opposes God at all times. It is not subject to the laws of God. This explains why the flesh and spirit's minds are in opposition.

Galatians 5:17 says, "For the flesh (mind of the body) lusteth (war) against the Spirit (mind of the spirit), and the Spirit lusteth against the flesh: and these are contrary to one, to the other: so that you cannot do the things you would (Emphasis mine). Even though the mind of the spirit is in oneness with the Holy Spirit, the soul's alignment with the mind of the body might set aside the spirit's mindedness since the spirit is subject to the man in control. 1st Corinthians 14:32 says, "The spirits of the prophets are subject to the prophets." However, the mind of the spirit man is permanently God-conscious because "he that is joined to unto the LORD is one spirit" (1st Corinthians 6:17).

You are either preoccupied with physical things or spiritual things of God. We live in a world where our dominant concerns are the things we can see, feel, touch, hear, etc.

We're often preoccupied with our five senses much of the time and seldom become conscious of the spiritual.

It is a fact that Spirit-mindedness produces death to carnal-mindedness, while carnal-mindedness produces death to Spirit-mindedness. "For to be carnally minded is death, but to be spiritually minded is life and peace" (Romans 8:6). When the scripture talks about carnal mindedness, it does not mean we should not invent things or focus on developing our world through science and technology. Or else the world would have remained in the dark ages. Carnal-mindedness here means walking according to the dictates of the sinful flesh, which affect our spiritual growth. It has nothing to do with man's inventions in airplanes, cars, computers, space travel, football, games, or circular work.

God enjoys our inventions as men, especially when men are happy, laughing, and playing together, devoid of violent intentions. Like football, volleyball, tennis, car racing, swimming, wrestling, etc. God enjoys these games and sometimes informs his prophets about the outcomes of such matches before they are played if the prophet heard correctly anyway. You saw how an angel wrestled with Jacob as in sporting activities. The essence of wrestling was just for fun, not a violent intention to kill. This is where so many Christians missed it. They are used to spiritual-dominated thought life only, failing to use their minds in creativity and life advancements, so they suffer defeats in life.

Spiritual-mindedness implies being Word and prayer minded, while carnal-mindedness implies pursuing fleshly desires, not necessarily avoiding educational, economic, social, political, and scientific developments in our world. The former produces hope of eternal life and peace, while the latter produces vanity. Both minds have varying perspectives on life. Scripture says, "Man shall not live by bread alone, but by every word that proceedeth out of the mouth of God" (Matthew 4:4). This implies that man shouldn't be dominated by his fleshly needs only, but his spiritual needs as well.

Chapter 23

Familiar Spirits

The defiled unregenerated spirit of man tends towards wickedness and sin because it became dormant to the things of God. Because of that, it was willed over to Satan and became a tool in his hands. There is a spiritual law that says, "...To whom you yield yourselves servant to obey, you become a servant to whom you obey" (Romans 6:16, emphasis mine). Once the spirit of God in man is dormant, man would resort to the study of nature, idol worshipping, wickedness, violence, cursing, carnality, drinking, smoking, immorality, drug addiction, malice, envy, lesbianism or homosexuality, witchcraft, occultism, etc.

In an attempt to fill the void of a broken relationship with God, man resorts to those mentioned above. In the process of time, Satan proceeded to fellowshipping with humanity teaching them spiritual things in a perverse manner, such as mind control and manipulating things in the Wicca world, which God abhors. Satan's objective is to have God hate and banish humans just as fallen spirits were banished, coupled with the fact that God didn't want the man of the dust to attain the knowledge of good and evil. I assumed someone just interjected, asking, "Why would God disapprove of man attaining such level of spiritism?" It is because it would further destroy the human race.

We were not made spirit beings like the angels with the flesh of beryls and brass. Remember, I told you that God was comfortable with Adam's childish mind at the beginning, void of violence or evil thoughts. Just as we all love children at their tender ages, the violence we all experience today is caused by higher knowledge acquisition, and there can never be an end to violence until Jesus returns to put an end to it. More so, the introduction of idolatry seems to have enhanced the spiritual violence world amongst us which has resulted in destruction of lives. Spiritual violence comes in forms of being hagged at night.

Many, if not most people at tender or adult age, have been hagged at night by witches or aliens in form of dwarfs during night or day time, for which many strive to gain consciousness during such encounters. The use of charms capable of destroying more lives on earth through sickness and diseases are also medium of spiritual violence undetected by scientific methods. Some sicknesses and diseases are infused into the human body through spiritual powers. Satan once afflicted Job with sore boils when he told God skin for skin. I told you earlier that God converting the man of the dust to run the affairs of this earth was the problem between God and Satan. And because Satan hated man, he will continue to kill and destroy lives. Satan, to date, trains and initiates more men and women who cooperate with him in this world to accomplish his mission through witchcraft and charms.

The satanic world is about acquiring powers to control and destroy humanity. Satan is corrupting humanity for God to see why man should also be banished forever, just as the pre-Adamic people were banished. Many think Satan empowers them to succeed because they have whatever they needed, ultimately, their soul is his target. Satan gives power to humans and makes them celebrities on earth. Humans are also collaborating with him to destroy fellow humans. We have seen people commit crimes using drugs or shooting at school children. In the Wicca world, the spirits of some idolatrous people change form into animals or birds, and many are happy thinking they have powers to destroy others.

Their transformed spirits enable them to move out of their bodies and operate in a different location while the silver cord connecting the soul remains. The genesis of this craft began when fallen spirits in human flesh taught people the power of manipulating others after calling on Satan. Some practice mind control in the occult world using special mirrors given to them in their secret societies. Others are on a mission to retard the prosperity of others aimed at impoverishing them. All such practitioners are heading to destruction, and the lake of fire is their final destination, with Lucifer as their god.

Those who practice or seek demonic powers to achieve fame, wealth, or protection know they serve Satan.

Many are practicing witchcraft, and even our higher institutions of learning have adopted witchcraft as a discipline. We already have Satan's church on earth long established. So why would anyone protest that God is sending people to hell? Some gullible people deceive others that God is not that wicked to send anyone to hell. If our governments would imprison deviant behaviors, is it God who would accommodate deviant behaviors? There is nothing you can do about it anyway. Humans practice spiritisms with demons, and you dare say God is not wicked to send them to hell? That's an unfair and absurd sense of judgment!

We saw the art of witchcraft in the scriptures among several, in which Saul consulted a woman with a familiar spirit at Endor. Scriptures recorded that the woman brought up the soul of the deceased Samuel – a prophet in Israel. She manipulated her own spirit to the land of the dead, using Saul's face. Hence, Samuel's soul, on seeing Saul in the land of the dead, followed and said unto Saul, "Why are you disturbing me?" She was at one spot when she traveled into the spiritual realms and called forth Samuel's soul under the earth before Jesus came and moved the saints. Communication ensued between Samuel and Saul, but such a medium led to Saul's early death. Saul died the following day after consulting a witch with a familiar spirit.

Some people contest, "It was a demon that spoke." Unfortunately, it was never a demon. It was Samuel's soul. Anyone contesting this event of Samuel talking to Saul might be shallow-minded. The words of Samuel were direct to the point, and every word of Samuel came to pass because God did not allow Samuel's word to fall to the ground. Samuel told Saul that he and his two children would be with him tomorrow, and it came to pass according to his word (See 1st Samuel 28:1- 25). The dead can commune with the living, as exemplified by Jesus, Moses, and Elijah.

This was an encounter in which the living and the 'living-dead' were communicating things that pertained to this life. When I talk about the living dead, I mean to say that those who died in the LORD are very much alive in the universe above, while those who died outside God are the dead. For this reason, Jesus said, "Let the dead bury their dead" (Matthew 8:22). In other words, let the dormant, defiled, and diminished in spirit of unregenerated man bury those who died without God. And Jesus also said that 'God is not the God of the dead, but the God of the living (Luke 20:38). The 'living' are those who died on planet earth, moved to the light zone universe above, being very much active as we are on earth.

I've found that many people have handed their spirits over to Satan. And Satan keeps teaching and exposing humans to destroy and utilize their powers to gain control. They obtained the power to live long from Satan. Some could see into the future of others as stargazers, necromancers, witch doctors, etc. Some have obtained powers to divert death meant for them to someone else, even though they would eventually die at a later time. Many have been fooled into thinking death won't come, so they fight all their life, struggling to live on.

The meaning of life

We must understand that life is transient at this level under the darkness. You must have seen people who labored and wearied all their lives trying to achieve feats as professors, top scientists, the wealthiest celebrities, presidents, bishops, etc., who, in their dying moment, asked critical questions as to what is the meaning of life. The longing to have humans live forever may have spurred the curiosity to ask about the meaning of life. While some people define life as giving your best to your world, others think there is something more to life that they cannot figure out! Some have described the concept of life based on the consciousness of death. So you hear people say, "Live your best, and impact humanity by giving to the poor." But these definitions are given in despair. They are not truly the definition of life. Many gave such definitions about life with the notions of cessation to life after death.

God exists to some, but pride is impeding their public declaration of the truth about his existence, probably, considering their prestige and personality in society. Everyone bears witness to God on the inside because the breath of life instilled the knowledge of God in all human races. The knowledge and laws of God went through all human races as soon as they started breathing from the womb, even without formal/informal education. The intuitive knowledge of God was registered in every human spirit that ever existed, even those who are proud of denying God's existence and claiming to have been atheists. They tell you, "I don't believe in God!" Yes, they can say that, but they intuitively know God exists because it is written on their hearts. Someone might say, "Why would you say that?" It is simply because that is what the scriptures say.

Every spirit or human has the intuitive knowledge of God, just that they don't have faith in God. An atheist cannot stop thinking about God once in a while because the life they breathe is actually from the spirit of God. Some might say, "But the scripture says, some have not the knowledge of God," citing 1st Corinthians 15:34. The scripture here implied people lack the depths of God as to the spiritual power of God capable of raising the dead after life experience. So this scripture isn't a backup for someone giving the excuse that he is ignorant of God's existence. Everything bears witness about God, but the proud chose to deny him.

Life came from Jesus, and they chose to reject and ridicule him. Scripture says that Jesus Christ is the life, and that life was the light of men, and that was the true Light which lighteth (touched or gave life) to every man that cometh into this world (John 1:4 and 9, emphasis mine). Jesus substantiated this when he said, I am... the life" (John 14:6). I have discussed the emergence of life in detail in this book, but you must understand that many are walking in ignorance, teaching what they know nothing about even as professors. The Scripture is not just an academic book, but a holy and spiritual book. So without the author's (Holy Ghost) interpretations, you may not be able to demystify the context of its scripts. From the same book, many have understood the scriptures and got miracles, while others see it from an academic or historical perspective.

Unfortunately, so many professors don't know there is a spirit called the spirit of life from Jesus, which they breathe. They might spite him, uttering derogative comments about Jesus, but that doesn't change the fact that he remains the breath of life. Fallen spirits and souls in hell or the seas are sustained by eternal breath under the deep darkness. Life as in existence is a concept imported from the everlasting into light realms. God dreamt of life as a concept and created things that would give him pleasure. It would have been boring for God to be alone all by himself. The concept of life becomes eternal since the originator is eternal. Life is not intended to be transient and was never meant to be short-lived, as many have concluded. It remains an eternal concept even if existence in this darkness zone was once interrupted for a period of time and would continue to be interrupted at His will. The light zone universe had been continuous from its inception uninterrupted, even when this zone was shut down for several million years.

The Adamic human race could be experiencing sickness, stress, aging, poverty, lack, depression, and death because they were scripted before recreation in Genesis to return to their source – God. Individual yearnings to continue life endlessly have led to exhaustion and despair by many people who see life as useless and meaningless. Some end up concluding like Solomon: Vanity and vexation of spirit (Ecclesiastes 4:16). Of course, it is extremely painful to have put in such efforts in this dispensation of temporal 'short life' and depart this world after 100 years or less. As I said, various definitions of life that are based on the premise of despair were wrongly defined. Life under the darkness was designed to be transient by God, but life in the light zone continues endlessly.

The scriptures buttressed this when it says, "For he will finish the work, and cut it short in righteousness: because a short work will the Lord make upon the earth" (Romans 9:28). Death was made to interrupt the process temporally, but we have hope to come back to eternal life. You will be back again if you join the bandwagon on the train of truth. Jesus promised us eternal life with everlasting joy. There is no meaninglessness to life when you think about the one who says he is the life. And Jesus had to demonstrate this hope by raising the dead. We read about Lazarus, who was dead for four days, being embalmed and buried in a sepulcher. He had a sister named Martha, who told Jesus how Lazarus must have stunk being in a grave for four days.

But "Jesus said unto her I am the resurrection and the life: he that believeth on me, though he were dead, yet shall he live" (John 11:25). This is an assurance given by the Life-giver himself. So simple and free without your money or property needed; just a free gift of salvation to everyone who believes. He had to demonstrate his ability to give life even to a dead bone. He is the life. And if Jesus is the life, it means he must be a Spirit. John 1:2 says, "For the life was manifested, and we have seen it, and bear witness unto you that the eternal life which was the Father, was manifested unto us." Jesus was trying to demonstrate that he is the life-giver. He can give life to dead things. You need not despair. Jesus is the breath everyone who existed tapped into whether they believe in him or not because everyone has the free will to do so.

Weak through flesh.

Now, let's get back on track as regards the breath of life which instilled the laws or knowledge of God in every creature. Scripture recorded that the Mosiac laws given to the Israelites were spiritual. Yet, their defiled-dormant Adamic nature could not sustain the commandment that was spiritually ordained to life. It became their destruction instead (Romans7:10). And since they were unable to fulfill the laws due to this defiled-dormant spirit in them, God had to promise them a new spirit and a new heart (Ezekiel36:26). Because God knew that they would not be able to keep the Mosaic laws perfectly. Jesus said, "Did not Moses give you the law, and yet none of you keepeth the law?" (John 7:19). It means nobody kept the laws 100%. God knew that the defiled-dormant Adamic spirit in man could not sustain the righteousness of the law. Hence he said, "O that there was such a heart in them, that they would fear me, and keep all my commandments..." (Deuteronomy 5:29).

In so far as the heart in the spirit was weak due to the dormant spirit, they cannot keep the laws perfectly. "For what the law couldn't do in that it was weak through the flesh, God sending his own Son in the likeness of sinful flesh, and for sin, condemned sin (dormant Adamic spirit) in the flesh" (Romans 8:3). The weak dormant spirit in them could not sustain the commandments (the law of righteousness) which was meant to make them live. The defiled-dormant spirit in Adam was what the scripture meant as sin condemned in the flesh. In other words, the old Adamic spirit in the midst of the body was destroyed, while the human body was still very much alive, as earlier explained.

Since the defiled-dormant spirit was weak, there must be a disannulling of the commandments because of the weakness and unprofitableness (Hebrews 7:18). There must be a new method of getting this problem solved. That was why Melchizedek would have to incarnate as Jesus, even after blessing Abraham and all his descendants who occupied the priestly office. This is in response to the question posed by Paul in the book of Hebrews. The second Adam's spirit was given and inserted into those who believed by the declaration of faith in Jesus Christ, who paid the price for the sins of all human races.

The first Adam became the child of the devil by obedience to the voice of deception, dand Adam's nature passed into all human races. The first Adam disobeyed, and death reigned upon all human races, but the second Adam – Christ, was obedient (Romans 5:17-21). How did the second Adam obey? Like the first Adam, he was tempted with food, pride, and fame, to have earthly kingdoms. He rejected those offers. He was sent to die, and he obeyed the command laying down his life willingly. Jesus is the second Adam foreordained, not from the seed of the first Adam. He was heavenly, not earthy. This second Adam birthed the new man after God who was created in righteousness and holiness (Ephesians 4:26). The new man (light energy in vapor form) is in everyone who accepted and believed in Jesus Christ.

Born again spirit.

Have you ever wondered how someone who was once a thief, drunkard, murderer, or prostitute, after genuinely accepting Jesus Christ as Lord and Savior, changes behavior and begins to witness for Jesus? They suddenly find peace and joy bubbling on the inside. Sure, there was an exchange on the inside. A new spirit has taken possession which made such a person obtain the power of the sons of God. The person suddenly behaves gently and does not like fighting, abusing, or causing trouble anymore. A new creature in him is in effect. "If any man be in Christ he is a new creature, old things are passed away, behold all things are become new" (2nd Corinthians 5:17). Old things mean the old Adamic spirit is passed away. The new creature is the second Adam seed deposited by the Holy Ghost on the inside of the believer in Christ. So is every one that is born of the Spirit (John 3:8).

The second Adam's spirit was inserted through the heart as well as the first Adam's spirit, but not aimed at activating the soul because the believer was alive when this exchange took place on the inside in a split second. The new creature had to replace the old man via actions of faith when the heart believed, and confession was made unto Jesus. It deposited the laws of the spirit into the heart, thereby generating love, joy, peace, longsuffering, gentleness, goodness, faith, meekness, and temperance (Galatians 5:22). There was this inexplainable ecstasy in the spirit associated with peaceful, gentle and loving behavior observed due to this new experience.

No more dormancy or insensitivity to God. It became a lively spirit that sings praises, worships, and often listens to the voice of the spirit. It's domiciled in everyone who is born again and fervent in God. This explains why most Christians are dominated by praying in tongues, singing, preaching, studying God's Word, etc. The new spirit is alive in them as a well of living water (John 7:38). It quickens them on the inside because, "If the spirit of him that raise Christ from the dead dwells you, it shall make lively your mortal bodies" (Romans 8:11). This quickening compels some preachers to say, 'Man is a spirit in error because of this injection of power from on high. It is ever rejoicing and bubbling in them. You see them sing praises while carrying out daily chores. It is a result of this born-again spirit. The new spirit inside a genuinely born-again child of God is the incorruptible seed from the Holy Ghost.

Incorruptible seed.

We were born of the second Adam by the Word of God. "Being born again, not of corruptible seed, but of incorruptible, by the word of God, which liveth and abideth forever" (1 Peter 1:23). Jesus was the incorruptible seed, which means the devil could not corrupt him. Adam was corruptible because he was earthly and taken from the dust of death. Jesus was the Word, which means Creation, as earlier explained. We got born again by Jesus (the Word), and Jesus sustains us; hence Jesus said, "Without me, you can do nothing" (John 15:5). The newborn spirit in a believer is an incorruptible seed which cannot sin, because it is born of God (1st John 3:9, 1st Peter 1:23). To be incorruptible means not capable of contamination. Sins of the flesh cannot contaminate the new spirit. It is sealed or protected from contamination by the Holy Ghost.

If the believer sinned, it might not affect the new spirit in him, but it does affect the soul. And whenever the soul is weak due to the sins of the body, it makes the believer to be dominated by sin since the new spirit is shut off temporally, and "fleshly lust wars against the soul's consciousness of the spirit" (Ephesians 4:30; 1st Peter 2:11, emphasis mine). Remember that we have proven from the scriptures that the soul is yet to be saved but will only be saved at the end of one's journey since its consciousness or alignment is paramount to the purchase of possessions of that believer. So when sin enters, it weakens the soul from an excited state back to a ground state until the believer comes in fellowship again and gets re-ignited.

For this reason, the scripture says, "There is therefore now, no condemnation to them who are in Christ Jesus who walk not after the flesh, but after the Spirit" (Romans 8:1). Spirit and Word-mindedness are proven recipes for maintaining healthy growth in the Lord. The first Adam's sin tainted his spirit affecting his soul's consciousness. But the new creature has the very nature of God. It cannot be tainted easily like the first Adam's spirit, although it can be tainted on the grounds of renouncements, with certain conditions attached. The soul's conformity to the new spirit is an ongoing process, coupled with the fact that the flesh (body) has not been changed from its Adamic nature as it were after the born-again experience.

We can see why Apostle Paul advocated and admonished us to renew the mind in the book of Romans. It means there is still a job to do running the race to the end. You are not adding to the work of Christ, but you have to keep on track regulating your consciousness per time since the soul often toed the mind of the spirit or the mind of the body. You are not guaranteed entry into God's kingdom just because you got born again. There is a journey which is called the pilgrimage.

The second Adam's seed in you does not guarantee that you may not sin in the flesh once you are born again. But the scripture says, "Sin shall no more have dominion over you..." (Romans 6:14). This addresses your spirit man who was regenerated, not your soul or flesh. We have seen many people who were born again struggling with sin or living in sin, even when they have a holier-than-thou attitude. It does not stop them from battling with sins of the flesh or being proud, greedy, using abusive words, thinking on evil thoughts, immoral, envious, depressed, wicked, etc.

Some believers think by the energy of the flesh, they can stop sinning; it does not work that way. They may stop one sin, but other sins from within still defile them. Some have given up their faith after being born again because they could not stop the sins programmed in their flesh by the old man. They throw in the towel, go back to the world and become worse than before. Don't struggle to stop sin on your own. Engage in fellowship, prayers, evangelism, and studying the scriptures. Let me explain what happened to a born-again child of God who may still fall into sin and repent often.

Flesh to contend with

The new regenerated spirit was swapped with the initial Adamic spirit (with which you were born) and was inserted into the human body (sinful flesh). It means the new creature was kept inside a corrupt (Adamic) flesh, necessitating the soul to interface between the flesh and the new spirit. It means the new creature is kept inside a corrupt (Adamic) flesh, necessitating the soul to interface between the flesh and the new spirit. "For the creature itself was made subject unto vanity (flesh) not willingly, but by reason of him who subjected the same in hope" (Romans 8:20, emphasis mine). It is obvious that after you accept Jesus Christ as Lord, God hopes you will make it to the end. That is the reason why the Holy Ghost is interceding for you.

In other words, the new creature has the flesh to contend with so long as the flesh desires sinful things and the new spirit desires righteousness and holiness. The soul wasn't saved when this new creature was infused into the human body; the soul was simply conscious of this new spirit. Hence, "the flesh wars against the spirit, and the new spirit wars against the flesh, and these are contrary one to another" (Galatians 5:17). The Holy Ghost is constantly "making intercession for us with groaning which cannot be uttered" so that you make it to the end (Romans 8:26).

The new spirit desires righteousness, living in the laws of the spirit of life, while the body desires immorality, drunkenness, lies, pride, wickedness, greed, envy, etc. The soul will cooperate whenever the flesh is engaged in sinful activities that please the flesh, and the new spirit may not be dominant. At this point, a person is said to be carnal. However, when the spirit wants to engage in spiritual activity, the soul will switch and cooperate with the spirit. The man is said to be spiritual at that point in time. The soul filters impulses at both ends.

This was Paul's frustration in Romans 7:7-24 when he wrote, "I know within me, that is in my flesh, nothing is good because I desire to please the inward man (new spirit), but I find a law (force) bringing me into captivity - that is my soul is aligning with my flesh to make me carnal and fall into sin" (Romans 7:18, emphasis mine). Then in Chapter 8, he wrote, "They that are after the flesh, do mind the things of the flesh, and they that are after the Spirit the things of the spirit." (Romans 8:5). This means when the born-again person is spiritually minded, they remain spiritual and victorious. However, the desire for sin surfaces when he switches to his fleshly mind. Hence, it is a battle between the flesh and the spirit mindedness.

The apostle Paul further said that he knew that "our outward man perish, yet our inward man (new spirit) is renewed day by day" (2 Corinthians 4:16). It means while the body is getting old, the new spirit is still glowing daily rejoicing to be clothed with the heavenly body that will forever keep it rejoicing. "For in this we groan earnestly desiring earnestly to be clothed upon with our house - new body from heaven" (2nd Corinthians 5:2). In other words, your soul will be perfected when it receives its glorified body after death or rapture. Your flesh profits nothing (John 6:63). It will be trashed and buried and can never enter heaven since 'flesh and blood cannot inherit the kingdom of God' (1 Corinthians 15:50).

You are righteous in your spirit once you have accepted Jesus Christ as your LORD and Savior. God deals with you now as a righteous person in your new spirit. He gave his righteousness to your new spirit man by which you are called into the fellowship of his dear Son. The new spirit has been perfected or sanctified forever. That does not imply once saved, always saved because the soul is yet saved. Though there is a covenant of not imputing sins to the born-again believer, many have been hardened through sin's deceitfulness, being overly dominated by the flesh in the course of their journey (2nd Corinthians 5:19, Hebrews 3:13, 10:29).

When a believer tenaciously holds his faith to the end, they are saved. Hebrews 10:23 says, "Let us hold fast to the profession (confession) of our faith without wavering or losing our confidence" (Emphasis mine). We shall be finally saved "if we hold fast the confidence and the rejoicing of the hope firm to the end" (Hebrews 3:5). Jesus further corroborated this when he said, "He that overcometh, and keepeth my works, to him will I give power over the nations (Revelation 2:26). The soul's alignment with your regenerated spirit guarantees redemption after death. No man of the dust will gain access to heaven by his own righteousness except by the mercies of God.

Remember, the new spirit of Christ entered the believer with the laws of the Spirit, just like Adam's spirit came with the knowledge of God. The knowledge of God was in Abimelech, who told God that he did not know Sarah was Abraham's wife. The knowledge of God is in the conscience of everyone born on earth. For instance, a believer who refuses to forgive cannot obtain forgiveness from God because the new spirit is the spirit of love. (1st Timothy 1:7). Also, a believer who joins a secret society or witchcraft can never be granted access into God's kingdom because one cannot drink of the LORD's table as well as the cup of the devil (1 Corinthians 10:21).

Perfection with God

But we have seen people interpret the Hebrews 10:14 out of context, supporting the notions of 'once saved, always saved.' God will never affirm such an idea to anyone. The scripture says, "For by one offering he had perfected forever them that are sanctified." Many are deluded, thinking the scriptures implies once saved, always saved. Jesus said, "Many are called, but few are chosen" (Matthew 22:14). In other words, being saved or born again does not guarantee entrance into heaven, which I've explained from the scriptures that your spirit was saved, but your soul is yet saved. Jesus also said, "Strive to enter, for many will strive and will not be able" (Matthew 7:13).

This shows the Christain journey requires your cooperation with the Holy Spirit. In the course of your journey, you are admonished not to grieve the person of the Holy Spirit. So God hopes that you will make it to the end. The interruptions caused by fleshly lusts or other factors during the Christain journey often impede the smoothness of the journey. Jesus counseled the churches in the book of Revelation about some attitudes found unpleasant amongst them and admonished them to repent. They were already saved, but Jesus knew that the soul was yet saved since he, who subjected the creature (new spirit) to vanity (the flesh), hoped the soul would abound in the Lord as well.

The apostle Paul also expounded on this when he wrote in 1st Corinthians 10:1-21, How the LORD, having saved some, destroyed those who didn't follow on to the end. Many were cut off by the LORD because, in the course of their walk, God was not pleased. I believe the LORD gives us a new spirit inside our body at salvation to experience the love for righteousness. Like the Israelites who were set free from bondage and quickly forgot what God had done for them, we go through certain situations which test our faith in him. Although, now, the scriptures make a provision for believers to confess sins and have them washed in the blood of Jesus Christ (John 2:1, 1:1:8-9). And this is one of the reasons Jesus became a high priest in the heavens. So when Jesus said, many are called, and few are chosen, it means not everyone that saith unto me Lord, Lord shalt enter into the kingdom of heaven. God will select his people from the multitudes that came.

Now, before expounding on the notions of 'once saved, always saved,' I'd like us to go through the old Testament patterns of appeasing God once more. The carnal services performed by sacrificing the blood of bulls and goats were meant to purify the flesh, not the heart's conscience. The first and second tabernacles had veils that signified a certain degree of consecration of altars of holiness. The Scriptures recorded that the second tabernacle is the holiest of all, to which the high priest had access only once a year. The high priest would have to offer blood sacrifices for himself first before entering the second tabernacle, indicating that the high priests under the law were subject to sin and death.

It was observed that the sacrifices of bulls and goats could not have made the high priests perfect as pertaining to the conscience of the heart. Perfection here is a state of being unconscious of sin. According to the scriptures, Job was a perfect man, not because he never sinned, but because he always prayed to God for forgiveness of sins for himself and his family, making sacrifices for sins. This brought him into perfection with God. Job became mature following God; that was what the scriptures meant by perfect. So many ignorant Christians think Job was sinless. Only the blood of Jesus guarantees perfection when you confess sins. No man attained perfection by works done on earth. The blood sacrifices of animals performed by the Israelites were made according to the laws, which present them as holy to God, just like Job.

Perfected forever

The blood of bulls and goats can't take away sins registered in the conscience of the heart (Hebrews 10:2-4). The congregations of the Israelites then were made to lay hands on the sacrifices signifying faith in those animal sacrifices for cleansing, which, when offered, made them 'clean' or 'holy' as pertaining to the flesh. But if the priest or high priest accidentally touches a dead body or comes in contact with a leprous man, he would be declared unclean.

The priests were not permitted to come near certain things to avoid being defiled in the flesh. The garments they put on portray holiness, but in their conscience, they retain guilt for sins committed. It is then evident that the blood of bulls couldn't take away sins from the conscience, or else the worshippers, once purged, should not have had the conscience of sins (Hebrews 10:2). For this reason, the scriptures say, "...Rend your hearts, and not your garments" (Joel 2:13).

When Jesus came on the scene, he said, "Woe unto you, scribes and Pharisees, hypocrites! For you are like unto whited sepulchers, which indeed appear beautiful outwardly, but are within full of dead men's bones, and of all uncleanness" (Matthew 23:27). Whited sepulchers denotes being clothed white like a ghost. Such outward white garment coverings couldn't stop the heart from thinking evil anyway. They were cleanly dressed outwardly, but their hearts were full of envy, greed, blood, cursing, immorality, deceit, cheating, lust, lies, wickedness, etc. So you can see that certain dress codes aren't what God is much concerned about but the state of the heart. It doesn't mean you dress inappropriately in the presence of God because you won't do that in congress or a courtroom. Decency is part of moral living.

Another thing of note is that the animal sacrifices offered by the Israelites were incapable of destroying the defiled spirit of Adam; hence they were repeated yearly. There was a need for a spotless body so that the blood from the undefiled body would purify the conscience of the heart that resides in every soul. Suppose you must work on the condition of your heart. In that case, you must also work on the spirit since the human spirit, as breathed from God, went through the nostrils connecting the vocal cords down to the heart to activate the cells of the heart and, at the same time, deposited the laws and nature of God inside man.

This is why God promised a new heart and a new spirit in Ezekiel 36:26. You cannot work on the spirit without the heart being involved. This means everyone knows what is required of them, even without the Mosiac laws. Those who were not Israelites knew God's requirements intuitively. "For as many that have sinned without law (Mosaic laws), shall also perish without law: and as many as have sinned in the law shall be judged by the law; For not the hearers of the law are justified before God, but the doers of the law shall be justified. For when the Gentiles which have not the law, do by nature the things contained in the law, these having not the law, are a law unto themselves: Which shows the work of the law written in their hearts, their conscience also bearing them witness, and their thoughts the mean while accusing or else excusing one another." (Romans 2:12-15).

You can see that nobody is excused or has an alibi for not knowing what to do as regards God's law. So long as you can breathe, the laws of God are deposited inside of you. Everyone knows what they are doing. Some people only show remorse when they are reprimanded. Many don't examine themselves to have a rethink before they are rebuked or apprehended. And so, the only qualified person, who could have sacrificed himself without sin, was Jesus Christ. His blood was spotless, which he offered once and for all to sanctify those who come unto God by him. His blood is still available in heaven to cleanse all sins; hence if we confess our sins, he is just and faithful to cleanse us from all unrighteousness (1 John 1:9).

The blood of Jesus Christ through the eternal Spirit will purge your conscience from sins to enable us to serve the living God (Hebrews10:14). Without the conscience being purged by the blood of Jesus Christ, and the old defiled spirit being destroyed (sanctified), you and I will not be able to draw near to God. God deals with us by mercy in the blood of Jesus Christ. You come to God based on his mercy, so exercising faith in him gives you confidence.

If you are born again and retain this Old Testament mentality of confessing sins you have confessed repeatedly, you need to renew your mind from such thinking. You cannot confess sins that have been thrown into forgetful seas. The blood of Jesus Christ was sacrificed once and for all - forever, but still available to cleanse sins committed. The sanctified ones are those who obtained the new creature (incorruptible seed) and have their conscience purged. Perfected forever means Jesus won't repeat his death. It was done once and for all. We can interchange the phrase "perfected forever" with "completed forever." That is what the scripture meant when it said, "you are complete in him" (Colossians 2:10).

It will amount to pride if we don't acknowledge our sins and confess them to God because we are born again and know we have sinned. What is the essence of Jesus being made a high priest forever? A typical example is the relationship between a father and a son. The fact that you had a son who bears your name does not mean that your son won't offend you. If the son does something wrong and seems unapologetic, you may not tolerate such arrogance from him. Why would your righteousness consciousness be unapologetic or unrepentant?

Chapter 24

The God Experience

    I didn't just get up out of bed and start writing. I have had many experiences that propelled me to write about these mysteries. When I was age 14, I had a dream. In the dream, I could remember cleaning up a sitting room. I saw a man who happened to be a friend of my manager approaching the house I was cleaning up. I saw my manager screaming at the top of his voice, "Shut that door! Shut that door!" He wanted me to shut the door against his friend. And I did shut the door in that dream. When I did that, I saw this friend of his chasing after me for shutting the door at him. When I woke up, it was already 6:00 am, and in less than an hour, I was cleaning up the same sitting room. Lo, and behold, the exact man I saw in my dream was approaching the house, and my manager with whom I passed the night started screaming, "Shut that door! Shut that door!" I immediately remembered my dream playing out and had to use my discretion. I was amazed at how such a thing would play out from the spiritual realm into reality. And from that moment forward, I was careful about what I saw in my dreams and visions. Of course, I also know when Satan infiltrates.

    Time will not permit me to tell you several dreams and visions I have had over the years which played out exactly, but I'd briefly tell you a little fraction that got me curious about God—of course, encountering God once is not enough. Knowing God daily is better. Experiencing God once in a while is not sufficient for a lifetime. You've got to stay on track daily. We saw Solomon had the God experience twice but was clouded with vain pursuits. I believe God showing up was a call to duty.

    God's appearance to Moses was a call to duty. You have got to know him daily by his current word and ways. Seeing someone for the first time doesn't mean you know the person in terms of their behavior. It is one thing to see a person well dressed and attractive, and it is another thing to know the person's behavior, the do's and don'ts, the likes and dislikes. We have seen people who loved themselves and swore their lives for each other as married couples, and when things began to fall apart, they had regrets about being in love. However, when it comes to God encounters, God doesn't hurt. Instead, he has a force of love more potent than our emotional feelings. God pulls you with a force of love that is too strong to resist.

The more you encounter God, the more you want more of him. Scripture calls it past findings and unsearchable. Romans 11:33 says, "O the depth of the riches both of the wisdom of God! How unsearchable are his judgments, and his ways are past finding out!" The truth is God is inexhaustible. You cannot get satisfied with the pursuit of God even when he is living in the same room as you. It is one level of glory to another. Even in heaven, the elders and angels still wonder about this God. Scripture says, "...In God's temple doth everyone speak of his glory" (Psalms 29:9).

One time, I was caught in a trance. I saw a spirit being in my room; when I looked at it, from top to bottom was fire. The hands and legs everywhere was fire. But it was in the shape of a man. At this time, I couldn't grasp the meaning. This spirit walked into the walls and disappeared. I was wondering what sort of thing this is!

At that time, I was working for an organization. It was Wednesday, July 6, 2011, and it happened that my manager had scheduled a meeting with someone about my work on July 11, 2011, the following Monday.

I had made a few errors, and I knew those errors might be discovered if that meeting was held as planned. So I was scared, praying that the meeting should not happen. Then I heard Holy Spirit say, 'The meeting would not occur as planned.' I was wondering how on earth an appointment already scheduled would be canceled. Then he told me, "Write this day down for a memorial." His words keep resonating in my spirit. So, I took up the pen and wrote in my diary the events of my vision on July 6th, not knowing what lies ahead.

When I got home, I lay on my bed to rest. Suddenly, I was caught in a trance. This occurred in less than 2 minutes of lying on the bed without sleeping. Is like my conscious mind was suspended, and I saw a cloud descend very close to my bed. I was wondering where the roof over me had gone. The cloud dropped down, overshadowing all substances in my room except the bed where I lay. I then saw the hand of God come out of the cloud. His hand was magnificently too big to behold.

One of the fingers was about 32 times bigger than the size of a mortal man. I'm not exaggerating. It came close to me and went back into the cloud. On regaining consciousness, I began to praise God. It then dawned on me that God is this big. I was pondering how great God could be! The meeting date (July 11) came, and the meeting was according to His words to me. At other times, God's hand will flash, and I will quake. I then took out time to search the scriptures to know who this God is.

At other times, I saw Father Abraham in heaven's clouds, coming alongside heaven's saints to welcome home believers on earth. I knew in the vision that this was Father Abraham, just like Peter, James, and John knew Moses and Elijah at the mount of transfiguration. At other times, I saw Jesus on a throne with multiple colors, like the rainbow. One time, I saw Jesus entering the earth through the cloud, and he walked in and out at will. At other times, I saw the tunnel to hell, which was very black, and I saw black glittering dragons. So I knew the spirit realm is real. As I said, I may not be able to tell you all my experiences, but these experiences got me curious to search the scriptures to know more about the universe in which we live.

Ministry of the prophets

Delving into abstract concepts seems difficult to the natural man who has been overly concerned with scientific ideologies. Trying to bridge the gap between abstract and natural concepts is complex. It has birthed two classes of individuals: some who believed in the existence of God and others who are being tutored and misled to discard the concept of God, especially at the elementary school through the college levels. However, it's being observed that many who might have attempted to disregard the existence of God often find the concept keeps resonating in their hearts. The reason may not be unconnected to the fact the intuitive knowledge of God is intrinsically witnessed by everyone who has the breath of life, including inanimate objects.

Unfortunately, those who disbelieved the existence of God for the simple fact that some top scientists had cajoled them into such belief systems have been deceived. In reality, science is the study of nature and is limited to carnal ways of reasoning. The carnal mind does not comprehend the supernatural. For instance, space exploration of planets in our universe would take several hours, days, months, or years to travel from the earth's surface, but demons cover such distances at the sleight of thought - less than a minute which is far greater than the speed of light. In addition, the supernatural world has been observed to supersede the natural world when one considers the ministry of the prophet. We have seen several cases in which someone may encounter the prophetic ministry, and a prophet unconnected to that individual would accurately describe the person's past and present and give insight into the future.

The prophet here operates from the supernatural realm and, in some cases, would call out individuals by their names, analyzing every bit of their life experiences, which the recipients affirmed. The prophetic ministry is capable of invading and interpreting the dream, dissecting as far as the thoughts of the heart. You must understand that our reasonings occur in abstract realms. As a result, our performances are conspicuously seen in the abstract world, which is playing alongside the natural world. To act, you must have reasoned or accepted any internal or external influence processed in your mind (abstract). Once the thought or suggestion goes through, it is examined on the grounds of good or evil in the realms of the spirit. Hence Jesus's remarks that thoughts are capable of defiling a man are correct.

The scripture says, "For from within, out of the heart of men, proceed evil thoughts, adulteries, fornications, thefts, covetousness, wickedness, deceit, lasciviousness, an evil eye, blasphemy, pride, foolishness: All these evil things come from within, and defile the man" (Mark 7:21-23). In other words, you were captured in a split second during the image formation before your soul cooperated with your body to effect the action. So when Jesus said that 'out of the abundance of the heart the mouth speaks, or whosoever looketh on a woman to lust after her, hath committed adultery with her already in his heart, it denotes the spiritual world revolves in and around us, and our intentions are manifest in the abstract world before they are materialized (Matthew 5:28 and 12:34).

It always begins with the abstract into the natural, making it clear that the spiritual is superior to the natural. Jesus said, "...For your heavenly Father knoweth what things you have need of, before you ask him" (Matthew 6:8). You can see here that your thoughts or reasonings were seen in the abstract world before you implemented them or even prayed for divine guidance or intervention. As mentioned earlier, there are varying dimensions of the spiritual world. Accessing the spiritual world doesn't automatically grant you access to seeing angels or God.

A discourse about the person of God can be explained by the word of God or the ministry of the prophet. God operates through the ministry of the prophets when it has to do with things pertaining to his personality and ways. The book of Hosea 12:10 says, "I have also spoken by the prophets, and I have multiplied visions, and used similitudes, by the ministry of the prophets." God affirmed that he uses prophetic ministry when revealing his personality. It shows prophets are special people gifted by God to see and hear what God is doing in the spiritual realms. A natural man is incapable of understanding the things of the spirit because they are spiritually discerned, just as science cannot understand inanimate objects of stones, waves, rocks, thunders, lightning, stars, sun, and planets.

God's mode of operation is known by the prophets or vessels he chooses to reveal certain mysteries. The prophetic gift is not necessarily given to those who have congregations, like Amos, who was not a prophet but was used by God. Amos confirmed this in the scriptures that he was not a prophet: "Then answered Amos, and said to

Amaziah, I was no prophet, neither was I a prophet's son; but I was an herdman, and a gatherer of sycomore fruit and the LORD took me as I followed the flock, and the LORD said unto me, Go, prophesy unto my people Israel" (Amos 7:14- 15). Amos was just a herdman gathering fruit. We saw Daniel, who was a gatekeeper that was mightily used by God in the prophetic. God dealt with wise men who were shepherds as stargazers from the east, opening their eyes to see angels who told them about the birth of Jesus Christ (See Luke 2:8-13). Abraham was a prophet like David, the king, who performed the priestly function of sacrificing directly to God.

The prophetic ministry is not an entitlement but a ministry with God where he communicates to certain individuals in visions, trances, and dreams. God confirmed that "if there be any prophet among you, I the LORD will make myself known unto him in a vision, and I will speak to him in a dream" (Numbers 12:6). God reveals his operations (workings) in visions to prophets. The gift of the word of knowledge is a shadow of the prophetic ministry. The prophetic gift deals with visions, trances, and dreams. Visions and trances have to do with God's opening of a man's spiritual eyes to align with the focal point of the eyes of the body. But then, God is not limited to visions or dreams only. He does reveal himself through his word as well.

God reveals himself through his word to Samuel. Scriptures say in 1st Samuel 3:1, "And the child Samuel ministered unto the LORD before Eli. And the word of the LORD was precious in those days; there was no opened vision." In other words, there was no open vision prior to Samuel's days. Samuel did experience open vision with his eyes opened. God spoke to Samuel in his right ear, not in a dream state. He did that by communicating to Samuel's spirit openly. Your spirit is the medium by which you can hear God. God, who is light, communicates to your spirit (light energy) infused inside of you. If you recollect, God does talk to your spirit man, which vibrates to your soul. Your spirit is the first contact point by which you hear God's still, small, audible voice. The word of God connects your spirit and vibrates to your soul, which brings you to awareness of His voice. "God revealed himself unto Samuel by the word of the LORD" (1st Samuel 3:21).

According to the scripture, every word from God is living. In context, God is not boxed to the cover pages of the Scriptures. He is not locked in. Hence he is a living God. The scriptures we referenced came through God's dealings with men in previous generations. God spake to men like you and I, who wrote down the scriptures. The Holy Spirit inspired them to write. That doesn't suggest they never added their reasonings in the process, as Paul wrote, "...to the rest speak I not the Lord" (1st Corinthians 7:12).

The conversations they had with God were written down for us to learn and know God's voice and ways. The manner of his instructions and the things he does in the lives of men were principles laid down for us to understand that God loves righteousness, and he does interfere in our affairs.

The scriptures confirmed God's word is pure and tried in a fire, just as impurity is refined by fire out of gold. Meaning he cannot say impure words. His word is rooted in truth which is life, and there has never been any form of flattery. You know, we've got people who are religious, incapable of discerning God's voice, yet possess head knowledge of the scriptures. Such religious people may analyze the scriptures academically but never hear the living God tell them what to do in their own lives. And this is where many missed it, not striving to hear God's voice. The Scripture is printed in a physical book in the natural world, but they are spiritually alive. Jesus said, "…The words that I speak unto you, they are spirit, and they are life" (John 6:63). God's word in the scripture is a living word activated by his spirit when faith exudes from an individual.

The adjective 'living' denotes the capacity of God's word to transform a deviant behavioral personality from drunkenness, prostitution, hooliganism, etc., to an upright person just by studying the scriptures. And since God's word is a living word, it is capable of being infused into a human, transforming that living soul.

The truth is you can use the scriptures to address insurmountable challenges, and such challenges will take the direction of your prayers. We have seen people who testified that medical doctors had given up hope on them due to cancer. But they took hold of the scriptures and held on to the promises of God by meditating and declaring the scriptures, which paid off, and they eventually got healed of cancer. While some would just read the same scriptures religiously, being unable to connect to God. I think they have a long way to go. Sorry, I don't mean to hurt anyone. I'm just being sincere. If God talks to people in the scriptures, then he can talk to you about your life because he is a living God, not a dead God. God is not dead, and neither can he die. He didn't get dumb as soon as the Bible was printed. Any thought that tells you God is dead is from Satan.

God talks to people daily. Some say miracles ended in the scriptures, and if that were true, the question is, why then would you still pray? There wouldn't have been any need for praying. But you've got a witness on the inside that God is very much around you and that you are talking to a living God who listens whenever you pray. And, of course, some have boxed the living God into a sculpture. They believe God is in a monument, so they religiously pray to a statue. God sometimes answer their prayers, not because of the sculpture but because of their words.

When you pray, you are speaking words that proceed from a living being, and God is a living God who heard your prayer, not the sculpture, which cannot hear or speak. So people who worship images or ancestral sculptures pray (by uttering words), which proceed from their spirit, as living beings, believing that their words were heard, and the spirits they prayed to acted upon their words. Spirits are around you right where you are, and your words have positive and negative effects on life.

Spirits listen to you

Words are powerful because they advance or destroy our world. Humans talk all the time. Our words run throughout the earth. Psalms 19:4 says, "... their words to the end of the world..." Whether in prayers or casual speaking, we release words from our spirits. Words proceed from things that have life. Man can speak because of the breath of life (spirit), so animals or birds have spirits in them as well, which causes them to make sounds or communicate amongst themselves. A robot cannot make sound without energy. The battery becomes the life of the robot. When we say words, we release words from our spirit, and such words go beyond the person we are speaking to, extending to spirit beings who also listen to our words.

Jesus said, "For by your words thou shalt be justified, and by your words, thou shalt be condemned." (Matthew 12:37). In other words, spirits listen to our words even if spoken in privacy. So you can see that your words were heard. That is why you got an answer, not because the sculpture answered you. Worshipping a sculpture is idolatry. And if your words were heard, it means spirits often listen to you.

Let's take an analogy of two persons in a relationship, in which one of the partners might say privately, "I don't need him or her anymore." And after a period of time, circumstances will arise that will cause the relationship to go south. Similarly, when demons prompt us to say words against someone we love or our business associates, we have to be careful not to speak against them, not even privately, as spirits could implement those words unless we renounce them. Although scriptures say, "...curse causeless shall not come (Proverbs 26:2)." If your words were borne out of envy, hatred, and jealousy unjustifiably, then your words will do them no harm. So words are powerful tools used by God and his creatures. Let's get back on track.

When God came to Abraham, he revealed himself to Abraham by his word. He instructed Abraham to leave his father's house and move to a land of promise. And as the relationship progressed, he appeared to Abraham in a vision. He approached Abraham in human form as Melchizedek, and at other times, as a man with an angelic body -

LORD. If you considered the progressions, you'd agree that God first communicated his word before moving on to visions. That doesn't mean God would go through every stage in dealing with man. His word comes first. God is known by his word. It then means God's word depicts his personality. The scriptures characteristically described God as a consuming fire, rock, light, living water, love, creator, and as a person who directs and as commander (LORD) of all creatures in the multiverse. If you want to know God, search the scriptures because the scriptures testify about God with the intent to draw you closer to God (John 5:39- 40).

God at first spoke to Abraham and subsequently made himself known unto him. God's word often goes before him. The scripture says, "...His word runs swiftly" (Psalms 147:15). God's word actively performs the function of a living being upon the earth. Isaiah 55:11 says, "So shall my word be that goeth out of my mouth: it shall not return unto me void, but it shall accomplish that which I please, and it shall prosper in the thing whereto I sent it." God's word is like a drone being monitored to accomplish a mission. When his word by way of counsel is released and obeyed, created things as nature favors the receiver, but when his word is rejected, nature rises against the receiver. The word of God came unto Abraham, and Abraham obeyed his words, which Adam disobeyed. Because Abraham obeyed his word, God was attracted to Abraham. Abraham came to know God in person when the LORD visited him.

God's visit to Abraham was because His word found a place in Abraham's heart. God values his word to man. When his word cannot find a place in you, it means you are doomed. Jesus told the Pharisees that his word has no place in them (John 8:37). If you cannot obey his voice, then he is not your Lord because he does not waste words. Refusing to take his instruction means you have another master you owe allegiance to, so he sends you to your master. Though Moses was one of the sons of God, when he first refused the instruction to return to Egypt, the scripture says God almost killed him. The next partial obedience of Moses was costly. Throughout the time Moses heard God and obeyed, he was attracted to God. Moses eventually saw God's back part due to obedience and fellowship. Just like Adam saw God one-on-one. I know this might cause a stir among some people who haven't studied the scriptures correctly, sticking to religious lines of thought. It's been established that God usually visited Adam and Eve directly in the Garden of Eden.

No sinful flesh can

In a sinless state, Adam's spirit eyes align with the focal point of the eye of the body, enabling him to see the abstract realms altogether. Just as a prophet under the influence of the Spirit of God in ministry can simultaneously see into the spiritual realm and see humans. The prophet's spiritual eyes must have been opened and thus aligned with his focal point of the body. The prophet can't open his spiritual eyes on his own. It is exclusive to God or the angels who have access to your spirit. Of course, Satan also does that since he can enter the heart, with some people consulting demons to be able to see. So when someone tells you that God opened his eyes to see into the spirit to behold God, it is not for you to criticize. You judge incorrectly because your mind has accepted that no man can see God, which is incorrect.

We have seen people discontent with others who may have had the God experience quoting the scripture which says, "No man hath seen God at any time" (John 1:18). Couple with some other scriptures saying, "God said, no man can see him" (Exodus 33:20). Another person might immediately quote, "Jesus said, no man hath seen the Father" (John 6:46). All scriptures quoted are acknowledged. We shall be looking into these scriptures one after the other to clarify the contexts in which they were used: So let's begin with the book of Exodus 33:20. "And he said, Thou canst not see my face: for there shall no man see me, and live." It is also clear God was referring to his face here. He told Moses that his face could not be seen. Moses prayed to God, saying, "Show me your glory" (Exodus 32:18). It means God's glory refers to God's face in this context. I will return to this point about 'the glory of God," in which God meant his face.

God said, "No man shall see me and live." Many don't know the context in which the scripture was used. We have established earlier that when the Father as LORD came down at Mount Sinai, the Lord (angel) was amongst the angels who accompanied him. This means that God the Father was the rock speaking to Moses at this time, while the Lord, as a star amongst the hosts of angels, was the commander. Moses testified about seeing God's back which we shall soon touch on. So when God said, No man shall see me and live, God was, in essence, saying Moses could not literally see his face and survive it. He was referring to God the Father's face as in rock. Mortal man looking into the face of God as a Rock would be absorbed into the spiritual realms.

No flesh shall see God the Rock in his core person literally and live. But the Lord God as LORD (a star transformed into man) was seen by Abraham. Truth is God the Father descended once upon Mount Sinai. Adam saw the Lord God (LORD) who appeared unto Abraham, which was the Son. When God came looking for Adam, the scriptures say,

"...Adam and his wife hid from the presence of the Lord God amongst the trees of the garden" (Genesis 3:8). That was the Lord, the same God as the bright and morning star here which I have touched on.

Face for identification

Let's go back to Exodus 19:9. "And the LORD God said unto Moses, Lo, I come unto thee in a thick cloud, that the people may hear when I speak with thee, and believe thee forever..." God descended on a mountain with fire, smoke, and clouds. God warned Moses to tell the people to beware, lest they break through to see who God (the Father) was, and many of them perished (Exodus 19:21, emphasis mine). So they were not permitted to see God as a rock, corroborating what Jesus meant by the Israelites have not seen God nor know his shape.

If you read further, the scriptures say God spoke audibly, and the people heard and were afraid of the voice of God. In Deuteronomy 5:25-26, "Now therefore, why should we die? for this great fire will consume us: if we hear the voice of the LORD our God anymore, then we shall die, For who is there among all flesh that hath heard the voice of the living God, speaking out of the midst of fire, as we have, and lived?" This shows they heard God's audible voice when God came down upon Mount Sinai. God's voice was thunderous, and they could not bear it; only Moses, whom God chose, heard it distinctly.

However, when God was still on Mount Sinai for forty days, scriptures say God later permitted Moses to come up with seventy elders and priests, namely Aaron, Nadab, and Abihu, to climb the mountain. This was only after the sacrifices were performed and blood was sprinkled upon the altars before they could meet with God. And the scriptures record, "And they saw the God of Israel: under his feet as it were a paved work of a sapphire stone and as it was the body of heaven in his clearness. And upon the nobles of the children of Israel, he laid not his hand: they saw God, and did eat and drink." (See Exodus 24:1-11).

So they saw God but could only see white clouds covering him. Hence they described what they saw. They didn't see God's face, but they saw God covered in a cloud and what was under his feet like the sapphire stone. This was no vision or dream. They literally saw God covered in a cloud; the scriptures said God didn't kill them. This brings us back to what God told Moses: His face cannot be seen. Correct? Yes. These elders didn't see God's body entirely. He was still covered with clouds seeing them, but they couldn't see through the cloud covering God. Having experienced this manifest form of God, Moses was still curious, wanting to know more about God. So Moses said to God, "Show me your glory." This implies showing me your face and how you looked physically.

Of course, when you scheduled a meeting with someone over the phone, and the person honored your invitation, but on getting there, your invitee remained inside a tinted glass car and only spoke to you. If you were asked what the person you visited looked like, you might not be able to describe the person. So Moses was curious to have the opportunity to know God in person since he literally came down to planet earth but was covered in a cloud. And God replied to him, saying, "Thou canst not see my face: for there shall no man see and live." So God knew Moses was asking about His facial identification, His glory.

God refused that request but granted Moses the opportunity to see his very back part (in rocky form) by displacing the cloud and used his hand to cover Moses's face (See Exodus 33:23). This shows God's hand is large to cover Moses's face even from a far distance completely. The scripture didn't say hands, but hand. The hand of God is not man's hand in size. From what I saw in my vision about God, one of his fingers is larger than 32 men clustering together in one spot. God, as a spirit, has a long hand that can be stretched from his throne to hell. His hands are very long, according to the scriptures. Psalms 89:13 says, "Thou hast a mighty arm: strong is thy hand, and high is thy right hand." God is everywhere, so his right hand can reach you wherever you go.

When the the Psalmist narrated his experience trying to flee from the presence of God, he realized that God is everywhere. He knew God's right hand was long enough to reach him wherever he could flee. "If I ascend to the heaven, thou are there: if I make my bed in hell, behold thou art there. If I take the wings of the morning and dwell in the uttermost parts of the sea, even there will thy hand lead me, and thy right hand shall hold me." (Psalms 139:8-10). The heaven here also means traveling to space. God's hand is great and high, which, when stretched, can project out to reach you. I told you the spiritual world is side by side with our natural realms.

Chapter 25

The Glory of God

Now, let's look back at John's epistle. John's gospel 1:18 says, "No man hath seen God at any time; which is the only begotten Son, which is in the bosom of the Father, he hath declared him." I believe this scripture is self-explanatory. John wasn't referring to God the Father here. Instead, he was talking about God the Son Jesus. The Scripture was emphatic here when it says,... "...which is the only begotten Son which is in the bosom of the Father." John repeated the same sentence in 1st John 4:12, referencing God the Son Jesus not being seen before he was born on earth. Jesus was described in the bible as the Son of God but was not yet seen by man.

John made this assertion based on his depth of understanding of the scriptures at the time of writing his epistle. Just as the apostle Paul refuted scientific concepts in his days. Although scientists also set aside the God factor in their experimental analysis, most of the developments on earth are 90% science and technology based. However, things being utilized and explored on the earth were created by God. They didn't show up on the earth. God is the creator of all things.

I presumed John might be wrong in this verse because Jesus said that he was before Abraham, and as Melchizedek implies, he is LORD and that Abraham rejoiced to see his day. This has been proven from the scriptures corroborating Paul's depths on Melchizedek from Old Testament. Conversely, John is presumed to have been correct on the condition that when Abraham met Jesus as Melchizedek, Jesus didn't show Abraham his face during the encounter in Genesis plausibly, or Melchizedek had a different facial appearance. Whatever the case, God, the only begotten of the Father, had been to planet earth before he incarnated as Jesus Christ.

Now, let's look at the third scripture reference on the subject. Jesus talked about God the Father not being seen yet. Jesus said, "Not that any man had seen the Father, save he which is of God, he hath seen the Father." (John 4:46). This, we can understand, means he was talking about God the Father's face, not being seen by any man because Moses saw God's back part but not his face. In essence, Jesus said God the Father's face had not been seen yet. Then in John 5:37, Jesus told the Jews present at that time that they had not heard God's voice nor seen God's shape. He was clearly talking to the Jews of his time because past generations heard God's voice, as we have seen in the scriptures about God's visitation at mountain Sinai, and Moses beheld the similitude of God.

Then he went further, informing the Jews, "...If you had known me, you should have known my Father also" (John 8:19). In other words, if you can see me, you can easily identify God the Father facially, who is a Spirit. In other words, I'm the facial expression of the Father. Which is I'm the Father in the flesh for you to see. To put things into perspective, he told his disciples plainly, "If you had known me, you should have known my Father also: and from henceforth, you know him, and have seen him....he that hath seen me, hath seen the Father; and how sayest thou then, Shew us the Father?" (John 14:7-9).

That does not mean the Father is flesh, but the Father as a Spirit is Jesus's face being a Rock. The true image of God's face is Jesus in the flesh. Please note that I am not referring to the portrait pictures of Bruce Machiano or Robert Powell, who portrayed Jesus in the Jesus film, which was seen by many religious people worldwide. The people who saw Jesus when he came to planet earth 2000 years ago saw the face of the invisible God in human flesh.

So when you see God the Father and look at Jesus who came to planet earth, you would understand what the scriptures meant by Jesus is God. Just like stars of heaven turned into humans on earth, leaving black holes in space, so also God begot himself as the bright and morning Star, who is now Jesus in the flesh. For this reason, the scriptures wrote that Jesus was the express image of God (Hebrews 1:3). In other words, if you have seen Jesus, you have seen God the Father (same Jesus) who dwells in the everlasting realms but a living Rock. Jesus Christ, who died and rose again, was God's expression in the flesh.

That is why the scripture says men have no excuse for not seeing God. Romans 1:20 says, "For the invisible things of him from the creation of the world are clearly seen, being understood by the things that are made, even his eternal power and Godhead; so that they (creatures) are without excuse" (emphasis mine). The invisible things of God mean the hidden things, as in facial recognition of God was clearly seen by the men he made; hence men are without excuse.

God had already revealed himself from the invisible realms unto man, in the person of Jesus, but some are still confused. How? Let's call to memory the time of Moses we talked about earlier. God said, his face could not be seen. And Moses requested to see God's glory, which we understood was God's face. In Isaiah 40:5, Scripture says, "And the glory of the LORD shall be revealed, and all flesh shall see it together: for the mouth of the LORD hath spoken it." This means God's glory, which Moses requested of the LORD in Exodus, was later revealed to men in the New Testament. And that is why Jesus said, "he who hath seen him hath seen God." Jesus face is the image of the invisible God.

Graced to relate

Moses was a man who sought God, and God showed him mercy. Scripture says Moses beheld the form of God. God would speak to Moses face to face. In other words, God came so close to Moses and talked with him. A typical example is someone wearing a tinted shield on his face who came near to your face while talking to you. That was a level of intimacy. This is spirit relating to mortal flesh named Moses (despite being one of the sons of God), unlike the disciples of Jesus, during his days on earth. Scripture says, "And the LORD spake unto Moses face to face as a man speaketh with his friend..." (Exodus 33:11). I know the direct contact of God's glory in the flesh is essential, as in John's epistle when he wrote that they have literally touched or handled eternal life in the flesh (1st John 1:1).

But God permitted Moses to behold his similitude or shape of God in an obscure manner was a higher level of encounter. God came so close that Moses could obscurely see through the cloud of glory covering God the Father for Moses to view the shape of God. Of course, God as a Spirit can diminish size to enter a temple, but that does not equal his actual height. He is massive in size, much more than the biggest star in space. This degree of intimacy between a mortal and a Spirit showed the level of affection God displayed to Moses. Numbers 12:8 says, "With him will I speak mouth to mouth, even apparently, and not in dark speeches; and the similitude (semblance) of the LORD shall he behold..." Moses was graced to have fellowship with God to the extent of seeing His likeness inside the cloud, but he did not see God's face.

He must have desired God wholeheartedly. He was passionate about God, so he spent 40 days twice (without food and water) on top of a mountain, waiting on God, while the people were busy waiting for what to eat and drink. There are people serving God for their belly sake, money, and miracles. Only a few people are drawn to him, seeking to know him more. When you seek God to an extent, you would then wish why God is not money being sought for. It's like seeking things distracts the mood. Moses was graced, and God said when it came to Moses, he revealed his ways, but to the Israelites, God revealed his acts (miracles, signs, wonders, butter, and bread). "He made known his ways unto Moses, his acts to the children of Israel" (Psalms 103:7).

I have learned that God initiates every move for those assigned. You cannot force yourself on God. If he is wooing you on the inside, you'd know it. Don't be mechanical about it. You may be trying to mimic someone else, but if God is not drawing you, you cannot pursue him in the manner in which Moses sought him. That is why everyone should abide by his calling (1st Corinthians 7:20). God will show mercy and compassion on whom he will. (Romans 9:15). Those who envied the drawn ones to discourage the called ones react like Cain, who envied Abel, his brother because God accepted Abel's sacrifice. So don't envy or become an impediment either. Moses was drawn to God, and God does his work on the inside of the human spirit. "No man can come to me, except the Father which hath sent me draw him..." (John 6:44).

But that doesn't mean you cannot desire the worship of God. God initiates this spiritual love attraction. It is the strongest force of love ever experienced. It pulls one's heart to a certain degree of sobbing like a child, no matter your age limits. Gospel musicians like Don Moen and Jimmy Swaggart, amongst others, may have experienced this power of love in their hearts, as evident in many of their songs that I have heard. As I said, many other gospel musicians love the LORD intimately. When you get into a love relationship with the LORD, you will begin to soar in the spirit of worship and tears. It's such a force of pure love attraction that exceeds any intimate physical desire, causing you to desire God more than earthly pleasures. God does the initiation process, while the drawn man or woman responds obsessively by heart.

This force of love attraction in pure worship of God once pulled a woman's heart who must have felt the holy nature of Jesus sobbing and wiping Jesus's feet with her hair. She's got no choice but to offer her expensive perfume - an alabaster box of ointment and break it open. Psalms 45:9-15 perfectly describes the union between Jesus and the church. I wouldn't know how God does it, but you can't stop thinking about him when you get into this realm. It's like you are married to God. Scripture talks about this union between Jesus as the husband and the church as the bride. God has a strong force of spirit love, clothed in majesty, covered in a cloud of light.

Everlasting burnings

When God led the children of Israel, he led them by a pillar of fire by night and a pillar of cloud by day. "And the LORD went before them by day in a pillar of cloud, to lead them the way; and by night in a pillar of fire, to give them light; to go by day and night" (Exodus 13:21). And these were the two elements God employed as his coverings. Of these two material elements, the scriptures confirmed God made the clouds himself. However, when it comes to fire, God is a consuming fire. In other words, the everlasting realm from which God emerged was fire. Isaiah 33:14 says, "...Who among us shall dwell with the devouring fire? Who shall dwell with everlasting burnings?" God is a devouring fire, as an everlasting burning.

The natural habitat of God is fire, and he breathes out fire. The book of Psalms 18:8 says, "There went up a smoke out of his nostrils, and fire out of his mouth devoured: coals were kindled by it." God spits fire from his mouth, and his eyes are like flames of fire. Coals are kindled when God exhales. It implies that the everlasting realm from which God emerged is known as the 'everlasting burning' universe, from which life (light and darkness) concepts evolved.

God existed in the timeless beginning, dwelling inside fire before forming light, clouds, earth, man, stars, darkness, etc., which have been discussed extensively. I also told you that God came from the everlasting realm, which is two steps away from our realm. This shows that the highest heights above the third heaven, where God is seated, is an environment of fire. You've got to understand that before God created water or clouds, referred to as the highest dust of the heavens, he had existed for several billion years. The scriptures substantiate this when it says, "...The clouds are the dust of his feet" (Nahum 1:3). God made the clouds to be the dust of his feet. The light zone universe above where the angels of God dwell far above our dark universe in space is under the holy mountain of God - the domain of stones of fire. That is why it becomes a multiverse, not a universe, since we have established the fire, light, and the darkness zones.

The visions seen by Daniel indicate God's throne is made of fire, and we saw God the Father was clothed in a white garment with pure white hair as pure as wool. Fire surrounds God's throne because those were his habitation. God is inseparable from fire. Fire runs in his body like a Rock of fire. Ezekiel saw God dwelling inside of fire. "And above the firmament that was over their heads was the likeness of a throne, as the appearance of a sapphire stone: and upon the likeness of the throne was the likeness as the appearance of a man above it. And I saw the color of amber, as the appearance of fire round about within it, from the appearance of his loins even upward, and from the appearance of his loins even downward, I saw as it were the appearance of fire, and it had brightness round about. As the appearance of the bow that was in the cloud in the day of rain, so was the appearance of the brightness round about. This was the likeness of the glory of the Lord. And when I saw it, I fell upon my face, and I heard the voice of one that spake." (Ezekiel 1:26- 28).

Ezekiel saw four cherubs who were God's ministers in a flash of fire, and he also saw

God covered in fire from top to bottom. That does not mean he is not a personality. When I mean person, I mean he has the attributes of man and possesses the shape of a man. He talks, walks, laughs, sees, feels, thinks, and forms things. He is a living God who was never created. He self existed alone as a burning spirit before forming all things. The fire inside and outside of God are the seven spirits. As a matter of fact, the seven spirits of God are the everlasting burnings. "And out of the throne proceedeth lightnings and thunderings and voices: and there were seven lamps of fire burning before the throne, which are the seven Spirits of God." (Revelation 4:5). God is inclosed of seven spirits. God exists as a Spirit by his seven spirits.

You cannot separate God from His Spirit. He emerged first in the everlasting realms by his seven spirits and functions by his Spirit. Everything God does revolve around his Spirit – the seven spirits. The bright and morning star (God) was formed by his seven spirits. The seven spirits formed God (the Son) as a personality. The word "God" means a Spirit. Isaiah 43:10 says, "Before me, there was no God formed" It means the seven spirits merged to form a personality God who was the firstborn of every creature. This explains what the scriptures implied in Proverbs 8:30 when it says, "Then I was by him, as one brought up with him: and I was daily his delight, rejoicing always before him." And the LORD possessed or utilized the power of the Spirit during creation. Hence the scripture says, "The LORD possessed me in the beginning of his way, before his works of old" (Proverbs 8:22). Here, the scripture is talking about the Son as the LORD.

The book of Genesis substantiates this when it talks about the Spirit of God moving upon the face of the deep. It also means that before the earth or deep or heavens (planets) were formed several billion years back, the Spirit of God existed alongside God the Father before replicating God the Son, called Lord God, who is the personality on the ground, who formed all things and created the stars. God is the first and last, which implies no other God existed elsewhere who is a creator. The lifeblood of God is the lamps of fire burning inside him. But ignorant people relegate the person of the Holy Spirit to a third person. They grossly erred, not knowing the scriptures.

When Jesus said the Holy Spirit would glorify him, it meant Jesus was God in the flesh that humans can see to be praised on earth.

We already saw how the Holy Ghost told Paul that he was the one who told the Israelites that they provoked Him in the wilderness (See Hebrews 3:7-11). And we also saw that Jesus spoke to John in the book of Revelation 3:13, saying, "He that hath an ear, let him hear what the Spirit saith unto the churches." It means the LORD is that Spirit (2nd Corinthians 3:17). That is why the composition of the bright and morning

Star God scheduled to incarnate on earth as Jesus was predicted to have the same composition of the Spirit of God. The operations of the Spirit are mysterious and unsearchable. The Holy Spirit transformed a full Star into semen and deposited it inside the womb of Mary, overshadowing her with light. As soon as this bright and morning Star was dropped, it gained a soul inside the womb developing.

The book of Isaiah 11:1-3 says, "And there shall come forth a rod out of the stem of Jesse, and a Branch shall grow out of his roots: And the spirit of the LORD (Father) shall rest upon him, the spirit of wisdom and understanding, the spirit of counsel and might, the spirit of knowledge and of the fear of the LORD; And shall make him of quick understanding of the fear of the LORD, and he shall not be judged after the sight of the eyes, neither reprove after the hearing of the ears" (Emphasis mine). I believe the bright and morning Star (LORD) was completely transformed into semen (child) named Jesus Christ.

This is because whenever stars descend into the earth or incarnate, they form black holes in space and sometimes return to space as new stars or appear as another star in another location. Of course, the bright and morning Star Jesus in the light zone universe couldn't have become a black hole on being transfused into the womb of Mary because black holes exist only in our universe under the darkness. I believe the operations of the bright and morning Star LORD were suspended until his assignment was over on earth, or the Star LORD continued while he was on earth, because all through the scriptures, Jesus was dealing with the Father directly. Hence he manifested the spirit's behavior of walking on water and transfigured himself back into his star light body at the mount of transfiguration. Either way, it is the same LORD as the Father replicated as the Son. And there is nothing impossible for him.

But then one thing of note is that the spirit of the fear of the LORD was upon the child Jesus which made him of quick understanding in the fear of the LORD. And this could have been why Jesus quickly recognized his earthly assignment on earth when he told his mother that he was about his Fathers' business. He had a quick understanding as the Son of God on earth, even at a tender age, which took Moses more than 80 years to realize his spiritual sonship. Paul said, there are things hard to be uttered, so also there are things which I cannot convey in this book. Let's get back on track concerning our discourse on God, who made a thorough search and declared there is no other God before Him.

Light generates current

Out of fire comes forth light. Light was created from fire. Burning fire provides light to its environment. God made light and formed darkness. So when the scripture says, "God is light," it means God shines far greater than our Sun planet. Psalms 50:2 says, "Out of Zion, the perfection of beauty, God hath shined." God is an everlasting fire and does shine as the sun. From light comes lightning and thundering.

Revelation 4:5 talks about 'lamps of fire. In context, lamps (lights) came from the fire, so also lightnings and thunderings and voices. Light is a form of energy, which means light generates a current. It then means God is full of high voltage (current), which I have also witnessed in one of my trances. I remember one time, I fell into a trance and saw the Holy Spirit standing on my right side. Though I couldn't grasp the picture clearly because he was in a transparent form, I could sense His presence around me, and I knew he was there. I then stretched out my hands to touch the tip of his garment, and I was suddenly electrocuted with a very high volt. It was scary to me! I didn't know such a high current moved in and around him.

Although that wasn't the first time I saw the Holy Spirit. I saw him in a white garment as a person embracing a minister I knew. It occurred to me that God is fathomless. The Holy Ghost generates a very high current which drives the planets in motion. The move of the Spirit was found to have been responsible for the rotation, orbiting, revolution, and drifting of planets in our universe. If these motions were not in place, mere mortals would have prided themselves. There is virtually no science or technology that can stop the earth's rotation. We have earlier discussed the move of the Spirit of God in the recreation in Genesis.

Jeremiah 33:20 - 21 says, "Thus saith the LORD; if you can break my covenant of the day and my covenant of the night, and that there should not be day and night in their seasons; then may also my covenant be broken with David, my servant..." It means nothing can stop the motions of planets in our solar system except God wrap it up. God knows the weight of each planet in our universe, including the loads therein. He once told me that his Word is heavier than the earth. I have been puzzled about it ever since!

God, by his Spirit, directs the cosmos. Isaiah 40:13 -17 says, "Who hath directed the Spirit of the LORD, or being his counselor hath taught him...Behold, the nations are as a drop of a bucket and are counted as a small dust of the balance...all nations before him are as nothing, and they counted to him less than nothing and vanity." God knows the weight of each planet under the darkness in space and planets above the darkness in space. The weight of the earth is tiny compared to all of the planets under the darkness universe. The entire human race on the earth, including the weight of the earth, is less than nothing in his sight. "Who hath measured the waters in the hollow of his hand, and meted (measured) with the span, and comprehended the dust (weight) of the earth in a measure, and weighed the mountains in a scales, and the hills in a balance?" (Isaiah 40:12). In other words, God knows the weight of each mountain, hill, and planet because God has his own rules by which the hills and planets are measured, including the volume of the waters. I believe this speaks of the planets being formed with precision.

God in Genesis dealt with the earth as a personality because he knows the earth is 'living' in the spiritual realms. Genesis 9:13 says, "I do set my bow in the cloud, and it shall be for a token of the covenant between me and the earth." In context, he is dealing with the earth as a being because he knows that the earth breathes out. The earth possesses certain organs, like the heart, face, belly, etc., which science cannot figure out. There is a cardiac-like rhythm of the earth, and I believe scientists will one day discover that the earth somehow functions like the human heart. Matthew 12:40 talks about the heart of the earth, which shows the earth is breathing; hence vegetation, just like human hair, grows. This doesn't mean life exists only on planet earth. There are planets where life exists in our universe, which the LORD showed me. And what I saw in my trance were (aliens) creatures capable of grabbing humans living on two different planets under the space darkness.

Massive in size

God is colossal and can diminish in shape at will. He can access your room like a normal person, but in an actual sense, he is massively great. Whenever God talks in his audible voice, it is like thunder mixed with many waters. Job 37:5 says, God thundereth marvelously with his voice...." He alone dwells in the secret place of thunder (Psalms 81:7). The children of Israel, on hearing God's voice in those days, were afraid. We saw a repeated scenario play out when Jesus was praying or communing with the Father before he went to the cross. Scripture confirmed God answered him from heaven directly. While praying, Jesus said, "Father, glorify thy name." Then came a voice from heaven, saying, I have both glorified it and will glorify it again. The people that stood by and heard it said that it thundered: others said, An angel spake to him." (John 12: 28-29). The people were used to angels because they dreaded God. They were used to angelic visitations instead of chasing after God. Their little minds ascribed God's voice to an angel.

Now, let's critically analyze the voice of God the people standing with Jesus heard. The voice, which came as thunder, had traveled some distance before getting to the earth. Though the spiritual realm is alongside the natural realm, we must understand that God's voice resonated from the spiritual realms. A simple analogy could be measuring the sun's temperature while standing on the earth's surface, considering that the actual heat energy radiating from the sun had gone through the ozone layer before reaching the earth's surface. Taking the sun's temperature on the earth is not equal to the sun's temperature at a close range in space. So when God spoke in response to Jesus's prayers, the people heard it thundered, but the voice had traveled from the heights of the heavens far above the darkness in space before getting to planet earth if distance was factored in.

It also dictates that lightning and thundering are by-product of God's voice replicated in nature. God did establish his bow (rainbow) upon the clouds in the days of Noah. Usually, lightning bolts have a very high magnitude of current compared to normal electric current, and you can do a mathematical computation of the magnitude of voltage and current in a lightning bolt. Considering that the lightning bolt had traveled some distances before discharge. So when the Jews heard it thundered, they heard God's audible voice like thunder, confirming what the Israelites in the days of Moses said about God's audible voice, which sounds like thunder. The reason is that God the Father is colossal. We can all attest that when a child speaks, you can almost always easily discern his voice from an adult. God the Father is taller than the sons of Anak, who were giants in those days, which the children of Israel saw and trembled, alleging the sons of Anak were tall like the cedar trees.

The book of Amos expounded further that the sons of Anak as giants whose heights were compared to cedar trees. And of a truth, the children of Israel were little in sight, just that they lacked faith in God. "And there we saw the giants, the sons of Anak, which come of the giants: and were in our own sight as grasshoppers, and so were we in their sight." (Numbers13:33). Spirit beings are mighty and taller than humans who are descendants of Adam. Although they also possess the capability to contract into the size of men, my encounter with God put things into proper perspective, seeing the size of his fingers.

Tall into the clouds

So when people talk about God, many are speaking in ignorance. The children of Israel saw the giant's offspring, whose parents once occupied the earth in the days of Noah. The sons of Anak were descendants of the Amorites that were of great heights like the cedar trees, but God destroyed them from off the earth through the Israelites and other nations because he had earlier told Lucifer that the seed of the fallen spirits (as giants) would not inherit this present earth already handed to the Adamic human race.

The reason for excluding the giants and their offspring who procreated the earth before and after the floods of Noah was for the reproduction of the human races with the same kind of flesh and to ensure the human race (not the giants) dominated and replenished the earth. The book of Amos 2:9 says, "Yet destroyed I the Amorite before them, whose height was like the height of the cedars, and he was strong as the oaks; yet I destroyed his fruit from above, and his roots from beneath." God is taller than all giants in height. Hence his voice thunders. In a literal sense, God the Father is higher than mountains but diminishes his size for man's sake.

The scriptures already described God. Psalms 89:6 says, "For who in heaven can be compared unto the LORD? Who among the sons of the mighty (fallen stars) can be likened unto the LORD?" In context, the actual height of God is far more than any creature. Psalms 97:9 says, "For thou, LORD, art high above all the earth: Thou art exalted far above all gods (spirit beings). And of a truth, the essence of God becoming flesh was to relate with us. Jesus was made a little lower than the angels. The scripture tells us that God beheld the people on earth as grasshoppers when compared to his actual height. Isaiah 40:22, "It is he that sitteth upon the circle (axis) of the earth, and the inhabitants thereof, are as grasshoppers...."

Just as the children of Israel were little as grasshoppers when compared to the sons of Anak, so is the actual size of the man of the dust Adam before God the Father. I believe the size of the rainbow is the size of his head because the rainbow is a crown upon God's head. It is like a king wearing a crown fitted into his head, so the bow or rainbow is the size of God's head. God said, "I do set my bow (crown) in the cloud, and shall be for token between me and the earth." (Genesis 9:13). God is not a man, which also implies God is not the size of man. Jesus said, "The earth is God's footstool." (Matthew 5:35). What does the scripture mean by the earth being God's footstool?

This implies God is seated on his throne while the sea of glass before his throne in heaven (representing the earth and universe under darkness) is under his footstool. In Exodus 24:10, the elders of Israel saw God in a cloudy pillar, and they saw sapphire stones as the pavement under his feet. And under the earth is found sapphire stones, gold, and fire (Job 28:5-6). It means the sapphire stones under God's foot (in his sitting position in heaven) represent the earth; therefore, he is the possessor of heaven and earth.

It causes us to appreciate when Jesus said, "My father is greater than I," he actually meant God, who is in the everlasting realm and is very tall (See John 14:28). Even God confirmed that he filled heaven and earth. "Do not I fill heaven and earth? saith the LORD." (Jeremiah 23:24). The question is, "Since God is this tall more than the giants, how come he accesses the temple in the old testaments?" Simple! God is a Spirit. He can diminish his shape at will or increase to His full size. The stars we see in the sky are mightier in size, but they turn humans and infiltrate the earth as normal humans.

Even Jesus as God, does change shape. Sometimes, he is perhaps 7ft, and other times very tall, reaching the clouds. Believers who died and have been privileged to return to earth have testified to this. Jesus is the same God all souls of men will see as God in the spiritual realm because he is God in the flesh. Hence the Father committed all judgment to him, the Son. Jesus can fit into God the Father and come out of God as a human, which we saw in the book of Revelation. God has three dimensions: the Father, Son, and Holy Ghost. I'd come back to this shortly, but let's take a brief look at the epoch of the giants after the flood of Noah.

Offspring of the giants

I have studied the scriptures to find the truth instead of relying on the teachings of leading theologians. With the help of the Holy Spirit, this study has led to many discoveries. When I got the revelation of what took place in the Garden of Eden, I rejoiced, saying, "Thank You, Jesus!" Whatever I have shared in this book are the fundamental truths of the multiverse and mysteries surrounding us. Before this study, I didn't believe in incarnation or reincarnation. But I discovered the truth, which I have shown you that spirit beings do incarnate into earth at will.

In my curiosity, I asked thus, "If the giants in the time of Noah were killed by the flood of waters, how come giants existed after the floods?" I took out time to research the scriptures, and this is what I have found. Remember, I shared with you that when God said he would shake the heavens once more, it meant he shook it during Noah's flood and also in the land of Egypt in the days of Pharoah and that the once more shaking implied the war that will take place in the future, written in the book of Daniel and Revelation 12:7. Of which, John the apostle of Jesus narrated what he saw in a vision hence he used the finite lexical verb "was" as in a narrative of the vision seen. And this singular verb "was" has resulted in many errors in the interpretation of scriptures in the body of Christ, attempting to interpret scriptures superficially without criticizing scriptural writings.

Now, let's get back to what God spoke about the giants - sons of Anak after the flood of Noah, with the question in mind: "How come there were giants after the flood of Noah if all flesh died except Noah and his family?" Let's get back to what God said in Amos 2:9, "Yet destroyed I the Amorite before them, whose height was like the height of the cedars, and he was strong as the oaks; yet I destroyed his fruit from above, and his roots from beneath." You could notice that God said he destroyed the Amorite seed from above and his roots from beneath. Two striking things here stand out. God destroyed from above and from beneath, which means God used rain as flood waters, as recorded in Genesis 7:16-24 to dislodge the seed of the renowned giant men of old. We have discussed this earlier. Now, let's see what God meant by destroying the roots of these giants from beneath.

After the flood of Noah, God discovered that Ham - one of Noah's sons- had a wife, and it happened that the wife of Ham was also preserved in the Ark with Noah. "And Noah went in, and his sons, and his wife, and sons' wives with him, into the ark, because of the waters of the flood." (Genesis 7:7). Ham's wife was a descendant of the giants destroyed by the floods of waters. She had the genes of these giants in her bloodlines, and that meant her children would become giants by the law of hereditary. God saw that there must be a ground operation to be carried out to decimate these giants from the face of the earth coming from Ham's copulation with his wife.

So, it wasn't a coincidence when Noah pronounced a curse upon Ham, his son, the Father of Canaan, for seeing his nakedness when he was drunk with wine. Noah cursed his son Ham saying, "Cursed be Canaan; a servant of servants shall he be to his brethren." (Genesis 9:25). God used Noah to curse the offspring of the giants in Ham (through his wife), which will come through copulation. God saw in advance that the descendants of Ham's wife would reproduce giants upon the earth. And we saw from the genealogy of Ham that the first son of Ham was Cush, who later begat Nimrod, of which the scripture told us that Nimrod was a mighty one. "And the sons of Ham; Cush, and Mizraim, and Phut, and Canaan...And Cush begat Nimrod: and he began to be mighty one (giant) in the earth" (See Genesis 10:6-8).

In other words, Nimrod was a Giant. Then we have Canaan, the last son of Ham, Canaan; who was the father of the Sidon, Heth, Jebusite, Amorite, Girgasite, Hivite, Arkite, and Sinite (Genesis 10:15-17). So God intending to root out the offspring of these giants from the earth beneath, told Abraham that Abraham's seed would return to the land of Canaan after 400 years to continue the war against these giants as ground operations were concerned. "But in the fourth generation they shall come hither again: for the iniquity of the Amorites is not yet full" (Genesis 15:16). The iniquity of the Amorites implies the violence of the giants (Amorites) is not yet due for destruction. God raised an army who would dislodge these giants breeding upon the earth through Abraham, which are the Israelites.

The descendants of Lot, which are the Moabites, were spared from being invaded by the Israelites simply because God used the Moabites to annihilate the Emims, who are also giants like the Anakims. "And the LORD said unto me, Distress not the Moabites, neither contend with them in battle: for I will not give you their land for a possession; because I have given Ar unto the children of Lot for a possession; The Emims dwelt therein in the time past, a people great, and many, and tall, as the Anakims." (Deuteronomy 2:9-10). This means the Emims (giants) were giants who the Moabites displaced because God didn't refurbish this earth again for giants who once lived on this earth before Adam to inhabit anymore. He made the earth for Adam and his descendants; hence he took the rib of Adam to form a woman so that one human race is produced in resemblance.

Predetermining individual

God empowered the Moabites, the descendants of Lot, whose ideology differs from the heathen nations around them, to accomplish the destruction of the Emims. Because the Moabites had eliminated those giants, God said, the children of Israel shouldn't attempt attacking the Moabites because they had done the will of God, destroying the giants they met. Moreso, Lot's descendants could be likened to Abraham's seed, who were righteous nations. When the children of Israelites saw the giants Amorites, they were scared, except for Joshua and Caleb, who encouraged themselves.

Let's go through the children of Israel's feedback to Moses: "And they told him and said, "We came into the land wither thou sentest us, and surely it floweth with milk and honey, and this is the fruit of it. Nevertheless, the people be strong that dwell in the land and the cities are walled, and very great: and we saw the children of Anak there. The Amalekites dwell in the land of the south: and the Hittites, and the Jebusites, and the Amorites dwell in the mountains: and the Canaanites dwell by the sea, and by the coast of Jordan...And there we saw the giants, the sons of Anak, which came of the giants: "... and we were in our own sight as grasshoppers, and so were in their sight." (Numbers 13:27-33). But thank my goodness, Joshua and Caleb invaded these giants and destroyed them at last.

However, from the period in which these giants were destroyed to date, there has been, as it were, a continuance of their offspring mingling with natural Adam's descendants in the course of procreation. That is the giant's seed procreating with Adam's natural descents to produce offsprings who may not be giants in size but of a mixed seed of the wicked. We can see that many people could be destined for destruction in their millions represented in every generation, which must be eliminated from earth based on God's prescription of Adam and Eve's actual descendants as the flesh of the same kind, not giant traced descendants.

For this reason, Jesus gave a parable of the reality of this world we live in that not all humans are natural Adam's descendants. "Another parable put he forth unto them, saying, The Kingdom of heaven is likened unto a man who sowed seed (Adam and Eve) in his field: But while men slept, his enemy came and sowed tares (fallen spirit beings offsprings) among the wheat (natural Adam's seed), and went his way. But when the blade sprung up and brought forth fruit (humans), then appeared the tares also. So the servants of the householder came and said unto him, Sir, didst not thou sow good seed in the field? From whence then hath it tares? He said unto them that an enemy had done this. The servants said unto him, Wilt thou then we go and gather them up? But he said, Nay; lest while you gather up the tares, you root up the wheat with them. Let both grow together until the harvest: and in the time of harvest, I will say to the reapers, Gather you together first the tares, and bind them in bundles to burn them: but gather the wheat into my barn." (Matthew 13:24-30, Emphasis mine).

The parable implies God is being patient, knowing fully well that the offspring of the wicked shall be thrown down at last. The fact that these offsprings of the wicked are in the world multiplying the evil doesn't make them the children of God. Of course, God made an open check that whosoever believeth shall not perish but have everlasting life. However, Jesus never debunked the reality of the mysteries of the end of the world, which I've just shared with you in Matthew 13:24-30. Fallen stars that turned humans, alongside ancient people (sons of God) together with their offspring, will be completely banished from God's kingdom, having reclaimed the earth from Satan and his hordes. They don't belong to God, including their offspring. A typical example is the land of Shinar, in which I've told you that the inhabitants of Mount Seir and their descendants shall be rooted out of the earth at last. Does that mean everyone from the Mount Seir region is destined for destruction? No. God will decide the criteria by which he selects those he has chosen based on his free gift offer of his Son Jesus in such regions. However, a majority will be cast out into darkness for the reasons given above.

More so, I think the interplay of what transpires in the spirit realm at the conception level also goes a long way in predetermining individual destiny. The idea is that a righteous father and a mother may conceive four children, and God will choose only one or two of the children as his very own. At some other time, a wicked father might marry a righteous mother, and their offsprings, say three children, might have one or two or even the three children chosen by God. Apostle Paul almost delved into this hidden mystery. He said, "For the unbelieving husband is sanctified by the wife, and the husband sanctifies the unbelieving wife: else were your children unclean, but now are they holy" (1st Corinthians 7:14).

This implies one righteous parent (between the husband and wife) is an avenue for God to choose holy children. Also, Paul expounded on this concept when he discussed Esau and Jacob, who were still in the womb, being predestinated even when they were yet born, and having done nothing good or evil, God already chose his own (See Romans 9:9-11). We can take a clue from Adam and Eve, Issac and Rebekah, and Eli, the priest. That is why I said God has criteria by which he would choose those that belong to him. Some religious people may not accept this raw truth, but they will tell you it doesn't matter. God loves everybody.

But I knew there was a mystery that Jesus declared. "Either make the tree good, and his fruit good, or else make the tree corrupt, and his fruit corrupt: For the tree is known by its fruit" (Matthew 12:33). An evil tree cannot produce good fruit, and neither can a good tree produce evil fruit.

The fruit here implies the offspring, which goes with the tendencies of the heart expressed through the mouth or actions. Jesus was forthright with the truth, saying the offspring of the wicked would be wicked as well. If the source of the tree is evil, the fruit cannot be good. I heard the Lord say, "Not all are mine." Remember, Jesus also said, "My sheep hear my voice, and they obey." It means some belong to the devil, even if they are humans. The scriptures kept emphasizing the destruction of fallen spirits alongside their offspring, which the scriptures recognized as the proud and the wicked.

Malachi 4:1 says, "For, behold, the day cometh, that shall burn as an oven; and all the proud, yea, and all that do wickedly, shall be stubble: and the day that cometh shall burn them up, saith the LORD of hosts, that it shall leave them neither root nor branch." The proud denotes those who outrightly reject God's salvation. The wicked denotes sinners or those that practiced wickedness. Sorry, this is not a conventional book, but God gave me these mysteries, and I wrote them. You and I can do nothing about what has gone wrong in our world. We have established from scriptures that all the seeds of the wicked shall be uprooted out of this earth at last.

The angels of God know the lineage of these fallen spirits. And this was what Paul talked about referencing "vessels fitted for destruction" in Romans chapter 9:22. So when the Scripture says, "...Now, if any man has not the Spirit of Christ, he is none of his." It shows there are people on earth, who cannot obtain the mercy of God, and the Spirit of God can never reside in them, and there is nothing anyone can do about it.

Of course, not all men have faith on earth. "That we may be delivered from unreasonable and wicked men: for all men have not faith." (2nd Thessalonians 3:2). These are people who persuade others from talking about God while they talk carelessly about God and ridiculing Jesus. They knew they were not Adam's descendants. Some people will never believe in Jesus in their hearts, even if they go to church and confess to Jesus as LORD. Don't be fooled into thinking everyone that confesses Jesus as Lord and savior is automatically God's own. They might confess him with their mouth but are insincere in their hearts, like Judas Iscariot, who never believed in Jesus even while working with Jesus as a cashier. Scripture says, "But there are some of you that believe not. For Jesus knew from the beginning who they were that believe not, and who should betray him." (John 6:64).

The Spirit of God couldn't remain in Judas Iscariot. He was excluded from continuing with God, even if he ate the LORD's super and did the work of the ministry in terms of evangelism and running around. Apostle Peter confirmed that Judas Iscariot took part in the work of the ministry (See Act 1:17). I'm not saying that Judas Iscariot was an offspring of the wicked, but I'm just pointing out the reality of hidden mysteries.

Science and the Pre-Adamic World

For more information contact:

Alfred Adjarho
C/O Advantage Books
info@advbooks.com

For further inquiries please send your emails to:
godsearch1@gmail.com

To purchase additional copies of this book visit our bookstore website at: www.advbookstore.com

Longwood, Florida, USA
"we bring dreams to life"™
www.advbookstore.com

www.ingramcontent.com/pod-product-compliance
Lightning Source LLC
Chambersburg PA
CBHW060939230426
43665CB00015B/2002